"*THE TEMPTING OF AMERICA S̶* SIC IN THE PUBLIC DEBATE A̶B̶O̶U̶T̶ ̶W̶H̶O̶ ̶C̶O̶ AMERICA AND HOW."
—William French Smith
Former Attorney General of the United States

"*The Tempting of America* is an intellectual history of the Supreme Court and the Constitution which is also Robert Bork's autobiography, so dedicated has been his entire life to the theory and practice of American justice. He formulates the issues of our time with clarity and precision, but, more than that, he provides a model of the love of ideas and discussion, as well as the capacity for friendship, in the service of the common good. He is never doctrinaire, for he is always concerned with the most difficult and awe-inspiring of endeavors, judging our citizens justly."
—Allan Bloom
Author of *The Closing of the American Mind*

"This book demonstrates the qualities of intellect and character that caused me to nominate Robert Bork to the Supreme Court."
—Ronald Reagan

"Seldom have high expectations been so completely fulfilled. It is a work of monumental dimension and addresses the central legal question of our time."
—*National Review*

THE
TEMPTING
OF
AMERICA

The Political
Seduction of the Law

Robert H. Bork

A TOUCHSTONE BOOK
Published by Simon & Schuster

TOUCHSTONE
Rockefeller Center
1230 Avenue of the Americas
New York, NY 10020

Copyright © 1990 by Robert H. Bork
All rights reserved,
including the right of reproduction
in whole or in part in any form.

First Touchstone Edition 1991

TOUCHSTONE and colophon are registered trademarks
of Simon & Schuster Inc.

Manufactured in the United States of America

5   7   9   10   8   6

Library of Congress Cataloging-in-Publication Data
Bork, Robert H.
The tempting of America: the political seduction of the law /
Robert H. Bork.
p.   cm.
Includes bibliographical references and index.
1. Judicial power—United States.   2. Judicial review—United
States.   3. Political questions and judicial power—United States.
4. United States—Constitutional law—Interpretation and
construction.   I. Title.
KF5130.B59   1991
347.73'12—dc20
[347.30712]   90–19275
CIP
ISBN 0-02-903761-1
ISBN 0-684-84337-4 (Pbk)

The author and the publisher gratefully acknowledge permission to reprint excerpts from the following publications:

Bruce A. Ackerman, *The Storrs Lectures: Discovering the Constitution.* 93 Yale L. J. (1984). Reprinted by permission.

Roy P. Basler, ed., 4 *The Collected Works of Abraham Lincoln* (1953). Copyright © 1953 by The Abraham Lincoln Association. Reprinted by permission of Rutgers, the State University of New Jersey.

Alexander M. Bickel, *The Least Dangerous Branch.* First published in 1962 by the Bobbs-Merrill Company, Inc. Copyright © 1986 by Josephine Ann Bickel. *The Morality of Consent.* Copyright © 1975 by Joanne (Josephine Ann) Bickel. Reprinted by permission.

Robert Bolt, *A Man for All Seasons* (1960). Copyright © 1960, 1962 by Robert Bolt. Reprinted by permission of Random House, Inc.

Hon. William J. Brennan, Jr., Georgetown University Speech (Oct. 12, 1985), reprinted in *The Great Debate: Interpreting Our Written Constitution* (1986). Reprinted by permission.

Paul Brest, *The Fundamental Rights Controversy,* 90 Yale L. J. (1981). Copyright © 1981 by Paul Brest. *The Misconceived Quest for the Original Understanding,* 60 B. U. L. Rev. (1980). Copyright © 1980 by Paul Brest. Reprinted by permission.

David P. Currie, *The Constitution in the Supreme Court: The First Hundred Years 1789–1888* (1985). Reprinted by permission of University of Chicago Press.

William A. Donohue, *The Politics of the American Civil Liberties Union* (1985). Copyright © 1985 by Transaction Publishers. Reprinted by permission of Transaction.

John Hart Ely, *Democracy and Distrust* (1980). Copyright © 1980 by the President and Fellows of Harvard College. Reprinted by permission of Harvard University Press.

Felix Frankfurter, ed., *The Commerce Clause under Marshall, Taney, and Waite* (1973). Copyright © 1937 the University of North Carolina Press. Reprinted by permission.

Thomas C. Grey, *Eros, Civilization, and the Burger Court,* 43 Law & Contemp. Prob. (1980). Reprinted by permission.

Milton Handler, *The Supreme Court and the Antitrust Laws: A Critic's Viewpoint,* 1 G. L. Rev. (1967). Reprinted by permission.

Maurice J. Holland, *A Hurried Perspective on the Critical Studies Movement: The Marx Brothers Assault the Citadel,* 8 Harv. J. L. & Pub. Pol'y. (1985). Reprinted by permission.

Paul Hollander, *The Survival of Adversary Culture* (1988). Copyright © 1988 by Transaction Publishers. Reprinted by permission of Transaction.

Robert W. Jenson, *Churchly Honor and Judge Bork,* DIALOG, vol. 27, no. 1, Winter 1988. Reprinted by permission.

To my wife, MARY ELLEN,
and to my children,
ROBERT, JR., CHARLES, and ELLEN

About the Author

Robert H. Bork received undergraduate and law degrees from the University of Chicago and served in the U.S. Marine Corps. He has been a partner in a major law firm, taught constitutional law as the Alexander M. Bickel Professor of Public Law at the Yale Law School, served as Solicitor General and as Acting Attorney General of the United States, and as Circuit Judge on the U.S. Court of Appeals for the District of Columbia Circuit, before his nomination by President Reagan to the Supreme Court. He and his wife live in Washington, D.C., where he is John M. Olin Scholar in Legal Studies at the American Enterprise Institute.

Contents

Acknowledgments

*T*his book could not conceivably have been finished without the assistance of a great many people.

Steven Calabresi, my research associate for the past year, was indispensable in every aspect of the work: discussion of ideas, suggestions, comments on drafts, research, and organizing volunteers. Mr. Calabresi was my law clerk during the 1984–85 term of the U.S. Court of Appeals for the District of Columbia Circuit.

Margaret Tahyar, Andrew McBride, and Clark Remington did extensive research and provided invaluable suggestions. They came to my chambers as clerks in the summer of 1987 and stayed with me as research associates upon my departure from the bench in February of 1988. Ms. Tahyar and Mr. McBride subsequently commented extensively on drafts of the manuscript. John Harrison and Peter Keisler, who clerked for me in 1982–83 and 1985–86, respectively, also read and commented upon drafts.

Judy Carper, who was also my secretary when I was a judge, prepared and repeatedly revised the manuscript on the word processor and also handled the seemingly endless administrative tasks with great skill.

The following individuals put in many arduous hours assisting in different phases of producing the manuscript: Daniel E. Troy, Brent O. Hatch, John F. Manning, and Bradford R. Clark, who clerked for me at the Court of Appeals in 1983–84, 1984–85, and 1985–86, respectively; Lawrence J. Block, Barbara K. Bracher, Allyson E. Dunn, Keith M. Dunn, Edward D. Hearst, John M. Kleeberg, Gary S. Lawson, Lee S. Liberman, David M. McIntosh, Eugene B. Meyer, Mark R.A. Paoletta, David B. Rivkin, Jr., Simon S. Saks, E. Jane Wallace, and Henry Weissmann.

My special thanks go to Irving Kristol and Gertrude Himmelfarb, who read the manuscript and offered both good advice and encouragement. My publisher at The Free Press, Erwin Glikes, was an extraordinarily skillful, perceptive, and sympathetic editor. Eileen DeWald, managing editor at The Free Press, and Shirley Kessel, who assisted with the index, also did a superb job in their respective tasks. Robert Barnett, as my lawyer and literary agent, gave excellent advice about the mysterious world of publishing and drafted a contract highly satisfactory to all concerned.

I owe a debt of gratitude that hardly can be repaid to the people who helped.

Thanks are due to the American Enterprise Institute, which houses and supports me, and to the John M. Olin Foundation, whose grant makes that support possible. My personal thanks go to Christopher C. DeMuth, the President of AEI, and to William Simon, President of the Olin Foundation. The views expressed in this book are my own and not necessarily those of the American Enterprise Institute, the Olin Foundation, or the persons who assisted in its production.

Introduction

*I*n the past few decades American institutions have struggled with the temptations of politics. Professions and academic disciplines that once possessed a life and structure of their own have steadily succumbed, in some cases almost entirely, to the belief that nothing matters beyond politically desirable results, however achieved. In this quest, politics invariably tries to dominate another discipline, to capture and use it for politics' own purposes, while the second subject—law, religion, literature, economics, science, journalism, or whatever—struggles to maintain its independence. But retaining a separate identity and integrity becomes increasingly difficult as more and more areas of our culture, including the life of the intellect, perhaps especially the life of the intellect, become politicized. It is coming to be denied that anything counts, not logic, not objectivity, not even intellectual honesty, that stands in the way of the "correct" political outcome.

The process by which this is accomplished may vary from field to field, from universities to the media to courts. In law, the moment of temptation is the moment of choice, when a judge realizes that in the case before him his strongly held view of justice, his political and moral imperative, is not embodied in a statute or in any provision of the Constitution. He must then choose between his version of justice and abiding by the American form of government. Yet the desire to do justice, whose nature seems to him obvious, is compelling, while the concept of constitutional process is abstract, rather arid, and the abstinence it counsels unsatisfying. To give in to temptation, this one time, solves an urgent human problem, and a faint crack appears in the American foundation. A judge has begun to rule where a legislator should.

The American people are tempted as well. Many of the results seem good, and they are told that the choice is between a cold, impersonal logic, on the one hand, and, on the other, morality and compassion. This has always been the song of the tempters, and now it is heard incessantly from those who would politicize the courts and the Constitution, as a necessary stage in the politicization of the culture at large.

The democratic integrity of law, however, depends entirely upon the degree to which its processes are legitimate. A judge who announces a decision must be able to demonstrate that he began from recognized legal principles and reasoned in an intellectually coherent and politically neutral way to his result. Those who would politicize the law offer the public, and the judiciary, the temptation of results without regard to democratic legitimacy.

This strategy, however, contains the seeds of its own destruction. Since the politicization of the law has, for half a century, moved results steadily to the left, a very large number of Americans do not like those outcomes. Increasingly, they are not deceived by the claim that those results are compelled by the actual Constitution. This perception delegitimizes the law in their eyes. There are signs that law may be at a tipping stage in the public perception of its legitimacy. Americans increasingly view the courts, and particularly the Supreme Court, as political rather than legal institutions. Perhaps a lesson may be learned from another great institution: the press. The political coloration of news reporting is easier for the public to see than is that of judicial decisionmaking, and, as the press has in fact become more political, it has lost legitimacy with large sections of that public. Something of the same thing may be happening to law, more slowly but perhaps as inexorably. Conservatives, who now, by and large, want neutral judges, may decide to join the game and seek activist judges with conservative views. Should that come to pass, those who have tempted the courts to political judging will have gained nothing for themselves but will have destroyed a great and essential institution.

The clash over my nomination was simply one battle in this long-running war for control of our legal culture. There may be legitimate differences about that nomination, but, in the larger war for control of the law, there are only two sides. Either the Constitution and statutes are law, which means that their principles are known and control judges, or they are malleable texts that judges may rewrite to see that particular groups or political causes win. Until recently, the American people were largely unaware of the struggle for dominance in law, because it was waged, in explicit form, only in the law schools. Now it is coming into the open.

In the clash of law and politics, the integrity of the law has already been seriously undermined and the quality of its future remains very much in doubt. The forces that would break law to a tame instrument of a particular political thrust are past midway in a long march through our institutions. They have overrun a number of law schools, including a large majority of America's most prestigious, where the lawyers and judges of the future are being trained. They have an increasing voice in our politics and in Congress. But the focus of the struggle, the commanding height sought to be taken, as indeed it partially has been, is control of the courts and the Constitution. The Constitution, or the law we call "constitutional"—they are by no means identical—is the highest prize, and control of the selection of judges is the last step on the path to that prize. Why? Because the Constitution is the trump card in American politics, and judges decide what the Constitution means. When the Supreme Court invokes the Constitution, whether legitimately or not, as to that issue the democratic process is at an end. That is why we witnessed the first all-out national political campaign with respect to a judicial nominee in our country's history.

My chambers, as a federal court of appeals judge on the District of Columbia Circuit, were on the third floor of the United States Courthouse and overlooked Constitution Avenue. Twice a year, along with my clerks and secretaries, I watched massive marches come down that wide street, one by anti-abortionists and one by pro-abortionists. The reason for those parades was, of course, *Roe* v. *Wade*,[1] the Supreme Court's 1973 decision making abortion a matter of constitutional right, thus largely removing the issue from state legislatures, where it had rested for all of our history. Each group first gathers to demonstrate outside the White House, then forms, carrying placards and sometimes chanting, to begin the lengthy walk down Pennsylvania Avenue to Constitution Avenue and on to Capitol Hill. There the demonstrators march past the Houses of Congress with hardly a glance and go straight to the Supreme Court building to make their moral sentiments known where they perceive those sentiments to be relevant. The demonstrators on both sides believe the issue to be moral, not legal. So far as they are concerned, however, the primary political branch of government, to which they must address their petitions, is the Supreme Court. There is something very disturbing about those marches, for, if the marchers correctly perceive the reality, and I think it undeniable that they do, a major heresy has entered the American constitutional system.

"Heresy," Hilaire Belloc reminds us, "is the dislocation of some complete and self-supporting scheme by the introduction of a novel denial of some essential part therein. We mean by 'a complete and self-supporting scheme' any system of affirmation in physics or mathematics or philosophy or what-not, the various parts of which are coherent and sustain each other."[2] The American design of a constitutional Republic is such a "complete and self-supporting scheme." The heresy that dislocates it is the introduction of the denial that judges are bound by law.

The foundation of American freedoms is in the structure of our Republic. The major features of that structure are the separation of the powers of the national government and the limitation of national power to preserve a large degree of autonomy in the states. Both are mandated by the Constitution. These dispersions of power, viewed historically, have guaranteed our liberties as much as, perhaps more than, the Bill of Rights itself. The phrase "separation of powers," briefly put, means that Congress has "All legislative Powers," as those are defined in article I of the Constitution, while the President possesses "The executive Power," which is outlined in article II, and article III sets forth the elements of "The judicial Power." Those powers are very different in nature, as those who adopted the Constitution recognized and intended. When powers are shared, as they sometimes are by the President and Congress, the Constitution is usually explicit on the subject. Thus, the Constitution specifies that the President may veto a bill enacted by Congress and that Congress may override the veto by a two-thirds vote of each House. Similarly, the President may negotiate treaties, but they must be ratified by a two-thirds vote of the Senate. There is no faintest hint in the Constitution, however, that the judiciary shares any of the legislative or executive power. The intended function of the federal courts is to apply the law as it comes to them from the hands of others. The judiciary's great office is to preserve the constitutional design. It does this not only by confining Congress and the President to the powers granted them by the Constitution and seeing that the powers granted are not used to invade the freedoms guaranteed by the Bill of Rights, but also, and equally important, by ensuring that the democratic authority of the people is maintained in the full scope given by the Constitution.

The Constitution preserves our liberties by providing that all of those given the authority to make policy are directly accountable to the people through regular elections. Federal judges, alone among our public officials, are given life tenure precisely so that they will not be accountable to the people. If it were otherwise, if judges were accountable, the people could, when the mood seized them, alter the separation of powers, do away with representative government, or deny basic freedoms to those out of popular favor. But if judges are, as they must be to perform their vital role, unelected, unaccountable, and unrepresentative, who is to protect us from the power of judges? How are we to be guarded from our guardians? The answer can only be that judges must consider themselves bound by law that is independent of their own views of the desirable. They must not make or apply any policy not fairly to be found in the Constitution or a statute. It is of course true that judges to some extent must make law every time they decide a case, but it is minor, interstitial lawmaking. The ratifiers of the Constitution put in place the walls, roofs, and beams; judges preserve the major architectural features, adding only filigree.

What does it mean to say that a judge is bound by law? It means that he is bound by the only thing that can be called law, the principles of the text, whether Constitution or statute, as generally understood at the enactment. The lay reader may wonder at the emphasis put upon this apparently simple point. Of course, the judge is bound to apply the law as those who made the law wanted him to. That is the common, everyday view of what law is. I stress the point only because that commonsense view is hotly, extensively, and eruditely denied by constitutional sophisticates, particularly those who teach the subject in the law schools.

In these matters, common sense is sound. As Joseph Story, who was both an Associate Justice of the Supreme Court and a professor of law at Harvard, put it in his famed *Commentaries on the Constitution of the United States,*

> The reader must not expect to find in these pages any novel views, and novel constructions of the Constitution. I have not the ambition to be the author of any new plan of interpreting the theory of the Constitution, or of enlarging or narrowing its powers by ingenious subtleties and learned doubts. . . . Upon subjects of government it has always appeared to me, that metaphysical refinements are out of place. A constitution of government is addressed to the common sense of the people; and never was designed for trials of logical skill, or visionary speculation.[3]

Story might have been addressing today's constitutional cognoscenti, who would have judges remake the historic Constitution from such materials as natural law, conventional morality, prophetic vision, the understanding of an ideal democracy, or what have you. There is a remarkable consistency about these theorists. No matter the base from which they start, they all wind up in the same place, prescribing a new constitutional law that is much more egalitarian and socially permissive than either the actual Constitution or the legislative opinion of the American public. That, surely, is the point of their efforts.

What the theorists want are courts that make major policy, courts that build a new structure rather than maintain the original. Story knew better. When he came to the role of the courts under the Constitution, he said: "The first and fundamental rule in the interpretation of all instruments is, to construe them according to the sense of the terms, and the intention of the parties."[4] Only by following that rule can our unelected guardians save us from themselves. Only in that way can the foundation of our freedoms, the separation of powers, be kept intact. Only so can judicial supremacy be democratically legitimate.

There is a story that two of the greatest figures in our law, Justice Holmes and Judge Learned Hand, had lunch together and afterward, as Holmes began to drive off in his carriage, Hand, in a sudden onset of enthusiasm, ran after him, crying, "Do justice, sir, do justice." Holmes stopped the carriage and reproved Hand: "That is not my job. It is my job to apply the law."[5] I meant something like that when I dissented from a decision that seemed to proceed from sympathy rather than law: "[W]e administer justice according to law. Justice in a larger sense, justice according to morality, is for Congress and the President to administer, if they see fit, through the creation of new law."[6]

That is the American orthodoxy. The heresy, which dislocates the constitutional system, is that the ratifiers' original understanding of what the Constitution means is no longer of controlling, or perhaps of any, importance. A variety of reasons are given for this extraordinary proposition, and these will be examined later. The result is a belief, widely held and propagated in the law schools and even by some Justices of the Supreme Court, that judges may create new principles or destroy old ones, thus altering the principles actually to be found in the Constitution. Courts then not only share the legislative power of Congress and the state legislatures, in violation both of the separation of powers and of federalism, but assume a legislative power that is actually superior to that of any legislature. The innovations are announced in the name of the Constitution—though they have little or nothing to do with it—and are therefore intended to be, and are accepted as, final. Courts have behaved in this way on occasion throughout our history, but never so often as in the modern era; what is more ominous, never before has such behavior been so popular in the law schools, in the press, and in the opinions of elite groups generally. Heresy sometimes becomes so pervasive that it becomes the new orthodoxy.

The heresy described is not peculiar to any political outlook. When it has suited their purpose, conservatives as well as liberals have surrendered to its temptation. Given the chance, no doubt many conservatives would be delighted to succumb again. If I address the failings of liberals more than those of conservatives, it is only because liberalism or ultraliberalism is currently in the ascendancy in constitutional theory and practice.

The orthodoxy of original understanding, and the political neutrality of judging it requires, are anathema to a liberal culture that for fifty years has won a succession of political victories from the courts and that hopes for more political victories in the future. The representatives of that culture hate the American orthodoxy because they have moral and political agendas of their own that cannot be found in the Constitution and that no legislature, or at least none whose members wish to be reelected, will enact. That is why these partisans want judges who will win their victories for them by altering the Constitution.

Americans, who know a great deal about presidents and something about Congress, are generally not well-informed about the third branch of government. They react, often in anger, to particular decisions but tend to regard them as aberrational rather than systemic failures. But the heresy of political judging is systemic. A great many judges subscribe to it, a large number of left-wing activist groups promote it, many senators insist upon it, and in the legal academy this heresy is dominant. The orthodoxy of original understanding is regarded as passé, and signs that it is stirring and may achieve an intellectual revival are viewed with alarm as a reactionary threat. The reader will, I think, be amazed at how political, how simultaneously sophisticated and anti-intellectual, is much of what passes for constitutional scholarship today. It is not, in truth, scholarship; it is, as one of its leading practitioners candidly states, the advocacy of political results addressed to courts. That is not what most people mean by "law." But that bothers the academicians not a bit. A few years ago I was invited to a small seminar of professors of constitutional law. During the discussion I argued that, the Constitution being law, there were some results courts could not legitimately achieve: rules cover some things and not others. A well-known Harvard law professor turned to me with some exasperation and said, "Your notion that the Constitution is in some sense law must rest upon an obscure philosophic principle with which I am unfamiliar." That attitude is common among our constitutional philosophers. It is fair to say, as Gary McDowell has, that in the law schools, "The question today is not so much how to read the Constitution as *whether* to read the Constitution."[7]

Those who now dominate public discourse on these matters recognize that, if the Constitution is law, departures from the principles the ratifiers understood themselves to be enacting are illegitimate. Yet such departures are essential if the results desired by the liberal culture are to be achieved through the courts. It follows that the Constitution cannot be law. Thus, the morality and politics of the intellectual or knowledge class, a class that extends well beyond the universities, can be made into constitutional law. The class I describe is not necessarily composed of people who are good at intellectual work. They are defined as a class because they work, however adroitly or maladroitly, with words and ideas. For reasons that will be discussed, they tend to have values antagonistic to a traditional, bourgeois society. It is not too much to say that these people see the Constitution as a weapon in a class struggle about social and political values.

Judges are by definition members of the intellectual class and, in addition, for professional and personal reasons, tend to be influenced by the culture of the law schools. Like most people, judges tend to accept the assumptions of the culture that surrounds them, often without fully understanding the foundations of those assumptions or their implications. If they can be persuaded to abandon the idea of original understanding, they are quite likely to frame constitutional rules that reflect the assumptions of modern liberal culture.

That has happened repeatedly in the past few decades. It probably explains, to cite only recent examples, the fact that the Supreme Court has approved reverse discrimination on the basis of sex and race under a statute that clearly forbids it, found a right to abortion in the Constitution without explaining even once how that right could be derived from any constitutional materials, and came within one vote of finding a constitutional right to engage in homosexual conduct. For a few years the Court even abolished the death penalty, though the Constitution several times explicitly assumes that penalty to be a matter of legislative choice. My point is not that these choices are necessarily morally or politically wrong; my point is simply that, under the Constitution, these are questions left for the people and their elected representatives, not for courts, to decide.

It seems significant that every departure from the original understanding on that list, be it a departure from the original meaning of a statute or of the Constitution, resulted in the judicial enactment, or attempted enactment, of an item on the modern liberal agenda. Though the Court once legislated results that may be called conservative (which was also an illegitimate judicial role), rarely, if ever, in the past fifty years has it done so. The abandonment of original understanding in modern times means the transportation into the Constitution of the principles of a liberal culture that cannot achieve those results democratically. This difference about the proper role of courts is what the battle over my confirmation was about underneath, but not what it was about in the public campaign.

The public campaign, designed to influence senators through public opinion polls, consisted of the systematic distortion of my academic writings and my judicial record and, it must be said, employed racial and gender politics of a most pernicious variety. The ferocity of the attack, the ideological stance of the assailants, and the tactics they used all showed that the opposition knew they were fighting over more than one judge. They were fighting for control of the legal culture. They knew that in reality and, perhaps even more important, symbolically, they must defeat a nominee who had for long expressed in writing the philosophy of original understanding and had tried to show the lack of any constitutional foundation for some of the liberal culture's most important victories. The liberal culture needed to preserve, if possible to intensify, and certainly to legitimate, the politicization of the Court and the Constitution.

These are matters worth discussing, for there will be many future nominees to the Supreme Court, and the philosophies of those who are confirmed will have much to do with the future of our constitutional form of government and with the direction of our politics and culture. One purpose of this book is to persuade Americans that no person should be nominated or confirmed who does not display both a grasp of and devotion to the philosophy of original understanding.

Nor should the American people put up with a political campaign about nominees that resorts to untruths or to a confirmation process in which senators demand that the nominee promise specified results. The way the campaign against my confirmation was waged, if it becomes the norm, will have long-term effects—effects on the judicial nomination process of the future, effects on the substance of our law, particularly our constitutional law, and effects upon the intellectual life of the law.

The liberal elites will not be satisfied with blocking the nomination of judges who may be expected to adhere to the historic principles of the Constitution. They intend to root that idea out of the intellectual life of the law, to make the philosophy of original understanding, and the associated idea of political neutrality in judging, disqualifying for the men and women who hold them. They have almost achieved that in the legal academic world; they are trying to achieve it in public discourse. They made much play with the claim that I was "outside the mainstream." But it is obvious from those who supported me, men and women whose legal careers define the mainstream, that the ultraliberal activists were, in actuality, trying to shift the mainstream radically to the left. If by vilification you can make people believe that the center is actually the extreme right, then you can get them to think that the left must be the center. That is the way the war for control of the legal culture is being fought.

But what I have just described is merely part of a larger war in our culture. As an integral part of that culture, law both reflects and influences trends and ideological movements there. In the last twenty-five years what we had thought were shared values and moral first principles have begun to disintegrate. There has always been a division between liberals and conservatives, of course, but part of liberal thought has evolved into something quite different from the liberalism of a quarter of a century ago. Now we seem to be experiencing in our law, our politics, and our culture something relatively new, a kind of restless and unprogrammatic radicalism that does not share but attacks traditional values and assumptions.

Thus, Alasdair MacIntyre states, "modern politics cannot be a matter of genuine moral consensus. . . . Modern politics is civil war carried on by other means."[8] If that is true—and it may be increasingly true—we may expect a politics that is increasingly polarized and divisive. Max Lerner wrote that he had not seen a time since the 1960s when our politics were so Jacobin.[9] There is a ferocity and irresponsibility about political struggle as practiced by a wing of modern liberalism that results in large measure from the arrival on the national scene of the activists of the 1960s, who have brought their ideological baggage with them intact. The left activists of that generation and those whom they have swayed hold only contempt for the limits of respectable politics and indeed for political neutrality in any institution, including the federal judiciary. When courts are viewed as political bodies, we may expect judicial confirmations that are increasingly bitter. We may also expect a constitutional law that lurches suddenly in one direction or another as one faction or another gains the upper hand, a constitutional law that is seen as too crucial a political weapon to be left to nonpolitical judges, and certainly too important to be left to the actual Constitution.

The judicial assumption of ultimate legislative power is deceptive and difficult to resist because that assumption takes the form of a judgment handed down like other judgments, claims to be "constitutional," and leaves the appearance of the separation of powers intact. Those who deny the validity of a jurisprudence of original understanding do not explicitly propose a rearrangement of our republican form of government. "The denial of a scheme wholesale is not heresy, and has not the creative power of a heresy," said Belloc. "It is of the essence of heresy that it leaves standing a great part of the structure it attacks. On this account it can appeal to believers. . . . Wherefore, it is said of heresies that 'they survive by the truths they retain.' "[10] We retain the reality of legislative and executive authority over wide areas of life. Moreover, we retain the institution of judicial review because we have found that it does much good. These are the truths that make the misuse of judicial power all the more insidious. For that reason, it is crucial to recognize a heresy for what it is and to root it out, for "heresy originates a new life of its own and vitally affects the society it attacks. The reason that men combat heresy is not only, or principally, conservatism . . . it is much more a perception that the heresy, in so far as it gains ground, will produce a way of living and a social character at issue with, irritating, and perhaps mortal to, the way of living and the social character produced by the old orthodox scheme."

This book is not, therefore, ultimately about legal theory. It is about who we are and how we live; it is about who governs us and how, about our freedom to make our own moral choices, and about the difference that makes in our daily lives and in the lives of generations yet to come.

A Word About Structure

The most active agent in transforming the federal courts has been the Supreme Court of the United States. For that reason, Part I of this book considers the increasing politicization of the Court and the Constitution in five chapters, four devoted to the Court from the beginning to the mid-1930s, the New Deal Court, the Court under Chief Justice Earl Warren, and the Court under Chief Justices Burger and Rehnquist. The fifth chapter draws conclusions about the path of the Court over time.

In recent decades, however, a new force has appeared in this arena: a herd of theoreticians of the Constitution, almost all of them professors of law. It is the enterprise of the large majority of this intelligentsia to justify the political behavior of the Court in the past and to provide theories that will draw the Court ever farther along the path of left-liberal Constitution rewriting. Part II is, therefore, devoted to theories of how constitutional judges should conduct themselves. It begins with a statement of the basic problem—defining the respective rights of majorities and minorities—that all theories of constitutional interpretation must solve. In the next two chapters I offer an argument that only by interpreting the Constitution according to the meaning it was understood to have when adopted can a judge solve the problem; I then turn to meet the numerous objections that have been offered to that conclusion. The next two chapters analyze the theories put forward by liberal and conservative theorists who want the Court to depart from the original meaning of the document. The theories of each set of revisionists are, and this may come as no surprise, found deficient, and seriously so. The following chapter examines some nonconstitutional ideas—both extreme moralism and extreme moral relativism—that have worked their way into constitutional decisions. I next argue that no theory that calls for departures from the original understanding can ever succeed. Part II closes with a chapter showing that rigorous legal reasoning is crucial to the maintenance of our form of government and our freedoms while a preference for "good results" over good reasoning subverts both the structure of government and freedom.

In Part III I place my own experience as President Reagan's nominee to a seat on the Supreme Court in the context of the wars that rage for control of our legal culture and our general culture, suggest what is at stake as those wars continue, and try to estimate what effects my experience may have on the future.

Because provisions of the Constitution are frequently discussed, that document is set out at the end of the book as an Appendix.

I

THE SUPREME COURT AND THE TEMPTATIONS OF POLITICS

A popular style in complaining about the courts is to contrast modern judges with those of a golden or, at least, a less tarnished age. Many people have a fuzzy impression that the judges of old were different. They did things like "follow precedent" and "apply the law, not make it up." There is a good deal to be said for that view. The practice of judicial lawmaking has certainly accelerated spectacularly in this century, particularly in the past four or five decades. Nevertheless, the whole truth is rather more complicated.

From the establishment of the federal judiciary at the end of the eighteenth century, some judges at least claimed the power to strike down statutes on the basis of principles not to be found in the Constitution. Judges who claimed this power made little or no attempt to justify it, to describe its source with any specificity, or to state what principles, if any, limited their own power. No more have the activist judges of our time. Justifications for such judicial behavior had, for the most part, to await the ingenuity of modern law faculties. But the actions of the federal judiciary, and in particular those of the Supreme Court, have often provoked angry reaction, though rarely a systematic statement of the appropriate judicial role. The appropriate limits of judicial power, if such there be, are thus the center of an ancient, if not always fruitful, controversy. Its confused and unfocused condition constitutes a venerable tradition, which is one tradition, at least, modern scholarship leaves intact. This part of the book traces the history of judicial revisions of the Constitution, identifies the social values revisionism served, and evaluates such justifications as were offered.

In a single volume, it is possible to examine only the most obvious or the most explicit revisions of the Constitution. But it is important to keep in mind that any court seen engaging in overt revisionism will, in all probability, have engaged in many more instances of disguised departures from the Constitution. A court that desires a result the law does not allow would rather, whenever possible, through misuse of materials or illogic, publish an opinion claiming to be guided or even compelled to its result by the Constitution than state openly that the result rests on other grounds. That is because popular support for judicial supremacy rests upon the belief that the court is applying fundamental principles laid down at the American founding. We would hardly revere a document that we knew to be no more than an open warrant for judges to do with us as they please.

Disguised or not, the habit of legislating policy from the bench, once acquired, is addictive and hence by no means confined to constitutional cases. The activist or revisionist judge, as we shall see, can no more restrain himself from doing "good" in construing a statute than when he purports to speak with the voice of the Constitution.

The values a revisionist judge enforces do not, of course, come from the law. If they did, he would not be revising. The question, then, is where such a judge finds the values he implements. Academic theorists try to provide various philosophical apparatuses to give the judge the proper values. We may leave until later the question of whether any of these systems succeed. The important point, for the moment, is that no judge has ever really explained the matter. A judge inserting new principles into the Constitution tells us their origin only in a rhetorical, never an analytical, style. There is, however, strong reason to suspect that the judge absorbs those values he writes into law from the social class or elite with which he identifies.

It is a commonplace that moral views vary both regionally within the United States and between socio-economic classes. It is similarly a commonplace that the morality of certain elites may count for more in the operations of government than that morality which might command the allegiance of a majority of the people. In no part of government is this more true than in the courts. An elite moral or political view may never be able to win an election or command the votes of a majority of a legislature, but it may nonetheless influence judges and gain the force of law in that way. That is the reason judicial activism is extremely popular with certain elites and why they encourage judges to think it the highest aspect of their calling. Legislation is far more likely to reflect majority sentiment while judicial activism is likely to represent an elite minority's sentiment. The judge is free to reflect the "better" opinion because he need not stand for reelection and because he can deflect the majority's anger by claiming merely to have been enforcing the Constitution. Constitutional jurisprudence is mysterious terrain for most people, who have more pressing things to think about. And a very handy fact that is for revisionists.

The opinions of the elites to which judges respond change as society changes and one elite replaces another in the ability to impress judges. Thus, judicial activism has had no single political trajectory over time. The values enforced change, and sometimes those of one era directly contradict those of a prior era. That can be seen in the sea changes constitutional doctrine has undergone in our history. There will often be a lag, of course, since judges who have internalized the values of one elite will not necessarily switch allegiances just because a new elite and its values have become dominant. When that happens, when judges are enforcing values regarded by the dominant elite as passé, the interim between the change and the replacement of the judges will be perceived as a time of "constitutional crisis." The fact of judicial mortality redresses the situation eventually, and new judges enforce the new "correct" values. This has happened more than once in our history. The intellectuals of the newly dominant elite are then highly critical of the activist judges of the prior era for enforcing the wrong values while they praise the activist judges of their own time as sensitive to the needs of society. They do not see, or will not allow themselves to see, that the judicial performances, judged as judicial performances, are the same in both eras. The Supreme Court that struck down economic regulation designed to protect workers is, judged as a judicial body, indistinguishable from the Court that struck down abortion laws. Neither Court gave anything resembling an adequate reason derived from the Constitution for frustrating the democratic outcome. So far as one can tell from the opinions written, each Court denied majority morality for no better reason than that elite opinion ran the other way.

In this chapter and the next, we shall see that the Supreme Court's activism was at various times enlisted in the protection of property, the defense of slave owners, the protection of business enterprise in an industrializing nation, the interests of groups in the New Deal coalition, and, today, the furtherance of the values of the elite or cluster of elites known as the "new class" or the "knowledge class."[1] The point ought not be overstated. We are discussing a strong tendency, not invariable conduct. No Court behaves in this way all of the time, in every case. Few judges are so willful as that. The structure of the law does have force, and, in any event, most cases do not present a conflict between elite morality and the law's structure. Yet such occasions arise in important matters, and it is those occasions that give the Court of each era its distinctive style.

Part of any revisionist Court's style, in addition to the nature of the nonconstitutional values enforced, is the rhetoric employed. The Court of each era is likely to choose different provisions of the Constitution or different formulations of invented rights as the vehicles for its revisory efforts. These are different techniques for claiming that what is being done is "law." The shifts in terminology do not alter the reality of the judicial performance as such. Still, the rhetoric employed will often disclose what values are popular with the elites to which the Court responds. Thus, the Court's shift from the use of the word "liberty" in the due process clause, popular in the closing decades of the last century and the opening decades of this century, to the idea of equality in the equal protection clause signified a shift in dominant values. It also signified a change in the social groups to which the Court responded, a decline in the influence of the business class and a rise in that of the New Deal political coalition and its intellectual spokesmen. Similarly, the change from "liberty of contract," used in striking down economic reform legislation, to the "right of privacy" employed to guarantee various aspects of sexual freedom, signals a change in dominant values from capitalist free enterprise to sexual permissiveness, and, again, a change in dominant elites from the business class to the knowledge class, though now with less concern than previously for the social values of those who made up the New Deal coalition.

1

Creation and Fall

The First Principles of the Social Compact

The Constitution was barely in place when one Justice of the Supreme Court cast covetous glances at the apple that would eventually cause the fall. The occasion was the Supreme Court's 1798 decision in *Calder* v. *Bull*.[1] A probate court of Connecticut refused to accept a will, but the legislature invalidated the court's refusal. The court then accepted the will, and those who would have inherited under the first decision appealed to the Supreme Court. They lost, but two Justices took the occasion to disagree profoundly about the scope and nature of judicial power. Justice Samuel Chase of Maryland was prepared to strike down laws that violated no provision of any constitution, federal or state. His extraordinary opinion was supported less by legal reasoning than by frequent recourse to the typographic arts.

I cannot subscribe to the *omnipotence* of a *State* Legislature, or that it is *absolute* and *without control*; although its authority should not be *expressly* restrained by the *Constitution,* or *fundamental law,* of the State. . . . The purposes for which men enter into society will determine the *nature* and *terms* of the *social* compact. . . . An ACT of the Legislature (for I cannot call it a *law*) contrary to the *great first principles* of the *social compact,* cannot be considered a *rightful exercise* of *legislative authority.* . . . The *genius,* the *nature*, and the *spirit*, of our State Governments, amount to a prohibition of *such acts of legislation*; and the *general principles of law and reason* forbid them. . . . To maintain that our Federal, or State, Legislature possesses *such powers,* if they had not been *expressly* restrained; would, in my opinion, be a

19

political heresy, altogether inadmissible in our *free republican governments.*

One gathers that Justice Chase felt strongly, and he certainly gave judicial activism an emotional, if not an intellectual, heritage. No modern Court has been quite so candid in claiming a power beyond any written law. But then no modern revisionist Court has offered any better explanation of its power than did Chase's italics. Chase was an intemperate and highly partisan judge, a trait that later led to his impeachment by the House, though he escaped conviction in the Senate. Given his later behavior, it seems likely that Chase identified the *"great first principles of the social compact"* with the politics of the Federalist Party. By 1798 the Jeffersonian Republicans had become an obvious threat at the polls, and it is possible Chase was preparing a rationale for defeating their legislation by summoning up an unwritten social compact known only to himself.

Justice James Iredell of North Carolina answered Chase.

If, then, a government . . . were established, by a Constitution, which imposed no limits on the legislative power, the consequence would inevitably be, that whatever the legislative power chose to enact, would be lawfully enacted, and the judicial power could never interpose to pronounce it void. It is true, that some speculative jurists have held, that a legislative act against natural justice must, in itself, be void; but I cannot think that, under such a government, any Court of Justice would possess the power to declare it so. . . . *The ideas of natural justice are regulated by no fixed standard: the ablest and the purest of men have differed upon the subject.* . . .[2]

In this case, the emphasis is mine, not the Justice's. It is noteworthy that the impulse to judicial authoritarianism surfaced and was resisted at the beginning of our constitutional history. The Justices' exchange did not affect the outcome of the case, but it set out opposing philosophies that remain with us today. It is somewhat disheartening, indeed, that, while the debate has grown increasingly complex, in almost two centuries the fundamental ideas have not been improved upon.

The Divided John Marshall

John Marshall, commonly thought the greatest judge in our history, was named the fourth Chief Justice of the United States in 1801.

Thomas Jefferson had just won the presidency but had not yet been sworn in, and President John Adams, fearful of Jefferson's principles, wished to preserve the national judiciary as a Federalist Party stronghold. The appointment of Marshall, who was Adams's Secretary of State, did much to accomplish that. The Federalists and the Republicans had very different ideas about how the young nation should develop. The Federalists stood for a much stronger national government than did the Jeffersonians. Today, it seems difficult to see the point in the struggle to draft and ratify the Constitution if Jefferson and his followers were correct. This conflict of visions probably does much to explain Marshall's performance as Chief Justice.

An explanation of some sort is required, for even those of us who deplore activism admire Marshall, and it is clear that Marshall was, in some respects, an activist judge. But his activism consisted mainly in distorting statutes in order to create occasions for constitutional rulings that preserved the structure of the United States. Although he may have deliberately misread the statutes, he did not misread the Constitution. His constitutional rulings, often argued brilliantly, are faithful to the document. Marshall's tactic may perhaps be understood, for the survival of the Union was probably in some part due to the centralizing and unifying force of Marshall and his Court. The threat was posed by the Jeffersonians' insistence upon an extreme version of state sovereignty. For a time Jefferson viewed the Constitution as a mere compact among the states, leaving each state with the right to decide for itself whether actions of the national government were unconstitutional. Jefferson's view of the power of judicial review was of a piece. He accepted judicial review that included review of the acts of the President and Congress, but he thought those branches had a right to decide for themselves whether to accept the Court's ruling.

These positions would certainly have made the national government unworkable. Indeed, the centrifugal forces in the new nation were so great that at times Marshall and others despaired of the Union's survival. Congress often behaved more like a bevy of ambassadors from separate nations than a national assembly. The Federalist judiciary was the one strong, centralizing branch of government. Marshall knew that and used his powers accordingly. Jefferson knew it too, and was determined to destroy the courts' independence. It is against this backdrop that one must evaluate Marshall's performance.

The Jeffersonians chose impeachment as the weapon to reduce the Federalist redoubt in the judiciary. They began with an easy target: John Pickering, a federal district judge in New Hampshire, who was apparently both insane and a drunkard. These characteristics may not, oddly enough, be sufficient grounds for impeachment. (Article II, section 4 requires "Treason, Bribery, or other high Crimes and Misdemeanors"[3] for the removal of civil officers. But article III, section 1 states that judges "shall hold their Offices during good Behavior,"[4] and it is not settled whether that standard is different from the standard stated under the general impeachment provision.)[5] The House impeached Pickering nonetheless, and the Senate convicted, thus removing him from office. The Federalists feared, correctly, that this was a trial run for the pursuit of more substantial prey. The Jeffersonians did in fact move on to the impeachment of a Justice of the Supreme Court, Samuel Chase. Chase, as we have seen, claimed the power to strike down laws that violated no provision of the Constitution but were, in his view, "contrary to the *great first principles* of the *social compact.*" One wishes the House had impeached and the Senate convicted him for those sentiments. He was chosen instead as a likely opening for a full-scale assault on the Court because he seemed, for other reasons, the most vulnerable of the Justices. A fierce Federalist, he displayed a raging partisanship both on and off the bench. In the event, the Jeffersonians could not muster the two-thirds of the Senate necessary to convict, and Jefferson, calling impeachment "not even a scare-crow," realized that it was not a weapon that could reach John Marshall and the other Federalist Justices.[6]

The Jeffersonian threat to the Court, which was obvious before the attempt on Chase, may have led Marshall to the then much-criticized opinion that has become his most famous. *Marbury* v. *Madison,*[7] the 1803 decision that rationalized, though it was not the first to assume, the Court's power of judicial review, is a curious blend, an essay resting the power to invalidate statutes of Congress on the original understanding of the Constitution and yet reaching the question of that power without justification.

Marshall himself precipitated the case. While serving both as Chief Justice and Secretary of State, he neglected, in his latter capacity, to deliver commissions to some Federalist judges appointed in a rush at the end of Adams's administration. One who failed to receive his commission was William Marbury, confirmed by the Senate for the post of justice of the peace for the District of Columbia.

Jefferson, annoyed at Adams's last-minute packing of the courts, directed his Secretary of State, James Madison, to withhold the undelivered commissions. Marbury and four others in the same situation brought an action in the Supreme Court, where Marshall now presided, seeking a writ of mandamus to compel Madison to deliver the commissions. (A writ of mandamus is a court order directing an official to perform his duty.) It was a very odd lawsuit, one with no chance of success, and it may have been a Federalist political gambit to embarrass the Republicans. Madison was so contemptuous of the suit that he did not even respond.

Marbury had clearly brought his case in the wrong court. Article III of the Constitution, which structures the federal judiciary, places certain classes of cases within the appellate jurisdiction of the Court. These are cases that originate in lower courts and come to the Supreme Court for review. Other classes of cases are placed within the Court's original jurisdiction. These cases begin and end in the Supreme Court. Cases placed in the original jurisdiction are those likely to be especially politically sensitive, such as cases affecting ambassadors or cases in which a state is a party. Though Marbury had filed directly in the Supreme Court, his claim obviously did not qualify to be placed in its original jurisdiction and should have been dismissed out of hand.

Instead, Marshall delivered a long opinion, part of which was designed to embarrass the Jeffersonians for not delivering Marbury's commission, to which he had a legal right, according to Marshall. The other part was a lengthy disquisition on the power of the Court to strike down statutes that were inconsistent with the Constitution. In order to reach that issue, Marshall had not only to ignore the fact that his Court had absolutely no jurisdiction, he had as well to distort the statute in order to make it a fit subject for a holding of unconstitutionality. Congress had authorized the Supreme Court "to issue writs of mandamus, in cases warranted by the principles and usages of law," to officers of the United States. There was nothing in the least controversial in this humdrum and inoffensive power to require an officer to do his duty. But Marshall argued, quite incorrectly, that a writ of mandamus could be issued only in the exercise of the Court's original jurisdiction; hence, Congress had added to the Court's original jurisdiction, which was defined by the Constitution, and had thus impermissibly attempted to alter the Constitution by statute. The statute must, therefore, be struck down.

None of this made much sense. Congress had clearly not attempted to do what Marshall claimed. Mandamus is a well-known writ and had long been used by courts of appellate jurisdiction. There might well, for instance, be cases on appeal in which the Court would wish to issue mandamus to prevent an officer from taking an action that would render the case moot before the Court could decide it. Before and after *Marbury,* courts have found that and other occasions for the issuance of mandamuses in aid of appellate jurisdiction. In fact, the language that supposedly tried to add to the Court's original jurisdiction came at the end of a sentence in which Congress was explicitly dealing with the appellate jurisdiction of the Court. Marshall and his Court had, apparently, deliberately misread a clear statute in order to write an essay on the constitutional power of the Court to declare an act of Congress void.

Contrary to common belief, it was not the first time members of the Court had asserted that power. Eleven years before, in *Hayburn's Case,*[8] most of the Justices had refused to comply with a statute because it assigned them duties not of the judicial nature specified by the Constitution, but no extensive explanations had been given. *Marbury* was decided after Pickering's impeachment but before his removal. Perhaps Marshall, knowing Jefferson's plans for the Court and the nation, was concerned to assert the Court's power more vigorously than the Justices had done in *Hayburn's Case* and to provide an intellectual foundation for judicial supremacy. If so, many commentators since have thought the foundation inadequate to support the structure. That is not to deny that the power claimed exists; there are better arguments than Marshall's for the legitimacy of judicial review.

The good news about *Marbury* is that Marshall placed the Court's power to declare laws unconstitutional directly upon the fact that the United States has a written Constitution. "The powers of the legislature are defined and limited; and that those limits may not be mistaken, or forgotten, the constitution is written. To what purpose are powers limited, and to what purpose is that limitation committed to writing, if these limits may, at any time, be passed by those intended to be restrained?"[9] He said that the theory of every government with a written Constitution "must be, that an act of the legislature, repugnant to the constitution, is void. This theory is essentially attached to a written constitution. . . ." Moreover, "it is apparent, that the framers of the constitution contemplated that instrument, as a rule for the government of *courts,* as well as of the legislature." Chase's speculations in *Calder* v. *Bull* were ignored.

Yet only seven years later, Marshall appeared to adopt, almost in passing, something very like Chase's position on principles of natural justice as a source of judicial power. The Georgia legislature, all but one of whose members appear to have been corrupted (and that member happened to be absent), sold millions of acres along the Yazoo River for prices that ranged between one cent and one and one-half cents per acre, an extraordinarily inadequate price. The Yazoo land fraud, as it came to be called, was the only issue in the next election; the rascals were relieved of any further concern with the people's affairs, and the next legislature rescinded the land grant. In the meantime, however, many of the original purchasers, who had themselves corrupted the prior legislature, resold to others who were apparently innocent. A purchaser sued his seller because the rescission of the grant deprived him of the land and the seller held his money. The case, *Fletcher* v. *Peck*,[10] eventually came to the Supreme Court.

Marshall thought the rescinding statute necessarily rested on a proposition he was unable to accept. "The principle is this; that a legislature may, by its own act, devest the vested estate of any man whatever, for reasons which shall, by itself, be deemed sufficient." Before coming to the conclusion that that principle was foreclosed by article I, section 10 of the Constitution, which provides that "No State shall . . . pass any . . . Law impairing the Obligation of Contracts,"[11] Marshall suggested another ground of invalidity: "It may well be doubted whether the nature of society and of government does not prescribe some limits to the legislative power; and, if any be prescribed, where are they to be found, if the property of an individual, fairly and honestly acquired, may be seized without compensation[?]"[12] He said it was "well worthy of serious reflection" whether transferring the property of an individual to the public "be in the nature of the legislative power." Marshall speculated that a court might enforce an inherent, but unwritten, limit on the legislative power arising from the nature of society and government. This is a remarkable performance, since Marshall, who intended to rely upon a provision of the federal Constitution, had to go well out of his way to float the idea that a court might strike down a statute even where "the constitution is silent."

But Marshall's speculations are tepid compared to the opinion of Justice William Johnson of South Carolina. He began with the sweeping pronouncement: "I do not hesitate to declare that a state does not possess the power of revoking its own grants. But I do it on a general principle, on the reason and nature of things: a principle which will impose laws even on the deity."[13] Marshall at least had suggested extra-constitutional power only over the legislature and left God alone. Given Johnson's extravagant beginning, one reads on with considerable anticipation. Unfortunately, the principle that controls both Georgia and the deity seems too confused for general application.

> When the legislature have once conveyed their interest or property in any subject to the individual, they have lost all control over it; have nothing to act upon; it has passed from them; is vested in the individual; becomes intimately blended with his existence, as essentially so as the blood that circulates through his system. The government may indeed demand of him the one or the other, not because they are not his, but because whatever is his is his country's.

That passage, which is thrown into utter incoherence by its last sentence, was, apparently, clearer to Johnson than article I, section 10. "I have thrown out these ideas that I may have it distinctly understood that my opinion on this point is not founded on the provision in the constitution of the United States, relative to laws impairing the obligation of contracts." Just so. That is the only thing that can be understood.

Fletcher v. *Peck* was, however, the end of the Marshall Court's flirtation with the idea that legislative acts could be overturned on grounds of natural justice or the nature of government and society. Moreover, none of the Justices—Chase, Marshall, and Johnson—who suggested that laws not barred by the Constitution might nevertheless be invalidated by the Court ever gave a reason for that conclusion or ever described how the Court should go about identifying the extra-constitutional principles that might apply. There was no theoretical argument even remotely comparable to the extended justification in *Marbury* for conventional review under the express provisions of the Constitution.

Aside from writing an extensive opinion in *Marbury,* attacking Madison and arguing for judicial review, in a case where the Court had no jurisdiction and where he had to misrepresent a statute in order to make his point, Marshall repeatedly ignored the actual legal materials before him in order to make points he thought important. In *Gibbons* v. *Ogden* (1824),[14] he wrote an opinion for the Court striking down a New York statute that granted a monopoly to operate steamboats on the state's waters. He strongly suggested the possibility that the power over commerce, given to Congress by the Constitution, though Congress had not exercised it, was sufficient to invalidate the law by its mere existence. That suggestion would have meant that the judiciary should assume a power that the Constitution lodges in Congress, and later in the century the suggestion was picked up, so that even today the Court does what Marshall suggested. But he went on in *Gibbons* to hold that Congress had in fact exercised the commerce power, thus preempting New York's law, by providing for the licensing of vessels in the coastal trade. Though the license was rather clearly intended only to exempt American ships from the burdens Congress imposed on foreign ships, Marshall, in a feat of construction reminiscent of his distortion of the mandamus statute in *Marbury,* construed the license as federal permission of unimpeded passage on all navigable waters of the United States.

Yet five years later, in *Willson* v. *Black Bird Creek Marsh Co.,*[15] he upheld Delaware's power to authorize a private company to block a navigable waterway with a dam. He made no mention of either his suggested inference from the existence of the congressional commerce power or of the coasting license, which was present in this case as well. Without explanation, and without authorization by Congress, Marshall simply decided which state regulations of commerce were reasonable and which were not.

It remains true, of course, that Marshall was a great judge and a powerful expositor of the Constitution. His opinion in *McCulloch* v. *Maryland* (1819),[16] upholding the power of Congress to establish the Second Bank of the United States, and denying the power of the state to tax the bank's notes, is a magnificent example of reasoning from the text and the structure of the Constitution. And in *Barron* v. *Baltimore* (1833),[17] Marshall wrote an excellent opinion refusing to apply the prohibitions of the Bill of Rights to the states, drawing inferences from the constitutional text, structure, and history. Yet, as David Currie, who very much admires Marshall, has said, "time and again he seems to have been writing a brief for a conclusion reached independently of the Constitution."[18] He seems, nonetheless, to have reached few conclusions that could not be justified by the Constitution. More objection may be taken to his way with statutes. But he seems to have abused them in order to create occasions for constitutional rulings that appeared essential to solidify the national power the Constitution had attempted to create. It would be wrong for those of us who have never faced the possible failure of the entire enterprise that is the United States to be too easily critical of Marshall's performance. It must be remembered that centrifugal forces remained strong in the United States throughout Marshall's tenure on the Court. Before he left, John C. Calhoun was elaborating his philosophy of virtual state independence, and not even the position of the Court was as secure as we have now come to take for granted. President Andrew Jackson is said to have remarked after the Court decided a land case in favor of an Indian tribe: "John Marshall has made his decision. Now let him enforce it!"[19] The state involved ignored the decision, and Jackson did leave it unenforced. If these conditions provide some justification, by the same token it would be a mistake for us to take Marshall's performance, in all its aspects, as a model for judges now that the basic structure and unity of our nation have been accepted. And it is well to remember that, when Marshall wrote his major essay justifying judicial power to strike down legislation, he did so on the ground that the Constitution is a written document, that it is law, that it governs courts as well as legislatures, and that its principles are those contemplated by the ratifiers and the framers who produced it.

Chief Justice Taney and Dred Scott: The Court Invites a Civil War

After *Marbury,* the Supreme Court did not hold another major federal statute unconstitutional for fifty-four years. If Marshall's cause was nationalism, that of the Supreme Court in 1857 was regionalism, and in *Dred Scott* v. *Sandford*[20] the politics and morality of the Justices combined to produce the worst constitutional decision of the nineteenth century. Speaking only of the constitutional legitimacy of the decision, and not of its morality, this case remained unchallenged as the worst in our history until the twentieth century provided rivals for that title.

The Court headed by Chief Justice Roger Taney of Maryland was dominated by Southerners, and to the South in 1857, as for many years previously, the overriding question of national politics was the "peculiar institution" of slavery. Slavery was attacked and defended on principles of morality, and the South had increasing cause to fear that the rising population and prosperity of the North would soon make it dominant and bring an end to the institution upon which the South's prosperity rested. The problem became particularly acute for both sections of the nation as Americans who moved west and settled territories petitioned Congress for admission to the Union as states. The balance of power in the Union would be determined by whether the new states were admitted as slave or free.

The crisis came to a head when Missouri sought statehood. Congress ultimately admitted Missouri as a state where slavery was permitted but balanced that by admitting Maine as a free state and by prohibiting the introduction of slavery into the rest of the territory acquired by the Louisiana Purchase north of Missouri's southern border. This was the Missouri Compromise of 1820. Congress subsequently followed the practice of admitting paired slave and free states so that the balance of power in the Senate was not altered. Though not satisfactory to the more ardent opponents and defenders of slavery, North and South, this compromise, whatever its morality, had the beneficial political result of allowing the United States to develop with a degree of stability. There is a body of dubious opinion that, had the slavery question been permitted to simmer without exploding, ultimately the institution would have declined and disappeared.[21] Abraham Lincoln was once of that view, "resting in the hope and belief that [slavery] was in course of ultimate extinction,"[22] a view he later abandoned. We may discuss the Court's performance, however, without assessing the accuracy of that belief.

Taney, a Southern partisan, resented the arrogance of the North on the slavery issue and most especially resented the principle, insulting to the South, that lay beneath the North's acceptance of the Missouri Compromise: slavery is an evil and must be limited so long as it cannot be ended. In 1857 he got the chance to make his resentments and his adherence to the cause of the slave states into constitutional law.

Dred Scott was a slave taken by his owner into the free state of Illinois and then to federal territory where slavery had been forbidden by the Missouri Compromise. Having been returned to Missouri, Scott sued for his freedom on the theory that he became free when taken to soil where slavery was outlawed. He first sued in the Missouri courts, where precedent was on his side, and initially won, only to have the decision overturned by the Missouri Supreme Court. Scott turned to the federal courts, lost in the trial court and appealed to the United States Supreme Court, where Taney and a Southern majority awaited him.

The Court produced a welter of opinions. It is sometimes unclear how many Justices joined Taney's "opinion of the Court" on the various grounds he advanced. The case takes up 241 pages in the Reports. There is no need to examine all of its dubious arguments; it was quite evident not only that Scott was to remain a slave but that Taney intended to read into the Constitution the legality of slavery forever. When he was done he had denied the power of the federal government to prevent slavery in any state or territory and the power of the federal government to permit a state to bar slavery within its territory. This, of course, had the result of declaring the Missouri Compromise unconstitutional. It had been repealed in 1854, but Taney's ruling was not entirely gratuitous, because Scott had been in free territory while the Compromise was in effect. What was important was the significance of the ruling for the future. The crucial passage comes near the end of his opinion, and it is as blatant a distortion of the original understanding of the Constitution as one can find.

Taney was determined to prove that the right of property in slaves was guaranteed by the Constitution. He led up to his crucial point by noting, unexceptionably, that when the federal government enters into possession of a territory, "It has no power of any kind beyond [the Constitution]; and it cannot . . . assume discretionary or despotic powers which the Constitution has denied to it."[23] He illustrated his point: "[N]o one, we presume, will contend that Congress can make any law in a Territory respecting the establishment of religion, or the free exercise thereof, or abridging the freedom of speech or of the press, or the right of the people of the Territory peaceably to assemble, and to petition the Government for the redress of grievances."

All well and good. But there is no similar constitutional provision that can be read with any semblance of plausibility to confer a right to own slaves. It may well have been the case that the federal government could not then have freed slaves in states where the law allowed slavery without committing a taking of property for which the fifth amendment to the Constitution would have required compensation. But that is a far different matter from saying that the Constitution requires the federal government to permit and protect slavery in areas under its control. The definition of what is or is not property would seem, at least as an original matter, a question for legislatures.

How, then, can there be a constitutional right to own slaves where a statute forbids it? Taney created such a right by changing the plain meaning of the due process clause of the fifth amendment. He wrote: "[T]he rights of property are united with the rights of person, and placed on the same ground by the fifth amendment to the Constitution, which provides that no person shall be deprived of life, liberty, and property, without due process of law. And an act of Congress which deprives a citizen of the United States of his liberty or property, merely because he came himself or brought his property into a particular Territory of the United States, and who had committed no offence against the laws, could hardly be dignified with the name of due process of law."

The first sentence quotes the guarantee of due process, which is simply a requirement that the substance of any law be applied to a person through fair procedures by any tribunal hearing a case. The clause says nothing whatever about what the substance of the law must be. But Taney's second sentence transforms this requirement of fair procedures into a rule about the allowable substance of a statute. The substance Taney poured into the clause was that Congress cannot prevent slavery in a territory because a man must be allowed to bring slaves there. The second sentence is additionally dishonest because it postulates a man who had "committed no offence against the laws," but a man who brings slaves and keeps them in a jurisdiction where slavery is prohibited does commit an offense against the laws. Taney was saying that there can be no valid federal law against slaveholding anywhere in the United States.

How did Taney know that slave ownership was a constitutional right? Such a right is nowhere to be found in the Constitution. He knew it because he was passionately convinced that it *must* be a constitutional right. Though his transformation of the due process clause from a procedural to a substantive requirement was an obvious sham, it was a momentous sham, for this was the first appearance in American constitutional law of the concept of "substantive due process," and that concept has been used countless times since by judges who want to write their personal beliefs into a document that, most inconveniently, does not contain those beliefs.

Taney did just that, and created a powerful means for later judges to usurp power the actual Constitution places in the American people.

It is clear that the text of the due process clause simply will not support judicial efforts to pour substantive rather than procedural meaning into it. As Professor John Hart Ely put it, "there is simply no avoiding the fact that the word that follows 'due' is 'process.' . . . [W]e apparently need periodic reminding that 'substantive due process' is a contradiction in terms—sort of like 'green pastel redness.' "[24] More than a century after Taney's legerdemain, Justice Hugo Black demonstrated in his *In re Winship* dissent that the constitutional phrase "due process of law" descended from the Magna Carta's guarantee that no freeman should be deprived of his liberty except by the law of the land.[25] Due process was satisfied, therefore, when government proceeded "according to written constitutional and statutory provisions as interpreted by court decisions." When the Court poured substantive content into this procedural provision, Black said, "our Nation ceases to be governed according to the 'law of the land' and instead becomes one governed ultimately by the 'law of the judges.' " He preferred to put his "faith in the words of the written Constitution itself rather than to rely on the shifting, day-to-day standards of fairness of individual judges." The latter is always, and only, what the notion of substantive due process means. But the Supreme Court will not abandon the notion, despite demonstrations of its utter illegitimacy, precisely because it is an ever flowing fount of judicial power.

Professor David Currie wrote that *Dred Scott* "was at least very possibly the first application of substantive due process in the Supreme Court, the original precedent for *Lochner* v. *New York* and *Roe* v. *Wade*."[26] *Lochner* employed substantive due process to strike down a state law limiting the hours of work by bakery employees.[27] *Roe* used substantive due process to create a constitutional right to abortion.[28] *Lochner* and *Roe* have, therefore, a very ugly common ancestor. But once it is conceded that a judge may give the due process clause substantive content, *Dred Scott, Lochner,* and *Roe* are equally valid examples of constitutional law. You may or may not like the judge's politics or his morality, but you have conceded, so far as the Constitution is concerned, the legitimacy of his imposing that politics and morality upon you. Lenin is supposed to have written: "Who says A must say B."[29] In that he was logically correct. Who says *Roe* must say *Lochner* and *Scott*. This is vehemently denied by today's proponents of judicial policymaking, but the denial is hollow and merely means that they like the policies now being made.

Justice Benjamin Curtis of Massachusetts dissented in *Dred Scott,* destroyed Taney's reasoning, and rested his own conclusions upon the original understanding of those who made the Constitution. At one point, complaining of divergent views on congressional power offered by counsel, he wrote: "No particular clause of the Constitution has been referred to. . . ."[30] One argument "rested upon general considerations concerning the social and moral evils of slavery, its relations to republican Governments, its inconsistency with the Declaration of Independence and with natural right." A second was drawn from "the right of self-government, and the nature of the political institutions which have been established by the people of the United States." The third rested upon "the equal right of all citizens to go with their property upon the public domain," so that a regulation excluding slavery from a territory was an "unjust discrimination."

The weight of these considerations, when presented to Congress, Curtis said, was not the concern of the Court. "The question here is, whether they are sufficient to authorize this court to insert into this clause of the Constitution an exception of the exclusion or allowance of slavery, not found therein, nor in any other part of that instrument. . . . To allow this to be done with the Constitution, upon reasons purely political, renders its judicial interpretation impossible—because judicial tribunals, as such, cannot decide upon political considerations."

Curtis went on to make essentially the same argument that Iredell had made in response to Chase, an argument that should have been conclusive: "Political reasons have not the requisite certainty to afford rules of juridical interpretation. They are different in different men. They are different in the same men at different times. And when a strict interpretation of the Constitution, according to the fixed rules which govern the interpretation of laws, is abandoned, and the theoretical opinions of individuals are allowed to control its meaning, we have no longer a Constitution; we are under the government of individual men, who for the time being have power to declare what the Constitution is, according to their own views of what it ought to mean." But Curtis's argument did not prevail then, and it does not deflect willful courts today.

Shortly afterward, Curtis resigned from the Supreme Court and returned to Boston to practice law. His motives were said to be partly financial and partly a loss of confidence in the Court. It would be good to think that he might have borne the financial sacrifice had *Dred Scott* not convinced him that the Court, far from being a serious judicial body, had become hopelessly political, and that he wanted no part of it. Since only one other Justice, John McLean of Ohio, had sided with him, Curtis was entitled to think he could not affect the balance of the Court.

The ruling in *Dred Scott* at once became an explosive national issue. As historian Don Fehrenbacher noted, Taney had ruled "in effect that the Republican party was organized for an illegal purpose. . . . No doubt it contributed significantly to the general accumulation of sectional animosity that made some kind of national crisis increasingly unavoidable."[31] There is something wrong, as somebody has said, with a judicial power that can produce a decision it takes a civil war to overturn.

The Spirit of the Constitution and the Establishment of Justice

Salmon P. Chase of Ohio was one of Lincoln's rivals for the Republican presidential nomination in 1860. Lincoln, once in office, made Chase Secretary of the Treasury. Among his accomplishments in that office was to help finance the Union's efforts in the Civil War by helping to make paper money legal tender of the United States. In 1864, Lincoln appointed him Chief Justice of the United States. Within a few years Chase wrote for a Court majority in *Hepburn* v. *Griswold*,[32] holding that the Constitution forbade making paper legal tender. The decision may well have been correct, though Chase's opinion does not persuade one of that. Of interest for present purposes is that Chase swept to his conclusion with arguments that justify absolutely unlimited judicial power.

In 1860, a Mrs. Hepburn gave a promissory note for 11,250 "dollars" to one Griswold. At the time the note was made, and when it fell due in 1862, gold and silver coins were the only legal tender of the United States. A few days later Congress authorized the issuance of paper money and made it legal tender for the payment of all public and private debts. In 1864, having been sued on the note by Griswold, Hepburn tried to pay the principal and interest with paper money, which Griswold refused because that currency was worth a good deal less than the gold and silver he had been entitled to previously. The question in the suit became whether the act making paper money legal tender for debts already incurred was constitutional.

The Supreme Court thought not, and Griswold received full value. That seems only fair, but the Court had some difficulty in explaining why that fairness was constitutionally mandated. Chase cited Marshall for the proposition that a claimed congressional power must be "consistent with the letter and spirit of the Constitution." Chase skirted the question of the "letter" in favor of the question whether Congress's statute was "consistent with the spirit of the Constitution." With that maneuver he was free of constraint and broke into the open field. It required only a little rhetoric to go the rest of the way. "Among the great cardinal principles of that instrument, no one is more conspicuous or more venerable than the establishment of justice." What was intended by "justice" was "happily, not a matter of disputation. It is not left to inference or conjecture, especially in its relations to contracts." The principle to be applied found "expression in that most valuable provision of the Constitution of the United States, ever recognized as an efficient safeguard against injustice, that 'no State shall pass any law impairing the obligation of contracts.'" Chase admitted, as he had to, that the provision bound only the states, not the federal government. But that was a minor difficulty since "we think it clear that those who framed and those who adopted the Constitution, intended that the spirit of this prohibition should pervade the entire body of legislation, and that the justice which the Constitution was ordained to establish was not thought by them to be compatible with legislation of an opposite tendency."

This would be an incredible performance had we not seen its like so many times since. The Constitution contains not only guarantees of liberty but also powers of government over individuals, including the power to define crimes and punish for them. It would appear to have a number of "spirits," not all of them of the same character. Matters are not helped by Chase's taking as expressing the "spirit" a clause in the Preamble, which is entirely hortatory and not judicially enforceable, stating that a purpose of the Constitution was to "establish Justice." If that states a criterion for judicial review, every judge is free to decide which laws are just and which not. Subjectivism is given free rein. Worse than that, however, there are any number of "spirits" within the Preamble itself: other stated purposes are to "form a more perfect Union," "insure domestic Tranquility, provide for the common defence, promote the general Welfare, and secure the Blessings of Liberty to ourselves and our Posterity."[33] That is a cornucopia of "spirits" for a judge to draw upon in making up his own Constitution. His freehand methodology permitted Chase to say that a provision barring the impairment of the obligation of contracts, which he admitted did not apply to the case, nevertheless applied to the case.

Not satisfied with this, Chase suggested that the legal tender law violated the "spirit" of the fifth amendment's prohibition of the "taking" of private property for public use without just compensation. He closed with a rousing *Dred Scott* finale. The statute, Chase said, deprived Griswold of property without due process of law. That there may have been a legitimate way to reach the same result (the power given Congress in article I, section 8, "To coin Money" may well have been intended to exclude paper money) hardly redeems Chase's irresponsibility.

Judicial Activism in the Service of Property and Free Enterprise

After the Civil War the nation entered upon a long period of growth and industrialization. The judicial devotion to private property and limited government, which had been evident from the beginning of the Republic, now began to face the challenge of new kinds of legislation, some of it designed to further economic development through public expenditures, some of it designed to curb what were thought to be the abuses of a free enterprise system. The Constitution did not easily lend itself to all that the judges' philosophy of the proper role of government and the limits of democratic choice might suggest.

In a great burst of constitution-making prompted by the Civil War, the nation from 1865 to 1870 adopted three major constitutional amendments designed, primarily, to provide the recently freed slaves with the same civil and political rights as all free citizens. The thirteenth amendment prohibited slavery and "involuntary servitude"; the fifteenth guaranteed the right to vote regardless of "race, color, or previous condition of servitude." But the fourteenth amendment, adopted in 1868, became and has remained the great engine of judicial power. The critical language of that amendment, for our purposes, is contained in three clauses: "No State shall make or enforce any law which shall abridge the privileges or immunities of citizens of the United States; nor shall any State deprive any person of life, liberty, or property without due process of law; nor deny to any person within its jurisdiction the equal protection of the laws."[34] The privileges and immunities clause, whose intended meaning remains largely unknown, was given a limited construction by the Supreme Court and has since remained dormant. The due process clause, now made applicable to the states, was, of course, copied from the fifth amendment, which applied only against the federal government. Unlike the other two clauses, it quickly displayed the same capacity to accommodate judicial constitution-making which Taney had found in the fifth amendment's version. The creative use of the equal protection clause for the same purpose had to await the Warren Court of the mid-twentieth century.

In 1869, Louisiana chartered a corporation and gave it a monopoly of slaughterhouses, landings for cattle, and stockyards in a large area that included New Orleans. Butchers precluded from practicing their trade, except on the corporation's land and terms, challenged the law under the thirteenth and fourteenth amendments. The Supreme Court, splitting five to four, sustained the law in the *Slaughter-House Cases*.[35] Justice Samuel Miller's opinion for the Court said that the text and history of the three post–Civil War amendments disclosed a unity of purpose, "the freedom of the slave race, the security and firm establishment of that freedom, and the protection of the newly-made freeman and citizen from the oppressions of those who had formerly exercised unlimited dominion over him." He interpreted privileges and immunities as referring to rights already protected elsewhere in the Constitution and thus, in effect, adding nothing. Of the due process clause, according to Miller, "it is sufficient to say that under no construction of that provision [as already contained in the fifth amendment] that we have ever seen, or any that we deem admissible, can the restraint imposed by the State of Louisiana upon the exercise of their trade by the butchers of New Orleans be held to be a deprivation of property within the meaning of that provision." Moreover, "[w]e doubt very much whether any action of a State not directed by way of discrimination against the negroes as a class, or on account of their race, will ever be held to come within the purview" of the equal protection clause. The fourteenth amendment thus had little reach beyond the protection of those who had been slaves. Though some have complained bitterly about this, Miller was following a sound judicial instinct: to reject a construction of the new amendment that would leave the Court at large in the field of public policy without any guidelines other than the views of its members. He said of the argument by the complaining butchers, "[S]uch a construction . . . would constitute this court a perpetual censor upon all legislation of the States, on the civil rights of their own citizens, with authority to nullify such as it did not approve as consistent with those rights. . . ." In a word, the history of the fourteenth amendment gave judges no guidance on any subject other than the protection of blacks. Beyond that, the Justices had nothing more to apply than their personal views. That, Miller thought, was reason enough to confine the amendment almost entirely to the subject of race.

What is striking about the *Slaughter-House Cases* is not the caution displayed by the majority but rather the radical position of the four dissenters. Justice Stephen Field wrote for them all, stating that the first clause designated "those [privileges and immunities] *which of right belong to the citizens of all free governments.*"[36] These were "natural and inalienable rights" and included "the right to pursue a lawful employment in a lawful manner, without other restraint than such as equally affects all persons." Field actually supported his constitutional position with a quotation from Adam Smith to the effect that hindering a working man from employing his skills as he thinks proper is "a plain violation of this most sacred property. It is a manifest encroachment upon the just liberty both of the workman and of those who might be disposed to employ him." One may be an unyielding admirer of Adam Smith, and of that moral principle in particular, without supposing that Smith wrote the fourteenth amendment or that judges are entitled to enforce *The Wealth of Nations* because its principles should have been in the Constitution.

Justice Joseph Bradley, in an additional dissent, agreed that the Louisiana law abridged the privileges of citizens and also deprived the butchers of liberty and property without due process of law. "Their right of choice is a portion of their liberty; their occupation is their property."[37] Bradley, like the Taney of *Dred Scott,* thus converted a constitutional requirement of just procedures into a prohibition of legislation whose substance he disliked. The difference is that Bradley's principles are admirable and Taney's despicable, but that is not a constitutional difference where nothing in the document authorizes judges to apply *either* principle. Bradley also found the statute in violation of the guarantee of the equal protection of the laws. The presence of three distinct clauses was apparently, in Bradley's view, an embarrassment of riches; any one of them was adequate as a vehicle for his political views. Indeed, he apparently did not even need the fourteenth amendment, for, in a passage remi- niscent of Chase in *Calder* v. *Bull,* Bradley said, "even if the Constitu- tion were silent, the fundamental privileges and immunities of citi- zens, as such, would be no less real and no less inviolable than they now are. It was not necessary to say in words. . . ." Speaking of the dissents in the *Slaughter-House Cases,* David Currie said, "The fundamental-rights notion reflects once again the incessant quest for the judicial holy grail; perhaps at long last we have discov- ered a clause that lets us strike down any law we do not like."[38]

Bradley also protested the limitation of the amendment almost entirely to blacks. "They may have been the primary cause of the amendment, but its language is general, embracing all citizens, and I think it was purposely so expressed."[39] This, too, as we shall see, can be read as an almost illimitable discretionary power in the courts.

The *Slaughter-House Cases* pose the interesting question of the appropriate judicial response to a constitutional provision whose meaning is largely unknown, as was, and is, the meaning of the privileges and immunities clause. It is quite possible that the words meant very little to those who adopted them and that, as Charles Fairman said, the clause came from Representative Bingham of Ohio. "Its euphony and indefiniteness of meaning were a charm to him."[40] Whether that is the case or not, that the ratifiers of the amendment presumably meant something is no reason for a judge, who does not have any idea what that something is, to make up and enforce a meaning that is something else.

The *Slaughter-House Cases* were a narrow victory for judicial moderation and, in the event, proved only a temporary one. The idea that there are rights that are not in the Constitution and yet are enforceable by courts had been gaining ground in some state courts. For example, in 1870 the Wisconsin Supreme Court, in *Whiting* v. *Sheboygan & Fond du Lac Railroad Co.,*[41] without citing a constitutional provision in point, held that the state legislature could not authorize taxes to aid the construction of a privately owned railroad even though a majority of the people should vote in the affirmative. The court simply limited the purposes for which people could be taxed according to the court's political philosophy: "It is obvious, if public benefits and advantages of this kind, and which may be properly called incidental, constitute a public use which will justify a resort to either of these sovereign powers of government, that then all distinction between public and private business, and public and private purposes, is obliterated, and the door to taxation is opened wide for every conceivable object by which the public interest and welfare may be directly or in any wise promoted. Such a doctrine would be subversive to all just ideas of the powers of government and destructive of all rights of private property, leaving every man's estate to be held by him as a mere grace or favor received at the hands of the legislative body."

Michigan's Supreme Court, in *People* v. *Township of Salem*,[42] an 1870 opinion by the distinguished Judge Thomas Cooley, struck down a similar law saying that "there are certain limitations upon this power [to tax], not prescribed in express terms by any constitutional provision, but inherent in the subject itself, which attend its exercise under all circumstances, and which are as inflexible and absolute in their restraints as if directly imposed in the most positive form of words." It was beyond the power of the state to furnish capital to set private parties up in business or to subsidize a going business since "when the State once enters upon the business of subsidies, we shall not fail to discover that the strong and powerful interests are those most likely to control legislation, and that the weaker will be taxed to enhance the profits of the stronger." Therefore, "the first and most fundamental maxim of taxation is violated by the act in question." The "first and most fundamental maxim of taxation," rather curiously had not been included in the constitution that gave the power to tax.

So appealing was this political philosophy disguised as constitutional law that, astonishingly, Justice Miller, who in the *Slaughter-House Cases*, refused to become a "perpetual censor" on all state legislation, one year later, in 1874, became just that. *Loan Association* v. *Topeka*[43] involved a Kansas statute which permitted cities to issue bonds and donate them to private businesses to encourage them to set up in the cities. The bonds would, of course, be paid out of tax revenues. Miller would have none of it. Like the state court judges, he insisted that people could not be taxed except for a public purpose, and it was up to the courts not only to impose this limitation but to define what such a purpose was. Unless such a limitation were imposed on the legislative power by judges, government would hold the lives, liberty, and property of its citizens subject to the most absolute despotism; "a despotism of the many, of the majority, if you choose to call it so, but it is none the less a despotism." It was not enough to have a Constitution that limited the powers of government and guaranteed specific freedoms of persons; it was necessary to have still further limitations invented by judges. "There are limitations on such power which grow out of the essential nature of all free governments. Implied reservations of individual rights, without which the social compact could not exist, and which are respected by all governments entitled to the name." No provision of any constitution was invoked for this remarkable performance. Miller closed with a recitation of state cases upholding the same principle and seemed to view with particular approbation a decision by the Supreme Judicial Court of Massachusetts striking down taxation to provide funds to aid owners to rebuild "after the disastrous fire in Boston, in 1872, which laid an important part of that city in ashes."

The sole dissenter in *Loan Association* was Justice Nathan Clifford, who wrote that

> . . . the better opinion is that where the constitution of the State contains no prohibition upon the subject, express or implied, neither the State nor Federal courts can declare a statute of the State void as unwise, unjust, or inexpedient, nor for any other cause, unless it be repugnant to the Federal Constitution. Except where the Constitution has imposed limits upon the legislative power the rule of law appears to be that the power of legislation must be considered as practically absolute, whether the law operates according to natural justice or not in any particular case, for the reason that courts are not the guardians of the rights of the people of the State, save where those rights are secured by some constitutional provision which comes within judicial cognizance; or, in the language of Marshall, C. J., "The interest, wisdom, and justice of the representative body furnish the only security in a large class of cases not regulated by any constitutional provision."
>
> Courts cannot nullify an act of the State legislature on the vague ground that they think it opposed to a general latent spirit supposed to pervade or underlie the constitution, where neither the terms nor the implications of the instrument disclose any such restriction. Such a power is denied to the courts, because to concede it would be to make the courts sovereign over both the constitution and the people, and convert the government into a judicial despotism.[44]

Of course the power claimed by the *Loan Association* majority would convert the government into a "judicial despotism"; in some degree, it has. The despotism is selective; it does not operate on all subjects of life all of the time. But it is there, ready to hand, when judges feel strongly enough. Clifford made the case for the correct judicial role about as well as it can be made. The security furnished by "the interest, wisdom, and justice" of the legislature is at least as good as that provided by free-ranging judges, with the added advantage that legislative despotism, if you, with Justice Miller, are pleased to call it that, can be cured at the polls. But logical demonstrations based upon the character of our republican form of government, in which courts do not rule as they see fit, is, apparently, no match for the passions of judges. In such behavior, of course, judges are encouraged not only by those who share their politics but by lawyers who see in the absence of law, and the existence of unguided judicial discretion, always the possibility of winning.

Indeed, Justice Miller saw what was happening and yet could not bring himself to cut it short. In *Davidson* v. *New Orleans*,[45] an 1877 decision, he managed to say both that the due process clause of the fourteenth amendment was satisfied by a fair judicial procedure and also that it was not, because the clause had substantive content. He and the Court held that "it is not possible to hold that a party has, without due process of law, been deprived of his property, when, as regards the issues affecting it, he has, by the laws of the State, a fair trial in a court of justice, according to the modes of proceeding applicable to such a case." Yet, a few pages earlier, he said that "a statute which declares in terms, and without more, that the full and exclusive title of a described piece of land, which is now in A., shall be and is hereby vested in B., would, if effectual, deprive A. of his property without due process of law, within the meaning of the constitutional provision." So a fair judicial proceeding would not be enough; the clause prohibits some undefined category of substantive legislation, of which Miller offered only one instance. The bar was thus invited to continue challenging the substance of statutes under the due process clause and simultaneously kept in the dark as to what the Court thought that clause might cover.

Given that performance, it required considerable gall for Miller to write, in the same brief opinion: "[T]here exists some strange misconception of the scope of this provision as found in the fourteenth amendment. In fact, it would seem, from the character of many of the cases before us, and the arguments made in them, that the clause under consideration is looked upon as a means of bringing to the test of the decision of this court the abstract opinions of every unsuc-

cessful litigant in a State court . . . of the merits of the legislation.
. . ." On the basis of Miller's own performance, that view of the
clause was not a "misconception" but a perfectly rational litigating
stance. And so it proved.

Substantive due process, though it had originated in the judicial
desire to protect slavery, had now been validated as constitutional
doctrine. Perhaps "doctrine" implies too much of rationality and
intellectual rigor. Since the clause was designed only to require
fair procedures in implementing laws, there is no original understanding that gives it any substantive content. Thus, a judge who insists
upon giving the due process clause such content must make it up.
That is why substantive due process, wherever it appears, is never
more than a pretense that the judge's views are in the Constitution.
That has been true from *Dred Scott* to today.

The doctrine took a new turn in *Allgeyer* v. *Louisiana*.[46] Justice
Rufus Peckham, writing for a unanimous Court, held that the word
"liberty" in the due process clause meant "liberty of contract." The
real Constitution, in an altogether different provision, had been interpreted to prevent states from impairing the obligation only of existing
contracts. Now, Peckham invented a provision preventing states
from forbidding the making of new contracts that the Justices thought
worthy. Louisiana enacted a statute imposing fines on persons who
did any act to effect marine insurance with any company that had
not complied with the laws of the state. Allgeyer made an open
marine insurance contract with a New York company calling for
insurance to go into effect when he notified the company that a
shipment was being made. He wrote a letter from New Orleans
notifying the company of a shipment of cotton and the state levied
fines upon him because the company had not complied with Louisiana
law.

Peckham conceded that Louisiana could put such conditions as
it pleased upon doing business within the state but insisted that it
could not punish the mailing of a letter from the state, where the
cotton was, to bring insurance coverage into effect. He said, in a
passage conspicuous for its circularity, "To deprive the citizen of
such a right as herein described without due process of law is illegal."
Why did the statute lack due process? "Such a statute as this in
question is not due process of law, because it prohibits an act which
under the Federal Constitution the defendants had a right to perform." Where in the Constitution is this right to be found? Why,
in the due process clause. How do we know that this right is in

the due process clause? Because Peckham and his brethren put it there. "The liberty mentioned in that amendment means . . . the right of the citizen to be free in the enjoyment of all his faculties; to be free to use them in all lawful ways; to live and work where he will; to earn his livelihood by any lawful calling; to pursue any livelihood or avocation, and for that purpose to enter into all contracts which may be proper, necessary and essential to his carrying out to a successful conclusion the purposes above mentioned."

Louisiana, through its legislature, had already decided that what Allgeyer did was unlawful. So Peckham's rule that citizens are free to do whatever is "lawful" meant that, without the assistance of any constitutional provision, he and not the legislature would decide what was lawful and what was not. The assumption of authority was open-ended and ad hoc, so it was not too surprising that Peckham wrote, "When and how far [the state's legislative] power may be legitimately exercised with regard to these subjects must be left for determination to each case as it arises." This was lawlessness. The Court made up an entire new set of freedoms, including a liberty to enter into contracts the legislature had prohibited, then refused to say what contracts were protected, but promised to go from case to case deciding in each whether the legislature or the Court would govern.

Peckham was as good as his word. In 1905 he wrote an opinion whose name lives in the law as the symbol, indeed the quintessence, of judicial usurpation of power: *Lochner v. New York.*[47] To this day, when a judge simply makes up the Constitution he is said "to Lochnerize," usually by someone who does not like the result. A New York statute set maximum daily and weekly hours for bakers. Six Justices struck the law down, calling statutes of this nature "mere meddlesome interferences with the rights of the individual." "The general right to make a contract in relation to his business is part of the liberty of the individual protected by the Fourteenth Amendment. . . . The right to purchase or sell labor is part of the liberty protected . . . unless there are circumstances which exclude the right." Peckham thought it proper to limit hours where the nature of the work made that reasonable, but baking, in his view, was not such work. Peckham employed another concept that judges have found useful in overturning legislation, the concept of "the police power." That is a term historically given to the general powers of legislatures. The better view of state legislative power is that, as Justice Iredell said in *Calder v. Bull,* it encompasses the power to make any enactment whatever that is not forbidden by a provision of a constitution.[48] In such cases, as Chief Justice Marshall said, the protection of citizens lies in the "interest, wisdom, and justice" of their elected representatives. But a different view of the police power, to which Peckham subscribed, came into being: that the power had inherent limits independent of any constitutional prohibition, and that judges could enforce those limits by invalidating legislation even where the Constitution was silent. That idea, of course, gave judges free rein to decide what were and were not proper legislative purposes.

Four Justices dissented in *Lochner,* but three of them accepted the notion that there was a liberty of contract to be found in the due process clause of the fourteenth amendment. Even the dissent of Justice Oliver Wendell Holmes, Jr., which has become famous in the law, was flawed in this manner. "I strongly believe," he wrote, "that my agreement or disagreement has nothing to do with the right of a majority to embody their opinions in law. It is settled by various decisions of this court that state constitutions and state laws may regulate life in many ways which we as legislators might think as injudicious or if you like as tyrannical as this, and which equally with this interfere with the liberty to contract. . . . The liberty of the citizen to do as he likes so long as he does not interfere with the liberty of others to do the same, which has been a shibboleth for some well-known writers, is interfered with by school laws, by the Post Office, by every state or municipal institution which takes his money for purposes thought desirable, whether he likes it or not."[49]

Holmes went on in an oft-quoted passage: "[A] constitution is not intended to embody a particular economic theory, whether of paternalism and the organic relation of the citizen to the State or of *laissez faire*. It is made for people of fundamentally differing views. . . ." But he spoiled it all by adding, "I think that the word liberty in the Fourteenth Amendment is perverted when it is held to prevent the natural outcome of a dominant opinion, *unless it can be said that a rational and fair man necessarily would admit that the statute proposed would infringe fundamental principles as they have been understood by the traditions of our people and our law.*" So Holmes, after all, did accept substantive due process, he merely disagreed with Peckham and the majority about which principles were fundamental. Nor did he explain why a free people could not decide to change or abandon principles supported by tradition but not by the Constitution. There was no Justice on the Court who was not prepared to substitute his opinions for those of elected representatives at some point. The difference was merely about when that point was reached.

It is hard to say why *Lochner* rather than *Allgeyer* became the symbol of judicial usurpation of power. Perhaps the reason is that to the modern liberal mind it is essential that the state have the power to protect labor while the regulation of the details of the insurance business are unimportant. Or perhaps it is that Holmes who, oddly enough, given most of his views, is a hero to liberals, wrote a dissent in *Lochner*. The fact remains, however, that, as judicial performances the two are indistinguishable and equally unjustifiable assumptions of power. But, even with *Lochner,* the Court had not yet hit its stride. It will be possible to discuss only a few representative cases. Both federal and state courts were producing lots of *Lochners*.

Adair v. *United States,*[50] in 1908, struck down, under the due process clause of the fifth amendment, a federal statute banning "yellow dog" contracts—contracts by which an employee agreed not to join a union—on interstate railroads. In 1915, *Coppage* v. *Kansas*[51] held unconstitutional a similar state law. *Adkins* v. *Children's Hospital,*[52] a 1923 decision, invalidated a District of Columbia law setting minimum wages for women. The statute was defended on the ground that women needed special protection. The majority opinion argued that the passage of the nineteenth amendment, giving women the vote, meant that their civil inferiority was almost at a "vanishing point," which in turn meant that their liberty of contract was equal to that of men. This enabled Holmes, in dissent, to give the case its one memorable remark: "It will need more than the 19th Amendment to convince me that there are no differences between men and women."[53]

The Court went on to strike down a Washington law forbidding employment agencies to collect fees from workers; a Pennsylvania enactment forbidding corporate ownership of pharmacies unless all the corporation's shareholders were licensed pharmacists; and an Oklahoma statute treating the manufacture of ice as a public utility and requiring any would-be entrant into the business to obtain from the state a certificate of public convenience and necessity. Many of these laws were pernicious. The pharmacy law was designed merely to prevent consumers from enjoying, and pharmacists from suffering, the competition of lower-cost services and medicines. The ice statute was an attempt to give existing ice manufacturers monopoly profits at the expense of consumers. The minimum wage law has the effect of putting less skilled workers out of work and limiting the competition of others with unionized labor. Perhaps there ought to have been a constitutional provision invalidating those laws. But there was not, and the Court had no business striking them down.

The Court's use of the concept of substantive due process was not limited to the protection of economic liberty, however. Immediately after the end of World War I, Nebraska and other states, including Iowa and Ohio, enacted laws that made it a criminal offense to teach a child who had not passed the eighth grade any language other than English. One Meyer was convicted in Nebraska of teaching a ten-year-old child attending a Lutheran parochial school to read German. The Supreme Court of Nebraska, in upholding the statute, made its purpose clear: foreigners who came to this country often reared and educated their children in the language of their native land; the children thus thought in that language and hence were inculcated with ideas and sentiments contrary to the best interests of the United States; for that reason, the children must be taught no language other than English.

In *Meyer* v. *Nebraska*,[54] the Supreme Court of the United States, in an opinion by Justice McReynolds, who is usually derided as a reactionary, and over a dissent by Justice Holmes, often mistakenly viewed as a liberal, held the statute unconstitutional under the due process clause of the fourteenth amendment. McReynolds began with the usual litany about the liberties protected by the due process clause—freedom from bodily restraint, the right to contract, to engage in the common occupations, to acquire useful knowledge, to marry, establish a home and bring up children, to worship God according to the dictates of one's own conscience, and "generally to enjoy those privileges long recognized at common law as essential to the orderly pursuit of happiness by free men." Some of the listed freedoms, of course, are protected explicitly by other clauses of the Constitution. To the degree that McReynolds would apply them against the states through the due process clause, he was anticipating the later doctrine of "incorporation." But he did not articulate that technique here.

McReynolds's opinion was short and uninformative. He did not doubt the power of the state to compel attendance at some school, require that schools give instruction in English, and prescribe a curriculum for schools it supports. But the prohibition went too far: "Mere knowledge of the German language cannot reasonably be regarded as harmful." Holmes, today viewed as a civil libertarian, dissented because he thought the statute reasonable: "Youth is the time when familiarity with a language is established and if there are sections in the State where a child would hear only Polish or French or German spoken at home I am not prepared to say that it is unreasonable to provide that in his early years he shall hear and speak only English at school."[55]

Two years later, in 1925, another case involving the states' power over education came to the Supreme Court in *Pierce* v. *Society of Sisters*.[56] Oregon's new Compulsory Education Act made it a misdemeanor for any parent to send a child who had not completed the eighth grade to any school other than a public one. The Society of Sisters operated primary schools that taught the subjects usually taught in the public schools and also provided systematic religious instruction and moral training according to the tenets of the Roman Catholic Church. The Hill Military Academy conducted primary schools in which the courses of study conformed to state requirements and also gave military instruction and training. Both institutions challenged the act under the fourteenth amendment. Justice McReynolds's opinion for a unanimous Court stressed that there was no challenge to the power of the state to require attendance at some school, that certain studies be taught, and that nothing be taught that was manifestly inimical to the public welfare. The state could, of course, regulate, inspect, test, and supervise to ensure that its regulations were followed. The statute failed, however, under the doctrine of *Meyer* v. *Nebraska*. "The fundamental theory of liberty upon which all governments in this Union repose excludes any general power of the State to standardize its children by forcing them to accept instruction from public teachers only."

This last sentence suggests that McReynolds could have decided *Meyer* and *Pierce* in the same way by using an actual constitutional value rather than a judge-invented one. That was what Justice Hugo Black later attempted when he persuaded the Court that the fourteenth amendment incorporated, and so enforced against the states, various provisions of the Bill of Rights. Whatever the historical merits of that approach, it had the potential of confining judges to rights specified in the Constitution. In the end, Black's strategy was unavailing. Court majorities accepted the power to enforce both the actual rights incorporated and new rights of their own invention.

In both *Meyer* and *Pierce,* it seems plain, the state was attempting to prevent the teaching of ideas not officially approved. In *Meyer,* learning German, or any other foreign language, at an early age was thought by the state to pose the danger of the inculcation of foreign ideas contrary to the best interests of the United States. Similarly, in *Pierce* the state wanted to do more than ensure that certain subjects and ideas were taught; it wanted to make sure that other ideas were not taught. Indeed, though it swept more broadly, the law was largely the product of anti-Catholic prejudice. So viewed, both of these decisions could have been laid under the guarantee of freedom of speech in the first amendment, and the application of Oregon's statute to the Society of Sisters might have been invalidated as well under that amendment's guarantee of the free exercise of religion.

It is unfortunate that the Court chose to use the undefined notion of substantive due process instead, because that notion, which is wholly without limits, as well as without legitimacy, provided a warrant for later Courts to legislate at will. The use of substantive due process to invalidate economic regulations became highly unpopular. The fact that it had been used in *Meyer* and *Pierce* to defend real constitutional rights lent a spurious legitimacy to later decisions using the due process clause to create new rights which are neither mentioned nor implied anywhere in the Constitution or its history.

In his 1905 *Lochner* opinion, Justice Peckham, defending liberty from what he conceived to be "a mere meddlesome interference," asked rhetorically, "[A]re we all . . . at the mercy of legislative majorities?"[57] The correct answer, where the Constitution is silent, must be "yes." Being "at the mercy of legislative majorities" is merely another way of describing the basic American plan: representative democracy. We may all deplore its results from time to time, but that does not empower judges to set them aside; the Constitution allows only voters to do that.

By the 1930s, with the deepening of the Depression and a consequent spectacular alteration of political forces, voters put in power an administration that had to change the Court's performance radically in order to accomplish its ends.

2

The New Deal Court and the Constitutional Revolution

*T*he Supreme Court's behavior, its systematic frustration of the political branches, eventually erupted in a constitutional crisis. But the crisis arose less because the Court's behavior was illegitimate than because the judge-made values it protected suddenly went out of political and intellectual fashion. The Court could not stand for long against the large majorities that now opposed its work.

Federalism and Sick Chickens

Prior to the New Deal, there had been many attempts at the state and federal level to regulate business in a variety of ways, and the Court had struck down scores of these laws. Most of the regulations were enacted by states, and the Court usually employed the substantive due process technique. But with the coming of the Great Depression and the election of Franklin D. Roosevelt, there was an outpouring of regulation at the national level. Here the Court had additional techniques for invalidating laws. The substantive due process notion was practically the only device the Court had for invalidating state regulation, but national regulation could be curbed by finding that it was not within the scope of the powers granted Congress in article I, section 8 of the Constitution.

That is precisely what the Court did, holding again and again that attempted national economic regulations went beyond the power to regulate interstate commerce or the power to lay and collect taxes. Roosevelt's programs for recovery from the Depression were severely imperiled. A keystone of the New Deal's strategy was the National Industrial Recovery Act of 1932, which gave the President power to approve and impose codes for various industries and trades. The Supreme Court found it unconstitutional in *Schechter Poultry Corp.* v. *United States*,[1] the "sick chicken case," which involved the application of a code's minimum wage, maximum hour, and trade practice provisions to a kosher poultry slaughterer in Brooklyn. The Court held that conditions in Schechter's plant had only an indirect effect upon interstate commerce and hence was not within congressional power. The opinion also said that giving the President the power to impose codes upon industry was an unlawful delegation of legislative power to the executive.

Both of these points had considerable merit, though the *Schechter* decision is now regarded as utterly obsolete. There is little doubt that those who framed and ratified the Constitution enumerated the powers given the national legislature—and for good measure added the tenth amendment, "The powers not delegated to the United States by the Constitution, nor prohibited by it to the States, are reserved to the States respectively, or to the people"[2]—so that the federal government could not govern many aspects of life. Leaving the states as the sole regulators of areas left beyond federal power is the constitutional doctrine of federalism. Today it is usually thought passé, quaint, or even tyrannical, this last because federalism, rephrased as "states' rights," permitted some states to legislate racial discrimination.

But federalism also had an important benign aspect, the protection of individual liberty. The geographical areas over which state governments rule are far smaller than that the federal government controls. People who found state regulation oppressive could vote with their feet, and in massive numbers they did. Blacks engaged in great migrations to Northern states at a time when Southern states blatantly discriminated. Businesses that found state taxation or regulation too burdensome moved elsewhere. Individuals moved to avoid heavy state income and estate taxes. Of course, this freedom to escape came at a price, but a far smaller one than moving away from national regulation, and many found the price worth paying. That freedom would be drastically curtailed if the national government had the power to impose all of the same burdens. Indeed, that was and is often the argument for national power: since people and businesses cannot be effectively coerced if they can flee the jurisdiction, we must enlarge the jurisdiction to make escape impractical.

Federalism is, moreover, the only constitutional protection of liberty that is neutral. The various amendments to the Constitution specify what freedom is protected—freedom of speech, press, religion, freedom from unreasonable searches, and so on. If a liberty you cherish does not fall within one of the specified categories (or does not appeal to judges who are making up new constitutional rights), you will receive no protection from the courts. But if another state allows the liberty you value, you can move there, and the choice of what freedom you value is yours alone, not dependent on those who made the Constitution. In this sense, federalism is the constitutional guarantee most protective of the individual's freedom to make his own choices. There is much to be said, therefore, for a Court that attempted to preserve federalism, which is a real constitutional principle, by setting limits to national powers.

The Court's behavior, however, enraged Roosevelt and the leading figures of the New Deal. The Court struck down the Railroad Retirement Act of 1934,[3] the Bituminous Coal Conservation Act of 1935,[4] and the Agricultural Adjustment Act of 1933,[5] and the administration feared for the validity of such laws as the National Labor Relations Act and the Social Security Act. Lower court judges had issued hundreds of injunctions against New Deal programs.

The New Deal was an economic and governmental upheaval. It stood for a sudden and enormous centralization of power in Washington over matters previously left to state governments or left in private hands, a centralization accomplished largely through the assumption of greatly expanded congressional powers to regulate commerce and lay taxes. Many judges, however, believed that the New Deal was assuming powers far beyond those the Constitution permitted. There was thus a collision between an emergent Zeitgeist, reflected in the political branches, and the old ideas, entrenched in the courts, that was regarded by both sides as a constitutional crisis. The same thing had happened when Jefferson's Republicans won the presidency and the Congress only to be faced by a solidly Federalist judiciary. The reaction by the politicians in both cases was the same: an assault upon the independence of the federal courts. Jefferson chose impeachments of the Justices, a tactic that quickly failed. Roosevelt chose enlargement of the Court so that his additional appointments would produce a majority sympathetic to New Deal legislation, a tactic that also failed.

Roosevelt Fails, Then Succeeds, in Remaking the Court

After his landslide victory in the 1936 election, Roosevelt decided not only to attack the Court directly but to do so disingenuously. The disingenuousness may well have cost him the fight. The attempt certainly cost him enormous political capital. Instead of announcing that the Court was killing essential legislation with, in his view, unjustifiably narrow interpretations of federal powers, and that he proposed, for that reason, to return the Court to a proper understanding of the Constitution, Roosevelt disguised his plan as one to help the Court with its workload, intimating that the elderly Justices could not keep up. His bill provided that when any judge of the United States reached the age of seventy and did not resign or retire, the President could, with Senate confirmation, appoint one additional judge to the court where the older judge served. Six Justices of the Supreme Court were then over seventy. Roosevelt could have appointed six more, and five-to-four decisions against the New Deal presumably would have gone for the administration, ten to five. The pretense that the bill was designed as assistance to aged judges was instantly denounced as a ruse, and Roosevelt later urged the measure on the actual grounds that motivated it—"the Court has been assuming the power to pass on the wisdom" of acts of Congress, and it was necessary to "take action to save the Constitution from the Court and the Court from itself." "We must," he continued in his radio address to the nation, "find a way to take an appeal from the Supreme Court to the Constitution itself."[6]

This is a problem that has baffled, frustrated, and enraged many a President, many a Congress, and, indeed, large numbers of citizens. The Supreme Court may be issuing rulings that have no basis in the Constitution, but how is the nation to cope with that unconstitutional assumption of power? Jefferson tried impeachment; Andrew Jackson ignored the Court when it suited him; Abraham Lincoln ignored Chief Justice Taney's writ of habeas corpus during the Civil War ("I must violate one provision of the Constitution so that all the rest may be saved");[7] Ulysses Grant did manage to enlarge the Court to alter its course; Senator LaFollette proposed a constitutional amendment that would allow two-thirds of the Senate to overrule a Court decision; Roosevelt tried to "pack" the Court; and in recent years there have been a number of proposals to eliminate the Court's jurisdiction over particular classes of cases under the congressional power, given in article III of the Constitution, to make exceptions to the Court's appellate jurisdiction.

Almost all such attempts have proved fruitless, and it is not hard to see why. Americans revere both the Constitution and an independent Court that applies the document's provisions. The Court has done many excellent things in our history, and few people are willing to see its power broken. The difficulty with all proposals to respond to the Court when it behaves unconstitutionally is that they would create a power to destroy the Court's essential work as well. If two-thirds of the Senate might have overruled *Dred Scott,* then perhaps it is imaginable that two-thirds might have overruled a case like *Brown* v. *Board of Education.*[8] That depends upon the passions of the moment, but it is obvious that unpopular proper rulings may as easily be overturned as improper ones. There is, after all, no reason to think that over time the Senate will be a more responsible interpreter of the Constitution than the Court.

This sense that once we start tampering with the Court there will be no end to the matter probably accounts for the vociferousness with which the Senate Judiciary Committee disapproved Roosevelt's bill. "We recommend the rejection of this bill as a needless, futile, and utterly dangerous abandonment of constitutional principle. . . . [I]ts practical operation would be to make the Constitution what the executive or legislative branches of the Government choose to say it is—an interpretation to be changed with each change of administration. It is a measure which should be so emphatically rejected that its parallel will never again be presented to the free representatives of the free people of America."[9]

The Court's power lies entirely in the fact that the American people choose to obey even its least defensible mandates rather than contemplate the alternative. In that sense, it is the Court's vulnerability that makes it invulnerable. If that is true, the only safeguard we have in the long run against the abuse of a judicial power, which we have agreed in advance to obey, is the formation of a consensus about how judges should behave, a consensus which, by its intellectual and moral force, disciplines those who are subject, and properly so, to no other discipline.

Roosevelt was fortunate, however, for there is, despite what I have just said, one other force that disciplines judges: mortality. The Justices who were trying to enforce constitutional limits on federal power were quite old. There is a dispute whether the threat of political retaliation against the Court induced Justice Roberts to look more favorably on New Deal legislation ("the switch in time that saved nine").[10] That is unimportant, however, for within four years resignations, retirements, and death allowed Roosevelt to remake the Court as he desired. In rapid succession he appointed Hugo Black, who had led the fight in the Senate to pack the Court, Stanley Reed, Felix Frankfurter, William O. Douglas, Frank Murphy, James Byrnes, and Robert Jackson, and elevated Harlan Stone from Associate Justice to Chief Justice. A few years later he appointed Wiley Rutledge. New Court decisions made congressional power over commerce virtually limitless as the Court simply stopped protecting federalism.

The Court Stops Protecting Federalism

Wickard v. *Filburn*[11] held that a farmer who raised wheat for consumption on his own farm could be penalized for exceeding the quota set by the Secretary of Agriculture in order to hold up the price of wheat. Even though the wheat is never marketed but is consumed on the farm, "it supplies a need of the man who grew it which would otherwise be reflected by purchases in the open market. Home-grown wheat in this sense competes with wheat in commerce." Hence the amount grown could be set by the national government under its power to regulate interstate commerce. Sound economics without doubt, but it meant that the most trivial and local activities could be regulated, a conclusion the Court that had just passed into history would never have countenanced.

It is well to be clear that the new, permissive attitude toward congressional power was a manifestation of judicial activism. The Constitution does indicate that there are defined national powers and that they have limits. The fact that the powers of Congress are enumerated in article I, section 8,[12] demonstrates that Congress was not intended to have unlimited powers, even aside from the specific limitations stated, primarily, in the Bill of Rights. That necessary inference is reinforced by the tenth amendment: "The powers not delegated to the United States by the Constitution, nor prohibited by it to the States, are reserved to the States respectively, or to the people."[13] There were two kinds of limits to Congress's power. To take the power to regulate commerce "among the several States" as an example, federal regulation was seen as confined to that commerce that affected more states than one, so that there was some intrastate commerce beyond Congress's reach. In addition, a regulation of commerce had to be done for commercial reasons and not as a means of effecting social or moral regulation. The new

Court's refusal to enforce limits of any kind simply abandoned this aspect of the Constitution. That worked a revolution in the relationship of the federal government to the state governments and to the people, and the revolution did not have to await a constitutional amendment. The lesson to be learned from this is that the Court cannot stand forever against a strong and persistent political movement.

Our concern, however, is less with the economic nationalizing thrust of the New Deal Court than with its employment of those techniques that had enabled prior Courts to make policy judgments in the guise of constitutional principle in the cases that came before them.

Economic Due Process Abandoned

The notion of substantive due process had been used by prior Courts to protect both economic and noneconomic liberties, but there had been some indication prior to the New Deal Court that the protection of economic freedom was likely to decline. In 1934, a five-to-four decision in *Nebbia* v. *New York*[14] upheld a New York statute empowering a Milk Control Board to fix maximum and minimum retail prices for milk. Nebbia was convicted of selling milk too cheaply in his grocery store. The effect of the statute, and its obvious purpose, was to transfer money from consumers to milk producers. There could hardly be a case that more clearly met Justice Miller's test in *Davidson,* that a statute transferring title in land from A to B would violate the due process clause. Justice McReynolds's dissent, without citing *Davidson,* paralleled it: "[F]ixation of the price at which 'A,' engaged in an ordinary business, may sell, in order to enable 'B,' a producer, to improve his condition, has not been regarded as within legislative power."[15] But Justice Roberts's majority opinion said that "a state is free to adopt whatever economic policy may reasonably be deemed to promote public welfare. . . . With the wisdom of the policy adopted . . . the courts are both incompetent and unauthorized to deal." McReynolds, consistently with the old substantive due process view, insisted that "this Court must have regard to the wisdom of the enactment."

That the Court's mood was changing became more apparent in 1937, before Roosevelt's appointments but after his proposal to pack the Court, when, in *West Coast Hotel Co.* v. *Parrish,*[16] a Washington law setting minimum wages for women was upheld despite the *Adkins*[17] decision of 1923 striking down a similar District of Columbia law. It was well that *Adkins* was overruled, since there is nothing in the Constitution that prohibits minimum wage legislation, though such legislation is certainly unwise. But Chief Justice Hughes took a different line. He related in considerable detail the conditions and economic arguments that made the law desirable.

There are three things wrong with that approach. The first is that it throws the Court's considerable prestige behind a political decision and endorses a line of economic argument, which in this case happened to be quite wrong. That tends to affect the balance of opposing contentions in the political marketplace. The second is that the concept of substantive due process was kept alive because the Court purported to examine the conditions that made the so-called liberty of contract inapplicable. Thus, an extraconstitutional idea was left to do damage in the future. Third, the performance lent itself to disingenuousness in the future. The Court purported to apply the constitutional doctrine of substantive due process to economic regulation, but in fact the Court abolished the doctrine, because from then on every such regulation of economic activity was upheld. The list of judicially fashionable human freedoms had changed.

The Discovery of "Discrete and Insular Minorities"

It quickly became apparent that *Nebbia* and *West Coast Hotel* were accurate weather vanes. In *United States* v. *Carolene Products Co.,*[18] the Court sustained Congress's prohibition of the interstate shipment of "filled milk," milk mixed with any fat or oil other than milk fat. The Court rejected a due process attack by saying that the judicial inquiry must be limited to the question of whether any state of facts either known or which could be reasonably assumed provided any support for the statute. This was to become a deadly formula, for the Court proved quite ready to engage in the most extended and improbable conjectures about why legislatures might have thought economic regulations rational. The result was the appearance of judicial review without the reality.

But *Carolene Products* gave birth to an even more pernicious approach to questions of individual liberty and legislative power. In the famous footnote four to that opinion, Justice Stone said for the Court:

There may be narrower scope for operation of the presumption of constitutionality when legislation appears on its face to be within a specific prohibition of the Constitution, such as those of the first ten amendments, which are deemed equally specific when held to be embraced within the Fourteenth.[19]

That there should be any presumption of constitutionality for legislation that on its face is prohibited by a provision of the Constitution seems decidedly odd. That the presumption should be narrower than when no prohibition of the Constitution applies would seem indisputable. In the latter case, there should be a conclusive presumption of constitutionality. One might suspect that Justice Stone was preparing the way for something not so indisputable.

It is unnecessary to consider now whether legislation which restricts those political processes which can ordinarily be expected to bring about repeal of undesirable legislation, is to be subjected to more exacting judicial scrutiny under the general prohibitions of the Fourteenth Amendment than are most other types of legislation. [He cited cases invalidating restrictions on the right to vote on racial grounds, restraints on the dissemination of information and on interferences with political organizations, and the prohibition of peaceable assembly.]

Even the suggestion that legislation of the types cited might not be subjected to more exacting scrutiny seems almost disingenuous. The Court had already shown that it was prepared to enforce such constitutional values against state legislation.

Nor need we enquire whether similar considerations enter into the review of statutes directed at particular religious [citing *Pierce*], or national [citing *Meyer*], or racial minorities [citing cases on exclusions from primary elections on the basis of race].

These instances are again obvious cases for judicial holdings of unconstitutionality, but then came the apparent point of the footnote:

. . . whether prejudice against discrete and insular minorities may be a special condition, which tends seriously to curtail the operation of those political processes ordinarily to be relied upon to protect minorities, and which may call for a correspondingly more searching judicial inquiry.

This is a very odd statement and has led to some highly questionable decisions. Recall that Stone was talking about reviewing statutes under the concept of due process. It is necessary to be clear about the distinction, already alluded to, between two forms of substantive due process. The first consists in applying the substance of various provisions of the Bill of Rights against state legislation on the theory that the fourteenth amendment's due process clause "incorporates" those provisions. But for that incorporation, the Bill of Rights would restrain only the federal government. This theory has at least the merit of confining the courts to the enforcement of principles actually in the Constitution.

There is, however, a second form of substantive due process in which the courts create principles of freedom—freedom to own slaves, freedom to make contracts—that are nowhere to be found in the Constitution. It is proper that the Court recede from its highly interventionist stance under this second version, because it involves pure judicial legislation. But one hardly knows what to make of the tentativeness with which Stone suggests that the Court might be less deferential to the legislature if the legislation appears to be specifically prohibited by the Constitution. Of course, review should be more stringent if the Constitution reads on a subject than if it does not. That distinction should spell the difference between review and no review.

Perhaps the point of leading off with these puzzling suggestions is the last clause, which places on a par with all that has gone before a special protection to be given to "discrete and insular minorities." Everything that has gone before in footnote four was referrable to actual provisions of the Constitution. The Constitution does protect religious, national, and racial minorities. They need not be classified as "discrete and insular" in order to get that protection. What minorities, then, could Stone be talking about? They are, apparently, minorities not protected by a constitutional provision who cannot win their point in the political process because of "prejudice." Though it may be unpopular to point it out, the Constitution does not prohibit laws based on prejudice *per se,* though, of course, it prohibits those based on specified prejudices by protecting individuals who are members of particular groups from governmental discrimination based on that membership. It does not otherwise ban "prejudice." In any event, how is the Court to know whether a particular minority lost in the legislature because of "prejudice," as opposed to morality, prudence, or any other legitimate reason? One judge may as easily call a law that forbids certain types of sexual behavior a manifestation of the community's morality as another may see in it a manifestation of the community's bigotry. The Court, of course, can "know" whether prejudice or morality is in play only by deciding whether it thinks the reason for the legislative action is good, that is, whether the minority in question (which by definition is not one singled out by the Constitution for special protection) should not have lost in the legislature.

Stone's formulation in footnote four means nothing more than that the Justices will read into the Constitution their own subjective sympathies and social preferences. The "discrete and insular minority" formula, like the others we have examined, allows just that. The new formula in the context of the *Carolene Products* decision had, however, an additional significance. The simultaneous abandonment of due process review of economic regulation, coupled with the suggestion that minorities, other than businessmen, would be given some form of special protection, signaled the decline of the free market as an ideal and of the business class as a dominant elite. These developments also adumbrated the rise not of the (as-yet-unspecified) minorities, but of elites advocating the causes of minorities, whether in genuine sympathy or out of the expectation of power—or both.

Footnote four, then, adumbrated a constitutional revolution. In those few lines the doctrinal foundation of the Warren Court was laid. The Constitution being, as I have said, the trump card in our politics, the Court's change of direction and its assumption of a power to be used for new ends meant a revolution in our society as well.

Laying the Foundation for Substantive Equal Protection

Due process protection of economic liberties has never returned. The Court upheld a statute fixing maximum employment agency fees in *Olsen* v. *Nebraska*.[20] In retrospect, it is amusing to see that Justice Douglas had what, in light of his subsequent performances, can only be called the bravado to write that differences of opinion on the wisdom, need, or appropriateness of legislation should be left where they were left by the Constitution—to the states and to Congress. "Since [those notions of public policy embedded in the Court's earlier decisions] do not find expression in the Constitution, we cannot give them continuing vitality as standards by which the constitutionality of the economic and social programs of the states is to be determined." That amounted to a vow to be governed by the original understanding of the Constitution. But Douglas soon proved willing to put his own notions of public policy, which also do not find expression in the Constitution, into his constitutional decisions. The difference was only that his notions of public policy did not relate to economic freedoms.

Douglas demonstrated that thirteen months later, in the very next term of the Court. Oklahoma enacted a statute providing for the sterilization of habitual criminals. A "habitual criminal" was defined as a person who had committed two "felonies involving moral turpitude." The act stated that "offenses arising out of the violation of the prohibitory laws, revenue acts, embezzlement, or political offenses" were not included.[21] A certain Skinner had been convicted of felonies three times, once for stealing chickens and twice for robbery with firearms.

The problem in analyzing the case, Skinner v. Oklahoma,[22] is that the statute strikes the modern sensibility as savage. There is a natural tendency to want to strike it down. But the Constitution is a legal document, one different in texture from almost all others, but still a legal document and not an expression of a mood or a general injunction to be "civilized." To nullify the Oklahoma legislature's policy on the grounds that it shocks the judge is to embed in the Constitution the judge's notions of public policy, which, as the Douglas of Olsen v. Nebraska had just informed us, is entirely improper.

The approach Douglas disavowed was not merely improper on the occasion on which it was used; it led to more judicial lawlessness in the future. Judges, whose authority rests upon the public belief that they apply law and not emotion, are not usually content to say that a statute is unconstitutional because it is abominable. They try, therefore, to frame doctrine so that the intolerable law may be disposed of on what sound like legal grounds. But when the case is gone and the abomination erased, the doctrine remains. Lawyers and lower court judges will rely upon it, new cases will be decided in reliance upon it, and, since the doctrine was created in the first place to reach a result that existing doctrine did not permit, judicial power will have expanded to yet new territory. That is precisely what happened in Skinner v. Oklahoma.

Justice Douglas, perhaps having his recent animadversions on due process in mind, chose to use the equal protection clause of the same fourteenth amendment, and achieved precisely the same kind of result with the same kind of methodology that he had condemned in *Olsen.* This is a common tactic. People tend to suppose that the use of a different provision of the Constitution means that the flaw in substantive due process has disappeared. But the problem goes with the judge from clause to clause; the question always remains whether the provision in question gives him a relevant principle or whether, once more, he is embedding his own notions of policy in the Constitution.

The choice of the equal protection clause was interesting. In the *Slaughter-House Cases,*[23] it will be recalled, that clause had, in accordance with its origins, been virtually confined to the prohibition of racial discrimination. So little regarded as a source of judicial authority was equal protection that, as Douglas mentioned, Justice Holmes, in *Buck* v. *Bell,* a nonracial case, had referred to the clause slightingly as "the usual last resort of constitutional arguments. . . ."[24] *Buck* v. *Bell,* coincidentally, upheld a Virginia statute authorizing sterilization of mental defectives. Carrie Buck was feebleminded, the daughter of a feebleminded woman held in the same institution, and the mother of a feebleminded illegitimate child, a circumstance that provoked Holmes to remark, "Three generations of imbeciles are enough."[25]

But the Court in *Skinner* revived and remade the equal protection clause in such a way that it soon became not the last but the first resort of constitutional argument. Justice Douglas began by noting that under the sterilization statute stealing and embezzling identical amounts of money were treated differently. The three-time larcenist was subject to sterilization, the three-time embezzler was not. States were typically free, however, to make such distinctions in legislation as they wished. As Douglas recognized, "if we had here only a question as to a State's classification of crimes, such as embezzlement or larceny, no substantial federal question would be raised."[26] But this legislation ran afoul of the equal protection clause, he said, because it affected "one of the basic civil rights of man." It was clear, of course, that nothing in the Constitution made the state of being fertile a civil right. Douglas tried to avoid that difficulty in a very confused passage in which he first said that marriage and procreation are fundamental to the very existence and survival of the race. That observation was, of course, wholly irrelevant to the Oklahoma statute, which did not propose to sterilize the entire population. He next invoked the horrors of sterilization used for racial genocide, which also had nothing to do with the case or the Oklahoma statute, then pointed out that the injury was irreparable, and finally reneged on the statement that the Court had nothing to do with the state's classification of offenses: "When the law lays an unequal hand on those who have committed intrinsically the same quality of offense and sterilizes one and not the other, it has made as invidious a discrimination as if it had selected a particular race or nationality for oppressive treatment."

Although the difficulty with the statute was said to be that a distinction had been made between embezzlers and larcenists, Douglas closed by suggesting that that might not be the problem at all: "It is by no means clear whether . . . this particular constitutional difficulty might be solved by enlarging on the one hand or contracting on the other . . . the class of criminals who might be sterilized." If the decision really had been based on the equal protection clause, the statute could have been made constitutional by either providing for the sterilization of embezzlers or excluding larcenists from the classes of felons covered. Douglas was warning that the Court, or at least he, would not allow sterilization of criminals under any circumstances. That warning meant that *Skinner* was really a substantive due process case masquerading as a decision under the equal protection clause. The Court disapproved of sterilization, not of the distinction between types of felons.

This was the beginning of what came to be known as "substantive equal protection," an extraordinarily deceptive and therefore powerful means by which judges can embed their notions of public policy in the Constitution without appearing to do so. Using the due process clause to strike down the substance of what a legislature enacted had obvious difficulties. The clause on its face required a fair process, not a fair substance. To say, for example, that sterilization was a deprivation of liberty without due process of law would have been transparently to add to the Constitution a principle that had not been there before. But to say that the law denied equal protection of the laws because people who had done similar things were treated differently sounds much more like the application of a real constitutional provision. It was not that in *Skinner,* because Douglas conceded that the Constitution did not interfere with the state's classification of crimes. But the problem goes deeper. Once the Court begins to employ its own notions of reasonableness in order to decide which classifications should be treated like race, it *cannot* avoid legislating the Justices' personal views. The most honest and intelligent judge the nation has ever known could not avoid it if the clause is so read.

This is a point that many people, including lawyers and judges, seem to have difficulty grasping, yet it is quite simple. All laws, all statutes, contain classifications. That is, they treat people or behavior differently or the same according to characteristics the legislature deems relevant. But which things are the same and which are different is rarely—in human affairs never—a question of fact. Rather, it is always a question of perception, and perception is formed by a wide variety of factors. That is why, until relatively recently, the law did not require the differences that a legislature acted upon to be demonstrable in any even remotely rigorous sense. The differences or similarities perceived by the legislature and incorporated in statutory classifications may reflect moral views about which reasonable men and women may differ, judgments about degrees of danger, or decisions about what degrees of risk are acceptable. They may reflect tradeoffs between desires. The classifications will certainly reflect compromises between legislators or constituencies with different views concerning all of these matters. For these reasons different states have different laws about crime, marriage and divorce, tortious infliction of injury, and so on. It was why different states had different laws about abortion. If there had to be objective proof of real differences between the classifications of the law, legislatures could not legislate. Very few of the distinctions any of us make in life are based on demonstrable factors that we can show others to be true in any objective sense. That is why the Supreme Court has said that the Constitution does not require things to be treated alike if they are different in fact *or opinion.*

When a judge assumes the power to decide which distinctions made in a statute are legitimate and which are not, he assumes the power to disapprove of any and all legislation, because all legislation makes distinctions. But does that not mean that the equal protection clause is either a nullity or a deliberate conferral of just such power upon judges? Not at all. The clause was aimed primarily at the protection of the newly freed slaves by requiring that the laws of the states treat blacks and whites equally. The men who ratified the fourteenth amendment had made the decision that statutory inequality between blacks and whites was immoral and was to be disallowed. It is true, as Justice Bradley said in the *Slaughter-House Cases,* that the fourteenth amendment's "language is general, embracing all citizens,"[27] but the language of many other provisions is general, and yet courts have recognized the need for limitations in terms of the primary purpose of the ratifiers. The case for confining the amendment to statutory distinctions drawn in terms of race or ethnicity is that permitting the judges to choose subjectively which grounds of classification they will treat like race confers upon the courts a power to tell legislatures how all of their statutes on every subject must be written. That, we may be certain, was not what the ratifiers of the fourteenth amendment had in mind.*

Justice Douglas and the Justices who joined his opinion were aware of this difficulty, of course, and sought to avoid it, or the appearance of it, but the method they chose did not cure anything. The *Skinner* opinion said that the Court would not interfere with most classifications made by law but that this classification was different because it touched a right that was "fundamental" and "basic."[28] (If that is true, it is impossible to see how Skinner would have been helped by the sterilization of embezzlers.) The problem is, how does the Court know which rights are fundamental and basic? One answer might be that rights guaranteed by the Constitution are fundamental, but that answer could be of no help to the Court, because the right to procreate is not guaranteed, explicitly or implicitly, by the Constitution. (If the right were a real one, presumably life imprisonment without conjugal visits would violate the Constitution.) Thus, to justify *Skinner*'s approach the Court must decide that there are fundamental rights that the Court will enforce and that it knows how to identify them without guidance from any written law. This is indistinguishable from a power to say what the natural law is and, in addition, to assume the power to enforce the judge's version of that natural law against the people's elected representatives.

I am far from denying that there is a natural law, but I do deny both that we have given judges the authority to enforce it and that judges have any greater access to that law than do the rest of us. Judges, like the rest of us, are apt to confuse their strongly held beliefs with the order of nature. If the only effect of *Skinner* were to prevent a few sterilizations in Oklahoma, these matters would

---

* This point, which I have made before, became a focal point of the opposition to my nomination. Many people and senators expressed horror at the possibility that I thought "the Constitution does not apply to women." Of course it does, just as it applies to everybody. What I had said in the past was that it did not forbid virtually all classifications based on gender as it forbids all classifications that disfavor racial minorities. Few things are clearer than that the ratifiers of the fourteenth amendment did not think racial and sexual groups needed special protection to the same degree. I will discuss my attempt to come to terms with the Court's treatment of women, and in some cases males, as special classes in Chapter 15.

not be worth discussion. We could shrug and forget it as an aberrational decision that was at least morally acceptable if not constitutionally justifiable. But that is not the way law works. Decisions are precedents; doctrines are applied to new cases; and what begins as an attitude of "Let's do it just this one time" grows into a deformation of constitutional government. *Skinner,* in its attempt to frame doctrine that would stop the operation of a law that the Court regarded as cruel, framed doctrine that gave judges a new power to read their likes and dislikes into the Constitution. That power did not come to its full fruition, however, until the appearance of the Warren Court.

3

The Warren Court:
The Political Role
Embraced

*T*he Court headed by Chief Justice Earl Warren from 1953 to 1969 occupies a unique place in American law. It stands first and alone as a legislator of policy, whether the document it purported to apply was the Constitution or a statute. Other Courts had certainly made policy that was not theirs to make, but the Warren Court so far surpassed the others as to be different in kind. Nor is this entirely, or even primarily, attributable to Earl Warren himself. The groundwork had been laid by a generation of legal scholars, the "legal realists," and a legal realist faction existed on the Court well before Warren arrived.

Arrested Legal Realism

While the New Deal Court was still largely intact, there developed within it sharply opposing views of the judicial function. As Arthur M. Schlesinger, Jr., described the situation in 1947, "the Black–Douglas wing appears to be more concerned with settling particular cases in accordance with their own social preconceptions; the Frankfurter–Jackson wing with preserving the judiciary in its established but limited place in the American system."[1] The Black–Douglas view, Schlesinger reported, rested upon ideas particularly dominant at the Yale law school.

The Yale thesis, crudely put, is that any judge chooses his results and reasons backward. The resources of legal artifice, the ambiguity of precedents, the range of applicable doctrine, are all so extensive that in most cases in which there is a reasonable difference of opinion a judge can come out on either side without straining the fabric of legal logic. A naive judge does this unconsciously and conceives himself to be an objective interpreter of the law. A wise judge knows that political choice is inevitable; he makes no false pretense of objectivity and consciously exercises the judicial power with an eye to social results.

As Schlesinger made clear, the Black–Douglas wing applied its social preconceptions to the interpretation of statutes as well to the Constitution.

This constitutes what I have called "disguised activism." Though they wrote opinions that purported to explain their results in terms of legal doctrine, "Black and Douglas," according to Schlesinger, "vote less regularly for doctrines than for interests—for the trade union against the employer, for the government against the large taxpayer, for the administrative agency against the business, for the injured workman, for the unprotected defendant, against the patent holder—so that, in the phrase of Professor Thomas Reed Powell, 'the less favored in life will be the more favored in law.' " Powell's was a romantic way of describing a redistributionist or Robin Hood ethic. In the examples given, legislatures had arduously drafted laws precisely in order to define the respective rights of unions and employers, the IRS and the taxpayer, the administrative agency and the business. Elected representatives had argued their policies and compromised their differences to arrive at a democratic result. Then judicial activists upset the compromises and the policies by deciding that, regardless of the outcome of the democratic process, certain groups should be still more favored. It is difficult to find in that any defensible theory of the judicial function.

Nor is it correct that law is so indeterminate that these results can be reached without straining the fabric of legal logic. The opinions of Justices Black and Douglas were frequently seen by lawyers not only to have strained but to have shredded that fabric. But nothing could be done about it. When a judge upsets a legislative compromise, the legislators who could not get their way entirely in the legislature, but who have won through a disingenuous Supreme Court interpretation, are most unlikely to agree that the law should be amended to restore the original compromise.

The old Yale thesis, as described by Mr. Schlesinger, is excessively cynical in another respect. Not all judges choose their result and reason backward. Alexander M. Bickel called this philosophy "arrested realism" and accurately observed: "It was never altogether realistic to conclude that behind all judicial dialectic there was personal preference and personal power and nothing else."[2] Any lawyer or judge who is honest with himself knows that he often intuits a conclusion and then goes to work to see if legal reasoning supports it. But the original intuition arises out of long familiarity with the structure and processes of law. A judge will have such intuitions in cases where he has not the remotest personal preference about the outcome. A process like that must occur in all intellectual disciplines. But the honest practitioner, including the lawyer or the judge, also changes his mind when the materials with which he works press him away from his first tentative conclusion. I have had, as many other judges have, the experience of reaching one result after reading the briefs and reversing my position at oral argument, or of voting one way at the judges' conference after argument and then changing my mind in the process of reading, discussion, and writing. I have had the even less pleasurable experience of publishing my opinion and then concluding I was wrong upon reading the petition for rehearing and having to change the result of the case. Many judges can testify to similar experiences. If that is true, and it is, then it is not true that all judges choose their results and reason backward.

But it is true for some judges. We have canvassed instances of it in this book. One can only say with Bickel, "[T]hat is a reality, if it be true, on which we cannot allow the edifice of judicial review to be based, for if that is all judges do, then their authority over us is totally intolerable and totally irreconcilable with the theory and practice of political democracy."[3] To accept that view of the judicial process is profoundly cynical, and yet it is regularly taught in our best law schools. Indeed, it is hard not to teach it even for a professor who explicitly condemns it; the casebook teaches cynicism. At Yale, constitutional law is taught in the student's first semester, and the casebook collects the opinions of Justices who did and do adhere to a philosophy of voting for interests and personal values. The students, who are highly intelligent, quickly come to see that the opinions they read rend the "fabric of legal logic." They see that much of constitutional law has in fact been politics. If some Justices of the Supreme Court of the United States regularly perform in this way, it is almost idle for the professor to insist that things need not be this way. In any event, many students find the casebook's lesson congenial. They like the political outcomes of the cases. It takes a great deal of self-discipline to renounce a philosophy that some of the most renowned figures in the law hold and that produces results you like. To quote Bickel once more, "The sin [of cynicism] is mortal, because it propagates a self-validating picture of reality. If men are told complacently enough that this is how things are, they will become accustomed to it and accept it. And in the end this is how things will be."[4]

That is, indeed, how things were during the era of the Warren Court. The judicial philosophy espoused by Black and Douglas came to be a majority philosophy with new appointments, particularly those of Earl Warren as Chief Justice, and Justices Tom Clark, William J. Brennan, Jr., Arthur Goldberg, Abe Fortas, and Thurgood Marshall. It would be unfair to say that each of these men consciously held the philosophy of "arrested realism" that Bickel described. Many judges and Justices come to their duties with no particular philosophy of judging in mind. Most careers in the law that lead eventually to the bench give no reason to ponder the subject, and by the time a man or woman becomes a judge it is too late. Judging these days is a very busy occupation; it would be very hard to lift your eyes from the briefs and memoranda long enough to work out a philosophy that it generally takes years to develop. A judge works with whatever intellectual capital he accumulated before coming to the bench; he is most unlikely to add appreciably to his store while there. Thus, whether a particular Justice consciously adheres to a philosophy of political judging is not always easy to say. Earl Warren himself was one of whom that was true. He was not known for his ease in the company of abstractions. Meaning to be kind, one observer said of him that he was "born to act, not to muse," which is rather an odd compliment for a man whose job is intellectual. Be that as it may, Warren found congenial the style of judging that Black and Douglas had made prominent— the mood of attack, reform, and impatience with considerations other than social results.

It must be said, however, that Justice Black came to have significantly more respect for the limits of the Constitution than Justice Douglas and the other leading members of the Warren majorities ever showed.

The catalogue of the Warren Court's legislative alterations of the Constitution is a thick one and is organized by the theme of egalitarianism. Aside from instances to be discussed at greater length in a moment, the Court: expanded the equal protection concept to strike down traditional state classifications, such as the difference in legal entitlements between legitimate or acknowledged children and unacknowledged illegitimate children;[5] found that access to justice was a fundamental interest, so that Illinois, which was not constitutionally required to allow any appeal from a criminal conviction, had to pay for written transcripts for indigents who wished to appeal;[6] and ruled that a state could not impose a length-of-residency requirement for welfare benefits.[7] Criminal law was remade as the constitutional rights of defendants were multiplied, including the requirement that persons arrested be given *Miranda* warnings, with which every TV watcher is familiar: "You have the right to remain silent," etc.[8] The rule excluding evidence the Court found improperly obtained, often on the most technical grounds, was expanded.[9] Antitrust law was made into an intellectual shambles as the Court ruled against almost every business defendant, no matter what the precedent, the economic reality, or the lower court's findings of fact.[10] This, too, was part of the interest-voting pattern that Schlesinger noted in the Justices who were the forerunners of the Warren Court. Justice Douglas, formerly a professor at the Yale law school, visited the school when he was a leading figure on the Warren Court. A student of mine asked him why the government won every antitrust case, and he replied that he was ashamed a Yale student had to ask such a question. This was a period when one who took law and justice seriously, as an intellectual discipline, as something more than ultra-liberal politics, had reason to be extremely unhappy with the Supreme Court of the United States.

An adequate discussion of the Warren Court's unprincipled activism, manifested in both constitutional and statutory law, would take up an entire book. I can touch on only a few instances, but my dissatisfaction with that Court's performance, far from being idiosyncratic, was widely shared at the time. Professor Milton Handler, of the Columbia law school, summed it up: "Eminent scholars from many fields have commented upon [the Warren Court's] tendency towards overgeneralization, the disrespect for precedent, even those of recent vintage, the needless obscurity of opinions, the discouraging lack of candor, the disdain for the fact finding of the lower courts, the tortured reading of statutes, and the seeming absence of neutrality and objectivity."[11] That catalogue is just, perhaps even merciful, and it described a Court that had spun out of control.

Oddly enough, the Warren era opened with one of constitutional

law's great triumphs, but it was a triumph so misperceived by the
Justices themselves that it led to some of the law's most blatantly
illegitimate decisions.

Brown v. Board of Education: Equality, Segregation, and the Original Understanding

Appointed by President Eisenhower, Earl Warren assumed the post
of Chief Justice in 1953 and was plunged at once into the greatest
case of the twentieth century, *Brown* v. *Board of Education,*[12] a
case that proved to be the defining event of modern American constitutional law. *Brown* was the culmination of years of litigation, primarily by the National Association for the Advancement of Colored
People, designed to persuade the Supreme Court to overrule the
1896 decision in *Plessy* v. *Ferguson.*[13] *Plessy* had declared the equal
protection clause of the fourteenth amendment satisfied by a Louisiana law that required "equal" but separate accommodations for black
and white railroad passengers. Justice Brown's opinion for the majority said the fallacy of the attack on the statute lay in "the assumption
that the enforced separation of the two races stamps the colored
race with a badge of inferiority. If this be so, it is not by reason of
anything found in the act, but solely because the colored race chooses
to put that construction upon it." To this, the first Justice Harlan's
dissent very sensibly replied that everyone knew the law had "the
purpose, not so much to exclude white persons from railroad cars
occupied by blacks, as to exclude colored people from coaches occupied by or assigned to white persons."[14] He went on to say, in a
sentence that has become famous, "Our Constitution is color-blind,
and neither knows nor tolerates classes among citizens." But he
was a minority of one.

The legal campaign to have *Plessy* overruled did not begin with
a flat-out assault on the principle of "separate but equal." Rather,
litigation was directed at particular segregated facilities to show
that they were not equal, that whites always had better facilities,
usually much better. Litigation of this sort succeeded again and
again, and, by demonstrating the invariable inequality of facilities,
the litigation began to undermine the legal as well as the moral
foundations of the separate-but-equal doctrine.

Brown v. *Board of Education* was actually one of several consoli-
dated cases involving state laws that required segregation of the

races in public schools. *Brown* itself came from Kansas. It was argued when Fred Vinson, a Truman appointee, was Chief Justice, but Vinson died before a decision was handed down, and Warren replaced him. In order to have a full Court, and to have the Chief Justice participate in a case of such magnitude and sensitivity, reargument was ordered in the next term. On May 17, 1954, the decision was handed down and created an immediate sensation; the public forum rang with vehement approval and disapproval. As was appropriate in such a case, the Court was unanimous and the Chief Justice wrote. The school segregation laws of the various states were declared to violate the equal protection clause of the fourteenth amendment. At least to that extent, *Plessy* v. *Ferguson* was overruled. It was not immediately apparent that all racial segregation by law was unconstitutional.

Brown was a great and correct decision, but it must be said in all candor that the decision was supported by a very weak opinion. Those two facts, taken together, have caused an enormous amount of trouble in the law.

The *Brown* Court found the history of the fourteenth amendment inconclusive because public education in 1868 was embryonic in the South and the effect of the amendment on public schools in the North was ignored in the congressional debates. The opinion did not choose to face the uncomfortable fact that the effect on public education was ignored because no one then imagined the equal protection clause might affect school segregation. The Chief Justice concluded for the Court that to "separate [children in grade and high schools] from others of similar age and qualifications solely because of their race generates a feeling of inferiority as to their status in the community that may affect their hearts and minds in a way unlikely ever to be undone. . . . Whatever may have been the extent of psychological knowledge at the time of *Plessy* v. *Ferguson,* this finding is amply supported by modern authority."[15] There followed a footnote citing psychological studies.

There are obvious difficulties with the opinion. In the first place, it failed to deal with the fact that a number of Northern states had ratified the fourteenth amendment and had continued to segregate their public schools without even supposing there was any conflict between the two actions. It was no answer to say, as Warren did, that public education had not then advanced to the condition it has achieved today. The inescapable fact is that those who ratified the amendment did not think it outlawed segregated education or

segregation in any aspect of life. If the ratifiers had intended segregation as the central meaning of the equal protection clause, it is impossible to see how later studies on the baleful psychological effects of
segregation could change that meaning. Indeed, *Plessy* had recognized that segregation could have a psychological impact and found
it essentially irrelevant. It is difficult to believe that those who ratified
the fourteenth amendment and also passed or continued in force
segregation laws did not similarly understand the psychological effects of what they did. They didn't care.

The second difficulty is that nobody who read *Brown* believed
for a moment that the decision turned on social science studies about
such matters as the preference of black children for white or black
dolls, which supposedly showed something about their self-esteem,
which in turn supposedly was related to the presence or absence
of legal segregation. This was disingenuous. The real rationale for
Brown was deeper, and the pretense that it was not cheapened a
great moment in constitutional law. Finally, in focusing on the effects
of segregation on young children's capacity to learn—a question
by no means as simple as the Court made it sound—the decision's
rationale limited its principle to primary and secondary public education.

That the Court had not been straightforward in *Brown* quickly
became apparent. Cases soon came up in which the professed rationale
of *Brown*, the psychological effects of segregation on children of
tender years, could not conceivably apply. Plaintiffs challenged legally
segregated beaches,[16] golf courses,[17] parks,[18] and courtrooms.[19] The
Supreme Court simply issued orders that such segregation was unconstitutional with nothing more than the citation of *Brown* v. *Board
of Education*. That necessarily meant that the rationale of *Brown*
was not the rationale offered in the opinion. Racial segregation by
order of the state was unconstitutional under all circumstances and
had nothing to do with the context of education or the psychological
vulnerability of a particular age group. The real meaning of *Brown*,
therefore, was far better than its professed meaning.

But the combined disingenuousness of the *Brown* opinion and
the obvious moral rightness of its result had, I believe, a calamitous
effect upon the law. This was massively ironic, because the result
in *Brown* is consistent with, indeed is compelled by, the original
understanding of the fourteenth amendment's equal protection clause.
The disastrous fact was that the Supreme Court did not think so.
The Court, judging by its opinion, thought that it had departed

from the original understanding in order to do the socially desirable thing. What is more, the Court triumphed over intense political opposition despite that fact. Those of us of a certain age remember the intense, indeed hysterical, opposition that *Brown* aroused in parts of the South. Most Southern politicians felt obliged to denounce it, to insist that the South would continue segregation in defiance of any number of Supreme Court rulings. We remember the television pictures of adult whites screaming obscenities at properly dressed black children arriving to attend school. We remember that at one point President Eisenhower had to send in airborne troops to guarantee compliance with the Court's rulings.

Imagine, then, what the Justices of the Supreme Court thought. They had issued, so they apparently believed, a ruling based on nothing in the historic Constitution, and that decision had prevailed despite the fact that it had ordered a change in an entrenched social order in much of the nation. Scholars used to worry that the Court would damage its authority if it acted politically. I have written a few such naïve lines myself. The fact is quite the contrary. The Court is virtually invulnerable, and *Brown* proved it. The Court can do what it wishes, and there is almost no way to stop it, provided its result has a significant political constituency. (These days the significance of a political constituency is greatly magnified if the constituency includes a large part of the intellectual or knowledge class, which means that the Court has greater freedom to the left than it has to the right.) Much of the rest of the Warren Court's history may be explained by the lesson it learned from its success in *Brown*.

But *Brown* taught lessons to others as well. It was accepted by law professors as inconsistent with the original understanding of the equal protection clause. That fact was crucial. The end of state-mandated segregation was the greatest moral triumph constitutional law had ever produced. It is not surprising that academic lawyers were unwilling to give it up; it *had* to be right. Thus, *Brown* has become the high ground of constitutional theory. Theorists of all persuasions seek to capture it, because any theory that seeks acceptance must, as a matter of psychological fact, if not of logical necessity, account for the result in *Brown*. In fact, those who wish to be free of the restraints of original understanding in the hope that courts will further a particular policy agenda regularly seek to discredit that philosophy by claiming that it could not have produced the outcome in *Brown*. Since *Brown* is the test, the argument runs, and since original understanding cannot meet that test, then the philosophy is discredited, and courts may do as they wish, or as the intellectual class wishes, in all future policy issues. The charge is false, but if it were correct, that would not affect the legitimacy of the philosophy. Constitutional philosophy is a theory of what renders a judge's power to override democratic choice legitimate. It is no answer to say that we like the results, no matter how divorced from the intentions of the lawgivers, for that is to say that we prefer an authoritarian regime with which we agree to a democracy with which we do not.

But so great is the allegiance to *Brown* that when a respected law professor, Herbert Wechsler of Columbia, questioned the case in a Holmes Lecture at Harvard, he created a sensation in academic circles, and many professors rushed into print to rebut him.[20] Wechsler did not actually say the case was wrong, but he had confessed to being unable to discern the "neutral principle" upon which it rested.[21]

Wechsler contended that the Supreme Court must not be merely a "naked power organ," which meant that its decisions must be controlled by principle. "A principled decision," he said, "is one that rests on reasons with respect to all the issues in the case, reasons that in their generality and their neutrality transcend any immediate result that is involved."[22] The legal principle to be applied is never neutral in its content, of course, because it embodies a value that is to be applied to the exclusion of other contending values. Wechsler's argument was that the value-laden principle must be *applied* neutrally. That is a requirement, as Louis L. Jaffe put it, that the judge "sincerely believe in the principle upon which he purports to rest his decision."[23] "The judge," said Jaffe, "must believe in the validity of the reasons given for the decision at least in the sense that he is prepared to apply them to a later case which he cannot honestly distinguish." Which is to say that the judge must not decide lawlessly. I would add, as I will argue later on, that neutrality in the *application* of principle is not enough. In order to avoid lawlessness, the principles a judge applies must also be neutrally *derived* and *defined*. It should be obvious that a court which picks a principle it likes, regardless of its source, does not then avoid lawlessness by applying that principle neutrally. It has begun by legislating the principle without warrant in legal materials and is, for that reason, merely a "naked power organ." Wechsler apparently disagreed with that, and it was this that caused his difficulties with the *Brown* decision.

Wechsler, along with many legal scholars, agreed that *Brown* did not rest on the ground advanced in Chief Justice Warren's opinion. The real principle was that government may not employ race as a classification, but Wechsler thought the genesis of that principle unclear. He then committed an error fatal to his argument. He said his problem with the desegregation cases was not that "history does not confirm that an agreed purpose of the fourteenth amendment was to forbid separate schools or that there is important evidence that many thought the contrary; the words [of the amendment: 'equal protection of the laws'] are general and leave room for expanding content as time passes and conditions change."[24] This is error because it leaves the judge without guidance. He observes that conditions have changed, but he has no way of finding a principle to apply except his own view of morality. That forces him into the position of exercising naked power, which it was the point of Wechsler's analysis to avoid. Noting that *Brown* has to do with freedom to associate and freedom not to associate, Wechsler said a principle must be found that solves the following dilemma:

> [I]f the freedom of association is denied by segregation, integration forces an association upon those for whom it is unpleasant or repugnant. Is this not the heart of the issue involved, a conflict in human claims of high dimension. . . . Given a situation where the state must practically choose between denying the association to those individuals who wish it or imposing it on those who would avoid it, is there a basis in neutral principles for holding that the Constitution demands that the claims for association should prevail? I should like to think there is, but I confess that I have not yet written the opinion. To write it is for me the challenge of the school-segregation cases.

I think no one will ever be able to write that opinion persuasively, for Wechsler cast the problem as one in moral philosophy. Moral philosophy will never be able to demonstrate, as a general principle, that coerced association is preferable to freedom not to associate, nor will philosophy be able to demonstrate the opposite, that the freedom from association is a principle of higher rank than the claim for association.

I speak with some feeling on this subject because I once engaged in the sort of enterprise Wechsler suggested. Very early in my career as a law professor I held two views that are relevant here. The first, which I continue to hold, is that there should be a presumption that individuals are free, and to justify coercion by government a case must be made that overcomes that presumption. The burden of persuasion is upon those who would regulate. The second was that legislation, which is coercion, must rest upon principles of general application. These were not views about constitutional law, though at one point I tried to convert them to that,[25] but rather tenets of an embryonic political outlook. The public accommodations provisions of the Civil Rights Act were proposed in 1963 as a means of giving racial minorities access to restaurants, hotels, and other facilities that excluded them. This was not a constitutional matter. The fourteenth amendment did not apply because the discrimination was done by private persons, not the state. The result of the law would be to favor the claims of association over the claims of freedom not to associate. There seemed to be no generally applicable principle of moral or political philosophy available to justify the legislative coercion and I opposed the bill on that ground. I was, in a word, phrasing the legislative issue much as Professor Wechsler had framed the constitutional issue. I argued the point with my good friend and colleague on the Yale law faculty, Alexander Bickel, and he suggested I write a piece for *The New Republic,* a magazine on which he was a contributing editor.[26] Though he disagreed with me, he was delighted with the piece and said it was a variation of the liberal tradition. It was in fact rooted in the libertarian strain of that tradition. Since I operated from a presumption of freedom and required a general principle to justify coercion, I also opposed state-enforced segregation as well as state-compelled association in the article. The article was used heavily twenty-four years later in the campaign waged against my confirmation as indicating that I was or had been opposed to civil rights. Nothing could be further from the truth. The position, as I later came to see, was wrong, but the argument proceeded from a concern with the civil rights of all persons. But, of all the people who argued with me, nobody made the sensible point that no legislation rests upon a principle that is capable of being applied generally.

My position was incorrect because, as I subsequently realized, there are no general principles to decide competing claims of association and nonassociation. There being no correct general answer, the proper approach for the legislator is necessarily ad hoc, to ask whether the proposed law will do more good than harm. What do I mean by "more good than harm"? I mean that society itself will come to see the legislation as beneficial and will do so in the relatively short term. It is a pragmatic test, but none the worse for that, and it is the only test available for legislation. The Civil Rights Act of 1964 passes it easily. I said as much at my confirmation hearings to be Solicitor General in 1973.

This test will not do for constitutional law, however. It is not the function of a judge to decide what is good for us. *Brown,* which has been good for us, cannot be justified on that ground. Nor can it be justified on a principle of the sort Wechsler sought if such principles do not exist. Wechsler's difficulty arose from the fact that he discarded the idea that the original understanding is the only legitimate basis for a constitutional decision and simultaneously asked for a neutral principle to decide *Brown.* But once a court abandons the intention of those who made the law, the court is necessarily thrust into a legislative posture. It must write the law. And if the court must legislate, we cannot ask it for neutral principles of the sort Wechsler thought essential. Wechsler was asking the Supreme Court to be two branches of government at once, which would require the Justices to perform incompatible functions and to maintain incompatible states of mind simultaneously. The modes of reasoning appropriate to legislators and to judges are quite different. In 1963, I made the opposite mistake of demanding that Congress reason like the Supreme Court and produce a neutral principle to support the public accommodations bill. Congress can properly require that hotels not turn away guests on the basis of race but make an exception for a person who rents a room or two in a private residence. It can enforce associations in restaurants but refuse to do so in law partnerships. It can make a thousand detailed tradeoffs and produce a complex code that articulates no general principle but reflects moral intuitions, political pressures, and compromises.

This means that, if we accept Wechsler's requirement that a court must apply neutral principles, and I think we must, *Brown* must rest, if it is a correct decision, on the original understanding of the equal protection clause of the fourteenth amendment. It is clear that it can be rested there. In 1971, in an article in the Indiana Law Journal, I offered two grounds that support *Brown,* the second of which I have since expanded and think completely adequate.

Let us suppose that *Plessy* v. *Ferguson* correctly represented the original understanding of the fourteenth amendment, that those who ratified it intended black equality, which they demonstrated by adopting the equal protection clause. But they also assumed that equality and state-compelled separation of the races were consistent, an assumption which they demonstrated by leaving in place various state laws segregating the races. Let us also suppose, along with the Court in *Plessy,* as I think we must, that the ratifiers had no objection to the psychological harm segregation inflicted. If those things are true, then it is impossible to square the' *opinion* in *Brown* with the original understanding. It is, however, entirely possible to square the *result* in *Brown* with that understanding.

Perhaps because of their anxiety to deny that *Brown* v. *Board of Education* could have been arrived at consistently with the original understanding of the fourteenth amendment, those who oppose that philosophy always talk as though segregation was the primary thrust of the equal protection clause. But, of course, it was not. Segregation is not mentioned in the clause, nor do the debates suggest that the clause was enacting segregation. The ratifiers probably assumed that segregation was consistent with equality but they were not addressing segregation. The text itself demonstrates that the equality under law was the primary goal.

By 1954, when *Brown* came up for decision, it had been apparent for some time that segregation rarely if ever produced equality. Quite aside from any question of psychology, the physical facilities provided for blacks were not as good as those provided for whites. That had been demonstrated in a long series of cases. The Supreme Court was faced with a situation in which the courts would have to go on forever entertaining litigation about primary schools, secondary schools, colleges, washrooms, golf courses, swimming pools, drinking fountains, and the endless variety of facilities that were segregated, or else the separate-but-equal doctrine would have to be abandoned. Endless litigation, aside from the burden on the courts, also would never produce the equality the Constitution promised. The Court's realistic choice, therefore, was either to abandon the quest for equality by allowing segregation or to forbid segregation in order to achieve equality. There was no third choice. Either choice would violate one aspect of the original understanding, but there was no possibility of avoiding that. Since equality and segregation were mutually inconsistent, though the ratifiers did not understand that, both could not be honored. When that is seen, it is obvious the Court must choose equality and prohibit state-imposed segregation. The purpose that brought the fourteenth amendment into being was equality before the law, and equality, not separation, was written into the text.

Had the *Brown* opinion been written that way, its result would have clearly been rooted in the original understanding, and its legitimacy would have been enhanced for those troubled by the way in which the Court arrived at a moral result without demonstrating its mooring in the historic Constitution. There might have been an even more important benefit. The Court might not have been encouraged to embark on more adventures in policymaking, which is what it thought it had done in *Brown,* and academic constitutional lawyers might not have gone on to construct the apparently endless set of theories that not only attempt to justify *Brown* on grounds other than the original understanding but, in order to do so, advance arguments that necessarily justify departure from the historic Constitution in general. Perhaps constitutional theory would be in a far happier state today if *Brown* had been written, as it could have been, in terms of the original understanding.

But not all the Court's segregation decisions could have been so rooted. At the same time it decided *Brown,* the Court decided a companion case, *Bolling* v. *Sharpe,*[27] in which plaintiffs challenged the school segregation laws of the District of Columbia. That posed a problem since the equal protection clause, under which *Brown* had been decided, applied only to the states; no similar clause applied to the federal government, which governed the District of Columbia. Had the Court been guided by the Constitution, it would have had to rule that it had no power to strike down the District's laws. Instead, it seized upon the due process clause of the fifth amendment, which does apply to the federal government, and announced that this due process clause included the same equal protection of the laws concept as the equal protection clause of the fourteenth amendment. This rested on no precedent or history. In fact, history compels the opposite conclusion.[28] The framers of the fourteenth amendment adopted the due process clause of the fifth amendment but thought it necessary to add the equal protection clause, obviously understanding that due process, the requirement of fair procedures, did not include the requirement of equal protection in the substance of state laws.

Bolling, then, was a clear rewriting of the Constitution by the Warren Court. *Bolling,* however much one likes the result, was a substantive due process decision in the same vein as *Dred Scott* and *Lochner.* The only justification offered in the opinion was that it would be unthinkable that the states should be forbidden to segregate and the federal government allowed to. Yes, it would be unthinkable, as a matter of morality and of politics. Most certainly, Congress would not and could not have permitted that ugly anomaly to persist, and would have had to repeal the District's segregation statutes. But there is no way to justify the Warren Court's revision of the Constitution to accomplish its reforms. This was not a revision for that case only, as some lawless decisions are. Lawyers and judges now regularly attack and scrutinize federal legislation under the Court-invented "equal protection component of the due process clause."[29] Ironically, given the motives for this innovation, the Court's fifth amendment equal protection clause is the main basis for attacking federal legislation compelling affirmative action or reverse racial discrimination. Without *Bolling*'s invention, it is not easy to think of how a constitutional challenge to such laws could be mounted. The Court made it abundantly clear that it was not applying the Constitution to controversies involving race. Instead, it was endeavoring to deal with what it conceived to be the country's racial problems. This was not law but social engineering from the bench.

One Person, One Vote: The Restructuring of State Governments

The Warren Court's philosophical thrust was, as I have mentioned, egalitarian and redistributionist. Sometimes, as in *Brown*, its results could have been reached on the historic principles of the Constitution, but quite often they could not; any correspondence between the original understanding and the Court's rulings was often accidental. There is no better example of the Court's egalitarianism and its disregard for the Constitution in whose name it spoke than the legislative reapportionment cases, which created the principle of one person, one vote.

It may sound obvious that every American's vote should have the same weight. The principle, stated in the abstract, sounds admirable. But it is neither obvious nor admirable when it is forced upon people who have chosen democratically to arrange their state governments in part upon a different principle. During the campaign against my confirmation, the charge was repeatedly made that I opposed the rule of one person, one vote. A number of senators gave as a reason for voting against me that I had criticized that principle, which was rather curious, since the senators, being from states with very different numbers of people, do not represent even approximately equally weighted votes. The senators from California represent more than 26 million people; those from Wyoming about 550,000. That is the very situation the Warren Court found intolerable in state senates. It could do nothing about the U.S. Senate since that body's departure from the one person, one vote principle is deliberately written into the Constitution. I did and do oppose the principle, *as a constitutional rule.* What those who purported to be horrified at that position neglected to mention is that Americans could always base their state governments on one person, one vote if they chose to do so. No law prevented that. No one was coerced to arrange government on any other theory. But the people of most states chose to structure their state governments on the same model as the federal government, in which representation in one house is based on population and in the other, the Senate, upon political units, though their populations differ. One person, one vote has never been the American practice, and it is certainly not compelled by political theory. Worse, it is not supported by the Constitution and is not, and cannot be, implemented consistently.

The story began with a case, *Baker* v. *Carr,*[30] coming out of Tennessee. That state's constitution allocated representation in the legislature on the basis of population, but the legislature had not been reapportioned since 1901. Since then, major population growth and shifts had occurred, so that a distinct minority of the citizens of Tennessee elected a majority of the state legislature. As one might expect, the legislative majority did not care to realign districts to represent the current distribution of the population, because reapportionment would endanger some of their seats. A majority of Tennessee's voters were being prevented from choosing the structure of representation they wanted. Plaintiff voters sued for a court-ordered reapportionment, lost, and appealed to the Supreme Court.

There is no doubt in my mind, though many commentators whom I respect disagree, that plaintiffs deserved to win. The crucial question was the constitutional theory on which they won, because that would determine what the Court ordered as a lawful method of apportionment. Since a majority of Tennessee voters could not govern, they were denied representative government. The most obviously relevant clause of the Constitution was article IV, section 4, which states, in part, "The United States shall guarantee to every State in this Union a Republican Form of Government. . . ."[31] More than a hundred years ago, the Court held that it could not apply that clause in a dispute about which of two rival groups was the lawful government of Rhode Island. Since then, for no very good reason, the Court has held that it may not enforce the clause under any circumstances. *Baker* v. *Carr* was a case in which the guarantee clause should have been applied, precisely because a situation in which the majority is systematically prevented from governing is not what the Founders meant by a republican form of government. Use of that clause would have resulted in an order that a majority of the state's voters be permitted to reapportion their legislature, whether by referendum, convention, or some other mechanism. The Court would not tell Tennessee's voters what system of representation they were required to "choose."*

The Warren Court, however, had something more revolutionary in mind and signaled the fact by saying that the standards of the equal protection clause should be applied when the case returned to the lower court. Equal protection is not a flexible standard: equality is required or it isn't. The choice of that clause made the ultimate conclusion inevitable. In *Reynolds* v. *Sims,*[32] the answer came: both houses of every state legislature had to be apportioned on a population basis so that, so far as possible, every vote had equal weight. At the time, and for years previously, bicameral American state legislatures usually had a house corresponding to the United States Senate, each county or similar political unit within the state having equal representation in the state senate. Representation in the other house was typically arranged on a population basis. Alabama, the state involved in *Reynolds* v. *Sims,* contended, not surprisingly, that the state legislature was constructed like Congress and therefore could hardly be unconstitutional. Chief Justice Warren's opinion found "the federal analogy inapposite and irrelevant," because the federal system of representation was "one conceived out of compromise and concession indispensable to the establishment of our federal republic." No such compromises had been necessary to form the states. This response effectively said that the composition of the United States Senate was illegitimate as a matter of political morality but was frozen by the compromise made to protect the smaller states at the Constitutional Convention. The notion that states might similarly want to provide representation for people in certain localities, perhaps because they had distinctive economic interests or social

---

* There is a theory that the guarantee clause requires states to avoid obvious and egregious deviations from their own laws, without imposing a uniform, federal standard. Note, *The Rule of Law and the States: A New Interpretation of the Guarantee Clause,* 93 Yale L.J. 561 (1984). If so, that would have solved *Baker,* since Tennessee had a constitutional provision requiring periodic reapportionments which the state had ignored.

views that might be overlooked in a purely majoritarian legislature, was impatiently brushed aside. "Citizens, not history or economic interests, cast votes. . . . [P]eople, not land or trees or pastures, vote." What those observations had to do with giving some interests greater weight in one house of the legislature was not explained.

So determined was the Court that in a companion case to *Reynolds v. Sims, Lucas v. Forty-Fourth General Assembly,*[33] the majority held unconstitutional a Colorado apportionment that had recently been overwhelmingly approved by the state's voters in a referendum, including majorities in every political subdivision of the state. Justice Stewart's dissent destroyed the majority's rationale that " 'the fundamental principle of representative government in this country is one of equal representation for equal numbers of people.' "[34] Stewart, quoting Frankfurter's dissent in *Baker* v. *Carr,* said, "It has been unanswerably demonstrated before now that this 'was not the colonial system, it was not the system chosen for the national government by the Constitution, it was not the system exclusively or even predominantly practiced by the States at the time of adoption of the Fourteenth Amendment, it is not predominantly practiced by the States today.' " The Warren majority's new constitutional doctrine was supported by nothing. As Stewart pointed out, "The very fact of geographic districting, the constitutional validity of which the Court does not question, carries with it an acceptance of the idea of legislative representation of regional needs and interests." If the goal was solely equally weighted votes, he said, "I do not understand why the Court's constitutional rule does not require the abolition of districts and the holding of all elections at large." He might have added that the rule should call into question other devices, such as the legislative committee system, the filibuster, and the requirement on some issues of two-thirds majorities, all of which give some representatives, and hence those whom they represent, more weight in determining outcomes than others.

Madison's writing on the republican form of government specified by the guarantee clause suggests that state governments, which were structured as representative democracies, could take many forms, so long as those forms do not become "aristocratic or monarchical." That is not easily translated into a rigid requirement of equal weight for every vote. It translates far more readily into Justice Stewart's position that the apportionment, or system of representation, chosen need only be rational and "must be such as not to permit the systematic frustration of the will of a majority of the electorate of the State."

Few people understand how court-ordered reapportionment works. In 1972, a three-judge district court struck down the reapportionment plan devised by the Connecticut legislature. The chief judge telephoned to ask if I would act as a special master for the court to draw a new plan. I replied that I had written critically of one-person, one-vote, had indeed referred to the doctrine as a "fiasco," but would apply the law if the court wished. Connecticut politicians were not pleased to learn that a bearded Yale law professor was going to remake the legislature. Yale professors, with some reason, were regarded as outlanders. When I met in Hartford with leaders of the Senate and General Assembly one of them pointed to a map and said sarcastically, "That is Connecticut, professor." I looked thoughtfully at the map for a moment and replied, "For now."

Experts in reapportioning by computer began calling. One offered to do the job, staying within the court's guideline of a 1 percent deviation in the population of all electoral districts, and assured me that he could still gerrymander along any lines I wanted; racial, ethnic, religious, political, or other. I declined all offers, hired two graduate students, got the census tracts for the state, and set to work creating electoral districts with no criterion other than population equality. The operation was highly arbitrary. For one thing, the census tracts showed population but not voting-age population or actual voters. These vary a good deal from area to area, so that it was impossible to achieve one person, one vote, even if the census numbers of people had been very accurate, which they were not. For another, given the merciless requirement of a 1 percent deviation per district, the disparities in population between census tracts, the inability to break the census tracts down further, and very uneven population concentrations across the state, the shape and size of electoral districts was determined by the corner of the state where we began work. Toward the end it looked as if I would have to ask the court to order out the Governor's Guard to annex a piece of Massachusetts to make the numbers work. We finally managed to submit a plan that had only a few districts with slightly more than a 1 percent deviation. The rigors of arithmetic and the inadequacies of the materials we had to work with meant that the new districts utterly ignored geographical and demographic facts. Small towns were split into two districts, people on opposite sides of rivers were lumped into single districts. There was no help for it, but editorial reaction around the state was often furious. One editorial was headed

"Bork's Fiasco," which seemed a little hard since I had labeled the one person, one vote doctrine a fiasco to begin with.

What worried me was that, since we had redistricted entirely by the numbers, I had no idea of the political impact of the plan. Since I was known as a conservative, and that label brings with it a lot of erroneous assumptions in a liberal academic community, I could only hope that the plan would not turn out greatly to favor Republicans or to disadvantage minority groups. When I went to Hartford for the court hearing I was told that a particular restaurant was good for lunch but was not informed that it was also a Democratic Party hangout. I had just lowered a spoon into the soup when a man at another table rose and came over. "Professor, that is a fine reapportionment. It shows great integrity. My name is John Bailey." John Bailey was then Chairman of the Democratic National Committee, and that was how I found out what my plan did. It was no surprise, after that, when the Republican Party's lawyer went after me as I presented the plan to the court at that afternoon's hearing. He seemed determined to get me to admit that my plan had political consequences and mildly disconcerted when I freely admitted it every time he raised the point. Any districting produces political results. How population groups are divided or combined affects the balance in the legislature. The only virtue I could claim was that the political effects of my plan were produced mindlessly rather than intentionally. The court accepted the plan in its entirety. It never went into effect, however, since the Supreme Court, now headed by Chief Justice Warren Burger, relaxed the arithmetical rigor of the Warren Court's rule and held that the Connecticut legislature's original plan was acceptable.[35] That was just as well.

The experience taught me several things. One was that the one person, one vote doctrine, aside from the dispositive objections raised by Justice Stewart, does not result in equality of representation. Another was that the doctrine in no way reduces gerrymandering, which means some persons' votes are deliberately submerged and made ineffective. Finally, the Court's deformation of the Constitution probably succumbed to the law of unintended consequences. It is said that the Warren majority created its constitutional rule in order to increase the representation of cities, particularly inner cities. Earl Warren is reported to have said that these cases were the greatest accomplishment of his Chief Justiceship.[36] But the rule's actual result, apparently, has been to increase the influence of the suburbs.

If so, the one man, one vote doctrine was not only illegitimate constitutional law but a political failure as well.

Poll Taxes and the New Equal Protection

Poll taxes were common in this country for many years. After the Civil War, some poll taxes were enacted to disenfranchise blacks, but such taxes had other purposes as well. They were imposed in colonial times and afterward, before there was any question of black voting. Such taxes were a means of raising revenue and also of ensuring that those who voted had some minimal interest in the franchise and the outcome of elections. In 1937, the Supreme Court in *Breedlove* v. *Suttles*[37] unanimously upheld Georgia's poll tax against a challenge laid under the equal protection clause. No racial discrimination was present in the case. In 1964, the states ratified the twenty-fourth amendment, which barred poll taxes in all elections for federal offices. The amendment was carefully confined to federal elections, leaving the question of poll taxes in state elections up to the states. In 1966, the Supreme Court decided to complete what the twenty-fourth amendment had deliberately left undone.

In *Harper* v. *Virginia State Board of Elections*,[38] a Court majority, in a case where no racial discrimination was alleged or shown, held that any poll tax violated the equal protection clause. The Virginia tax amounted to $1.50 annually. Justice Douglas's opinion changed the law of the Constitution by stating that the right to vote was a fundamental interest, like the right to procreate in *Skinner* v. *Oklahoma,* so that close scrutiny of the law was required. (The invocation of the phrases "fundamental interest" and "close scrutiny" in Warren Court jurisprudence were not aids to analysis but the first ring of the death knell for the law under scrutiny. Once those phrases appeared, there was no need to read the rest of the opinion.) Voting qualifications, he said, have no relation to wealth or to paying or not paying a poll tax or any other tax. The fact that such a tax had previously been unanimously upheld was of no significance. "Notions of what constitutes equal treatment for purposes of the Equal Protection Clause *do* change. [He cited *Brown* v. *Board of Education.*] Our conclusion, like that in *Reynolds* v. *Sims,* is founded not on what we think governmental policy should be, but on what the Equal Protection Clause requires."[39]

Douglas must have enjoyed that line. The equal protection clause had required neither the result in *Reynolds* v. *Sims* nor that in *Harper* until the Court decided "what governmental policy should be." The practice of stating emphatically that the Court was not doing precisely what the Court was doing was common in the years of the Warren Court. Attention should be paid to the remarkable statement that "notions" of equality under the equal protection clause "*do* change." Whose notions? The Justices', obviously, which means that the content of the equal protection clause changes with the notions of five or more Justices. It is significant, too, that Douglas cited *Brown* for the proposition that the equal protection clause changes, showing that the Court did not think *Brown* was consistent with the original understanding of the clause and further that *Brown* justified the Court in ignoring that understanding.

Justices Black, Harlan, and Stewart dissented.[40] Black noted that racially nondiscriminatory poll taxes rested on a number of state policies that the Court had not proved to be "irrational," including: a desire to collect revenue; a belief that voters who pay a poll tax will be interested in the state's welfare; and the rationality of the tax as shown by its history. He thought Douglas was manipulating the equal protection clause to "write into the Constitution [the Court's] notions of what it thinks is good governmental policy," just as it had done under the idea of substantive due process. Harlan wrote that the poll tax was "not in accord with current egalitarian notions"[41] but that "legislatures should modify the law to reflect such changes in popular attitudes."

Congress's Power to Change the Constitution by Statute

The effort to reach liberal results routinely deformed the Constitution. The Constitution, in article I, section 2, unambiguously leaves with the states the authority to set the qualifications of voters in federal and state elections. One qualification states have regularly required for voting is literacy. There is clearly a valid state interest in literate electors, and the Supreme Court had held that literacy tests are constitutionally valid if not misused to disfranchise racial minorities. But one provision of the Voting Rights Act of 1965 stated that no person who had completed the sixth grade in Puerto Rico, having been instructed in a language other than English, could be denied the right to vote in any election because of inability to read or write in English. New York had a literacy test for voting. It was challenged and came before the Supreme Court the next year in *Katzenbach* v. *Morgan.*[42] The Court had a problem. The statute could not be upheld unless the Court was prepared to say that Congress could take from the states a power given them by the Constitution. The Court majority managed to do just that. Justice Brennan's opinion first noted that the states could not, of course, grant or withhold the franchise on conditions forbidden by the fourteenth amendment. That is true, but the Court had held that a literacy test was not forbidden by the fourteenth amendment. How to get around that? By saying that Congress in the Voting Rights Act had redefined the meaning of the amendment's equal protection clause. How can Congress change the meaning of a constitutional provision by a mere statute? The Court said Congress could because the act was a valid exercise of Congress's power to "enforce" the fourteenth amendment, given in section 5.

There were manifold difficulties with that. The power to "enforce" a law is not the power to change the law's content. The power to enforce is the power to provide remedies, such as criminal sanctions, damage actions, injunctions, and the like. Had the ratifiers intended to reserve to Congress the authority to alter the concept of equal protection, they could have said so much more plainly. Indeed, there would have been no need for a constitutional amendment if the subject of the liberties of the newly freed slaves was to be left to such statutes as Congress might see fit to pass in the future. Still worse, if Congress's power to enforce was a power to change the substance, why could it not do something like overrule *Brown* v. *Board of Education* and reinstitute the separate-but-equal doctrine so that states might segregate? Justice Brennan was forced into the position that the power to enforce was a liberal ratchet, it could go only in one direction. He said that section 5 "does not grant Congress power to exercise discretion in the other direction and to enact 'statutes so as in effect to dilute equal protection and due process decisions of this Court.' We emphasize that Congress's power under § 5 is limited to adopting measures to enforce the guarantees of the Amendment; § 5 grants Congress no power to restrict, abrogate, or dilute these guarantees."[43] No evidence is cited for the proposition that the ratifiers intended to give Congress power to amend the fourteenth amendment by statute but only by expanding the definitions of what states are constitutionally forbidden to do. The passage states that Congress can change the meaning of the clause only if it requires more equality rather than less. Only liberal, egalitarian statutes need apply. The notion that Congress can change the meaning given a constitutional provision by the Court is subversive of the function of judicial review; and it is not the less so because the Court promises to allow it only when the Constitution is moved to the left.

Applying the Bill of Rights to the States

There is no occasion here to attempt to resolve the controversy concerning the application of the Bill of Rights to the states. As an original matter, of course, the Bill of Rights was entirely a set of guarantees directed against the power of the national government. The Federalists, who sought the ratification of the Constitution, had not included a Bill of Rights because they thought the limited powers assigned the national government made such protections unnecessary. But the state constitutions had explicit declarations of rights, and the Anti-Federalists attempted to block ratification on the ground that, without such guarantees, the Constitution was fatally defective. To what extent the complaint about the lack of a Bill of Rights was merely a debating tactic by those who opposed ratification in any event is not entirely clear, but once ratification was accomplished, interest in the subject subsided remarkably. But Madison and others had promised to submit amendments guaranteeing rights during the ratification debates. Very little notice was taken when Madison submitted his amendments or when they were proposed and ratified.

That lack of attention seemed justified for most of our history, for the rights specified received almost no judicial enforcement until this century. Rights against state governments continued to be governed by state constitutions. Federal enforcement of rights against the states came to seem important only after the Civil War, when it became essential to guarantee the liberties of the freed slaves against hostile Southern state governments. The adoption of the due process clause in the fourteenth amendment soon provided, as we have seen, a temptation to judicial constitution-making the Justices could not resist. Soon they were using the concept of substantive due process, invented in *Dred Scott* for use against the federal government, to strike down state laws in no way related to race on grounds reflecting nothing but the personal views of the Justices.

Some of the values enforced, but by no means all, were those in the federal Bill of Rights, and it ultimately came to seem, primarily to Justice Hugo Black, that it would be best to hold that all of the federal Bill of Rights was "incorporated" in the due process clause and so applied to state laws and actions.[44] Among Black's reasons was the desire to end judicial legislation under the due process clause by substituting the provisions of the Bill of Rights for the vague formulas used in substantive due process. The Court ultimately did incorporate most of the Bill of Rights, but Black's hopes were not realized, because the Court also continued to make up new rights under the fourteenth amendment.

The controversy over the legitimacy of incorporation continues to this day, although as a matter of judicial practice the issue is settled. Nevertheless, the application to the states of the Bill of Rights enormously expanded the Court's power. That meant making its interpretations of the various amendments the uniform law throughout the nation, which had never occurred before. This process, though it started much earlier, was completed during the years of the Warren Court and created the occasions for some of its most controversial rulings.

The Court had, for example, devised a rule that evidence must be excluded in federal criminal trials if it had been obtained by a police search later held to have been unreasonable under the fourth amendment. In *Wolf* v. *Colorado*[45] in 1949 the Court held that the fourth amendment applied to the states but that the rule excluding evidence improperly obtained was not required. In 1961, however, the Court switched its position in *Mapp* v. *Ohio*,[46] and held that the state courts must use the exclusionary rule exactly as the federal courts applied it. Extending the reach of the principle that criminals should go free because the evidence of guilt was obtained in an unreasonable search was, it need hardly be said, a highly debatable and hotly debated development. A number of commentators have doubted the effectiveness of the rule in preventing improper searches and whether the deterrence achieved is worth the cost in decisions not to prosecute the obviously guilty. The Warren Court extended the principle in *Miranda* v. *Arizona*[47] by laying down a body of rules governing police questioning of subjects. *Miranda* reads more like the work of a legislative drafting committee than a judicial opinion, and it was extremely controversial. Four Justices dissented from the holding.[48]

Perhaps the most fiercely resented extension of the Court's Bill of Rights jurisprudence to the states arose under the first amendment clause forbidding the "establishment" of religion. As an original matter, the clause might have extended no further than a prohibition against the government's recognition of an official church or the favoring of some religions over others. The first Congress, many of whose members were also members of the Philadelphia convention or of the various state ratifying conventions, and hence aware of what the clause was intended to mean, adopted legislation that demonstrated they did not think the "wall of separation between church and state," a phrase that does not appear in the Constitution, was as severe and complete as the Court has now made it. The Court has adopted a rigidly secularist view of the establishment clause, which would not have disturbed too many people if the clause had not been incorporated to prohibit religious practices that the states had employed for many years. The sense of outrage was particularly intense when the Court prohibited prayer in the public schools,[49] and years later even disapproved some moments of silence.[50] The application of the Bill of Rights to the states in this and other matters has done much to alter the moral tone of communities across the country.

The Right of Privacy: The Construction of a Constitutional Time Bomb

The 1965 decision in *Griswold* v. *Connecticut*[51] was insignificant in itself but momentous for the future of constitutional law. Connecticut had an ancient statute making it criminal to use contraceptives. The state also had a general accessory statute allowing the punishment of any person who aided another in committing an offense. On its face, the statute criminalizing the use of contraceptives made no distinction between married couples and others. But the statute also had never been enforced against anyone who used contraceptives, married or not. There was, of course, no prospect that it ever would be enforced. If any Connecticut official had been mad enough to attempt enforcement, the law would at once have been removed from the books and the official from his office. Indeed, some Yale law professors had gotten the statute all the way to the Supreme Court a few years previously, and the Court had refused to decide it precisely because there was no showing that the law was ever enforced. The professors had some difficulty arranging a test case but finally managed to have two doctors who gave birth control information fined $100 apiece as accessories.

Such enforcement in the area as there was consisted of the occasional application of the accessory statute against birth control clinics, usually clinics that advertised. The situation was similar to the enforcement of many antigambling laws. They may cover all forms of gambling on their faces, but they are in fact enforced only against commercial gambling. An official who began arresting the priest at the church bingo party or friends having their monthly poker game at home would have made a most unwise career decision and would be quite unlikely to get a conviction. There are a number of statutes like these in various state codes, such as the statutes flatly prohibiting sodomy and other "unnatural practices," which apply on their faces to all couples, married or unmarried, heterosexual or homosexual. The statutes are never enforced, but legislators, who would be aghast at any enforcement effort, nevertheless often refuse to repeal them.

There is a problem with laws like these. They are kept in the codebooks as precatory statements, affirmations of moral principle. It is quite arguable that this is an improper use of law, most particularly of criminal law, that statutes should not be on the books if no one intends to enforce them. It has been suggested that if anyone tried to enforce a law that had moldered in disuse for many years, the statute should be declared void by reason of desuetude or that the defendant should go free because the law had not provided fair warning.

But these were not the issues in *Griswold*. Indeed, getting off on such grounds was the last thing the defendants and their lawyers wanted. Since the lawyers had a difficult time getting the state even to fine two doctors as accessories, it seems obvious that the case was not arranged out of any fear of prosecution, and certainly not the prosecution of married couples. *Griswold* is more plausibly viewed as an attempt to enlist the Court on one side of one issue in a cultural struggle. Though the statute was originally enacted when the old Yankee culture dominated Connecticut politics, it was now quite popular with the Catholic hierarchy and with many lay Catholics whose religious values it paralleled. The case against the law was worked up by members of the Yale law school faculty and was supported by the Planned Parenthood Federation of America, Inc., the Catholic Council on Civil Liberties, and the American Civil Liberties Union. A ruling of unconstitutionality may have been sought as a statement that opposition to contraception is benighted and, therefore, a statement about whose cultural values are dominant. Be that as it may, the upshot was a new constitutional doctrine perfectly suited, and later used, to enlist the Court on the side of moral relativism in sexual matters.

Justice Douglas's majority opinion dealt with the case as if Connecticut had devoted itself to sexual fascism. "Would we allow the police to search the sacred precincts of marital bedrooms for telltale signs of the use of contraceptives? The very idea is repulsive to the notions of privacy surrounding the marriage relationship."[52] That was both true and entirely irrelevant to the case before the Court. Courts usually judge statutes by the way in which they are actually enforced, not by imagining horrible events that have never happened, never will happen, and could be stopped by courts if they ever seemed about to happen. Just as in *Skinner* he had treated a proposal to sterilize three-time felons as raising the specter of racial genocide, Douglas raised the stakes to the sky here by treating Connecticut as though it was threatening the institution of marriage. "We deal with a right of privacy older than the Bill of Rights— older than our political parties, older than our school system." The thought was incoherent. What the right of privacy's age in comparison with that of our political parties and school system had to do with anything was unclear, and where the "right" came from if not from the Bill of Rights it is impossible to understand. No court had ever invalidated a statute on the basis of the right Douglas described. That makes it all the more perplexing that Douglas in fact purported to derive the right of privacy not from some pre-existing right or law of nature, but from the Bill of Rights. It is important to understand Justice Douglas's argument both because the method, though without merit, continually recurs in constitutional adjudication and because the "right of privacy" has become a loose canon in the law. Douglas began by pointing out that "specific guarantees in the Bill of Rights have penumbras, formed by emanations from those guarantees that help give them life and substance." There is nothing exceptional about that thought, other than the language of penumbras and emanations. Courts often give protection to a constitutional freedom by creating a buffer zone, by prohibiting a government from doing something not in itself forbidden but likely to lead to an invasion of a right specified in the Constitution. Douglas cited *NAACP* v. *Alabama*,[53] in which the Supreme Court held that the state could not force the disclosure of the organization's membership lists since that would have a deterrent effect upon the members' first amendment rights of political and legal action. That may well have been part of the purpose of the statute. But for this anticipated effect upon guaranteed freedoms, there would be no constitutional objection to the required disclosure of membership. The right not to disclose had no life of its own independent of the rights specified in the first amendment.

Douglas named the buffer zone or "penumbra" of the first amendment a protection of "privacy," although, in *NAACP* v. *Alabama,* of course, confidentiality of membership was required not for the sake of individual privacy but to protect the public activities of politics and litigation. Douglas then asserted that other amendments create "zones of privacy." These were the first, third (soldiers not to be quartered in private homes), fourth (ban on unreasonable searches and seizures), and fifth (freedom from self-incrimination). There was no particularly good reason to use the word "privacy" for the freedoms cited, except for the fact that the opinion was building toward those "sacred precincts of marital bedrooms." The phrase "areas of freedom" would have been more accurate since the provisions cited protect both private and public behavior.

None of the amendments cited, and none of their buffer or penumbral zones, covered the case before the Court. The Connecticut statute was not invalid under any provision of the Bill of Rights, no matter how extended. Since the statute in question did not threaten any guaranteed freedom, it did not fall within any "emanation." *Griswold* v. *Connecticut* was, therefore, not like *NAACP* v. *Alabama.* Justice Douglas bypassed that seemingly insuperable difficulty by simply asserting that the various separate "zones of privacy" created by each separate provision of the Bill of Rights somehow created a general but wholly undefined "right of privacy" that is independent of and lies outside any right or "zone of privacy" to be found in the Constitution. Douglas did not explain how it was that the Framers created five or six specific rights that could, with considerable stretching, be called "privacy," and, though the Framers chose not to create more, the Court could nevertheless invent a general right of privacy that the Framers had, inexplicably, left out. It really does not matter to the decision what the Bill of Rights covers or does not cover.

Douglas closed the *Griswold* opinion with a burst of passionate oratory. "Marriage is a coming together for better or for worse, hopefully enduring, and intimate to the degree of being sacred. It is an association that promotes a way of life, not causes; a harmony in living, not political faiths; a bilateral loyalty, not commercial or social projects. Yet it is an association for as noble a purpose as any involved in our prior decisions."⁵⁴ It is almost a matter for regret that Connecticut had not threatened the institution of marriage, or even attempted to prevent anyone from using contraceptives, since that left some admirable sentiments, expressed with rhetorical fervor, dangling irrelevantly in midair. But the protection of marriage was not the point of *Griswold*. The creation of a new device for judicial power to remake the Constitution was the point.

The *Griswold* opinion, of course, began by denying that any such power was being assumed. "[W]e are met with a wide range of questions that implicate the Due Process Clause of the 14th Amendment. Overtones of some arguments suggest that [*Lochner* v. *New York*] should be our guide. But we decline that invitation. . . . We do not sit as a super-legislature to determine the wisdom, need, and propriety of laws that touch economic problems, business affairs, or social conditions."⁵⁵ *Griswold,* as an assumption of judicial power unrelated to the Constitution is, however, indistinguishable from *Lochner*. And the nature of that power, its lack of rationale or structure, ensured that it could not be confined.

The Court majority said there was now a right of privacy but did not even intimate an answer to the question, "Privacy to do what?" People often take addictive drugs in private, some men physically abuse their wives and children in private, executives conspire to fix prices in private, Mafiosi confer with their button men in private. If these sound bizarre, one professor at a prominent law school has suggested that the right of privacy may create a right to engage in prostitution. Moreover, as we shall see, the Court has extended the right of privacy to activities that can in no sense be said to be done in private. The truth is that "privacy" will turn out to protect those activities that enough Justices to form a majority think ought to be protected and not activities with which they have little sympathy.

If one called the zones of the separate rights of the Bill of Rights zones of "freedom," which would be more accurate, then, should one care to follow Douglas's logic, the zones would add up to a general right of freedom independent of any provision of the Constitution. A general right of freedom—a constitutional right to be free of regulation by law—is a manifest impossibility. Such a right would posit a state of nature, and its law would be that of the jungle. If the Court had created a general "right of freedom," we would know at once, therefore, that the new right would necessarily be applied selectively, and, if we were given no explanation of the scope of the new right, we would know that the "right" was nothing more than a warrant judges had created for themselves to do whatever they wished. That, as we shall see in the next chapter, is precisely what happened with the new, general, undefined, and unexplained "right of privacy."

Justice Black's dissent stated: "I like my privacy as well as the next one, but I am nevertheless compelled to admit that government has a right to invade it unless prohibited by some specific constitutional provision."[56] He found none. "The Court talks about a constitutional 'right of privacy' as though there is some constitutional provision or provisions forbidding any law ever to be passed which might abridge the 'privacy' of individuals. But there is not." He pointed out that there are "certain specific constitutional provisions which are designed in part to protect privacy at certain times and places with respect to certain activities." But there was no general right of the sort Douglas had created. Justice Stewart's dissent referred to the statute as "an uncommonly silly law" but noted that its asininity was not before the Court.[57] He could "find no such general right of privacy in the Bill of Rights, in any other part of the Constitution, or in any case ever before decided by this Court." He also observed that the "Court does not say how far the new constitutional right of privacy announced today extends." That was twenty-four years ago, and the Court still has not told us.

4

After Warren: The Burger and Rehnquist Courts

*T*he moral imperialism of the Supreme Court did not end with Chief Justice Warren's resignation nor with the departures of the Justices who made up his distinctive majority. The Courts headed by Chief Justice Warren Burger and now by Chief Justice William Rehnquist, while perhaps less relentlessly adventurous than the Warren Court, displayed a strong affinity for legislating policy in the name of the Constitution. As before, departures from the Constitution invariably incorporated part of the modern liberal agenda.

Though the popular press portrayed the Court after Warren as relatively conservative, that was an error of parallax, akin to the misreading of time that occurs when a clock's hands are viewed from the side rather than straight on. From the media's perspective, the Burger and Rehnquist Courts *were* conservative. In truth, judging by decisions that are not compelled by or that run contrary to the Constitution and statutes, those Courts were more liberal than the American people.

Examination must again be confined to a few typical examples of judicial revisionism. The themes around which such decisions cluster in this era are those at the center of modern liberalism's imperatives: questions of race, gender, and sexual freedom.

The Transformation of Civil Rights Law

We may begin with examples concerning gender and race. These cases demonstrate that judicial revisionism, once let loose, does not confine itself to rewriting the Constitution but imposes its political stamp on statutes as well. Though it is said that Congress is free to correct a judicial misinterpretation of a statute, that is often not in fact true. Drafting, amending, and enacting a bill can be a highly contentious affair that succeeds only because of compromises within the legislature. The final statute reflects the balance of forces in Congress, which in turn reflects the various states and intensities of legislative sentiment in the electorate. The legislation that results may be compared to a contract in which each side gives the other something in order to get some of what it wants. When the Supreme Court distorts a statute, one side gets more than its bargain and the other gets less. And, when the statute deals with intensely political matters, there is little or no disposition on the part of the legislators to whom the judges have given a free victory to return to the matter and give the other side what it bargained for. The Court's alteration of the law becomes permanent.

The Court's transformation of an important antidiscrimination statute, Title VII of the Civil Rights Act of 1964, illustrates the point. The change began in 1973 in *Griggs* v. *Duke Power Co.*[1] A group of black employees challenged the company's requirement of a high school diploma and a satisfactory intelligence test score for certain jobs previously given only to white employees. There was no doubt the company had discriminated in the past, but the trial court found, and the finding was not overturned, that such conduct had ended. The case turned on the facts that neither the requirement of a high school diploma nor the intelligence test had been shown to "bear a demonstrable relationship to successful performance of the jobs for which it was used," and both requirements had a disparate racial impact. Though Duke Power had no discriminatory intent, the fact that both requirements disqualified blacks at a substantially higher rate than they did whites served to show a violation of the antidiscrimination statute. The problem is that the rule as framed requires the employer to demonstrate that the requirement predicts performance on the job, and the employer must do that to the satisfaction of any one of hundreds of district judges it may draw at trial. The employer is thus given a strong incentive, in order to avoid incessant, and often hopeless, litigation, to adopt a quota system so that there can be no allegation that its hiring procedures have a disparate racial impact.

The *Duke Power* decision, made by a unanimous Court, tended to press in the direction of equality of results rather than equality of opportunity,[2] though Chief Justice Burger, who wrote the opinion, certainly did not intend that. Indeed, the rationale of his opinion was clearly one of equal opportunity, the results to be determined by individual merit. In light of what came afterward, however, it is instructive to read his interpretation of what the law commanded. "Discriminatory preference for any group, minority or majority, is precisely and only what Congress has proscribed."[3] Moreover, "Far from disparaging job qualifications as such, Congress has made such qualifications the controlling factor, so that race, religion, nationality, and sex become irrelevant."

By 1979, the Chief Justice's view had become a minority position. In *United Steelworkers of America* v. *Weber,*[4] the Court decided that racial preferences were, after all, allowed by the Civil Rights Act. The Steelworkers and Kaiser Aluminum and Chemical Corporation entered into a master collective-bargaining agreement that included a plan to eliminate racial imbalances in Kaiser's almost exclusively white craftworkers. To that end, hiring goals were set for each of Kaiser's fifteen plants. The percentage of black craft workers was to be made to equal the percentage of blacks in the various local labor forces. The plan reserved for blacks 50 percent of the openings in the in-plant training programs until the requisite proportions were reached. At the plant in Gramercy, Louisiana, thirteen trainees were selected from the production work force, seven blacks and six whites. The most senior black had less seniority than several white workers who were rejected. One of the latter, Brian Weber, sued under the 1964 Act.

A majority of the Supreme Court, in an opinion by Justice Brennan, held that Congress's purpose had been to break down barriers to black employment, and therefore Congress could not have intended to prevent an employer from giving preference to blacks. Of course, the first statement does not lead to the second. If Congress intended to prevent discrimination against any "individual," which is what the statute said, a prohibition of discrimination on grounds of race would follow. In that case, Weber would win, as the trial court and court of appeals had held he should. The Court made of the 1964 Civil Rights Act a law that Congress had not written, one that allowed employers to prefer individuals, who had not been discriminated against, because of their membership in a racial group which was not proportionally represented in the work force. Chief Justice Burger's dissent said the majority's position was "contrary to the explicit language of the statute,"[5] accomplished "precisely what both its sponsors and its opponents agreed the statute was *not* intended to do," and was "wholly incompatible with long-established principles of separation of powers." Justice Rehnquist's lengthy dissent demonstrated beyond question that everybody in Congress understood that the act would not permit employers to prefer any individual because of race, no matter what that race was.[6] The transformation of Title VII of the Civil Rights Act of 1964 into a group entitlement law rather than an antidiscrimination law was completed in *Johnson* v. *Transportation Agency, Santa Clara County.*[7] The Transportation Agency adopted an Affirmative Action Plan that applied, among other things, to employee promotions. The plan's rationale was that " 'mere prohibition of discriminatory practices is not enough to remedy the effects of past practices and to permit attainment of an equitable representation of minorities, women and handicapped persons.' " The plan therefore permitted consideration of a person's membership in one of these groups in making decisions about employment and promotion. The persons to be favored because of membership in a named group were not persons who had been discriminated against. Nor was there any showing that there had been any discrimination against any persons in the past. Preference for individuals was given simply because the group to which he or she belonged was not "equitably" (read "proportionately") represented in a job category.

The agency announced a vacancy for the position of road dispatcher. Seven employee applicants were found qualified and received scores above 70 in an interview, which meant they were eligible for selection by the appointing authority. Paul Johnson received a score of 75, which tied him for second. Diane Joyce scored 73. A second interview was conducted by three supervisors, who recommended that Johnson be promoted. But Joyce had gone to the county's Affirmative Action Office, which then communicated with the agency's Affirmative Action Coordinator, who in turn recommended to the agency's director that Joyce receive the promotion. She did. Nobody claimed the recommendation of Johnson was discriminatory. Joyce received the promotion instead because she was female. There had not been a female road dispatcher, and the agency wanted a "balanced" work force.

The Court majority, in an opinion by Justice Brennan, upheld the preference: "the Agency appropriately took into account as one factor the sex of Diane Joyce. . . . The decision to do so was made pursuant to an affirmative action plan that represents a moderate, flexible, case-by-case approach to effecting a gradual improvement in the representation of minorities and women in the Agency's work force. Such a plan is fully consistent with Title VII, for it embodies the contribution that voluntary employer action can make in eliminating the vestiges of discrimination in the workplace."

That last sentence should be read again. Taking sex or ethnicity into account is consistent with the statute, because the employer is contributing to eliminating the vestiges of discrimination. No discrimination had been shown, of course, and the trial court found as a fact that there had been none. But these days discrimination in the past is assumed. That assumption is then used to justify actual discrimination in the present. Johnson won a promotion because of his merits, then lost it because of his sex. Even if that were an equitable social policy, that policy, as enunciated by the Court majority, plainly violates Title VII of the Civil Rights Act. Compare the passage quoted from Justice Brennan's opinion above with the actual language of the statute the Court was to apply.

The statute makes no allowance for "moderate, flexible, case-by-case" methods of preferring women or minorities to white males. Instead, it states:

It shall be an unlawful employment practice for an employer—

(1) to fail or refuse to hire or to discharge any individual, or otherwise to discriminate against any individual with respect to his compensation, terms, conditions, or privileges of employment, because of such individual's race, color, religion, sex, or national origin; or

(2) to limit, segregate, or classify his employees or applicants for employment in any way which would deprive or tend to deprive any individual of employment opportunities or otherwise adversely affect his status as an employee, because of such individual's race, color, religion, sex, or national origin.[8]

The statute could not be plainer. What happened to Johnson violated the statute. His employer discriminated against him because of his sex. At the time Title VII was debated, adversaries and doubters expressed the fear that it would allow reverse discrimination, discrimination against whites and males in favor of blacks and females. The proponents of the law, including such leaders in its passage as Senator Hubert Humphrey, emphatically denied that such discrimination would be legal. Those assurances were necessary to the passage of the statute. There could be no better example of a statute that was a bargained contract between persons of differing views. Nor could there be a better illustration of the Court's willingness to undo that contract and award a victory to one side that it could not win democratically. There could also be no better example of a statute's deformation that will not be repaired by new legislation. To try to bring Title VII back to its actual meaning would result in a major political war, with the opposition charging hostility to "civil rights," if not outright sexism and racism.

It makes little sense, or justice, to sacrifice a white or a male who did not inflict discrimination to advance the interests of a black or a female who did not suffer discrimination. No old injustice is undone, but a new injustice is inflicted. If it is impossible to understand what rational or defensible purpose such a policy serves, it is possible to see the state of society toward which the policy moves us. It is one of quotas for groups, regardless of individual merit. The goal of the plan was to mirror the racial and sexual composition of the entire county labor force in every individual job category at the agency. That balance would never come about naturally. As Justice Scalia, writing for three dissenters, noted, "Quite obviously, the plan did not seek to replicate what a lack of discrimination would produce, but rather imposed racial and sexual tailoring that would, in defiance of normal expectations and laws of probability, give each protected racial and sexual group a governmentally determined 'proper' proportion of each job category."[9] That is a radical social policy, one that sacrifices both individuals and the ideal of merit to the new fashion of group entitlements.

Martin Mayer described the results for civil rights when "the leadership of American society fell into the hands of the intellectual community. . . . [N]ondiscrimination became equal opportunity became affirmative action became goals became quotas became 'equality of outcomes.' "[10] This progression in intellectual and political fashion proved so powerful that a Court majority could be persuaded to hold that a statute means the opposite of what its words say and its proponents promised.

To say that government may impose quotas does not answer the crucial question: quotas for whom? Johnson attacked the plan because the quota excluded him. Some future plaintiff may choose to attack a government plan under the equal protection clause on the ground that his or her group deserved a quota as much as the favored group and may not be treated differently by government. President Gerald Ford convened a small group at the White House to discuss the problem of affirmative action or quotas in general. One man startled at least some of us by urging quotas for Americans of Slavic descent. He pointed out that various Slavic groups had a lower proportional representation among college students than did blacks. I thought the idea of quotas pernicious to begin with and that it would completely undermine the ideal of merit to extend quotas to yet more groups. But the extension is difficult to resist once you accept the idea of any quotas. If lack of proportional representation is inequitable, it becomes impossible to see why all groups whose proportion in employment, college, or what have you falls below its proportion of the population should not benefit from the principle. Of course, there is the problem that there are an almost endless number of such groups. As Thomas Sowell has reminded us, we tend to talk of "blacks" or "whites," but in fact there is great ethnic diversity within each of those groups and even within such subgroups as Slavs or Catholics or Jews.[11] Government could not single out these groups for less favorable treatment, but of course it does just that when it excludes them from the list of groups that get more favorable treatment. If the lawsuits start coming, the courts are going to have to decide that government cannot give preferences according to sex or ethnicity, or that it can discriminate as it wishes, or the courts themselves will have to decide which groups are entitled to preferential quotas and which not. The latter two options could hardly be more at odds with the promise of the equal protection clause, the 1964 Civil Rights Act, or, indeed, of America. But these choices are where the politics of ultraliberalism seemed to be driving the law.

That direction is no longer so apparent; at least, a counter-current has become visible. In the spring of 1989, 5-to-4 Court majorities made some moderate, and overdue, adjustments in civil rights doctrine. In *Richmond* v. *J. A. Croson Co.*[12] the Court this year struck down the city's minority set-aside program. Richmond required prime contractors who were given city construction contracts to subcontract at least 30 percent of the dollar amount to businesses at least 51 percent owned by U.S. citizens who were "Blacks, Spanish-speaking, Orientals, Indians, Eskimos, or Aleuts." It was less than clear why Richmond wanted to extend its quota to minorities from anywhere in the nation, and it requires an effort to imagine the rationale for putting Orientals, Indians, Eskimos, and Aleuts, on the preferred list. So far as one can tell, they had lost very few construction jobs in Richmond because of discrimination. What was clear was that whites were to be discriminated against. The Court found that to be a violation of the equal protection clause. The quota was not an allowable remedy because there was no evidence that the city or anyone in the Richmond construction industry had illegally discriminated against anyone. Justice Sandra Day O'Connor's opinion is marred only by the argument that the federal government can impose quotas that states and cities may not because the fourteenth amendment gives Congress the power to "enforce" its substantive provisions. The power to enforce, however, is the power to prescribe remedies and sanctions, for violations of equal protection, not the power to change what "equal protection" means. As Justice Anthony Kennedy wrote in concurrence, "The process by which a law that is an equal protection violation when enacted by a State becomes transformed to an equal protection guarantee when enacted by Congress poses a difficult proposition for me. . . ."[13] It is, in truth, an impossible proposition.

In *Croson,* three members of the *Johnson* majority, Justices Brennan, Marshall, and Blackmun, dissented vigorously.[14] Though the legality of racial preferences less bizarre than Richmond's may not be clear, and though the Court may draw a wavering line in these matters in the future, at least until new appointments alter the Court's composition, for the time being we may accept George Will's assessment of *Croson:* "The Court is gingerly backing out of a swamp."[15]

Shortly after *Croson,* in *Wards Cove Packing Co.* v. *Atonio,* the Court modified the harsh law of statistical racial imbalances it had made in *Griggs.*[16] Statistical imbalances are everywhere in our society since entirely innocent social processes and cultural differences guarantee that there will not be proportional representation of each ethnic group in each occupation. *Wards Cove* involved Alaskan salmon canneries with predominantly white work forces in skilled jobs and predominantly non-white work forces in unskilled jobs. Intentional discrimination was not at issue, only the consequences of business practices. The court of appeals held that imbalance created a case against the companies which they could rebut only by proving that the business practices that produced these disparities were essential to their businesses. This version of the law, Justice White wrote in reversing, "at the very least, would mean that any employer who had a segment of his work force that was—for some reason—racially imbalanced, could be haled into court and forced to engage in the expensive and time-consuming task of defending the 'business necessity' of the methods used to select the other members of his work force." Thus, the "only practicable option for many employers will be to adopt racial quotas . . . ; this is a result that Congress expressly rejected in drafting Title VII."

The Court held that the proper comparison was between the proportion of a racial group in the work force and the proportion of qualified members of that race in the population available to the employer. Plaintiffs must also identify the employment practices they contend are responsible for the statistical imbalance of the races. When the plaintiff has done that, the employer must come forward with evidence of business justifications for the practices challenged but the ultimate burden of persuading the court that the racial imbalances remain unjustified remains with the plaintiff.

The outcry of civil rights activists and the liberal press was loud and shrill, as, indeed, had been the dissenting opinions in both *Croson* and *Wards Cove*. Ignoring the question of whether the decisions were justified in law, the groups and the press launched a moral assault upon the Court majority. The American left regularly bypasses rational argument to challenge the moral character of those with whom it has substantive differences. The technique is one of intimidation and it has sometimes been at least partially effective with Courts that were sensitive about their image with the press and in public perception. It is important to understand, therefore, that the issue between the Court and its detractors on the left is simply one of quotas and other racial preferences. Most Americans, though thoroughly in favor of civil rights, are opposed to quotas. And they are right on policy as well as legal grounds. When non-whites who have not suffered discrimination are preferred to whites who have not inflicted discrimination, racial resentments are certain to be inflamed. The problem is likely to grow more acute if preferences are legalized because the question of race and ethnicity is no longer simply a black–white issue.

The composition of the American population is changing; in some areas it is changing rapidly. We now see competition for group entitlements among whites of European ancestry, blacks, Hispanics, and Asians. That competition quickly becomes bitter, and we now see alarmed articles about the eruption of racist sentiments and expressions on campuses and in workplaces. The only possibility of avoiding still more racial and ethnic antagonism, with largely unforeseeable but certainly unhappy results, is to drop the entire notion of group entitlements. That means an end to racial, ethnic, and sexual quotas. Fortunately, the relevant constitutional and statutory law, properly interpreted, supports that position.

Judicial Moral Philosophy and the Right of Privacy

The years of the Burger and Rehnquist Courts also saw the "right of privacy" invented by the Warren Court mature into a judicial power to dictate moral codes of sexual conduct and procreation for the entire nation. The Court majority adopted an extreme individualistic philosophy in these cases, seeming to assert that society, acting through government, had very little legitimate interest in such matters.

Griswold v. *Connecticut*[17] invalidated a law prohibiting the use of contraceptives on the ground that government must not enter the marital bedroom. That focus, spurious as it was, at least seemed to confine the "right of privacy" to areas of life that all Americans would agree should remain private. But almost at once a Court majority began to alter the new right's rationale and hence to expand its coverage in unpredictable ways.

Massachusetts enacted a law regulating the distribution rather than the use of contraceptives. The law provided that married persons could obtain contraceptives to prevent pregnancy on prescription only, and single persons could not obtain contraceptives for the purpose of preventing pregnancy but only to prevent the spread of disease. It was not apparent that the law made much sense, but that is not the same as being unconstitutional. In 1972, in *Eisenstadt* v. *Baird,*[18] the Supreme Court invalidated the statute under the equal protection clause of the fourteenth amendment and began the transformation of the right of privacy:

> If under *Griswold* the distribution of contraceptives to married persons cannot be prohibited, a ban on distribution to unmarried persons would be equally impermissible. It is true that in *Griswold* the right of privacy in question inhered in the marital relationship. Yet the marital couple is not an independent entity with a mind and heart of its own, but an association of two individuals each with a separate intellectual and emotional makeup. If the right of privacy means anything, it is the right of the *individual,* married or single, to be free from unwarranted governmental intrusion

into matters so fundamentally affecting a person as the decision whether to bear or beget a child.

Griswold did not, of course, deal with distribution of contraceptives but with a prohibition of use. That case, moreover, rested upon a rhetorical appreciation of marriage and the marital bedroom. Now that rhetorical line was dropped because the Massachusetts statute treated married couples and single persons differently, and the Court wanted to strike down the law as to unmarried people. Significantly, the argument of the Court shifted from the sanctity of a basic institution, marriage, to the sanctity of individual desires. The unmarried individual has, as a matter of fact, the freedom to decide whether to bear or beget a child, of course, because he or she has the right to choose whether or not to copulate. But that did not seem enough to the Court, perhaps because copulation should not be burdened either by marital status or by abstinence from its pleasures. There may or may not be something to be said for this as a matter of morality, but there is nothing to be said for it as constitutional law. The Constitution simply does not address the subject.

Nor after *Eisenstadt* were we much further along in knowing what it is that the right of privacy does cover. In order to apply the precedent to the next litigant's claim to be free of a law on the grounds of privacy, one would have to know whether the challenged governmental regulation was "unwarranted," which is in no way defined by the opinion, and whether the regulation concerned a matter "so fundamentally affecting a person as the decision whether to bear or beget a child." The opinion gives no guidance for deciding that issue either. It was impossible to tell from *Eisenstadt* where the right of privacy might strike next. We soon learned.

The subject of abortion had been fiercely debated in state legislatures for many years. It raises profound moral issues upon which people of good will can and do disagree, depending upon whether they view a fetus as fully human, and therefore not to be killed for anyone's convenience, or whether they think the fetus less than human so that the desires of the pregnant woman should be paramount. Whatever the proper resolution of the moral debate, a subject which there is no need to address here, few people imagined that the Constitution resolved it. In 1973 a majority of the Supreme Court did imagine just that in *Roe* v. *Wade*.[19]

In an opinion of just over fifty-one pages, Justice Blackmun, writing for a majority of seven Justices, employed the right of privacy to strike down the abortion laws of most states and to set severe limitations upon the states' power to regulate the subject at all. From the beginning of the Republic until that day, January 22, 1973, the moral question of what abortions should be lawful had been left entirely to state legislatures. The discovery this late in our history that the question was not one for democratic decision but one of constitutional law was so implausible that it certainly deserved a fifty-one-page explanation. Unfortunately, in the entire opinion there is not one line of explanation, not one sentence that qualifies as legal argument. Nor has the Court in the sixteen years since ever provided the explanation lacking in 1973. It is unlikely that it ever will, because the right to abort, whatever one thinks of it, is not to be found in the Constitution.

The *Roe* opinion began with a brief recitation of the statute challenged, the appealability of the orders below, and the power of the Court to decide the issue, and then turned to the history of abortion and the interests of the state in regulating the topic through its criminal code. Justice Blackmun canvassed ancient attitudes, including those of the Persian Empire, the Greeks, the Romans, and the "Ephesian, Soranos, often described as the greatest of the ancient gynecologists. . . ."[20] He placed the Hippocratic Oath, which forbids aiding an abortion, in historical context, suggesting that the oath was not at first highly regarded and that its later popularity was due in large measure to the rise of Christianity. The opinion then traced the English common and statutory law as well as the American law on the subject before devoting sections to the positions of the American Medical Association, the American Public Health Association, and the American Bar Association. None of this, it will be noted, is of obvious relevance to the Constitution. Nor was any of this material employed as history that might illuminate the meaning of any provision of the Constitution.

The *Roe* opinion next discussed three reasons said to explain the enactment of laws limiting the right to abort: "a Victorian social concern to discourage illicit sexual conduct";[21] concern for the hazards abortion posed for women; and concern for prenatal life. Note that the very concept of sexual conduct that is "illicit" is dismissed with the pejorative "Victorian." This accurately reflects the Court majority's allegiance to untrammeled individualism and its position in our cultural wars. And the Court did not decide that the statutes were invalid because obsolete—that, for example, state legislatures had been moved by concern for women's health that modern medicine had rendered irrelevant. A statute may be enacted for one reason, retained for another, and be none the less constitutional for that. Had that rationale for invalidity been advanced, moreover, states could have responded by reenacting their laws out of an expressed desire to protect the unborn. That was not what the Court had in mind.

The explanation of the true basis for the unconstitutionality of so many statutes begins with the sentence, "The Constitution does not explicitly mention any right of privacy."[22] The existence of such a right is nonetheless defended by citing a series of cases to demonstrate that "the Court has recognized that a right of personal privacy, or a guarantee of certain areas or zones of privacy, does exist under the Constitution." Nobody has ever quarreled with the proposition that certain zones or aspects of privacy or freedom are protected by the Constitution. Justice Blackmun cited cases decided under the first, fourth, and fifth amendments. But those differed entirely from the right he was creating in that they had specific textual support. He got closer to his solution when he moved to concepts previously employed by Courts that lacked support in the actual Constitution for what they wanted to do. The opinion cited the "penumbras of the Bill of Rights," relied upon by Justice Douglas in *Griswold* v. *Connecticut,* Justice Goldberg's reliance upon the ninth amendment in the same case, and the concept of liberty in the due process clause of the fourteenth amendment. *Roe* continued:

> These decisions make it clear that only personal rights that can be deemed "fundamental" or "implicit in the concept of ordered liberty [*Palko* v. *Connecticut*]," are included in this guarantee of personal privacy. They also make it clear that the right has some extension to activities relating to marriage [*Loving* v. *Virginia*]; procreation [*Skinner* v. *Oklahoma*]; contraception [*Eisenstadt* v. *Baird*]; family relationships [*Prince* v. *Massachusetts*]; and child rearing and education [*Pierce* v. *Society of Sisters; Meyer* v. *Nebraska*].

Skinner[23] and *Eisenstadt,*[24] as we have seen in this chapter and the one preceding, involved the Court's creation of new rights without support in constitutional text or history. *Pierce*[25] and *Meyer,*[26] as we saw two chapters back, used the same methodology of creating rights but at least reflected the first amendment. *Prince*[27] denied claims by a Jehovah's Witness to be free of the state's child labor laws on grounds of religious freedom and the equal protection of the laws. The case related to marriage, *Loving*,[28] struck down an antimiscegenation law on the grounds that the racial classification violated the equal protection clause and also the right of liberty under the due process clause, though the latter holding also seemed to depend upon the invidious racial classification. This is not a very impressive list of cases to support the claimed right of abortion. They do not bear upon the subject at all. Some of the cases were clearly instances of judicial rewriting of the Constitution, others at least enforced values found in actual provisions of the Constitution, and still others denied the rights claimed. None of them remotely addresses the issue of abortion, and none of them even mentions a right of privacy. It is difficult, therefore, to understand why the *Roe* opinion supposes that these cases show the extension or reach of the right of privacy. They do nothing of the sort. Marshaling these decisions as if they were precedents merely emphasized the absence of support for the right. The invented right of privacy had not been applied in any Supreme Court case other than ones involving contraception.

Nonetheless, without any analysis, the *Roe* opinion then immediately decided the issue before the Court by simple assertion:

> This right of privacy, whether it be founded in the Fourteenth Amendment's concept of personal liberty and restrictions upon state action, as we feel it is, or, as the District Court determined, in the Ninth Amendment's reservation of rights to the people, is broad enough to encompass a woman's decision whether or not to terminate her pregnancy.[29]

That is it. That is the crux of the opinion. The Court did not even feel obliged to settle the question of where the right of privacy or the subsidiary right to abort is to be attached to the Constitution's text. The opinion seems to regard that as a technicality that really does not matter, and indeed it does not, since the right does not come out of the Constitution but is forced into it. The opinion does not once say what principle defines the new right so that we might know both why it covers a liberty to abort and what else it might cover in the future. We are told only that wherever the right may be located and whatever it may cover, it is "broad enough" for present purposes. This is not legal reasoning but fiat.

The *Roe* opinion then legislated the rules the Court considered appropriate for abortions by balancing the interests of the woman and those of the state. To do that, of course, the Court had implicitly to decide which interests were legitimate and how much weight should be ascribed to each one. That, being unguided by the Constitution, was an exercise in moral and political philosophy, or would have been if some reasoning had been articulated. The upshot, in any event, was that in the first trimester of pregnancy the abortion decision must be left to the woman and the medical judgment of her physician. After that and up to the point where the fetus can live outside the womb, the point of viability, the state may regulate the abortion procedure but only in ways related to the health of the mother. Subsequent to viability, "the State in promoting its interest in the potentiality of human life may, if it chooses, regulate, and even proscribe, abortion" except where it is necessary to preserve the mother's life or health.

Justice Rehnquist's dissent pointed out that it was very curious to decide the case under the rubric of privacy since a transaction resulting in an operation by a physician is not "private."[30] Justice White's dissent, which Justice Rehnquist joined, summed up the trouble with *Roe:*

> I find nothing in the language or history of the Constitution to support the Court's judgment. The Court simply fashions and announces a new constitutional right for pregnant mothers and, with scarcely any reason or authority for its action, invests that right with sufficient substance to override most existing state abortion statutes. The upshot is that the people and the legislatures of the 50 States are constitutionally disentitled to weigh the relative importance of the continued existence and development of the fetus, on the one hand, against a spectrum of possible impacts on the mother, on the other hand. As an exercise of raw judicial power, the Court perhaps has authority to do what it does today; but in my view its judgment is an improvident and extravagant exercise of the power of judicial review that the Constitution extends to this Court.[31]

In the years since 1973, no one, however pro-abortion, has ever thought of an argument that even remotely begins to justify *Roe* v. *Wade* as a constitutional decision. Justice Blackmun frequently discusses the case in public, but the only justification he offers is not legal but moral: the case, he says, is a milestone on women's march to equality. There is certainly room for argument about that. There is no room for argument about the conclusion that the decision was the assumption of illegitimate judicial power and a usurpation of the democratic authority of the American people.

On the last day it sat in 1989, a bitterly divided Court decided *Webster* v. *Reproductive Health Services,*[32] a challenge to statutory restrictions Missouri has placed upon the abortion procedure. The crucial restriction was the law's requirement that before performing an abortion on a woman twenty or more weeks pregnant, the physician first determine whether the unborn child is viable. Five Justices upheld that regulation, which seemed to narrow the scope of *Roe.* Three Justices, Rehnquist, White, and Kennedy, employed a standard of review which necessarily, though not explicitly, completely undermines *Roe,*[33] while one Justice, Scalia,[34] stated that *Roe* should expressly be overruled. Justice O'Connor upheld the statute but stated that that could be done without bringing *Roe* into question.[35] Both sides in the abortion controversy at once announced that the Court had made a momentous decision. It is true enough that states now appear to have some unknown degree of additional power to control the incidents of abortion but *Webster* was neither the calamity that the pro-abortion groups bewailed ("the Court is waging war on women") nor the great victory that the anti-abortionists proclaimed ("we will produce an avalanche of legislation"). Though *Webster* altered little that was fundamental, it does signal the potential for such change. In *Roe,* the Justices split seven to two in favor of a right to abort. Now there are four Justices who favor that right, four who think it does not exist, and one who does not reach the issue.

Attempts to overturn *Roe* will continue as long as the Court adheres to it. And, just so long as the decision remains, the Court will be perceived, correctly, as political and will continue to be the target of demonstrations, marches, television advertisements, mass mailings, and the like. *Roe,* as the greatest example and symbol of the judicial usurpation of democratic prerogatives in this century, should be overturned. The Court's integrity requires that. But even if the case is relegated to the dustbin of history where *Dred Scott* and *Lochner* lie, the right of privacy and the judicial techniques and attitudes it represents are likely to remain. A more fundamental rethinking of legitimate judicial power than the mere demise of *Roe* would signify is required.

The privacy right had come to another crucial point three years earlier in *Bowers* v. *Hardwick.*[36] A narrow majority of the Court there upheld, at least as to homosexual sodomy, a Georgia statute making all sodomy criminal. This was significant, and may even have presaged *Webster,* for there seems little doubt that the impulse, it was no more than that, underlying *Roe* would have struck down the sodomy statute in *Hardwick.*

A police officer, who entered Hardwick's home lawfully, observed Hardwick engaged in homosexual sodomy and made an arrest. The district attorney, however, decided not to prosecute—there had been no criminal prosecutions under the statute for decades—and so Hardwick brought suit to have the law declared unconstitutional. Though he alleged that he was in imminent danger of arrest as a practicing homosexual, that was obviously not so, and the suit was surely brought to seek a declaration that would equate the constitutionality, and hence the presumed morality, of homosexual and heterosexual conduct. Hardwick's suit, in a word, rested upon nothing in the Constitution and so was one more sortie in our cultural war.

The Supreme Court upheld the law by a five-to-four vote. Justice White, writing for the majority, stated: "The issue presented is whether the Federal Constitution confers a fundamental right upon homosexuals to engage in sodomy and hence invalidates the laws of the many States that still make such conduct illegal and have done so for a very long time."[37] This statement of the issue was somewhat problematical, because the statute on its face applied to all forms of sodomy, heterosexual as well as homosexual, and, given the history of its enforcement, Hardwick was in no greater danger of prosecution than any heterosexual.

The court of appeals had found the statute unconstitutional by relying on Supreme Court precedent that we have already canvassed in this and previous chapters. Justice White found those precedents inapplicable, however, by categorizing them as dealing with child rearing and education, family relationships, procreation, marriage, contraception, and abortion. There was, he said, no connection between those subjects and homosexual sodomy. That was true enough, though, since those cases never did offer a rationale, it is hard to put them into categories except retroactively and as a matter of description rather than analysis.

But Hardwick, quite aside from the precedent, asked the Court to announce a fundamental right to engage in homosexual sodomy. Justice White's response showed that he knew the Court had long been performing a questionable function in this area. "It is true that despite the language of the Due Process Clauses of the Fifth and Fourteenth Amendments, which appears to focus only on the processes by which life, liberty, or property is taken, the cases are legion in which those Clauses have been interpreted to have substantive content. . . . Among such cases are those recognizing rights that have little or no textual support in the constitutional language."[38] Then:

> Striving to assure itself and the public that announcing rights not readily identifiable in the Constitution's text involves much more than the imposition of the Justices' own values on the States and the Federal Government, the Court has sought to identify the nature of the rights qualifying for heightened judicial protection.

That passage contains no suggestion that the Court had succeeded in its striving. Justice White noted two formulations of the Justices' attempts to assure themselves, and us, that they were not merely imposing their own values. In *Palko* v. *Connecticut,* a 1937 decision, it was said that the fundamental liberties to be protected, though not found in the text of the Constitution, included those "implicit in the concept of ordered liberty," so that "neither liberty nor justice would exist if [they] were sacrificed."[39] Forty years later, in *Moore* v. *East Cleveland,* the formulation of protected freedoms was those that are "deeply rooted in this Nation's history and tradition."[40]

This is pretty vaporous stuff. Compare the phrases used by *Palko* and *Moore* with the provisions of the Bill of Rights. The latter at least specify what liberty is to be protected. Whatever line-drawing must be done starts from a solid base, the guarantee of freedom of speech, of freedom from unreasonable searches and seizures, and the like. By contrast, the judge-created phrases specify no particular freedom, but merely assure us, in sonorous phrases, that they, the judges, will know what freedoms are required when the time comes. One would think something more is required as the starting place for a line of reasoning that leads to the negation of statutes duly enacted by elected representatives. "Ordered liberty" is a splendid phrase but not a major premise. It might be thought that ordered liberty is just what the Constitution was intended to establish for the nation and that it is therefore more than a little surprising, and perhaps presumptuous, that Justices should describe their task in a way that suggests they are completing a design the Founders left unfinished. Both the amendment process, specified in the Constitution, and the processes of legislation are means by which the design of order and liberty can be elaborated and improved. The phrase *Palko* used rather too clearly indicates that the Justices may rewrite the Constitution. Nor is it terribly reassuring to be told they will rewrite it only to save liberties the Founders overlooked but which are nevertheless so essential that neither liberty nor justice can exist without them. The suggestion that such rights were overlooked in the Constitution and then systematically overlooked through two centuries of amendments is, to be candid, preposterous.

The *Moore* formulation is less grandiose but hardly offers more guidance. Liberties that are deeply rooted in our history and tradition and that now need protection must be matters the Founders left to the legislature, either because they assumed no legislature would be mad enough to do away with them or because they wished to allow the legislature discretion to regulate the area as they saw fit. In any event, history is not binding, and tradition is useful to remind us of the wisdom and folly of the past, not to chain us to either. No constitutional doctrine holds that history and tradition may not be departed from when the people think there is good reason to do so. Our history and tradition, like those of any nation, display not only adherence to great moral principles but also instances of profound immorality. Opinions about which is which will differ at any one time and change over time. The judge who states that tradition and morality are his guides, therefore, leaves himself free to pick through them for those particular freedoms that he prefers. History and tradition are very capacious suitcases, and a judge may find a good deal pleasing to himself packed into them, if only because he has packed the bags himself.

Because homosexual sodomy has been proscribed for centuries, Justice White said the claim that such conduct was "deeply rooted in this Nation's history and tradition" was "at best, facetious."[41] He expressed the *Bowers* majority's unwillingness to take a more expansive view of its authority to discover new fundamental rights in the due process clause. "The Court is most vulnerable and comes nearest to illegitimacy when it deals with judge-made constitutional law having little or no cognizable roots in the language or design of the Constitution." That is quite right, or almost so. Perhaps he had to put the matter as one of coming "nearest to illegitimacy" in order not to offend members of the majority who had joined decisions that had no roots in the "language or design of the Constitution," but on this topic there is no question of near or far. When constitutional law is judge-made and not rooted in the text or structure of the Constitution, it does not approach illegitimacy, it *is* illegitimate, root and branch.*

Justice Blackmun wrote for the four dissenters.[42] His opinion has been widely praised by the commentators of the popular press with such terms as "eloquent" and "passionate." Those things it may be. But eloquence and passion are poor substitutes for judicial reasoning, and the *Bowers* dissent, the natural outcome of *Griswold* v. *Connecticut* and *Roe* v. *Wade,* is a constitutional debacle. The opinion will repay close examination nonetheless, for here, for the first time, a Justice embarks upon the enterprise law school theorists have been urging upon the Court as its proper function—the enterprise of articulated moral philosophy. Blackmun began with the observation that the case was not about a fundamental right to engage in homosexual sodomy but about " 'the most comprehensive of rights and the right most valued by civilized men,' namely, 'the right to be let alone.' " There is, of course, no general constitutional right to be let alone, or there would be no law. This was merely the general, undefined right of privacy again. Though it is difficult to be sure, Justice Blackmun seems to have located this free-floating right, or rather free-floating judicial power, alternatively in the due process clause of the fourteenth amendment or in the ninth amendment. We have discussed the due process clause's lack of substance, and the ninth amendment, as will be shown in Chapter 8, simply does not create any rights a court may enforce against any government. In *Roe,* Justice Blackmun had attached privacy to the due process clause of the fourteenth amendment. But, as in *Roe,* where in the Constitution a Justice chooses to insert a right he has made

---

* As a judge, I had earlier reached the same result by a somewhat different route. The Navy had discharged a petty officer for engaging in such conduct in the barracks with a young recruit. The former petty officer challenged his discharge and contended before our court that the right of privacy cases created a general rule that government may not interfere with an individual's intimate decisions regarding his or her own body. My opinion examined those cases, found in them "no explanatory principle that informs a lower court how to reason about what is and what is not encompassed by the right of privacy," and refused to invent a right to homosexual conduct, saying that "If the revolution in sexual mores that appellant proclaims is in fact ever to arrive, we think it must arrive through the moral choices of the people and their elected representatives, not through the ukase of this court." *Dronenburg* v. *Zech,* 741 F.2d 1388, 1395, 1397 (1984). Since the right of privacy cases rest upon no constitutional principle, but are themselves mere judicial ukases, that position still seems to me correct.

up is of small importance, more a matter of aesthetic preference than of legal significance.

Justice Blackmun went on to explain that the Court construed the right to privacy by proceeding along two lines. "First, [the Court] has recognized a privacy interest with reference to certain decisions that are properly for the individual to make. [He cited *Roe* v. *Wade* and *Pierce* v. *Society of Sisters*]. Second, [the Court] has recognized a privacy interest with reference to certain *places* without regard for the particular activities in which the individuals who occupy them are engaged."[43] Neither of these withstands even cursory examination.

The first line of argument gives itself away at once with the qualification that the Court protects the right to make those decisions that are "*properly*" the individual's to make. What is proper is not an objective fact but a moral choice to be made by someone, and the *Bowers* dissent says the moral choice is for judges. That is bad enough, but the next question is whether the judges can at least frame criteria that guide them to their choice and explain to us why the choice is correct and what is likely to be the judges' next choice on behalf of the individual against society. From the evidence of Blackmun's *Roe* opinion there are no such criteria, or at least none that the Justices care to share with us. *Bowers,* on the other hand, confirms the conclusion that there are no such criteria by trying to explain them to us. The dissent chastises the majority for stating that prior cases had related to the protection of the family. That may be so, Blackmun said in a truly startling argument, but the rights to be protected extend beyond that, because "We protect those rights [associated with the family] not because they contribute, in some direct and material way, to the general public welfare, but because they form so central a part of an individual's life. '[T]he concept of privacy embodies the "moral fact that a person belongs to himself and not others nor to society as a whole." ' " It is doubtful that there are any moral "facts," as opposed to moral convictions, but if there are, this is not one of them and cannot be so long as we live in a society. If the opinion meant what it said, four members of the Court viewed the state of nature, in which every individual is free to be for himself and no one else, as the moral condition contemplated by the Constitution. That view of the individual and his obligations can hardly be taken seriously. In our view of morality and responsibility, no husband or wife, no father or mother, should act on the principle that a "person belongs to himself and not others."

No citizen should take the view that no part of him belongs to "society as a whole." Under that notion, there would be no moral obligation to obey the law and it would certainly be impossible to draft an army to defend the nation. Here and elsewhere some Justices have enunciated a position of extreme individualism, which amounts necessarily to an attitude of moral relativism. If all that counts is the gratification of the individual, then morality is completely privatized and society may make no moral judgments that are translated into law.

The dissent cannot really mean what it said and, indeed, no Justice takes any such position consistently. None could since all law is based upon moral judgments. There is, for example, no basis for worker safety laws other than the moral judgment that it is wrong to endanger workers' lives and limbs in order to produce goods at lower cost. There is no objection to segregation or even to slavery other than moral disapproval. No one suggests that the fourteenth amendment, which ended the one, and the thirteenth amendment, which ended the other, are based on anything other than morality. Justice White rejected Justice Blackmun's point as phrased by Hardwick. Hardwick made the argument that has become common in these cases. White said he asserted that "there must be a rational basis for the law and that there is none in this case other than the presumed belief of a majority of the electorate in Georgia that homosexual sodomy is immoral and unacceptable. This is said to be an inadequate rationale to support the law. The law, however, is constantly based on notions of morality, and if all laws representing essentially moral choices are to be invalidated under the Due Process Clause, the courts will be very busy indeed."[44]

Justice Blackmun attempted to repair his position somewhat by claiming that "what the Court really has refused to recognize is the fundamental interest all individuals have in controlling the nature of their intimate associations with others."[45] "Intimate associations," of course, means sex. It has never been thought, until the rampant individualism of the modern era, that all individuals are entitled, as a matter of constitutional right, to engage in any form of sexual activity that appealed to them. The dissent had no real reply to the majority's observation that if the constitutional argument is "limited to the voluntary sexual conduct between consenting adults, it would be difficult, except by fiat, to limit the claimed right to homosexual conduct while leaving exposed to prosecution adultery, incest, and other sexual crimes even though they are committed in the home." Indeed it would. When the community decides that certain sexual conduct is permissible and other conduct is not, courts have no way of disagreeing about the line drawn except by saying that the judges' morality is superior to that of the majority of the citizenry and is, for that reason, to be transformed into a constitutional standard.

The dissent's second line of argument, that a right of privacy attached because Hardwick's behavior occurred in his own home, "a place to which the Fourth Amendment attaches special significance,"[46] fares no better. The fourth amendment states that citizens are to be secure in their homes from unreasonable searches and seizures; it does not even remotely suggest that anything done in the home has additional constitutional protection. Moreover, that amendment specifically recognizes the government's right to enter a home under a proper warrant, or if the search is reasonable. That certainly suggests that the privacy of the home is less than absolute. Many actions taken entirely in one's home can nonetheless be punished by law. Of course the Constitution and much legislation protect the privacy of the home in many respects, but they also leave much that is done in the home unprotected. When Justice Blackmun extrapolates from protections that exist to create a new protection not to be found in existing law, he performs precisely the same logical leap that enabled Justice Douglas to invent a right of privacy in the first place. Thus, it is appropriate that Justice Blackmun should end this section of his opinion with the observation that the "right of an individual to conduct intimate relationships in the intimacy of his or her own home seems to me to be the heart of the Constitution's protection of privacy."

The dissent makes a point of the fact that Hardwick's behavior was not physically dangerous to those engaged in it or to others and refers to "victimless" activity. That, as we have reason to know, is not true. But, in any event, physical danger does not exhaust the categories of harms society may seek to prevent by legislation, and no activity that society thinks immoral is victimless. Knowledge that an activity is taking place is a harm to those who find it profoundly immoral. That statement will be taken as repressive by many, but only because they really do not disapprove of the conduct involved in *Bowers*. If the sexual conduct involved was bestiality, they might agree that it could be prohibited by law, although the only objection to it is moral.

There is vast confusion upon this point. In the seminar on constitutional theory I taught with Alex Bickel, I took the position at one time that it was no business of society what conduct that did not harm another person took place out of sight. Indeed, my position then, though not my reasons, was almost identical to that of the *Bowers* dissent. Bickel posed a hypothetical. Suppose, he said, that on an offshore island there lived a man who raised puppies entirely for the pleasure of torturing them to death. The rest of us are not required to witness the torture, nor can we hear the screams of the animals. We just know what is taking place and we are appalled. Can it be that we have no right, constitutionally or morally, to enact legislation against such conduct and to enforce it against the sadist? I cannot now remember what, if any, answer I gave; certainly, whatever it was it was not a very good one. Bickel was right. Moral outrage is a sufficient ground for prohibitory legislation.

Many people will argue that Bickel's hypothetical does not at all resemble a law against consensual homosexual sodomy since cruelty to animals is involved in the former. We have already dealt with that argument. There is no objection to the torturing of puppies for pleasure except that it outrages our morality. There is, indeed, no objection to forcible rape in the home or to the sexual abuse of a child there, except a moral objection. But, it will be said, those cases do not involve consent or do not involve a consent the person is mature enough to give intelligently. Those are not objections to the comparison. They are merely statements that the speaker perceives a moral distinction in consent. But the perception of a moral distinction does not affect the point being made that morality, standing alone, is a sufficient rationale to support legislation. In fact, for most people, consent does not solve everything: they would favor laws punishing the torture of a consenting masochist or the provision of cocaine to a willing purchaser. I am sure to be attacked on the ground that I see no moral distinction between forcible rape and consenting sexual activity between adults. That is not true. I do see a clear moral difference. But the subject for discussion is not my morality. Nor is it the case that the moral difference between consent and non-consent means that only behavior involving the latter may be punished by law. If a majority of my fellow citizens decide that the cases, while not alike, are nevertheless similar enough so that both actions should be made criminal, while I may disagree with them morally, the fact that I am a judge does not mean that I am entitled to displace their moral judgment with my own. A robe is entirely irrelevant to the worth or power of one's moral views. A judge is also a voter, and it is in the polling booth that his moral views count.

The dissenting opinion also made the elementary error of confusing its power to override legislated morality when that morality conflicts with the Constitution and its power to override legislated morality when that morality conflicts with nothing in the Constitution but only with the judge's preferences. I have heard this argument when I sat on the bench: why, if you allow people to legislate their morality, it is said, they can decide that morality requires racial segregation. The argument is that if courts allow people to legislate on the basis of morality, the people will legislate immoral laws. There could hardly be a clearer statement that what those who want activist courts actually fear is rule by the people. The people cannot, of course, reflect any racist morality in law, because that notion of morality is placed out of bounds by the fourteenth amendment.

But the dissent went beyond denying that morality could be a basis for law and contended that if the morality was based in religion, that fact made the law worse. The Georgia Attorney General had argued that traditional Judeo-Christian values proscribed homosexual sodomy. The dissent correctly noted that conformity to religious doctrine is not enough to sustain secular legislation, but the opinion went further:

> [F]ar from buttressing his case, [the Attorney General's] invocation of Leviticus, Romans, St. Thomas Aquinas, and sodomy's heretical status during the Middle Ages undermines his suggestion that [the statute] represents a legitimate use of secular coercive power. *A State can no more punish private behavior because of religious intolerance than it can punish such behavior because of racial animus.*[47]

The fact that a moral view is embodied in religious doctrine does not convert either the view or the doctrine into religious intolerance. The Constitution prohibits punishing a person because of his religious beliefs; to do that would be religious intolerance. All religions of which I am aware condemn murder. One supposes that the dissenters would not find a homicide statute undermined by that fact. Indeed, if a religious parallel or basis for a law makes the law suspect, the Court should reexamine statutes punishing perjury since Jews and Christians believe that God has commanded, "Thou shalt not bear false witness."

There is a further paradox in the judicial objection to morality as the basis for legislation. Judges who vigorously deny elected representatives the right to base law on morality simultaneously claim for themselves the right to create constitutional law on the basis of morality, their morality. There being nothing in the Constitution prohibiting legislated morality, the only opposition to it rests upon a moral view. The *Bowers* dissent said as much when it stated as a "moral fact" that a person belongs to himself and not to others or to society. Moral relativism is, after all, one moral position. But the imposition of moral relativism upon legislatures by judges is not, strictly speaking, moral relativism in itself. It is more accurately described as the belief that the only valid and trustworthy morality is the judges'. That being the case, even should *Roe* be overruled, we have no idea what the "right of privacy"—or some other judge-made moral principle—may accomplish next.

The First Amendment and the Rehnquist Court

There will be no attempt here at a comprehensive survey of the first amendment rulings of the Supreme Court during William Rehnquist's tenure as Chief Justice. Rather, a few of the most recent decisions are discussed in order to make one point. The press, both print and electronic, have announced that the Court has a "working conservative majority," that the present Court is imposing the "conservative social agenda" on the country, and that the Court has taken a "sharp turn to the right." These things are simply not true. We have become so used to a left-liberal Court that any move toward the center is immediately proclaimed a right-wing threat to our basic liberties. We may pass by the point that what is seen from the left as a threat to American liberty is almost any instance in which the Court allows the American people to decide a question in a way the left dislikes. The point to be made is that we have recently gone from having a reliably left-liberal Court to having a mildly and somewhat inconsistently left-liberal Court. This is not because a majority of the Justices are liberal—although certainly there is no majority of conservatives either, except from the perspective of the left. The major reason for the course of the Court is, I think, that in the past four decades so much constitutional doctrine has been remolded on left-liberal assumptions that only a self-consciously and determinedly centrist Court could gradually, over a period of years, extricate itself. In any event, the cases discussed next should dispel any notion that the Court is now imposing conservative values upon the nation.

Forty-eight states and the federal government had laws prohibiting the desecration or defilement of the American flag. They do no longer. In *Texas* v. *Johnson,* five Justices ruled that a man who burned the flag in public to express his hatred for the United States was protected from prosecution by the first amendment's guarantee of the freedom of speech.[48] Justice Brennan's opinion rests upon two propositions, neither of which can be maintained. The first was that enforcement of the statute violated the "bedrock principle underlying the First Amendment," that being: "the Government may not prohibit the expression of an idea simply because society finds the idea itself offensive or disagreeable." If we accept that formulation, nothing follows. Texas had not prohibited the desecration of the American flag because the idea expressed was offensive but because the mode of expression was. Johnson and his companions chanted while the flag burned, "America, the red, white, and blue, we spit on you." Nobody suggested they could be punished for that, although the idea, or rather the emotion, is the same as that expressed by the burning. There were dozens of ways for Johnson to express his sentiments. Nor is it unusual for the first amendment to allow the prohibition of particular modes of expression. One supposes that the delivery of a political view in obscenities could be barred, as could its delivery by a sound truck in a residential neighborhood at two in the morning, or indecent exposure as forceful symbolism for a point of view.

The opinion's second proposition fares no better:

> To conclude that the Government may permit designated symbols to be used to communicate only a limited set of messages would be to enter territory having no discernible or defensible boundaries. Could the Government, on this theory, prohibit the burning of state flags? Of copies of the Presidential seal? Of the Constitution? In evaluating these choices under the First Amendment, how would we decide which symbols were sufficiently special to warrant this unique status? To do so, we would be forced to

consult our own political preferences, and impose them on the citizenry, in the very way that the First Amendment forbids us to do.[49]

This is a claim that the Court cannot make distinctions, a function it performs continually. The national flag is different from other symbols. Nobody pledges allegiance to the Presidential seal or salutes when it goes by. Marines did not fight their way up Mount Suribachi on Iwo Jima to raise a copy of the Constitution on a length of pipe. Nor did forty-eight states and the United States enact laws to protect these symbols from desecration.

To see how far the Court has moved, it is necessary only to recall, as Chief Justice Rehnquist's dissent did, that Chief Justice Earl Warren and Justices Hugo Black and Abe Fortas, a trio unlikely to be enshrined in any conservative pantheon, all expressed strong views that the Constitution did not prevent the states and the federal government from prohibiting the burning of the flag.[50]

In its most recent term, the Court also found that the first amendment protected the delivery of pornographic messages by telephone, thus throwing the mantle of the Constitution around the multi-million-dollar "dial-a-porn" industry.[51] Contrary to the historic meaning of the first amendment's prohibition of the establishment of religion, the Court held that a creche could not be displayed in a public building during the Christmas season.[52] And, contrary even to its own precedent, the Court declared invalid a state tax exemption on the sale of the Bible and religious literature.[53]

It seems clear that the drive of judicial revisionism has by no means ended.

5

The Supreme Court's Trajectory

*W*e have now surveyed the most explicit of the Supreme Court's rewritings of law, most particularly the law of the Constitution. Though the survey has been necessarily partial, it has, I think, been representative. Almost two centuries of constitutional adjudication discloses several characteristics of the Court's performance.

From first to last the Court has been a strong force for centralization in our national life. With the Marshall Court that was a deliberate strategy of solidifying national powers. But any Court that imposes values not found in the Constitution to that degree makes national policy that obliterates local and state policies. The New Deal Court centralized with gusto by refusing to limit Congress's powers over commerce, taxation, and spending. The Court in the era of Earl Warren and after has imposed political and moral uniformity across wide areas of American life.

It is somewhat unclear whether the modern Court is more politicized than Courts of previous eras. Certainly it makes more political decisions each year than was true in any year in the nineteenth century, but that is largely due to the number of occasions for such decisions presented to it. Before the post–Civil War amendments, particularly the fourteenth amendment, the Court had little opportunity to impose rules on the states. The development of substantive content in the fourteenth amendment's due process clause, and subsequently the incorporation of the Bill of Rights in that clause, enormously expanded the Court's power over the states. It is conceivable, though unlikely, that the Courts of the nineteenth century, given the opportunities that this legal structure presented, would have appeared as activist and political as do the Courts of the past five or six decades.

From era to era, the values the Court writes into the Constitution change. As new values are added, the old ones are dropped. The Court's performance, in terms of favored values, displays no single political trajectory over time. Moreover, the style of the Court's theorizing varies, as does the provision of the Constitution used to provide an appearance that what is being done is related in some legitimate manner to the actual document. The pace of judicial revision of the Constitution has accelerated over the Court's history, as has the exertion of judicial power, revisionist or not. The Court struck down no federal statutes between *Marbury* in 1803 and *Dred Scott* in 1857, a period of more than fifty years. The post–Civil War Courts did strike down a number of laws. The rate of constitutional revisionism picked up with the New Deal Court and became explosive with the Warren Court. The Courts after Warren's, those of Burger and Rehnquist, showed little significant slowing. We observe, therefore, the increasing importance of the one counter-majoritarian institution in the American democracy. That, by itself, would be worthy of remark, though not worrisome, if it merely reflected the number of occasions that the Court had to apply the Constitution to governmental incursions into more and more areas of American life. What is worrisome is that so many of the Court's increased number of declarations of unconstitutionality are not even plausibly related to the actual Constitution. This means that we are increasingly governed not by law or elected representatives but by an unelected, unrepresentative, unaccountable committee of lawyers applying no will but their own.

At the outset, I suggested that in each era the Court responded to the ideology of the class to which the Justices felt closest. By observing the values the Court chooses to enforce, it is often possible to discern which classes have achieved dominance at any given time in our history. "Dominance," as I use the word here, is not an entirely clear concept. It refers to the tendency of a class's ideas and values to be accepted by the elites that form opinion. In this century, we have seen the Court allied to business interests and the ideology of free enterprise. We have seen that ideology lose its power with the arrival of the New Deal and the effect of that ideological shift on the Supreme Court. The intellectual class has become liberal, and that fact has heavily influenced the Court's performance. For the past half-century, whenever the Court has departed from the original understanding of the Constitution's principles, it has invariably legislated an item on the modern liberal agenda, never an item on the conservative agenda.

The prospects for the immediate future are unclear. The present Court is divided in its approach to constitutional law, and it seems likely that the more extreme revisionists of a liberal persuasion will be replaced in the not too distant future. It is not obvious how the new Justices will affect the Court's behavior, however. Our political parties have become polarized on the issue of desirable judicial behavior, as on so many other issues. The Republican Party has become more conservative, just as the Democratic Party has become more liberal. In the modern era, liberals have favored revisionist judges. The President's nominees will have to be confirmed by a heavily Democratic Senate. That fact may mean that only persons with views acceptable to the left will be nominated or, more likely, that people will be nominated who have made no public record of their judicial philosophies. Their performance on the Court, for that reason, may not be predictable by either the President or the Senate. There was no reason to think that Earl Warren was not a moderate conservative when he was nominated, but on the bench he became a judicial radical. There have been more recent examples of judicial transformations. It is well to remember that the Supreme Court that produced liberal constitutional revisions in recent years had seven members who were appointed by Republican presidents. Nevertheless, the mood of the country is generally conservative, and that fact may in time tell on the performance of the Court.

If the performance of the Court changes, it is to be hoped that liberal revisionism will not be replaced by conservative revisionism. The two are equally illegitimate. The Constitution is too important to our national well-being and to our liberties to be made into a political weapon. Departure from its actual principles, whether in *Dred Scott, Lochner,* or *Roe,* is inconsistent with the maintenance of constitutional democracy.

There are those, and they are many, who prefer results to everything else, including democracy and respect for the legitimacy of authority. It is that view that Alexander Bickel addressed in his essay on civil disobedience.[1] He wrote of the moral imperatives that fueled the major episodes of civil disobedience in our recent history, including Southern resistance to desegregation orders, some of the opposition to the war in Vietnam, and the complex of events we call "Watergate." But he continued:

The assault upon the legal order by moral imperatives was not only or perhaps even most effectively an assault from the outside. . . . [I]t came as well from within, in the Supreme Court headed for fifteen years by Earl Warren. When a lawyer stood before him arguing his side of a case on the basis of some legal doctrine or other, or making a procedural point, or contending that the Constitution allocated competence over a given issue to another branch of government than the Supreme Court or to the states rather than to the federal government, the chief justice would shake him off saying, "Yes, yes, yes, but is it (whatever the case exemplified about law or about the society), is it *right?* Is it *good?*" More than once, and in some of its most important actions, the Warren Court got over doctrinal difficulties or issues of the allocation of competences among various institutions by asking what it viewed as a decisive practical question: If the Court did not take a certain action which was *right* and *good,* would other institutions do so, given political realities? The Warren Court took the greatest pride in cutting through legal technicalities, in piercing through procedure to substance.[2]

What Bickel said of the Warren Court may be said of all courts in our history that cut through procedure to substance, and through substance to political outcome. They engaged in civil disobedience, a disobedience arguably more dangerous, because more insidious and hence more damaging to democratic institutions, than the civil disobedience of the streets.

As Bickel also said, "It is the premise of our legal order that its own complicated arrangements, although subject to evolutionary change, are more important than any momentary objective. . . . The derogators of procedure and of technicalities, and other anti-institutional forces who rode high, on the bench as well as off, were the armies of conscience and of ideology."[3] They were also, he said, the armies of a new populism, and the "paradox is that the people whom the populist exalts may well—will frequently—not vote for the results that conscience and ideology dictate. But then one can always hope, or identify the general will with the people despite their votes, and let the Supreme Court bespeak the people's general will when the vote comes out wrong."[4]

There are heavy costs for the legal system, heavy costs for our liberty to govern ourselves, when the Court decides it is the instrument of the general will and the keeper of the national conscience. Then there is no law; there are only the moral imperatives and self-righteousness of the hour.

II

THE THEORISTS

Only recently has a body of writing appeared that can be called a literature of constitutional theory. Beginning a few decades back with a book here and an article there, this literature now qualifies as a torrent. Books, articles, and symposia taking up entire issues of law journals appear in such profusion and with such prolixity that it seems impossible anybody is reading all of the literature.

One might suppose that the sheer volume of writing coming out of our best law schools is a cause for optimism, that it is a sign of renewed vigor in scholarship and, therefore, in American constitutionalism. A more somber view is possible, however, even before sampling the writings characteristic of this genre. So much theory, theory in amounts dwarfing anything we have ever had before, suggests a need to shore something up. We are not talking, after all, about a field like mathematics or physics in which continual theoretical advances are a sign of health. We are talking about law, a field whose substantive rules often change but in which, one would suppose, the basic question of how judges and lawyers should go about deriving doctrine from legal materials would have been settled long ago. Indeed, one would have thought that the basic question of what *are* legal materials would hardly arise except in the most unusual cases. Yet that is the core of the controversy. The fact of a massive and rapidly growing literature about just such matters is, to say the least, puzzling, if not disturbing. Perhaps something has gone awry in law and courts. Self-confident legal institutions do not require so much talking about. If this is so, then the rising flood of innovative theories signifies not the health of scholarship and constitutionalism but rather a deep-seated malaise and, quite possibly, a state of approaching decadence.

To read the literature is to have one's worst fears confirmed. The sense that something in constitutional theory has gone high begins with the style of argumentation. The older constitutional commentators, secure in their commonsense lawyers' view of the Constitution, wrote prose that remains clear, to the point, self-confident, and accessible to the nonprofessional reader.[1] The modern theorists are different. Their concepts are abstruse, their sources philosophical, their arguments convoluted, and their prose necessarily complex.[2] These writers are in fact undertaking what Justice Story forswore, the alteration of the Constitution by "ingenious subtleties," "metaphysical refinements," and "visionary speculation" to make it not a document "addressed to the common sense of the people" but one addressed to a specialized and sophisticated clerisy of judicial power.[3]

To understand the new constitutions being built in the law schools, it is necessary to be a philosopher, at least an amateur one. If the literature were to be taken seriously, it would be necessary for lawyers and judges to study the vast outpouring of words that comes from the law professors and to choose among their methodologies. More than that, however, since many of the professors regard themselves as philosophers, it would be necessary to read widely in moral philosophy, hermeneutics, deconstructionism, Marxism, and who-knows-what-will-come-next. The reader is supposed to be familiar with utilitarianism, contractarianism, Mill, Derrida, Habermas, positivism, formalism, Rawls, Nozick, and the literature of radical feminism. It turns out, though previously it had never been suspected, that in order to understand the American Constitution ratified in 1787, one must study not John Locke or even James Madison, but a modern German Marxist. Working lawyers and judges can only despair in the realization that they will never be able to master even a significant fraction of what they are given to understand to be a very important body of theory. Indeed, some of the uninitiated appear not a little intimidated by the academic consensus that only comprehension of such profound and arcane inquiries can lead to a proper understanding of the way judges should deal with the Constitution. Given this state of affairs, it should come as no surprise that, in what I am increasingly tempted to call the real world, the literature remains largely unread.

This may sound like the description of a perfectly anemic academic genre, one without the potency to alter the practical workings of our legal system. In fact, that is not true. This philosophic enterprise has acquired great prestige in the law schools. Few students will master the complexities of the particular systems taught by the constitutional gurus in their schools, but that is not important. What is learned is an attitude. Many ardent Marxists, after all, have never read much Marx, and perhaps few of those who wear Adam Smith neckties have gotten very far into *The Wealth of Nations*. It is not necessary to become an adept to acquire a mind-set. Generations of law students are being trained to believe that one or another method of reasoning from nonlegal sources provides the method proper to constitutional argument. Law school moral philosophy—which deserves the same respect as what has been called "law office history"—turns out upon examination to be only a convoluted way of reaching the standard liberal or ultra-liberal prescriptions of the moment. One of my colleagues suggested that a professor of this bent change the name of his course from "Constitutional Law" to "Trendiness Made Complex." What the students learn, to put it bluntly, is that legal reasoning of the sort that served us for centuries is now utterly outmoded, and a verbal formulation can always be devised to reach the correct political result. Many will carry that attitude with them, first as clerks to judges, then as lawyers, professors, and judges themselves.

There is also the effect of the written word. Although it is unlikely that many persons outside the academy are even aware of this literature's existence, much less its content, that does not mean it is ineffective. Its very inaccessibility may, paradoxically, be a source of its influence. Because the public at large and the legal profession as a whole are unaware of what is being taught and written, the reaction of ridicule and hostility that might have been expected has not been forthcoming. But judges are aware that there is an enormous literature and that it is almost entirely disapproving of the idea that courts are bound by the original understanding of the Constitution. The message arrives where it counts. Because it is in effect coded, it is not read by outsiders.

Ideas, or at least attitudes, developed in the law schools do influence courts. As Schlesinger noted, the version of legal realism that infested the Yale law school earlier had a great influence upon the Justices who later became the center of the Warren Court majority. The new attitudes reach courts in various ways. Professors steeped in the revisionist liberal culture of the law schools may themselves become judges. This, of course, was the case with William O. Douglas, who had been a Yale law professor and became a powerful force on both the New Deal and Warren Courts. Many students become judicial clerks for a year or two after law school and carry the attitudes of the revisionist academic culture directly to federal judges. For some judges, the message that comes from the law schools reinforces their natural inclinations. The relationship between law school faculties and the federal judiciary is closer than many people realize. Professors are likely to have been clerks to federal judges, and they send their best students to clerkships. It is, moreover, important to federal judges to be well-thought-of and well-written-about in the law schools. Over time, disdain for the original meaning of the Constitution has a considerable impact.

The impact is all the greater upon judges who come to the bench with no developed view of the judicial role, of its scope and its limits. We frequently hear judges say, often with a surprising degree of satisfaction, that they have no theories of jurisprudence but are pragmatists who decide each case on its facts. Such statements are false, though not intentionally so, because the facts of a case mean nothing until the judge supplies an organizing principle that leads him to a conclusion about their meaning. Too often the judge is not conscious of the organizing principles that guide him, which means that he is likely to be led to a decision by sentiment rather than reason.

There was a time when the ideas of the law, particularly constitutional law, were fully accessible to educated people. That is no longer the case. Legal thought has become an intellectual enclave inhabited primarily by academics whose efforts are directed at influencing courts. The nature and extent of that influence are unsuspected by the general public and even by public policy intellectuals.

The new theorists of constitutional law deserve to be better known than they are, not because their theories are good but because, as a group, they are influential and their enterprise involves nothing less than the subversion of the law's foundations. Some of them are quite explicit about their intention to convert the Constitution from law to politics, and judges from magistrates to politicians. Others have no such conscious intent, but their prescriptions would have the same effect. The politics and the robed politicians, it need hardly be added, in nine cases out of ten are to be of the left-wing variety.

If they do not fully understand the extent to which the "life of the intellect" has become political rather than intellectual, many Americans do have a sense that something has gone very wrong in education. That probably accounts both for the phenomenal success of Allan Bloom's book *The Closing of the American Mind: How Higher Education Has Failed Democracy and Impoverished the Souls of Today's Students*[4] and for the acid reception accorded to it in the academy. Speaking of two disciplines, Hilton Kramer said what could be said of almost all university departments:

> We all know—and certainly our enemies know—that the assault on the study of the arts and the humanities . . . is, above all, a political assault—an attempt on the part of the radical Left first to discredit and then to do away with what in our most exalted artistic and humanistic traditions may be seen to offer resistance, either directly or by implication, to the total politicization of culture and life. We know the assault is at bottom political, no matter under what other temporary banners the assault may at times be mounted and regardless of what unexceptionable virtues it may at times be mounted in the name of.[5]

Kramer has perfectly described the situation in law as in many other fields.

Upon reading my description of the state of legal theory, the intellectual historian Gertrude Himmelfarb wrote me: "This is precisely the situation in literature and history—abstract, abstruse, highly methodological—the point of which is to relativize the disciplines thoroughly. Any methodology becomes permissible (except, of course, the traditional one), and any reading of the texts becomes legitimate (except, of course, that of the author). The purpose is not only to create a new privileged mandarin class who alone are competent to interpret the texts, but also to re-create the discipline *de novo* so as the better to politicize it, to create a *tabula rasa* upon which anything can be written. Original understanding is to the law what traditional, factual, documentary history is to the historian."[6]

Law is a critical battleground because, like the arts and humanities, like sociology, history, political science, and other areas that have become politicized, law has the capacity to affect ways of thinking and our culture through its educative and symbolic influence. When a court, especially the Supreme Court, pronounces in the name of the Constitution upon the meaning of racial justice, sexual morality, or any other subject, a cultural lesson is taught. Most people revere the Constitution as a basic compact that defines American civic morality. A decision does more than decide a case; it adds weight to one side of our cultural war, even when the decision is in fact not supported by the actual Constitution. But law, unlike other politicized fields, such as literature and philosophy, has the power to coerce, and when the law in question is the Constitution, the coercion is absolute: The people and their democratic institutions are, for all immediate practical purposes, helpless before the authority wielded by judges. Herbert Schlossberg, writing about the influence of the new class on the bureaucracy, makes a point that applies as well to its influence on judges. Through constitutional decisions that are not related to the historic Constitution, that class "has found a vehicle for giving its values the force of law without bothering to take over the political authority of the state."[7]

That is why what is being written and taught in our law schools matters. That is why it is important to understand that the spectacular efflorescence of modern constitutional theory is not a sign of vigor and health but in reality is the brilliant flower of decay.

6

The Madisonian Dilemma
and the Need for
Constitutional Theory

*T*he central problem for constitutional courts is the resolution of the "Madisonian dilemma." The United States was founded as a Madisonian system, which means that it contains two opposing principles that must be continually reconciled. The first principle is self-government, which means that in wide areas of life majorities are entitled to rule, if they wish, simply because they are majorities. The second is that there are nonetheless some things majorities must not do to minorities, some areas of life in which the individual must be free of majority rule. The dilemma is that neither majorities nor minorities can be trusted to define the proper spheres of democratic authority and individual liberty. To place that power in one or the other would risk either tyranny by the majority or tyranny by the minority. The Constitution deals with the problem in three ways: by limiting the powers of the federal government; by arranging that the President, the senators, and the representatives would be elected by different constituencies voting at different times; and by providing a Bill of Rights. The last is the only solution that directly addresses the specific liberties minorities are to have. We have placed the function of defining the otherwise irreconcilable principles of majority power and minority freedom in a nonpolitical institution, the federal judiciary, and thus, ultimately, in the Supreme Court of the United States. The task of reconciliation cannot be accomplished once and for all. The freedom of the majority to govern and the freedom of the individual not to be governed remain forever in tension. The resolution of the dilemma must be achieved anew in every case and is therefore a never ending search for the correct balance.

There is, of course, more to the Court's constitutional function than defining in so direct a fashion the rights of the individual against the state. There is the related task of maintaining the system of government the Constitution creates. The Court must often discern the powers of Congress and those of the President when the claims of each come into conflict, as, it appears, they increasingly do. Similarly, though the Court has largely abandoned the role, there is the job of defining the respective spheres of national and state authority. These questions of governmental structure, competence, and authority are, of course, closely related to the resolution of the Madisonian dilemma and may in fact amount to much the same thing. When the President and Congress come into a conflict requiring resolution by the Court, or when such a dispute arises between the national and a state government, it is usually because the contending bodies would decide an issue in different ways. It matters greatly to the individual, therefore, which arm of government has legitimate authority in a field that affects him. It matters not only in terms of the result that one branch of government ordains but, since different governmental bodies have constituencies of different sizes and compositions, it matters to the citizen's chances of participating in decision-making.

The functions assigned the Court impose a need for constitutional theory. How is the Court to reason about the resolution of the disputes brought before it? If we have no firm answer to that question, it will not be possible to know, or even rationally to discuss, whether judicial decisions are within the range of the acceptable. In resolving the Madisonian dilemma, courts must be energetic in protecting the rights of individuals while being equally scrupulous to respect the rights of majorities to govern. Should judges make serious mistakes in either direction, they abet either majority or minority tyranny. Should they make serious mistakes in structural issues, they also alter the balance of freedom and power. Modern debate about constitutional theory, however, is less about structural questions and the allocation of authority between arms of government than it is about the individual's right to be free of democratic governance.

We need a theory of constitutional adjudication, then, that defines the spheres of the majority and the individual in a sense that can be called "correct." If there is no correct solution, there is no dilemma to be resolved; there is no way to assess the work of the courts;

there is no way to choose among a constitutional theory that calls for complete majoritarianism, one that demands unlimited power for the judiciary, and a theory that insists upon freedom so extreme that it approaches anarchy. This means that if there is no single correct solution, there must be at least a limited range of outcomes that can be called correct. That, in turn, means that any theory worthy of consideration must both state an acceptable range of judicial results and, in doing that, confine the judge's power over us. It is as important to freedom to confine the judiciary's power to its proper scope as it is to confine that of the President, Congress, or state and local governments. Indeed, it is probably more important, for only courts may not be called to account by the public. For some reason unintelligible to me, Lord Acton's dictum that "Power tends to corrupt and absolute power corrupts absolutely"[1] is rarely raised in connection with judges, who, in our form of government, possess power that comes closer to being absolute than that held by any other actors in our system. The theory must, therefore, enable us to say what is the limit of the judge's legitimate authority.

In the following chapters we shall examine the leading academic theories of constitutional law, starting with the traditional and once dominant theory of the original understanding. We then turn to the competing theories, all of them revisionist in one way or another. No single revisionist theory has established dominance. One of the more entertaining features of the literature is that the revisionists regularly destroy one another's arguments and seem to agree only on the impossibility or undesirability of adherence to the Constitution's original meaning.

7

The Original Understanding

What was once the dominant view of constitutional law—that a judge is to apply the Constitution according to the principles intended by those who ratified the document—is now very much out of favor among the theorists of the field. In the legal academies in particular, the philosophy of original understanding is usually viewed as thoroughly passé, probably reactionary, and certainly—the most dreaded indictment of all—"outside the mainstream." That fact says more about the lamentable state of the intellectual life of the law, however, than it does about the merits of the theory.

In truth, only the approach of original understanding meets the criteria that any theory of constitutional adjudication must meet in order to possess democratic legitimacy. Only that approach is consonant with the design of the American Republic.

The Constitution as Law: Neutral Principles

When we speak of "law," we ordinarily refer to a rule that we have no right to change except through prescribed procedures. That statement assumes that the rule has a meaning independent of our own desires. Otherwise there would be no need to agree on procedures for changing the rule. Statutes, we agree, may be changed by amendment or repeal. The Constitution may be changed by amendment pursuant to the procedures set out in article V. It is a necessary implication of the prescribed procedures that neither statute nor Constitution should be changed by judges. Though that has been done often enough, it is in no sense proper.

143

What is the meaning of a rule that judges should not change? It is the meaning understood at the time of the law's enactment. Though I have written of the understanding of the ratifiers of the Constitution, since they enacted it and made it law, that is actually a shorthand formulation, because what the ratifiers understood themselves to be enacting must be taken to be what the public of that time would have understood the words to mean. It is important to be clear about this. The search is not for a subjective intention. If someone found a letter from George Washington to Martha telling her that what he meant by the power to lay taxes was not what other people meant, that would not change our reading of the Constitution in the slightest. Nor would the subjective intentions of all the members of a ratifying convention alter anything. When lawmakers use words, the law that results is what those words ordinarily mean. If Congress enacted a statute outlawing the sale of automatic rifles and did so in the Senate by a vote of 51 to 49, no court would overturn a conviction because two senators in the majority testified that they really had intended only to prohibit the *use* of such rifles. They said "sale" and "sale" it is. Thus, the common objection to the philosophy of original understanding—that Madison kept his notes of the convention at Philadelphia secret for many years—is off the mark. He knew that what mattered was public understanding, not subjective intentions. Madison himself said that what mattered was the intention of the ratifying conventions. His notes of the discussions at Philadelphia are merely evidence of what informed public men of the time thought the words of the Constitution meant. Since many of them were also delegates to the various state ratifying conventions, their understanding informed the debates in those conventions. As Professor Henry Monaghan of Columbia has said, what counts is what the public understood.[1] Law is a public act. Secret reservations or intentions count for nothing. All that counts is how the words used in the Constitution would have been understood at the time. The original understanding is thus manifested in the words used and in secondary materials, such as debates at the conventions, public discussion, newspaper articles, dictionaries in use at the time, and the like. Almost no one would deny this; in fact almost everyone would find it obvious to the point of thinking it fatuous to state the matter—except in the case of the Constitution. Why our legal theorists make an exception for the Constitution is worth exploring.

The search for the intent of the lawmaker is the everyday procedure of lawyers and judges when they must apply a statute, a contract, a will, or the opinion of a court. To be sure, there are differences in the way we deal with different legal materials, which was the point of John Marshall's observation in *McCulloch* v. *Maryland* that "we must never forget, that it is *a constitution* we are expounding."[2] By that he meant that narrow, legalistic reasoning was not to be applied to the document's broad provisions, a document that could not, by its nature and uses, "partake of the prolixity of a legal code." But he also wrote there that it was intended that a provision receive a "fair and just interpretation," which means that the judge is to interpret what is in the text and not something else. And, it will be recalled, in *Marbury* v. *Madison* Marshall placed the judge's power to invalidate a legislative act upon the fact that the judge was applying the words of a written document.[3] Thus, questions of breadth of approach or of room for play in the joints aside, lawyers and judges should seek in the Constitution what they seek in other legal texts: the original meaning of the words.[4]

We would at once criticize a judge who undertook to rewrite a statute or the opinion of a superior court, and yet such judicial rewriting is often correctable by the legislature or the superior court, as the Supreme Court's rewriting of the Constitution is not. At first glance, it seems distinctly peculiar that there should be a great many academic theorists who explicitly defend departures from the understanding of those who ratified the Constitution while agreeing, at least in principle, that there should be no departure from the understanding of those who enacted a statute or joined a majority opinion. A moment's reflection suggests, however, that Supreme Court departures from the original meaning of the Constitution are advocated *precisely because* those departures are not correctable democratically. The point of the academic exercise is to be free of democracy in order to impose the values of an elite upon the rest of us.

If the Constitution is law, then presumably its meaning, like that of all other law, is the meaning the lawmakers were understood to have intended. If the Constitution is law, then presumably, like all other law, the meaning the lawmakers intended is as binding upon judges as it is upon legislatures and executives. There is no other sense in which the Constitution can be what article VI proclaims it to be: "Law."[5] It is here that the concept of neutral principles, which Wechsler said were essential if the Supreme Court was not to be a naked power organ, comes into play. Wechsler, it will be recalled, in expressing his difficulties with the decision in *Brown* v.

Board of Education,[6] said that courts must choose principles which
they are willing to apply neutrally, apply, that is, to all cases that
may fairly be said to fall within them.[7] This is a safeguard against
political judging. No judge will say openly that any particular group
or political position is always entitled to win. He will announce a
principle that decides the case at hand, and Wechsler had no difficulty
with that if the judge is willing to apply the same principle in the
next case, even if it means that a group favored by the first decision
is disfavored by the second. That was precisely what Arthur M.
Schlesinger, Jr., said that the Black–Douglas wing of the Court
was unwilling to do. Instead, it pretended to enunciate principles
but in fact warped them to vote for interest groups.[8]

The Court cannot, however, avoid being a naked power organ
merely by practicing the neutral application of legal principle. The
Court can act as a legal rather than a political institution only if it
is neutral as well in the way it derives and defines the principles it
applies. If the Court is free to choose any principle that it will
subsequently apply neutrally, it is free to legislate just as a political
body would. Its purported resolution of the Madisonian dilemma
is spurious, because there is no way of saying that the correct spheres
of freedom have been assigned to the majority and the minority.
Similarly, if the Court is free to define the scope of the principle as
it sees fit, it may, by manipulating the principle's breadth, make
things come out the way it wishes on grounds that are not contained
in the principle it purports to apply. Once again, the Madisonian
dilemma is not resolved correctly but only according to the personal
preferences of the Justices. The philosophy of original understanding
is capable of supplying neutrality in all three respects—in deriving,
defining, and applying principle.

Neutrality in the Derivation of Principle

When a judge finds his principle in the Constitution as originally
understood, the problem of the neutral derivation of principle is
solved. The judge accepts the ratifiers' definition of the appropriate
ranges of majority and minority freedom. The Madisonian dilemma
is resolved in the way that the founders resolved it, and the judge
accepts the fact that he is bound by that resolution as law. He
need not, and must not, make unguided value judgments of his
own.

This means, of course, that a judge, no matter on what court he sits, may never create new constitutional rights or destroy old ones. Any time he does so, he violates not only the limits to his own authority but, and for that reason, also violates the rights of the legislature and the people. To put the matter another way, suppose that the United States, like the United Kingdom, had no written constitution and, therefore, no law to apply to strike down acts of the legislature. The U.S. judge, like the U.K. judge, could never properly invalidate a statute or an official action as unconstitutional. The very concept of unconstitutionality would be meaningless. The absence of a constitutional provision means the absence of a power of judicial review. But when a U.S. judge is given a set of constitutional provisions, then, as to anything not covered by those provisions, he is in the same position as the U.K. judge. He has no law to apply and is, quite properly, powerless. In the absence of law, a judge is a functionary without a function.

This is not to say, of course, that majorities may not add to minority freedoms by statute, and indeed a great deal of the legislation that comes out of Congress and the state legislatures does just that. The only thing majorities may not do is invade the liberties the Constitution specifies. In this sense, the concept of original understanding builds in a bias toward individual freedom. Thus, the Supreme Court properly decided in *Brown* that the equal protection clause of the fourteenth amendment forbids racial segregation or discrimination by any arm of government, but, because the Constitution addresses only governmental action, the Court could not address the question of private discrimination. Congress did address it in the Civil Rights Act of 1964 and in subsequent legislation, enlarging minority freedoms beyond those mandated by the Constitution.

Neutrality in the Definition of Principle

The neutral definition of the principle derived from the historic Constitution is also crucial. The Constitution states its principles in majestic generalities that we know cannot be taken as sweepingly as the words alone might suggest. The first amendment states that "Congress shall make no law . . . abridging the freedom of speech,"[9] but no one has ever supposed that Congress could not make some speech unlawful or that it could not make all speech illegal in certain places, at certain times, and under certain circumstances. Justices

Hugo Black and William O. Douglas often claimed to be first amendment absolutists, but even they would permit the punishment of speech if they thought it too closely "brigaded" with illegal action. From the beginning of the Republic to this day, no one has ever thought Congress could not forbid the preaching of mutiny on a ship of the Navy or disruptive proclamations in a courtroom.

But the question of neutral definition remains and is obviously closely related to neutral application. Neutral application can be gained by defining a principle so narrowly that it will fit only a few cases. Thus, to return to *Griswold*,[10] we can make neutral application possible by stating the principle to be that government may not prohibit the use of contraceptives by married couples. But that tactic raises doubts as to the definition of the principle. Why does it extend only to married couples? Why, out of all forms of sexual behavior, only to the use of contraceptives? Why, out of all forms of behavior in the home, only to sex? There may be answers, but if there are, they must be given.

Thus, once a principle is derived from the Constitution, its breadth or the level of generality at which it is stated becomes of crucial importance. The judge must not state the principle with so much generality that he transforms it. The difficulty in finding the proper level of generality has led some critics to claim that the application of the original understanding is actually impossible. That sounds fairly abstract, but an example will make clear both the point and the answer to it.

In speaking of my view that the fourteenth amendment's equal protection clause requires black equality, Dean Paul Brest said:

> The very adoption of such a principle, however, demands an arbitrary choice among levels of abstraction. Just what *is* "the general principle of equality that applies to all cases"? Is it the "core idea of *black* equality" that Bork finds in the original understanding (in which case Alan Bakke [a white who sued because a state medical school gave preference in admissions to other races] did not state a constitutionally cognizable claim), or a broader principle of "*racial* equality" (so that, depending on the precise content of the principle, Bakke might have a case after all), or is it a still broader principle of equality that encompasses discrimination on the basis of gender (or sexual orientation) as well? . . .

> . . . The fact is that all adjudication requires making choices

among the levels of generality on which to articulate principles, and all such choices are inherently non-neutral. No form of constitutional decisionmaking can be salvaged if its legitimacy depends on satisfying Bork's requirements that principles be "neutrally derived, defined and applied."[11]

If Brest's point about the impossibility of choosing the level of generality upon neutral criteria is correct, we must either resign ourselves to a Court that is a "naked power organ" or require the Court to stop making "constitutional" decisions. But Brest's argument seems to me wrong, and I think a judge committed to original understanding can do what Brest says he cannot. We may use Brest's example to demonstrate the point.

The role of a judge committed to the philosophy of original understanding is not to "*choose* a level of abstraction." Rather, it is to find the meaning of a text—a process which includes finding its degree of generality, which is part of its meaning—and to apply that text to a particular situation, which may be difficult if its meaning is unclear. With many if not most textual provisions, the level of generality which is part of their meaning is readily apparent. The problem is most difficult when dealing with the broadly stated provisions of the Bill of Rights. It is to the latter that we confine discussion here. In dealing with such provisions, a judge should state the principle at the level of generality that the text and historical evidence warrant. The equal protection clause was adopted in order to protect the freed slaves, but its language, being general, applies to all persons. As we might expect, and as Justice Miller found in the *Slaughter-House Cases*,[12] the evidence of what the drafters, the Congress that proposed the clause, and the ratifiers understood themselves to be requiring is clearest in the case of race relations. It is there that we may begin in looking for evidence of the level of generality intended. Without meaning to suggest what the historical evidence in fact shows, let us assume we find that the ratifiers intended to guarantee that blacks should be treated by law no worse than whites, but that it is unclear whether whites were intended to be protected from discrimination in favor of blacks. On such evidence, the judge should protect only blacks from discrimination, and Alan Bakke would not have had a case. The reason is that the next higher level of generality above black equality, which is racial equality, is not shown to be a constitutional principle, and therefore there is nothing to be set against a current legislative majority's decision to favor blacks. Democratic choice must be accepted by the judge where the Constitution is silent. The test is the reasonableness of the distinction, and the level of generality chosen by the ratifiers determines that. If the evidence shows the ratifiers understood racial equality to have been the principle they were enacting, Bakke would have a case. In cases concerning gender and sexual orientation, however, interpretation is not additionally assisted by the presence of known intentions. The general language of the clause, however, continues to subject such cases to the test of whether statutory distinctions are reasonable. Sexual differences obviously make some distinctions reasonable while others have no apparent basis. That has, in fact, been the rationale on which the law has developed. Society's treatment of sexual orientation is based upon moral perceptions, so that it would be difficult to say that the various moral balances struck are unreasonable.

Original understanding avoids the problem of the level of generality in equal protection analysis by finding the level of generality that interpretation of the words, structure, and history of the Constitution fairly supports. This is a solution generally applicable to all constitutional provisions as to which historical evidence exists. There is, therefore, a form of constitutional decisionmaking that satisfies the requirement that principles be neutrally defined.

To define a legal proposition or principle involves simultaneously stating its contents and its limits. When you state what *is* contained within the clause of the first amendment guarantee of the free exercise of religion, you necessarily state what is *not* contained within that clause. Because the first amendment guarantees freedom of speech, judges are required reasonably to define what is speech and what is its freedom. In doing these things, the judge necessarily decides that some things are not speech or are not abridgments of its freedom. As to things outside the proposition, the speech clause gives the judge no power to do anything. Because it is only the content of a clause that gives the judge any authority, where that content does not apply, he is without authority and is, for that reason, forbidden to act. The elected legislator or executive may act where not forbidden; his delegation of power from the people through an election is his authority. But the judge may act only where authorized and must do so in those cases; his commission is to apply the law. If a judge should say that the freedom of speech clause authorizes him to abolish the death penalty, we would unanimously say that he had exceeded the bounds of his lawful authority. The judge's performance is not improved if, following *Griswold* v. *Connecticut,* he adds four more inapplicable provisions to his list of claimed authorizations and claims that five inapplicable provisions give him the authority one alone did not. Where the law stops, the legislator may move on to create more; but where the law stops, the judge must stop.

Neutrality in the Application of Principle

The neutral or nonpolitical application of principle has been discussed in connection with Wechsler's discussion of the *Brown* decision.[13] It is a requirement, like the others, addressed to the judge's integrity. Having derived and defined the principle to be applied, he must apply it consistently and without regard to his sympathy or lack of sympathy with the parties before him. This does not mean that the judge will never change the principle he has derived and defined. Anybody who has dealt extensively with law knows that a new case may seem to fall within a principle as stated and yet not fall within the rationale underlying it. As new cases present new patterns, the principle will often be restated and redefined. There is nothing wrong with that; it is, in fact, highly desirable. But the judge must be clarifying his own reasoning and verbal formulations and not trimming to arrive at results desired on grounds extraneous to the Constitution. This requires a fair degree of sophistication and self-consciousness on the part of the judge. The only external discipline to which the judge is subject is the scrutiny of professional observers who will be able to tell over a period of time whether he is displaying intellectual integrity.

An example of the nonneutral application of principle in the service of a good cause is provided by *Shelley* v. *Kraemer,*[14] a 1948 decision of the Supreme Court striking down racially restrictive covenants. Property owners had signed agreements limiting occupancy to white persons. Despite the covenants, some whites sold to blacks, owners of other properties sued to enforce the covenants, and the state courts, applying common law rules, enjoined the blacks from taking possession.

The problem for the Supreme Court was that the Constitution restricts only action by the state, not actions by private individuals. There was no doubt that the racial restrictions would have violated the equal protection clause of the fourteenth amendment had they been enacted by the state legislature. But here state courts were not the source of the racial discrimination, they merely enforced private agreements according to the terms of those agreements. The Supreme Court nonetheless held that "there has been state action in these cases in the full and complete sense of the phrase."[15]

In a 1971 article in the Indiana Law Journal,[16] I pointed out the difficulty with *Shelley,* for which I was severely taken to task in my Senate hearings and elsewhere. That criticism consisted entirely of the observation that I had disapproved of a case that favored blacks and was therefore hostile to civil rights. Both the fact that many commentators had criticized *Shelley* and my approval of other cases that favored blacks were ignored. The implicit position taken by some senators and activist groups was that a judge must always rule for racial minorities. That is a position I reject, because it requires political judging. Members of racial minorities should win when the law, honestly applied, supports their claim and not when it does not. *Shelley* v. *Kraemer* rested upon a theory that cannot be honestly applied, and, in the event, has not been applied at all.

The Supreme Court in *Shelley* said that the decision of a state court under common law rules constitutes the action of the state and therefore is to be tested by the requirements of the Constitution. The racial discrimination involved was not the policy of the state courts but the desire of private individuals, which the courts enforced pursuant to normal, and neutral, rules of enforcing private agreements. The impossibility of applying the state action ruling of *Shelley* in a neutral fashion may easily be seen. Suppose that a guest in a house becomes abusive about political matters and is ejected by his host. The guest sues the host and the state courts hold that the property owner has a right to remove people from his home. The guest then appeals to the Supreme Court, pointing out that the state, through its courts, has upheld an abridgment of his right of free speech guaranteed by the first amendment and made applicable to the states by the fourteenth. The guest cites *Shelley* to show that this is state action and therefore the case is constitutional. There is no way of escaping that conclusion except by importing into the rule of *Shelley* qualifications and limits that themselves have no foundation in the Constitution or the case. Whichever way it decided, the Supreme Court would have to treat the case as one under the first amendment and displace state law with constitutional law.

It is necessary to remember that absolutely anything, from the significant to the frivolous, can be made the subject of a complaint filed in a state court. Whether the state court dismisses the suit out of hand or proceeds to the merits of the issue does not matter; any decision is, according to *Shelley,* state action and hence subject to constitutional scrutiny. That means that all private conduct may be made state conduct with the result that the Supreme Court will make the rules for all allowable or forbidden behavior by private individuals. That is not only a complete perversion of the Constitution of the United States, it makes the Supreme Court the supreme legislature. The result of the neutral application of the principle of *Shelley* v. *Kraemer* would be both revolutionary and preposterous. Clearly, it would not be applied neutrally, and it has not been, which means that it fails Wechsler's test.

Shelley was a political decision. As such, it should have been made by a legislature. It is clear that Congress had the power to outlaw racially restrictive covenants. Subsequently, in fact, in a case in which as Solicitor General I filed a brief supporting the result reached, the Supreme Court held that one of the post–Civil War civil rights acts did outlaw racial discrimination in private contracts.[17] That fact does not, however, make *Shelley* a proper constitutional decision, however much its result may be admired on moral grounds.

Judicial adherence to neutral principles, in the three senses just described, is a crucial element of the American doctrine of the separation of powers. Since the Court's invocation of the Constitution is final, the judiciary is the only branch of the government not subject to the ordinary checks and balances that pit the powers of the other branches against each other. If it is to be faithful to the constitutional design, therefore, the Court must check itself.

The Original Understanding of Original Understanding

The judicial role just described corresponds to the original understanding of the place of courts in our republican form of government. The political arrangements of that form of government are complex, its balances of power continually shifting, but one thing our constitutional orthodoxy does not countenance is a judiciary that decides for itself when and how it will make national policy, when and to what extent it will displace executives and legislators as our governors. The orthodoxy of our civil religion, which the Constitution has aptly been called, holds that we govern ourselves democratically, except on those occasions, few in number though crucially important, when the Constitution places a topic beyond the reach of majorities.

The structure of government the Founders of this nation intended most certainly did not give courts a political role. The debates surrounding the Constitution focused much more upon theories of representation than upon the judiciary, which was thought to be a comparatively insignificant branch. There were, however, repeated attempts at the Constitutional Convention in Philadelphia to give judges a policymaking role. The plan of the Virginia delegation, which, amended and expanded, ultimately became the Constitution of the United States, included a proposal that the new national legislature be controlled by placing a veto power in a Council of Revision consisting of the executive and "a convenient number of the National Judiciary."[18] That proposal was raised four times and defeated each time. Among the reasons, as reported in James Madison's notes, was the objection raised by Elbridge Gerry of Massachusetts that it "was quite foreign from the nature of ye. office to make them judges of policy of public measures."[19] Rufus King, also of Massachusetts, added that judges should "expound the law as it should come before them, free from the bias of having participated in its formation."[20] Judges who create new constitutional rights are judges of the policy of public measures and are biased by having participated in the policy's formation.

The intention of the Convention was accurately described by Alexander Hamilton in *The Federalist* No. 78: "[T]he judiciary, from the nature of its functions, will always be the least dangerous to the political rights of the Constitution; because it will be least in a capacity to annoy or injure them."[21] The political rights of the Constitution are, of course, the rights that make up democratic self-government. Hamilton obviously did not anticipate a judiciary that would injure those rights by adding to the list of subjects that were removed from democratic control. Thus, he could say that the courts were "beyond comparison the weakest of the three departments of power," and he appended a quotation from the "celebrated Montesquieu": "Of the three powers above mentioned [the others being the legislative and the executive], the JUDICIARY is next to nothing." This is true because judges were, as King said, merely to "expound" law made by others.

Even if evidence of what the founders thought about the judicial role were unavailable, we would have to adopt the rule that judges must stick to the original meaning of the Constitution's words. If that method of interpretation were not common in the law, if James Madison and Justice Joseph Story had never endorsed it, if Chief

Justice John Marshall had rejected it, we would have to invent the approach of original understanding in order to save the constitutional design. No other method of constitutional adjudication can confine courts to a defined sphere of authority and thus prevent them from assuming powers whose exercise alters, perhaps radically, the design of the American Republic. The philosophy of original understanding is thus a necessary inference from the structure of government apparent on the face of the Constitution.

The Claims of Precedent and the Original Understanding

The question of precedent is particularly important because, as Professor Henry Monaghan of Columbia University law school notes, "much of the existing constitutional order is at variance with what we know of the original understanding."[22] Some commentators have argued from this obvious truth that the approach of original understanding is impossible or fatally compromised, since they suppose it would require the Court to declare paper money unconstitutional and overturn the centralization accomplished by abandoning restrictions on congressional powers during the New Deal.[23] There is in these instances a great gap between the original understanding of the constitutional structure and where the nation stands now. But the conclusion does not follow. To suppose that it does is to confuse the descriptive with the normative. To say that prior courts have allowed, or initiated, deformations of the Constitution is not enough to create a warrant for present and future courts to do the same thing.

All serious constitutional theory centers upon the duties of judges, and that comes down to the question: What should the judge decide in the case now before him? Obviously, an originalist judge should not deform the Constitution further. Just as obviously, he should not attempt to undo all mistakes made in the past. Whatever might have been the proper ruling shortly after the Civil War, if a judge today were to decide that paper money is unconstitutional, we would think he ought to be accompanied not by a law clerk but by a guardian. At the center of the philosophy of original understanding, therefore, must stand some idea of when the judge is bound by prior decisions and when he is not.[24]

Many people have the notion that following precedent (sometimes called the doctrine of *stare decisis*) is an ironclad rule. It is not, and never has been.[25] As Justice Felix Frankfurter once explained, "*stare decisis* is a principle of policy and not a mechanical formula of adherence to the latest decision, however recent and questionable, when such adherence involves collision with a prior doctrine more embracing in its scope, intrinsically sounder, and verified by experience."[26] Thus, in Justice Powell's words, "[i]t is . . . not only [the Court's] prerogative but also [its] duty to re-examine a precedent where its reasoning or understanding of the Constitution is fairly called into question."[27] The Supreme Court frequently overrules its own precedent. In 1870, *Hepburn* v. *Griswold*[28] held it unconstitutional to make paper money legal tender for antecedent debts, but in 1871 *Hepburn* was overruled in the *Legal Tender Cases*.[29] The New Deal Court swiftly began overruling or ignoring precedent, some of it of fifty years' standing, and often did so by five-to-four votes. Indeed, the Court has overruled important precedent in cases where nobody asked it to do so. *Swift* v. *Tyson* held in 1842 that federal courts could apply a "general law" independent of the state law that would apply had the suit been brought in a state court sitting nearby.[30] The rule lasted for ninety-six years until *Erie Railroad Co.* v. *Tompkins* did away with it in 1938.[31] *Plessy* v. *Ferguson*,[32] and the rule of separate-but-equal in racial matters, lasted fifty-eight years before it was dispatched in *Brown* v. *Board of Education*.[33] In a period of sixteen years the Court took three different positions with respect to the constitutionality of federal power to impose wage and price regulations on states and localities as employers.[34] Indeed, Justice Blackmun explained recently in the last of these decisions that prior cases, even of fairly recent vintage, should be reconsidered if they "disserve[] principles of democratic self-governance."[35] Every year the Court overrules a number of its own precedents. As the examples given show, both recent and ancient precedents are vulnerable.

The practice of overruling precedent is particularly common in constitutional law, the rationale being that it is extremely difficult for an incorrect constitutional ruling to be corrected through the amendment process. Almost all Justices have agreed with Felix Frankfurter's observation that "the ultimate touchstone of constitutionality is the Constitution itself and not what we have said about it."[36] But that, of course, is only a partial truth. It is clear, in the first place, that Frankfurter was talking about the Supreme Court's obligations with respect to its own prior decisions. Lower courts are not free to ignore what the Supreme Court has said about the

Constitution, for that would introduce chaos into the legal system as courts of appeal refused to follow Supreme Court rulings and district courts disobeyed their appellate courts' orders. Secondly, what "the Constitution itself" says may, as in the case of paper money, be irretrievable, not simply because of "what [the Justices] have said about it," but because of what the nation has done or become on the strength of what the Court said.

It is arguable that the text of the Constitution counsels some ambivalence about precedent. Article VI states: "This Constitution, and the Laws of the United States which shall be made in Pursuance thereof" are to be "the supreme Law of the Land."[37] That could be taken to mean that recourse is continually to be had to the text of the Constitution and statutes without regard to prior judicial decisions since the latter are not given the status of supreme law. But article III vests the "judicial Power" in the Supreme Court and lower federal courts.[38] At the time of the ratification, judicial power was known to be to some degree confined by an obligation to respect precedent. Whatever may be made of that, it has been commonly understood that a judge looking at an issue for the second time is, or should be, less free than one who looks at it for the first time. In constitutional law, as in all law, there is great virtue in stability. Governments need to know their powers, and citizens need to know their rights; expectations about either should not lightly be upset.

The law currently has no very firm theory of when precedent should be followed and when it may be ignored or overruled. It is an important subject nonetheless, and it is particularly so to a judge who abides by the original understanding, because, as Monaghan said, so much of our constitutional order today does not conform to the original design of the Constitution. If we do not possess anything worthy of being called a theory of precedent, it is possible at least to suggest some of the factors that should be considered when facing a question of following or overruling a prior decision.

No question arises, of course, unless the judge concludes that the prior constitutional decision, which is urged as controlling his present decision, was wrong. In making that determination, particular respect is due to precedents set by courts within a few decades of a provision's ratification since the judges of that time presumably had a superior knowledge of the original meaning of the Constitution. Similarly, precedents that reflect a good-faith attempt to discern the original understanding deserve far more respect than those that do not. Here, there are not only the claims of stability and continuity in the law, but respect for the knowledge and intelligence of those who have gone before. Today's judge should reflect that if the prior court has been wrong, he too may fall into error.

But if the judge concludes that a prior decision was wrong, he faces additional considerations. The previous decision on the subject may be clearly incorrect but nevertheless have become so embedded in the life of the nation, so accepted by the society, so fundamental to the private and public expectations of individuals and institutions, that the result should not be changed now. This is a judgment addressed to the prudence of a court, but it is not the less valid for that. Judging is not mechanical. Many rules are framed according to predictions of their likely effects, and it is entirely proper for a decision to overrule or not to overrule to be affected by a prediction of the effects likely to flow from that. Thus, it is too late to overrule not only the decision legalizing paper money but also those decisions validating certain New Deal and Great Society programs pursuant to the congressional powers over commerce, taxation, and spending. To overturn these would be to overturn most of modern government and plunge us into chaos. No judge would dream of doing it. It was never too late to overrule the line of cases represented by *Lochner*, because they were unjustifiable restrictions on governmental power, and allowing additional regulation of economic matters did not produce any great disruption of institutional arrangements. Similarly, it will probably never be too late to overrule the right of privacy cases, including *Roe* v. *Wade,* because they remain unaccepted and unacceptable to large segments of the body politic, and judicial regulation could at once be replaced by restored legislative regulation of the subject.

To say that a decision is so thoroughly embedded in our national life that it should not be overruled, even though clearly wrong, is not necessarily to say that its principle should be followed in the future. Thus, the expansion of Congress's commerce, taxing, and spending powers has reached a point where it is not possible to state that, as a matter of articulated doctrine, there are any limits left. That does not mean, however, that the Court must necessarily repeat its mistake as congressional legislation attempts to reach new subject areas. Cases now on the books would seem to mean that Congress could, for example, displace state law on such subjects as marriage and divorce, thus ending such federalism as remains. But the Court could refuse to extend the commerce power so far without overruling its prior decisions, thus leaving existing legislation in place but not giving generative power to the faulty principle by which that legislation was originally upheld. It will be said that this is a lawless approach, but that is not at all clear. The past decisions are beyond reach, but there remains a constitutional principle of federalism that should be regarded as law more profound than the implications of the past decisions. They cannot be overruled, but they can be confined to the subject areas they concern. Similarly, there may be no real point in overturning the decision in *Griswold* v. *Connecticut*. It was unimportant in its immediate consequences since no jurisdiction wants to enforce a law against the use of contraceptives by married couples. But that does not mean that *Roe* v. *Wade* should not be overruled or that the spurious right of privacy that *Griswold* created should ever be used to invalidate a statute again. *Griswold* has had generative power, spawning a series of wrong decisions, and will certainly bring a series of new and unjustifiable claims before the federal courts. But should it become apparent that the Court will not apply it again, the stream of claims will dwindle and ultimately dry up. A case like *Shelley* v. *Kraemer* has generated no subsequent decisions and is most unlikely to. The Supreme Court has refused to follow its rationale, and there would be no point in overruling the decision. There are times when we cannot recover the transgressions of the past, when the best we can do is say to the Court, "Go and sin no more."[39]

Finally, it should be said that those who adhere to a philosophy of original understanding are more likely to respect precedent than those who do not. As Justice Scalia has said, if revisionists can ignore "the most solemnly and democratically adopted text of the Constitution and its Amendments . . . on the basis of current values, what possible basis could there be for enforced adherence to a legal decision of the Supreme Court?"[40] Indeed, it is apparent from our recent history that the Justices most inclined to rewrite the Constitution have the least patience with precedent that stands in their way. If you do not care about stability, if today's result is all-important, there is no occasion to respect either the constitutional text or the decisions of your predecessors.

*   *   *

The interpretation of the Constitution according to the original understanding, then, is the only method that can preserve the Constitution, the separation of powers, and the liberties of the people. Only that approach can lead to what Felix Frankfurter called the "fulfillment of one of the greatest duties of a judge, the duty not to enlarge his authority. That the Court is not the maker of policy but is concerned solely with questions of ultimate power, is a tenet to which all Justices have subscribed. But the extent to which they have translated faith into works probably marks the deepest cleavage among the men who have sat on the Supreme Bench. . . . The conception of significant achievement on the Supreme Court has been too much identified with largeness of utterance, and too little governed by inquiry into the extent to which judges have fulfilled their professed role in the American constitutional system."[41]

Without adherence to the original understanding, even the actual Bill of Rights could be pared or eliminated. It is asserted nonetheless, and sometimes on high authority, that the judicial philosophy of original understanding is fatally defective in any number of respects. If that were so, if the Constitution cannot be law that binds judges, there would remain only one democratically legitimate solution: judicial supremacy, the power of courts to invalidate statutes and executive actions in the name of the Constitution, would have to be abandoned. For the choice would then be either rule by judges according to their own desires or rule by the people according to theirs. Under our form of government, under the entire history of the American people, the choice between an authoritarian judicial oligarchy and a representative democracy can have only one outcome. But this is a false statement of alternatives, for judicial interpretation of the Constitution according to its original understanding is entirely possible. When that course is followed, judges are not a dictatorial oligarchy but the guardians of our liberties. I turn next to the objections that have been raised to this conclusion.

8

Objections to Original Understanding

A great many objections have been raised to the idea that the judge should be guided in applying a provision of the Constitution by the principles the ratifiers of that provision understood themselves to be enacting. The original understanding, as already noted, is the method by which we interpret and apply other legal texts, and, as Dean John Hart Ely has noted, it "does seem to retain the substantial virtue of fitting better our ordinary notion of how law works: if your job is to enforce the Constitution then the Constitution is what you should be enforcing, not whatever may happen to strike you as a good idea at the time."[1] Ely himself finds that view inadequate for reasons to which we shall return at the end of this chapter. But it is the fact that applying what was originally understood does fit our idea of how law works that makes it necessary for revisionists to clear the idea out of the way before getting on with their own theories of why the Constitution does embody what strikes them as a good idea at the time. In this chapter I shall deal with the more common objections to the original understanding to show that none of them bear examination.

The Claim that Original Understanding Is Unknowable

A very frequent objection to the idea of original understanding is that it is impossible of application since we at the end of the twentieth century cannot know what was intended by those who adopted the Constitution at the end of the eighteenth century. In its most severe form, this objection makes demands that no legal document can possibly satisfy. Thus, Justice William J. Brennan, Jr., in a speech at Georgetown University in 1985, attacked the view that legitimate judicial review consisted in applying what some call "the intentions of the Framers."[2]

> In its most doctrinaire incarnation, this view demands that Justices discern exactly what the Framers thought about the question under consideration and simply follow that intention in resolving the case before them. It is a view that feigns self-effacing deference to the specific judgments of those who forged our original social compact. But in truth it is little more than arrogance cloaked as humility. It is arrogant to pretend that from our vantage we can gauge accurately the intent of the Framers on application of principle to specific, contemporary questions.[3]

Of course the view described by Justice Brennan is arrogant, or would be, if anybody took such a position. The requirement that the judge know what the specific intention of the lawgiver was regarding the case at hand would destroy all law. Judges almost never know intentions with such particularity in applying statutes, contracts, or other judges' opinions. If they had to have such knowledge, they could never decide. If such specific knowledge were available, judges would never disagree with one another, there would be no need to allow appeals from the trial judge's decision, and no court would need more than one judge. Justice Brennan demolished a position no one holds, one that is not only indefensible but undefended.

The position of the proponent of original understanding was well described by John Hart Ely, who, in accordance with current academic fashion, called that view "interpretivism":

> What distinguishes interpretivism [original understanding] from its opposite is its insistence that the work of the political branches is to be invalidated only in accord with an inference whose starting point, whose underlying premise, is fairly discoverable in the Constitution. That the complete inference will not be found there—because the situation is not likely to have been foreseen— is generally common ground.[4]

In short, all that a judge committed to original understanding requires is that the text, structure, and history of the Constitution provide him not with a conclusion but with a major premise. That major premise is a principle or stated value that the ratifiers wanted to protect against hostile legislation or executive action. The judge must then see whether that principle or value is threatened by the statute or action challenged in the case before him. The answer to that question provides his minor premise, and the conclusion follows. It does not follow without difficulty, and two judges equally devoted to the original purpose may disagree about the reach or application of the principle at stake and so arrive at different results, but that in no way distinguishes the task from the difficulties of applying any other legal writing.

This version of original understanding certainly does not mean that judges will invariably decide cases the way the men of the ratifying conventions would if they could be resurrected to sit as courts. Indeed, the various ratifying conventions would surely have split within themselves and with one another in the application of the principles they adopted to particular fact situations. That tells us nothing other than that the ratifiers were like other legislators. Any modern congressional majority would divide over particular applications of a statute its members had just enacted. That does not destroy the value of seeking the best understanding of the principle enacted in the case either of the statute or of the Constitution.

We must not expect too much of the search for original understanding in any legal context. The result of the search is never perfection; it is simply the best we can do; and the best we can do must be regarded as good enough—or we must abandon the enterprise of law and, most especially, that of judicial review. Many cases will be decided as the lawgivers would have decided them, and, at the very least, judges will confine themselves to the principles the lawgivers intended. The precise congruence of individual decisions with what the ratifiers intended can never be known, but it can be estimated whether, across a body of decisions, judges have in general vindicated the principle given into their hands. If they accomplish that, they have accomplished something of great value.

Of at least equal importance, the attempt to adhere to the principles actually laid down in the historic Constitution will mean that entire ranges of problems and issues are placed off-limits for judges. Courts will say of particular controversies that no provision of the Constitution reaches the issues presented, and the controversies are therefore not for judges to resolve. The statute or executive action will be allowed to stand. That abstinence has the inestimable value of preserving democracy in those areas of life that the Founders intended to leave to the people's self-government. In both its vindica-

tion of principle against democratic majorities and its vindication
of democracy against unprincipled judicial activism, the philosophy
of original understanding does better by far than any other theory
of constitutional adjudication can. If that is not good enough, judicial
review under the Constitution cannot be legitimate. I think it is
good enough.

There are, however, persons who make more radical objections
to the idea of seeking the historic meaning of the Constitution.
They contend not that we cannot know in detail the Founders'
intentions, but that we cannot even understand the principles they
intended, because they lived in an entirely different society. The
argument is that we of this generation cannot know what the ratifiers
of 1797 meant by the Bill of Rights or what those of 1868 meant
by the fourteenth amendment.*

The claim is preposterous. Compare it with the treatment we
give other writings not of our generation. In a commencement address
at Duke University, Ted Koppel spoke to the issue, albeit in a
different context: "What Moses brought down from Mt. Sinai were
not the Ten Suggestions. They are commandments. *Are,* not *were.*
The sheer brilliance of the Ten Commandments is that they codify
in a handful of words acceptable human behavior, not just for then
or now, but for all time. Language evolves. Power shifts from one
nation to another. Messages are transmitted with the speed of light.
Man erases one frontier after another. And yet we and our behavior
and the commandments governing that behavior remain the same."[5]
The Commandments were written in another language, given to a
people of an entirely different culture, and are almost four thousand
years old, and yet the claim is that we can understand them. The
constitutional originalist asks only for two hundred years concerning
a document written in English and coming out of our culture, however much material conditions may have changed.

If the incomprehensibility of the past were a notion to be taken
seriously, the study of Aristotle, Plato, and all ancient authors would
be utterly fruitless, as would all historical investigation. Those who
are willing to assert the incomprehensibility of a document whose

---

* The best proof of the point I have ever heard occurred when I quoted a professor,
who did not believe original understanding could be discerned, as not believing
that the Constitution is law. He at once protested that he did. I said, "But you
wrote that it was not." He responded, "I may have written that but I didn't mean
that. Which proves we cannot know what was intended by words." The argument,
being circular, was irrefutable, and I was defeated.

relevant parts are from eighty to two hundred years old ought to admit that we can have no idea what the National Bank Act of 1864 means and that the Sherman Act of 1890 is already so much gibberish or is rapidly slipping into that condition. Under this view, we cannot be sure that the 1803 decision in *Marbury* v. *Madison*[6] intended to legitimate judicial review under the Constitution. It is also too bad that we have no means of deciphering Washington's Farewell Address or Lincoln's speech at Gettysburg. There is an ancient tradition that those orations were admirable, though of course we cannot really know what an ancient tradition means either. Nonsense is nonsense however heavily weighted with academic robes.

We have abundant sources for an understanding of particular provisions of the Constitution. Of course, some meanings will be doubtful or even lost, but much that is certain or probable remains. We have, after all, the constitutional text, records of the Philadelphia convention, records of ratifying conventions, the newspaper accounts of the day, the Federalist Papers, the Anti-Federalist Papers, the constructions put upon the Constitution by early Congresses in which men who were familiar with its framing and ratification sat, the constructions put upon the document by executive branch officials similarly familiar with the Constitution's origins, and decisions of the early courts, as well as treatises by men who, like Joseph Story, were thoroughly familiar with the thought of the time. Judges can also seek enlightenment from the structure of the document and the government it created. This mode of reasoning goes back to Chief Justice John Marshall and can be extremely fruitful. Finally, we must remember that the document to be construed is a constitution. A constitution is supposed to produce workable government, as Story observed. Results that are particularly awkward, in the absence of evidence to the contrary, were probably not intended. About much of the Constitution, therefore, we know a good deal; about other parts less; and, in a few cases, very little or nothing.

What is the judge to do on those rare occasions when he does not know and cannot discover what a constitutional provision means, when the original understanding really is lost? Early in my career as a judge I sat on a case governed, if that is the word, by a statute enacted in 1789 whose meaning was almost completely mysterious. The late Judge Henry Friendly called the law "a kind of legal Lohengrin; . . . no one seems to know whence it came."[7] The three-judge panel on which I sat split three ways.[8] One of the judges took the position that we had to give the statute content because it was meant to have content. He proceeded to construct a fairly reasonable piece of legislation.[9] I took the opposite stance, writing that "when courts go beyond the area in which there is any historical evidence, when they create the substantive rules for topics . . . , then law is made with no legislative guidance whatever. When that is so, it will not do to insist that the judge's duty is to construe the statute in order not to flout the will of Congress. On these topics, we have, at the moment, no evidence what the intention of Congress was. When courts lack such evidence, to 'construe' is to legislate, to act in the dark, and hence to do many things that, it is virtually certain, Congress did not intend. Any correspondence between the will of Congress in 1789 and the decisions of the courts in 1984 can then be only accidental."[10]

The same reasoning applies to constitutional law. The judge who cannot make out the meaning of a provision is in exactly the same circumstance as a judge who has no Constitution to work with. There being nothing to work with, the judge should refrain from working. A provision whose meaning cannot be ascertained is precisely like a provision that is written in Sanskrit or is obliterated past deciphering by an ink blot. No judge is entitled to interpret an ink blot on the ground that there must be something under it. So it has been with the clause of the fourteenth amendment prohibiting any state from denying citizens the privileges and immunities of citizens of the United States. That clause has been a mystery since its adoption and in consequence has, quite properly, remained a dead letter. There are, of course, academics who bemoan this and urge the Court to revive privileges and immunities, apparently on the theory that every part of the Constitution must be used, even if that means judges are writing their own Constitution.

Enough has been said, I trust, to show that we can understand the principles of the Constitution and that, on those rare occasions where we cannot, we have acceptable ways of dealing with our ignorance. The case for general incomprehension because of the passage of time is foolishness. Oddly enough, the people who relish agnosticism about the meaning of our most basic compact do not explore the consequences of their notion. They view the impossibility of knowing what the Constitution means as justification for saying that it means anything they would prefer it to mean. But they too easily glide over a difficulty fatal to their conclusion. If the meaning of the Constitution is unknowable, if, so far as we can tell, it is written in undecipherable hieroglyphics, the conclusion is not that the judge may write his own Constitution. The conclusion is that judges must stand aside and let current democratic majorities rule, because there is no law superior to theirs.

The Claim that the Constitution Must Change as Society Changes

The notion of a "living Constitution" seems to appeal to a great many people, possibly because the phrase makes it seem that the alternative is a "dead Constitution." Indeed, I have no difficulty with the idea of a Constitution that lives, only with the notion that it keeps sprouting new heads in accordance with current intellectual and moral fashion.

The philosophy of original understanding does not produce a rigid Constitution or a mechanical jurisprudence. Instead, it controls the process of growth in constitutional doctrine in ways that preserve the document's relevance and integrity. The fact that doctrine changes unsettles some who, like myself, object to courts that go beyond constitutional principle. It should not. I tried to explain this in *Ollman* v. *Evans*,[11] a case involving the relationship of the law of libel to the first amendment's guarantee of freedom of the press. One dissent complained that I was creating new law. In a sense, I was, as all judges must. I attempted to explain the degree to which that is both desirable and inevitable and the degree to which it is impermissible. The following three paragraphs are taken, with slight adaptations, from my opinion.

The dissent had implied that the idea of evolving constitutional doctrine should be anathema to judges who adhere to a philosophy of judicial restraint (by which I meant adherence to the original understanding). "But most doctrine is merely the judge-made super-structure that implements basic constitutional principles. There is not at issue here the question of creating new constitutional rights or principles. When there is a known principle to be explicated the evolution of doctrine is inevitable. Judges given stewardship of a constitutional provision—such as the first amendment—whose core is known but whose outer reach and contours are ill-defined, face the never-ending task of discerning the meaning of the provision from one case to the next. There would be little need for judges— and certainly no office for a philosophy of judging—if the boundaries of every constitutional provision were self-evident. They are not. It is the task of the judge in this generation to discern how the framers' values, defined in the context of the world they knew, apply to the world we know. The world changes in which unchanging values find their application. The fourth amendment, which prohibits unreasonable searches and seizures, was framed by men who did not foresee electronic surveillance. But that did not make it wrong for judges to apply the central value of that amendment to electronic invasions of personal privacy. The power of Congress to regulate commerce was established by men who did not foresee the scope, technologies, and intricate interdependence of today's economy. But that did not make it wrong for judges to forbid states the power to impose burdensome regulations on the interstate movements of trailer trucks. The first amendment's guarantee of freedom of the press was written by men who had not the remotest idea of modern forms of communication. But that does not make it wrong for a judge to find the values of the first amendment relevant to radio and television broadcasting.

"So it is with defamation actions. We know very little of the precise intentions of the framers and ratifiers of the speech and press clauses of the first amendment. But we do know that they gave into the judges' keeping the value of preserving free expression and, in particular, the preservation of political expression, which is commonly conceded to be the value at the core of these clauses. Perhaps the framers did not envision libel actions as a major threat to that freedom. I may grant that, for the sake of the point to be made. But if, over time, the libel action evolves so that it becomes a threat to the central meaning of the first amendment, why should not judges adapt their doctrines? A change in the legal environment provided by common law or statutory law is surely no different from a constitutional judge's standpoint than is a change in the technological environment. It is no different to refine and evolve doctrine here, so long as one is faithful to the basic meaning of the amendment, than it is to adapt the fourth amendment to take account of electronic means of surveillance, the commerce clause to adjust to interstate motor carriage, or the first amendment to encompass the electronic media. To say that such adjustments must be left to the legislature is to say that changes in circumstances must be permitted gradually to render constitutional guarantees meaningless. It is to say that not merely the particular rules but the entire enterprise of the Supreme Court in *New York Times* v. *Sullivan,* which laid down new rules making it more difficult for public figures to maintain actions for defamation, was illegitimate.

"Judges must never hesitate to apply old values to new circumstances, whether those circumstances spring from changes in technology or changes in the impact of traditional common law actions. *Sullivan* was an instance of the Supreme Court doing precisely that, as *Brown* v. *Board of Education* was more generally an example of the Court applying an old principle according to a new understanding of a social situation. It is not that a court may apply an old principle in new ways because its or the society's views on race have changed, but, as already explained, because it became evident over time that the racial separation the ratifiers of the fourteenth amendment assumed was completely inconsistent with the equal protection of the laws they mandated. The important thing, the ultimate consideration, is the constitutional freedom that is given into the judge's keeping. A judge who refuses to see new threats to an established constitutional value, and hence provides a crabbed interpretation that robs a provision of its full, fair, and reasonable meaning, fails in his judicial duty. That duty, it is worth repeating, is to ensure that the powers and freedoms the founders specified are made effective in today's altered world. The evolution of doctrine to accomplish that end contravenes no postulate of judicial restraint."[12]

I have since heard my argument quoted to justify the creation of new constitutional principles, such as the right to abortion invented in *Roe* v. *Wade*. The argument does no such thing. No doubt there is a spectrum along which the adjustments of doctrine to take account of new social, technological, and legal developments may gradually become so great as to amount to the creation of a new principle. But that observation notes a danger; it does not justify letting the process slide out of control. Judges and lawyers live on the slippery slope of analogies; they are not supposed to ski it to the bottom. *Roe* became possible only because *Griswold* had created a new right, and anyone who reads *Griswold* can see that it was not an adjustment of an old principle to a new reality but the creation of a new principle by *tour de force* or, less politely, by sleight of hand. When we say that social circumstances have changed so as to require the evolution of doctrine to maintain the vigor of an existing principle we do not mean that society's values are perceived by the judge to have changed so that it would be good to have a new constitutional principle. The difference is between protecting that privacy guaranteed by the fourth amendment—the "right of the people to be secure in their persons, houses, papers, and effects, against unreasonable searches and seizures"[13]—by requiring a warrant for government to listen electronically to what is said in the home and expanding that limited guarantee of privacy into a right not only to use contraceptives but to buy them, into a right to have an abortion, into a right, as four Justices of the Supreme Court would have it, to engage in homosexual conduct, into rights, as a number of professors would have it, to smoke marijuana and to engage in prostitution. If one cannot see where in that progression the adjustment of doctrine to protect an existing value ends and the creation of new values begins, then one should not aspire to be a judge or, for the matter of that, a law professor.

The Claim that There Is No Real Reason the Living Should Be Governed by the Dead

Quite often, when I speak at a law school on the necessity of adhering to the original understanding, a student will ask, "But why should we be ruled by men who are long dead?" The same thought is sometimes expressed by law professors, which I find particularly discouraging. The question, by the way, is never asked about the main body of the Constitution, where we really are governed by dead men in such crucial matters as the powers of the President, Congress, and the judiciary, as well as the timing and manner of elections and other central features of our republican form of government. Nor is the question ever asked about the continuing validity of the Sherman Act of 1890, the National Bank Act of 1864, the precedents of the Supreme Court, or ancient contracts or trusts. Instead, the question is asked only about those amendments to the Constitution that guarantee individual rights.

A related objection to the original understanding is that the men who wrote, proposed, and ratified the Constitution were not representative of the society at large, and in these days, when the suffrage has been vastly expanded, there is no reason to be bound by the Constitution the Founders gave us. Again, the idea is not that judges should feel free to alter the composition of the House of Representatives or decide that senatorial elections should occur every two years but that they should be free to create new individual rights and so strike down legislation that would be valid under the Constitution as written.

One answer is that with respect to the individual rights amendments we are not governed by our dead and unrepresentative Founders unless we wish to cut back or eliminate the freedoms they specified and to do so by simple legislative majorities. But that is never what the questioner means. The question is really meant to indicate that courts should be free to write into the Constitution freedoms from democratic control that the Framers omitted. Yet that is the one proposition that the objection to rule by the dead, if it had any validity, does not support. The dead, and unrepresentative, men who enacted our Bill of Rights and the Civil War amendments did not thereby forbid us, the living, to add new freedoms. We remain entirely free to create all the additional freedoms we want by constitutional amendment or by simple legislation, and the nation has done so frequently.

What the questioner is really driving at is why judges, not the electorate but judges, should be bound to protect against democratic choice only those liberties actually mentioned in the Constitution. The real objection is not to rule by dead men who were not fully representative of their society but to rule by living majorities. Though it is disguised, the unrepresentative-dead-men argument is nothing more than an attempt to block self-government by the representatives of living men and women.

The Claim that the Constitution Is Not Law

The assertion that judges may depart from the actual Constitution because it is not law came as a very considerable surprise to me. The natural first response is that the proposition undercuts the institution of judicial review, for how can a judge set aside a statute, which is law, in the name of a Constitution that is not law? There is a sense, of course, in which the assertion is merely a description of what has actually happened. Dean Terence Sandalow's comment may be understood in this way: "[T]he evolving content of constitutional law is not controlled, or even significantly guided, by the Constitution understood as an historical document."[14] To a similar effect is Dean Paul Brest's remark that our relationship to the documentary Constitution is "rather like having a remote ancestor who came over on the Mayflower."[15] The same point is made by the anecdote, which one hopes is not apocryphal, about the new chief justice of a state supreme court who, upon first meeting a United States Supreme Court Justice, said, "I'm delighted to meet you in person because I have just taken an oath to support and defend whatever comes into your head."

But the assertion that the Constitution is not law is advanced by people who want a dramatic expansion of judicial governance in the name of the Constitution. Their point is not that the Constitution does not authorize judicial power but rather that the Constitution does not limit that power, as of course it would if it were law. That was certainly the meaning of the Harvard professor who told me that my notion of the Constitution as law must rest upon an obscure philosophic principle with which he was not familiar. He said that in response to my argument from the idea of law that there were some results a constitutional court could not properly reach. But he is by no means alone. Among the various academics who have said similar things is Dean Paul Brest of Stanford, who wrote:

> What authority does the written Constitution have in our system of constitutional government? This is not an empty question. . . . [A]lthough article VI declares that the Constitution is the "supreme law of the land," a document cannot achieve the status of law, let alone supreme law, merely by its own assertion.
>
> According to the political theory most deeply rooted in the American tradition, the authority of the Constitution derives from the consent of its adopters. Even if the adopters freely consented to the Constitution, however, this is not an adequate basis for continuing fidelity to the founding document, for their consent cannot bind succeeding generations. We did not adopt the Constitution, and those who did are dead and gone.[16]

Apparently thinking this dead-men argument sufficient to undermine the Constitution as law, Brest immediately went on to argue that this justified courts in departing from it.

> Given the questionable authority of the American Constitution . . . it is only through a history of continuing assent or acquiescence that the document could become law. Our constitutional tradition, however, has not focused on the document alone, but on the decisions and practices of courts and other institutions. And this tradition has included major elements of nonoriginalism. . . . [T]he practice of supplementing and derogating from the text and original understanding is itself part of our constitutional tradition.[17]

This is the best argument I have seen that the Constitution cannot be regarded as law, and the argument is none too good.

The dead-men argument proves too much. It would serve as an excuse for a judge who decided not to enforce the Bill of Rights because James Madison and his colleagues are no longer among us. The judge would be justified in ignoring the Bill of Rights so long as the rest of us assented or acquiesced, which we might well do since the judge would be refusing to enforce the Constitution against a legislative majority's actions. Beyond that, however, the argument is not clear about who it is that assents to a judge's alteration of the Constitution. They certainly do not, for example, include the pro-life marchers who demonstrate each year before the Supreme Court on the anniversary of *Roe* v. *Wade*. It is also unclear how we actually know that the polity has assented or acquiesced. What choice have those who do not? Civil disobedience? Revolution? Americans would have to overthrow the Court as an institution in order not to be said to have acquiesced in the practice of ignoring the original understanding. The fact that we have not done any such thing is an extraordinarily slender reed upon which to base a continuing judicial power to remake the Constitution.

But that is not the end of the difficulties in which Professor Brest entangles us. One would assume that an effective assent or acquiescence for Brest's purposes would have to be by a majority of voting-age citizens. That is a very peculiar method of giving the Court authority to redo the Constitution, for it means that the Constitution may be amended if a simple majority of the American people delegate, or do not protest the delegation of, that authority to the Court. But the whole point of the Constitution is to establish law that cannot be amended by majority vote, much less by mute acquiescence. *Marbury* v. *Madison,* of course, justified the Court's power of judicial review by the statement that simple legislative majorities could not be permitted to rewrite the Constitution. Indeed, the entire theory of the guarantees of liberties in the Constitution is that they are countermajoritarian, that if even one person demands his constitutional rights, though the entire nation would deny them, the Court must give him justice.

It is of course true that no document can become law merely by its own assertion. The Constitution did not become law merely by its own assertion. Neither does any statute become law merely because near the beginning of the text it says something like, "Be it therefore enacted that. . . ." Neither does any judgment of a court become law merely because the court states: "It is therefore ordered that. . . ." All these writings become law because they

are made in ways that the people of this nation assume to be ways
of making law. Why should that assumption produce law? I do
not know of any ultimate philosophic reason why it should. A legal
system cannot operate if we must rethink the perplexed issue of
the nature of political obligation every time somebody cites a statute
or a case. Law is a very practical instrument for organizing a society
into a polity, and it is necessary to any polity that there be ground
rules or assumptions that identify certain propositions as laws if
they are produced in certain ways. It is clear that this nation has
always treated the Constitution as law.

Those who drafted, proposed, and ratified the Constitution meant
it to be law. That is why article VI, clause 2 states:

> This Constitution . . . shall be the supreme Law of the
> Land. . . .[18]

Even those who opposed the adoption of the Constitution did not
suggest after it had been ratified that it was not law. Clause 3 continues:

> The Senators and Representatives before mentioned, and the
> Members of the several State Legislatures, and all executive and
> judicial Officers, both of the United States and of the several
> States, shall be bound by Oath or Affirmation, to support this
> Constitution. . . .[19]

This Constitution, not one they make up themselves, is to bind
federal judges, and they are bound to the same thing that Senators
and Representatives are bound to, along with all state officers, legislators, and judges. It would be extremely odd if all of these functionaries
are equally bound but one set of them, the federal judges, is authorized
to keep changing what it is everybody is bound to. That would
mean, contrary to the text, that federal judges are not bound and
all other classes of persons mentioned are bound to the judges
and not to "this Constitution."

Every state subsequently admitted to the union accepted the
Constitution as law as a condition of admission. All the statutes
that Congress has ever passed have been enacted and accepted as
law under the authority of the Constitution as law. If the Constitution
were of "questionable authority," then Congress's authority is questionable, and with it every statute that body ever enacted. So, too,
are all the treaties the President has ever negotiated and the Senate
has ever ratified. And, since the federal judiciary are created and

empowered entirely by the questionable Constitution, all of the decisions handed down in the past two centuries must now be regarded as questionable. If decisions that come out of the historic Constitution are of questionable authority, how much more so must be those decisions that lack even that support? These decisions have only the support of a "constitutional tradition" of departing from a document that has dubious authority. On this thesis, it is difficult to see why anybody should pay any attention to the Supreme Court. Brest's argument must be that the Supreme Court has authority because, though the actual Constitution is all but irrelevant, the Court has established an easement across the body politic in much the same way that the public gains the right to use a footpath across private property because people have trespassed for so long.

Brest's second argument is no more convincing. What does it matter to the Constitution's status as law that we did not adopt it and those who did are dead? The dead-men-make-no-laws argument has already been examined. If it were valid, we might as well say of a statute that it is not law because at the last election so many of those who enacted the statute were defeated that there is no current majority in Congress who voted for the law. Much of our law, statutory and common law, and that growing out of private contracts, was made by men and women dead and gone. Brest's argument must rest on the unstated premise that no law is legitimate that cannot at any moment be altered or repealed by a simple majority vote. Everything but the Constitution can be altered by majority vote, and it is only the Constitution's legitimacy that he is at pains to question.

Yet it cannot be that Brest finds legitimacy only in majoritarianism since he wants judges, without even the warrant provided by the actual Constitution, to strike down laws made by majority decisions. If his point were taken seriously, judges would be free to change or ignore the structural provisions of the main body of the Constitution, allowing the President to legislate and Congress to act as commander in chief, as well as to eliminate both elections and the freedoms guaranteed in the Bill of Rights. They were declared to be law in a document of questionable authority by men long dead. If a majority of Americans should want to eliminate religious freedom or authorize searches of private homes without warrants or good cause, there is, on Brest's view of the Constitution, no particular reason why judges should not let them.

The argument that the Constitution is not law quickly becomes incoherent and chaotic. But if it is law, the tradition of judicial departures from it is profoundly illegitimate.

The Claim that the Constitution
Is What the Judges Say It Is

There exists a fatigued cynicism among lawyers and judges that frequently finds expression in the quotation of words attributed to Chief Justice Charles Evans Hughes: "The Constitution is what the judges say it is."[20] Hughes was hardly the first to make the point. "[W]hoever hath an absolute authority to interpret any written or spoken laws, it is he who is truly the lawgiver, to all intents and purposes, and not the person who first wrote or spoke them," said Bishop Hoadly in 1717.[21] The statements are sometimes taken to ratify cynicism. They should not be. Nobody familiar with Hughes's career would suppose he meant that power is all. It is essential to bear in mind the distinction between the reality of judicial power and the legitimacy or morality of the use of that power.

It is not more than a truism that, for practical purposes, at any given moment the Constitution is what the Justices say it is. Right or wrong, the statute you petitioned your legislature to enact has suddenly become a nullity because the Justices say it is. But behind that realism lies another fact just as real, and one with normative meaning: there is a historical Constitution that was understood by those who enacted it to have a meaning of its own. That intended meaning has an existence independent of anything judges may say. It is that meaning the judges *ought* to utter. If law is more than naked power, it is *that* meaning the Justices had a moral duty to pronounce. Hoadly and Hughes, far from reconciling us to cynicism, emphasize the heavy responsibility judges bear. Power alone is not sufficient to produce legitimate authority.

G. K. Chesterton is said to have illustrated the distinction between power and authority while engaged in discussion in a restaurant. "If a rhinoceros came in through that door," he said, "it would have considerable power. I should be the first to rise, however, and to assure the creature that it had no authority."

The Claim that the Philosophy of Original
Understanding Involves Judges in Political Choices

It has been argued, by Ronald Dworkin among others, that the claim of proponents of original understanding to political neutrality is a pretense since the choice of that philosophy is itself a political decision.[22] It certainly is, but the political content of that choice is not made by the judge; it was made long ago by those who designed and enacted the Constitution. It was a choice between a judicial branch that is a policymaking arm of government and a judicial branch that implements the policies made by others. That, as we have seen, is what the separation of powers was designed to accomplish as it affected the courts.

Another version of the inevitability-of-political-choice argument is that the adoption of a philosophy of original understanding would have political consequences. Thus, it was said that President Reagan's nomination of me was intended to alter the direction of the Supreme Court, which was a political intention on his part, and which would have produced results of a different political complexion from those the Court had been producing. This argument is made to justify the political campaign against my confirmation. If that campaign is to be justified, it will have to be done on more intelligent grounds.

Constitutional philosophies always have political results. They should never have political intentions. The proper question is not what are the political results of a particular philosophy but, under that philosophy, who chooses the political results. The philosophy of original understanding means that the ratifiers of the Constitution and today's legislators make the political decisions, and the courts do their best to implement them. That is not a conservative philosophy or a liberal philosophy; it is merely the design of the American Republic. A theory of judging that allows the courts to choose political results is wrong, no matter in which direction the results tend. When the Supreme Court was dominated by conservative activists, prior to the coming of the New Deal Court, adherence to original understanding and judicial self-restraint was urged by liberals. Since the Supreme Court of the past several decades has been more likely to create constitutional rights that liberals like, those views are likely to be espoused by conservatives. Constitutional philosophy too often depends on which political view dominates the Court.

In one sense, the liberal activists of today are right: the philosophy of original understanding does have political consequences, though not political content or intention, and my presence on the Court would have tended to make outcomes more conservative. But that would not have been because I imposed my politics. Rather, it would have been because when the Court of the past fifty years departed from the historic Constitution it consistently did so in order to legislate liberal results. A slowing or cessation of that tendency, a return to political neutrality, would mean fewer liberal results legislated in the name of the Constitution. It would also mean that no conservative results would be legislated in the name of the Constitution. Only those who think that the Court is properly a political body can object to that.

Perhaps those liberals who want a political Court are correct in their confidence that in the modern era judges will usually be more liberal than the electorate. If so, they are right, in terms of their immediate self-interest, to oppose original understanding and judicial nominees who insist upon it. That stance is, however, profoundly antidemocratic, and it is dangerous to the long-term health of the American Republic. A few years ago, I summed up my own view this way: "In a constitutional democracy the moral content of law must be given by the morality of the framer or the legislator, never by the morality of the judge. The sole task of the latter—and it is a task quite large enough for anyone's wisdom, skill, and virtue— is to translate the framer's or the legislator's morality into a rule to govern unforeseen circumstances. That abstinence from giving his own desires free play, that continuing and self-conscious renunciation of power, that is the morality of the jurist."[23]

It is, as well, a morality important to American liberty. The Constitution assumes the liberties of self-government, not merely those liberties that consist in being free of government. The freedom to govern is enormously important to the individuals who make up a community, for it is freedom to control the environment— physical, aesthetic, and moral—in which they and their families live. When a court rewrites the Constitution by creating a new constitutional right or, without warrant, unduly expands an existing right, it does not create additional freedom but merely shifts freedom from a larger group to a smaller one. There is no intrinsic merit in that.

"The Impossibility of a Clause-Bound Interpretivism"

The title of this subsection is a chapter heading in *Democracy and Distrust*[24] by the former dean of the Stanford law school, John Hart Ely. He argues that interpretation of the Constitution cannot be confined to discerning the meaning of its various clauses. "Interpretivism" is the usual academic word for the philosophy of original understanding. It was Ely's concern to escape that philosophy in order to offer his own version of the Constitution, which will be examined in Chapter 9. He begins his escape by conceding the philosophy's strength in a passage I have already quoted: "Interpretivism [or original understanding] does seem to retain the substantial virtue of fitting better our ordinary notion of how law works: if your job is to enforce the Constitution then the Constitution is what you should be enforcing, not whatever may happen to strike you as a good idea at the time."[25]

Indeed, Ely puts the matter so strongly that he sets himself a very considerable obstacle to overcome. "Thus stated," he writes, "the conclusion possesses the unassailability of a truism, and if acceptance of *that* were all it took to make someone an interpretivist, no sane person could be anything else." Since one must accept *that,* what the rest of the sentence suggests about the vast majority of academic theorists is best not dwelt upon. But, Ely points out, "interpretivism involves a further claim, that 'enforcing the Constitution' necessarily means proceeding from premises that are explicit or clearly implicit in the document itself." This proposition, which seems to me clearly correct, seems to Ely to be the problem.

> The suggestion . . . is usually that the various provisions of the Constitution be approached essentially as self-contained units and interpreted on the basis of their language, with whatever interpretive help the legislative history can provide, without significant injection of content from outside the provision. . . . [T]his standard form of interpretivism runs into trouble—trouble precisely on its own terms, and so serious as to be dispositive. For the constitutional document itself, the interpretivist's Bible, contains several provisions whose invitation to look beyond their four corners—whose invitation, if you will, to become at least to that extent a noninterpretivist—cannot be construed away.[26]

This is the only kind of claim that judges are not bound by the original understanding of the Constitution's provisions that makes any possible sense. It is not a claim that judges may depart from the document because they are better moral philosophers than are legislators or that they may create new constitutional rights because the Constitution is not law. It *is* a claim that the *law* of the Constitution commands judges to find rights that are not specified in the Constitution. If true, the Founders envisaged a much more dominant role for the judiciary than has commonly been supposed. For that reason, we must examine Ely's evidence with some care. The provisions he relies on are the fourteenth and ninth amendments.

The fourteenth amendment was adopted shortly after the Civil War, and all commentators are agreed that its primary purpose was the protection of the recently freed slaves. As we have seen, of the amendment's three clauses, two have been pressed into the service of judicial imperialism—the due process and equal protection clauses—while the third, the privileges and immunities clause, has remained the cadaver that it was left by the *Slaughter-House Cases*. It is this corpse that Ely proposes to resurrect.

The due process clause will not do as a warrant for the creation of new constitutional rights because, as Ely notes, it is simply a requirement that government not do certain things to people without fair procedures, not a statement of what things may not be done. The fifth amendment's due process clause, which applied only against the federal government, was later copied in the fourteenth amendment, which applied to the states. "There is general agreement that the earlier clause had been understood at the time of its inclusion to refer only to lawful *procedures*. What recorded comment there was at the time of replication in the Fourteenth Amendment is devoid of any reference that gives the provision more than a procedural connotation."[27] That is true, and it is more than enough to condemn the hundreds of cases, stretching from *Dred Scott* to today, in which the courts have given the due process clause substantive content in order to read their own notions of policy into the Constitution.

Ely's attempt to make the privileges and immunities clause do the work that has been improperly assigned to the due process clause is, however, unsuccessful. He points out that "there is not a bit of legislative history that supports the view that the Privileges or Immunities Clause was intended to be meaningless."[28] That is hardly surprising. One would not expect ratifying conventions to enact a constitutional provision they intended to mean nothing. But that hardly solves the problem, and the problem is that we do not know what the clause was intended to mean. But Ely leaps from that fact to a stunning delegation to courts to say what it means:

Thus the most plausible interpretation of the Privileges or Immunities Clause is, as it must be, the one suggested by its language— that it was a delegation to future constitutional decision-makers to protect certain rights that the document neither lists, at least not exhaustively, nor even in any specific way gives directions for finding.[29]

Since we can hardly be talking about ratifiers of future amendments, "future constitutional decision-makers" must be legislators, executives, or judges. If the first two groups are intended, the clause is precatory only. Before legislating, signing legislation, or taking action, legislators and executives are to think about what they would regard as privileges and immunities (meaning "liberties") that ought not to be infringed. But that is not Ely's meaning, since he is describing why judges must go beyond the particular provisions of the Constitution in finding rights. And here the argument falters. It is true that Representative Bingham and Senator Howard, who introduced the fourteenth amendment in their respective Houses of Congress, referred to *Corfield* v. *Coryell,* a singularly confused opinion in 1823 by a single Justice of the Supreme Court setting out his ideas of what the original privileges and immunities clause of article IV of the Constitution meant.[30] Most people have always thought that the article IV clause simply prevented a state from discriminating against out-of-staters in favor of their own citizens, but *Corfield* lists rights already secured by the Constitution against adverse federal action and goes on to suggest a number of others.

Bingham and Howard meant these additional rights. That the ratifiers did is far less clear. But even the full list of rights set out by one Justice in *Corfield* is something far different from a judicial power to create unmentioned rights by an unspecified method. Certainly there is no evidence that the ratifying conventions intended any such power in judges, and it is their intent, not the drafters', that counts. Nor is it easy to imagine that Northern states, victorious in a Civil War that led to the fourteenth amendment, should have decided to turn over to federal courts not only the protection of the rights of freed slaves but an unlimited power to frustrate the will of the Northern states themselves. The only significant exercise of judicial review in the past century had been *Dred Scott,*[31] a decision hated in the North and one hardly likely to encourage the notion that courts should be given carte blanche to set aside legislative acts. Ely supposes that the ratifiers of the fourteenth amendment intended two constitutional revolutions rather than one, applying the restrictions of the United States Constitution to the states, which had not been done prior to the Civil War, and also subordinating the legislatures of all the states, Northern as well as Southern, to the uncontrolled discretion of judges. We know the ratifiers intended the former revolution; there is not a shred of evidence that they contemplated the latter. Had any such radical departure from the

American method of governance been intended, had courts been intended to supplant legislatures, there would be more than a shred of evidence to that effect. That proposal would have provoked an enormous debate and public discussion. Whatever the intended meaning of the privileges and immunities clause may have been, it cannot be taken as commanding judges to abandon clause-bound interpretation.

Ely performs a similar transformation of the equal protection clause. The reason he gives is peculiar. The clause deals with discriminations among classes of persons, but that is no limitation because

> [A]ny case, indeed any challenge, can be put in an equal protection framework by competent counsel. If you wish to challenge the fact that you're not getting good X (or are getting deprivation Y) it is extremely probable that you will be able to identify someone who *is* getting good X (or is not getting deprivation Y). . . . [Thus] the limitation to cases involving differential treatment turns out to be no significant limitation at all, [and] the Equal Protection Clause has to amount to what I claimed the Privileges or Immunities Clause amounts to, a rather sweeping mandate to judge of the validity of governmental choices.[32]

That conclusion follows only if the reasonableness of all classifications under the equal protection clause is evaluated as if those classifications were ones based on race or ethnicity. If the latter meaning of the clause is accepted, we get a rule flatly prohibiting discrimination against blacks, whites, Americans of Polish descent, and so forth. We do not get Ely's "rather sweeping mandate," and we do not get cases applying the clause with the same severity to legislative restrictions on aliens, illegitimate children, or young males not allowed to drink at as early an age as young females.[33] Once matters of race and ethnicity are passed, the clause is indeed sweeping and, if reasonableness is denied to the same degree, allows courts the ultimate governance of society. That is particularly true because in *Bolling* v. *Sharpe* the Supreme Court read the equal protection concept into the due process clause of the fifth amendment so that it applies to federal as well as state legislation.[34]

The objection to the mandate Ely finds are the same as the objection to the judicial power he finds in the privileges and immunities clause. We know that the occasion for the fourteenth amendment was the desire to protect blacks from discriminatory laws and law enforcement. We know there is no evidence that the ratifiers imagined they were handing ultimate governance over to courts. We know that a constitutional revolution of that magnitude would have provoked widespread and heated (to put it mildly) discussion but that there is no record of any such discussion. The rather sweeping mandate must be judged counterfeit.

The last source Ely cites for a direction to judges to look outside the provisions of the Constitution for new rights is the ninth amendment. The ninth was in the original Bill of Rights and states simply, if enigmatically, that "[t]he enumeration in the Constitution, of certain rights, shall not be construed to deny or disparage others retained by the people."[35] The eight preceding amendments, of course, specify rights retained by the people, and the immediately following and last amendment, the tenth, states that "[t]he powers not delegated to the United States by the Constitution, nor prohibited by it to the States, are reserved to the States respectively, or to the people."[36]

There is almost no history that would indicate what the ninth amendment was intended to accomplish. But nothing about it suggests that it is a warrant for judges to create constitutional rights not mentioned in the Constitution. Ely, along with a great many other people, thinks that it is precisely such a warrant. Nothing could be clearer, however, than that, whatever purpose the ninth amendment was intended to serve, the creation of a mandate to invent constitutional rights was not one of them. The language of the amendment itself contradicts that notion. It states that the enumeration of some rights shall not be construed to deny or disparage others retained by the people. Surely, if a mandate to judges had been intended, matters could have been put more clearly. James Madison, who wrote the amendments, and who wrote with absolute clarity elsewhere, had he meant to put a freehand power concerning rights in the hands of judges, could easily have drafted an amendment that said something like "The courts shall determine what rights, in addition to those enumerated here, are retained by the people," or "The courts shall create new rights as required by the principles of the republican form of government," or "The American people, believing in a law of nature and a law of nature's God, delegate to their courts the task of determining what rights, other than those enumerated here, are retained by the people." Madison wrote none of those things, and the conventions ratified none of them. If the Founders envisioned such a role for the courts, they were remarkably adroit in avoiding saying so.

Once again, the problem is that a people who believed that their liberties depended upon the system of representation they created spent their time debating that and spent very little time discussing the role of the courts. Had so momentous a role for judges been contemplated, it would have been the center of discussion. It would not, as is the fact, have gone wholly unmentioned. In all of the controversies about the Court's assumption of powers, from Jefferson's complaints about Marshall to the uproar over *Dred Scott,* nobody, including the Justices of the Court, ever thought to say that such powers were given by the ninth amendment. Indeed, Ely, in discussing elsewhere Hamilton's view that the judiciary was "the least dangerous" branch of government, writes: "This must have made a good bit of sense at the outset of our nation: in the absence of precedent, the lack of independent enforcement machinery and the various constitutional checks on the judiciary must have seemed sufficient to ensure that it would play a quite insignificant role."[37] Now the Founders could not have contemplated both that the judiciary would play a quite insignificant role and, simultaneously, that they had delegated to judges the power to create new constitutional rights not mentioned in the Constitution. As before, the claim that the Founders intended judges to make up rights not specified in the Constitution itself is obviously inconsistent with the historical record.

What, then, can the ninth amendment be taken to mean? If it meant what Ely and others have suggested, it would have stated that the enumeration of certain rights "shall not be construed to mean that judges may not find that other rights exist and are protected by this Constitution." The words "retained by the people" at the end do not quite fit the suggested meaning. That sounds as if there are known rights that the people currently have. "Retained by the people" how? One suggestion, advanced by Russell Caplan and supported by some historical evidence, is that the people retained certain rights because they were guaranteed by the various state constitutions, statutes, and common law.[38] Thus, the enumeration of certain rights in the federal Constitution was not to be taken to mean that the rights promised by the state constitutions and laws were to be denied or disparaged.

This meaning is not only grammatically correct, it also fits the placement of the ninth amendment just before the tenth and after the eight substantive guarantees of rights. The tenth amendment is clearly a guarantee of federalism. It confirms that federal powers were intended to be limited and that the powers not lodged in the national government remained with the states, if the states had such powers under their own constitutions, and, if not, the powers were still held by the people. The ninth amendment appears to serve a parallel function by guaranteeing that the rights of the people specified already in the state constitutions were not cast in doubt by the fact that only a limited set of rights was guaranteed by the federal charter. Both the ninth and tenth amendments appear to be protections of the states and the people against the national government. The anti-Federalists feared the power of the United States, and Madison had promised them amendments to allay their fears.

This is also supported by Madison's explanation of the ninth amendment to Congress:

> It has been objected also against a bill of rights, that, *by enumerating particular exceptions to the grant of power,* it would disparage those rights which were not placed in the enumeration; and *it might follow by implication, that those rights that were not placed in that enumeration,* that those rights which were not singled out, *were intended to be assigned into the hands of the General Government,* and were consequently insecure.[39]

Though Ely sees some confusion in the explanation, it seems to me a perfectly straightforward statement that the ninth amendment guaranteed that rights already held by the people under their state charters would remain with the people and that the enumeration of rights in the federal charter did not alter that arrangement.

When all else is said, however, it is inconceivable that men who viewed the judiciary as a relatively insignificant branch could have devised, without even discussing the matter, a system, known nowhere else on earth, under which judges were given uncontrolled power to override the decisions of the democratic branches by finding authority outside the written Constitution. Neither the Revolution nor the Civil War was fought to establish that form of autocracy. It must be concluded that clause-bound interpretation of the Constitution is possible.

*　　　*　　　*

No doubt other objections to the idea of the original understanding have been raised, but those just discussed seem the most commonly voiced, which means, I would suppose, that they are the objections regarded as most persuasive. An examination of the objections, however, discloses that they do not succeed, so that the original understanding remains a viable approach to the Constitution. It will next be shown that other approaches are not viable.

9

The Theorists of Liberal Constitutional Revisionism

*I*t is my purpose in this chapter and the next to examine some of the most prominent theories of constitutional law now regnant in the law schools. The writers to be examined base their theories upon a rejection of the original meaning of the document and would substitute various other methods for guiding constitutional adjudication. Not all of them would agree that they have rejected the original understanding, but I think it can be shown that they have generalized that understanding so greatly, stated it at such a high level of abstraction, that virtually no one who voted to ratify the document would recognize the principles of the theorists as his own. Each chapter closes with an analysis of Supreme Court Justices' essays into explicit constitutional theorizing: here Justice William J. Brennan, Jr.; in Chapter 10, John Marshall Harlan, and then a debate among the Justices in a recent decision.

It is to be hoped that no professor will be offended at being left out, but the theorists are so many that it is possible to look at only a representative sample.

Alexander M. Bickel

Pride of place belongs to a man who was my very close friend and my guide in beginning constitutional studies when I undertook to teach the subject at Yale. The reader may be surprised that I should be critical of Alexander Bickel's theory of the Constitution since I have quoted him repeatedly to this point. The truth is that Bickel was a great man of the law, had insights that were invariably stimulating, and taught me more than anyone else about this subject. He wrote his theory, in *The Least Dangerous Branch,*[1] when he was a very young professor and, I think, came to be quite dubious about it in later years, though perhaps not for the reasons I became dubious about it. One thing should be set straight at the outset. I once criticized Bickel's theory in print and another judge referred, a trifle caustically, to what I had said of my friend. That reaction is wholly inappropriate. Bickel, who died at the age of fifty, was the last man who would have wanted his thought to stand immune from discussion as a sort of fossilized monument to his memory. He once said to me that he viewed all writing as an experiment. So it is, and the success of every experiment must be judged. I shall deal with him here as I did in life: with the utmost respect but with no disagreement hidden.

Indeed, it is hard to imagine not discussing Bickel here. He was one of the first law professors, if not the first, to set out a complete justification for and theory of nonoriginalist judging. His arguments, moreover, framed the constitutional debate on both sides. As Gary McDowell has said, "Bickel's work was at once seminal and paradoxical. On the one hand, Bickel sought to establish the legitimate grounds for a kind of judicial activism; on the other, he offered praise for a kind of judicial restraint."[2] His activist arguments seem to me the best that have ever been made for the view that the courts may proceed in constitutional adjudication without being bound by the original meaning of the document.

Bickel began by seeking a justification for judicial review. "The root difficulty," he said, "is that judicial review is a counter-majoritarian force in our system."[3] He therefore sought a justification which would legitimate this "deviant institution"[4] by bringing it into an acceptable accommodation with democratic rule. That is required because "democracies do live by the idea, central to the process of gaining the consent of the governed, that the majority has the ultimate power to displace the decision-makers and to reject any part of their policy. With that idea, judicial review must achieve some measure of consonance."[5]

The search must be for a function which might (indeed, must) involve the making of policy, yet which differs from the legislative and executive functions; which is peculiarly suited to the capabilities of the courts; which will not likely be performed elsewhere if the courts do not assume it; which can be so exercised as to be acceptable in a society that generally shares Judge [Learned] Hand's satisfaction in a "sense of common venture;" which will be effective when needed; and whose discharge by the courts will not lower the quality of the other departments' performance by denuding them of the dignity and burden of their own responsibility.[6]

One sees in that passage both the policymaking role Bickel would assign the Court and the requirement that the role be modest and played with caution. But why should the Court have any policymaking function? One answer might be that such a function is inevitable because the application of even an agreed principle will often involve the making of judgments that could be made the other way. That would be my answer, but it assumes only interstitial policymaking in the elaboration of principle and denies the Court the authority to choose the principle itself. That is not what Bickel had in mind. He spoke for the legitimacy of a Court that created the principles to be applied.

His justification for judicial policymaking was that courts have capacities that legislatures do not have and that these are valuable to society. Society needs both principle and expediency. "No society, certainly not a large and heterogeneous one, can fail in time to explode if it is deprived of the arts of compromise, if it knows no ways of muddling through. No good society can be unprincipled; and no viable society can be principle-ridden."[7] Bickel thought of elected officials as the spokesmen for the expedient, short-run solution, while judges had a greater institutional capacity to deal with principles of long-run importance. "[C]ourts have certain capacities for dealing with matters of principle that legislatures and executives do not possess. Judges have, or should have, the leisure, the training, and the insulation to follow the ways of the scholar in pursuing the ends of government."[8]

Bickel told us what it meant to follow the ways of the scholar:

The function of the Justices . . . is to immerse themselves in the tradition of our society and of kindred societies that have gone before, in history and in the sediment of history which is law, and . . . in the thought and the vision of the philosophers and the poets. The Justices will then be fit to extract "fundamental presuppositions" from their deepest selves, but in fact from the evolving morality of our tradition.[9]

"Fundamental presuppositions are not merely to be alluded to . . . or even merely intoned, but are to be traced and evaluated from the roots up, their validity in changing material and other conditions convincingly demonstrated, and their application to particular facts carried to the last decimal."[10]

Now this is fairly antidemocratic stuff. Bickel tried to accommodate the role he assigned the Court to the practice and theory of democracy, as just seen, by arguing that the Court served the function of injecting principle into government in a way that other governmental bodies were less equipped to do. He offered two other mitigating factors. The first was that the Court was not to get too far ahead of the society: The "Court should declare as law only such principles as will—in time, but in a rather immediate foreseeable future—gain general assent."[11] The other factor was Bickel's argument that the Court's commands are not really final.

> The Supreme Court's law . . . could not in our system prevail—not merely in the very long run, but within the decade—if it ran counter to deeply felt popular needs or convictions, or even if it was opposed by a determined and substantial minority and received with indifference by the rest of the country. This, in the end, is how and why judicial review is consistent with the theory and practice of political democracy. This is why the Supreme Court is a court of last resort presumptively only.[12]

Bickel was led to those reflections by the fact that the Court's decision in *Brown* v. *Board of Education* had, he thought, come close to being undone by passionate resistance and was saved only by strong public support in other quarters.

This is the structure of Bickel's argument but by no means the whole of his book. If the argument now looks inadequate, as I think it does, it should be said that the book as a whole is elegant, thought-provoking, and, in a number of ways, profound.

The trouble begins with Bickel's assignment to judges of the injection of long-term principles, principles other than those found in the Constitution itself, into our governmental processes. Federal judges will sigh wistfully as they read his description of their situation. Courts are immensely and increasingly burdened with case loads. They have no leisure. They are manned, moreover, by lawyers, usually very able lawyers, but not philosophers. Few have the training to do what Bickel asked, and none have the leisure for philosophic reflection or for immersion in tradition, history, and the thought and vision of philosophers and poets. If all of that could be done by men and women who had the characteristics required, it is not clear that the "fundamental presuppositions" that rose from the Justices' deepest selves would in fact represent the "evolving morality of our tradition."[13] The prescription leaves the Justices quite unmoored. A man or woman who read everything Bickel suggests could easily vote either way on such questions as whether the Court should create constitutional rights to abortion, to engage in homosexual conduct, to receive welfare payments, to take addictive drugs in the home, and on and on through the list of things that various practitioners of moral-philosophy-cum-law have suggested. Our most divisive political battles reflect the war in our culture about what should be the evolving morality of our tradition. There seems to be no reason why citizens rather than Justices should not extract fundamental presuppositions from their deepest selves.

The requirement that the validity of these fundamental presuppositions be demonstrated convincingly in other conditions and applied to the facts to the last decimal place sounds reassuring. But no one can point to any opinion by any court in which that has been done. One reason may be that such an opinion would require two or three volumes, if not a five-foot shelf.

But if we assume that the task is actually doable and that there are enough judges to staff the federal judiciary, or at least the Supreme Court, who can do it, further difficulties arise. The Constitution itself states fundamental presuppositions. These may not be transgressed by any legislature or executive. But the Constitution leaves all else to the legislative arena. It is not evident why the Justices should say that that is not good enough because legislatures are not as good as the Court in taking long-term principle into account. Legislative decisions involve a mix of, or a tradeoff between, principle and expediency. The Constitution holds that in decisions left to the democratic processes, the tradeoff we are entitled to is the one the legislature provides. Courts have no apparent mandate to impose a different tradeoff merely because they would arrive at a mix that weighed principle more heavily. There is no objectively correct balance between principle and expediency, so it is meaningless to say that legislatures inherently fall short of the right balance.

Bickel attempted to answer the question of how the judge could know that his principles were better than those of the democratic majority. He made an analogy to aesthetic issues and quoted Dwight MacDonald on the question of what standards could be applied to prove that William Faulkner was an important artist and that J. P. Marquand was not.[14] MacDonald said that could not be proved but it could be demonstrated by "an appeal—by reason, analysis, illustration, and rhetoric—to cultural values which critic and reader have in common."[15] That is all very well, but what is to be done if citizens persist in voting that Marquand is the better novelist? MacDonald could deplore that outcome and appeal once more to common values, but why should MacDonald be made into a court that can order Marquand removed from the shelves and replaced by Faulkner? The definition of democracy is that, after hearing argument, citizens can vote their tastes and need not bow to elite opinion. If the Court's principle's superiority can be demonstrated by an appeal to common cultural values, there is no need for the coercive power of the Court's judgment. The Justices should go instead into the political arena and, by the strength of their demonstration, ensure that the better principle is enacted. Bickel himself later recognized that he had once exemplified the danger that elite opinion would prevail by fiat rather than persuasion of MacDonald's sort, for he wanted the Court to declare the death penalty unconstitutional. If he had been right that the abolition of capital punishment is the better view, according to our common cultural values, then, given the intensity of the advocates for that view in the political arena, there should by now be no death penalty statutes.

The modesty commanded by the prescription that the Court is to anticipate the evolution of the morality of our tradition, but not by much, does not solve Bickel's problem. If it is "our" tradition that is evolving, it is not clear why the Court should get ahead of the evolution. The Court is not us, and it is sure to make mistakes about where we are going. Although it would be good if the Court enunciated only principles that will gain acceptance in the near future, there is no particular reason to think that it will so confine itself, or be prescient enough to do so if it wished.

The contention that the Court is not final and hence is not undemocratic, or at least not unacceptably so, must also be deemed to fail. It is true that an outraged citizenry, if it persists long enough, can overturn a Supreme Court decision, probably through the selection of new Justices as the old ones depart. That is what happened to the conservative pre–New Deal Court. But that is a rare instance, and it is clear that there would be little democratic control over a Court that followed Bickel's suggestions. Given the number of decisions to be scrutinized, the people would either have to focus upon perhaps one every five or ten years in order to be effective or else exist in a state of permanent apoplexy. As we know from history, moreover, it may take decades to accomplish the overturning of a single decision or line of decisions. Even then, an overturning cannot be forced if a substantial and influential minority supports the result. *Dred Scott, Lochner,* and *Roe* all lasted a long time, or long enough at least to work considerable damage, and so have many other decisions that many people intensely disliked and that were not based on anything in the Constitution. The argument that a Supreme Court decision is not really final, and so not at odds with the theory and practice of democracy, assumes, as one of my clerks put it, that in the long run none of us will be dead. John Maynard Keynes held the contrary view, which, unhappily, is more accurate.

It would be unfair to leave the impression that *The Least Dangerous Branch* was Alexander Bickel's last or even his major work in constitutional law. It was merely an early and provocative attempt to justify a Court that invalidates the acts of elected representatives without appealing to the historic Constitution. Even as I have changed my mind on a number of topics over the years, so did he. We experimented separately and together with a great many ideas about law. Bickel, being a man of intellectual integrity, changed his mind when the argument or the evidence went against him. Later in his all-too-brief career he came to doubt the capacity of the Supreme Court to manage principles of the sort his early work envisioned. When we taught together and I insisted upon adherence to the original understanding, he fell back upon the Court's tradition as an adequate and only available guide. Still later, contemplating the wreckage wrought by the Warren Court, he said to me, "All we ever had was a tradition, and now that is shattered." I wish we could teach together again. It would be fascinating to know what his final thoughts would have been.

If, as I think, Bickel's early argument—for a Court that makes policy in the broad sense of adopting principles not found in the Constitution—ultimately fails, that is only because no such argument can ever succeed. Bickel's argument is reasonable, honest, humane, at times even poetic, but in the end he could not clear the hurdle he set himself: accommodating a value-choosing Court to the theory and practice of democracy.

John Hart Ely

John Hart Ely, who also taught constitutional law at Yale for a time and later became dean at Stanford, in an interval at Harvard made a major attempt to provide a theoretical framework to support the Warren Court. That attempt is contained in his book *Democracy and Distrust,* subtitled *A Theory of Judicial Review.*[16] Ely begins by denying that it is possible to interpret the Constitution by sticking to its clauses since a number of open-ended provisions seem to require the judge to look outside the document. This argument is essential to the remainder of his theory, for it is all he offers to justify departures from the original understanding. I have already explained, in Chapter 8, why I think this foundational argument fails. Ely moves on to attack various theories that allow the judge to apply "fundamental values" not found in the document. His critique is devastating and, for some of us, highly entertaining. I recommend it highly. But our present endeavor is to scrutinize Ely's own version of a judicial power that is not bound to the historic meaning of the various clauses of the Constitution. It will be seen, I think, that Ely's judge would engage in the very method of choosing fundamental values that Ely had just laid waste.

Because he thinks the open-ended clauses show that "we have a Constitution that needs filling in,"[17] and because the "fundamental values" approach is not satisfactory,[18] Ely searches for an alternative source for new constitutional law that does not leave judges at large to impose their own policies. He thinks the Warren Court found such an approach and that it was foreshadowed in the infamous (he says "famous")[19] footnote four in the *Carolene Products* opinion written by Justice Stone for the New Deal Court. The second and third paragraphs of that footnote, it will be recalled from Chapter 2, reserved the possibility that two kinds of legislation might be subject to more exacting judicial scrutiny than other legislation. The first class was legislation that "restricts those political processes which can ordinarily be expected to bring about repeal of undesirable legislation";[20] the second included cases where "prejudice against discrete and insular minorities may be a special condition, which tends seriously to curtail the operation of those political processes ordinarily to be relied upon to protect minorities."[21]

Ely first takes up what he calls "representation-reinforcing,"[22] which corresponds roughly to Stone's first class. Judges are to ensure participation in decisionmaking by minorities whose interests differ from those of the rest of us. The minorities in question are not necessarily racial or ethnic but simply interest groups who lose in the legislative process although, in Ely's view, they should not have lost. He supposes that the protection of such groups is a proper function for judges because it is merely an extension of what the Constitution already does by way of ensuring broad participation in the processes and distributions of government. Thus, the open-ended clauses of the Constitution, those that he thinks require the judge to look beyond the content of the specific clauses, are given meaning by the surrounding document rather than by values the judge plucks from somewhere else. The function he thinks also proper because, unlike value-protecting theories of judicial review, representation-reinforcing supports the underlying premises of the American system of government.

Ely then takes the reader through the provisions of the Constitution to make a case that most of them are really concerned with process and participation rather than with substantive values.[23] His case has been controverted, and is certainly problematical, but that is not the line on which I wish to attack. He points out that the post–Civil War amendments are primarily aimed at broadening participation by, for example, forbidding abridgment of the right to vote on account of race.[24] And of the eleven amendments since 1913, five extended the franchise (direct election of senators, abolition of the poll tax in federal elections, female suffrage, etc.). "Extension of the franchise to groups previously excluded has therefore been the dominant theme of our constitutional development since the Fourteenth Amendment, and it pursues both of the broad constitutional themes we have observed from the beginning: the achievement of a political process open to all on an equal basis and a consequent enforcement of the representative's duty of equal concern and respect to minorities and majorities alike."[25]

Obviously, Ely does not wish to assign the courts the unfinished task of requiring participation by every human being in every decision that affects them. "The approach to constitutional adjudication recommended here is akin to what might be called an 'antitrust' as opposed to a 'regulatory' orientation to economic affairs—rather than dictate substantive results it intervenes only when the 'market,' in our case the political market, is systematically malfunctioning."[26] From there, without much argumentation, Ely proceeds to adopt all of the Warren Court results under the first amendment's clause guaranteeing freedom of speech, without, however, explaining the links between the representation-reinforcing approach and, for example, his condemnation of the Smith Act cases which originally upheld the power of Congress to ban speech that advocated the violent overthrow of the government.[27] One might as easily have argued that banning the advocacy of an end to democracy to be accomplished by minority violence tended to reinforce representation, especially since representation is not a prominent feature of Communist regimes.

But the real problems with the representation-reinforcing approach are more basic than Ely's use of that rationale to enact the standard liberal line. The approach need not be so used. As I have just suggested, it could be used to uphold restrictions on certain speech, which may suggest that the criterion has not a great deal of real meaning. The real problems, however, are more fundamental. The fact that the United States Constitution has provisions that require participation by certain groups and that we have a constitutional history of steadily expanding the suffrage does not give courts any warrant to go further than the Constitution already does in ensuring representation and suffrage. That expansion of participation and suffrage was accomplished politically, and the existence of a political trend cannot of itself provide the Court with a warrant to carry the trend beyond its own stopping point. How far the people decide *not* to go is as important as how far they *do* go.

The idea of representation-reinforcement is, therefore, internally contradictory. As an approach to constitutional adjudication it tends to devour itself. It calls upon judges to deny effect—to deny representation or participation, if you will—to those who have voted to enhance the representation of some people but have equally voted to deny representation to others. Since, by definition, there is no provision of the Constitution that requires the extension to these others, the Court, acting on its own, nullifies half the result of the vote that has been taken. What is reinforced is not democratic representation so much as it is judicial power to redistribute the polity's goods.

Nor is the argument assisted greatly by the analogy to antitrust. It has been suggested from time to time that antitrust courts should intervene when the economic market is, in Ely's words, "systematically malfunctioning" or, in other words, displays "market failure." The difficulty is that, except in cases where avoidable monopoly replaces competition, the concept of market failure usually means no more than that the market is producing results the critic disapproves of on grounds that ultimately turn out to be moral or aesthetic. The market failure concept has not proved to be very useful in antitrust. When an economist found an industry structure he did not like, he immediately pronounced market failure. General Motors once had about half of the American automobile market, and the literature was rife with market failure analyses by people unwilling to entertain the notion that GM had that share because more customers wanted its cars than other makes. Then the Japanese arrived, and the market's failure disappeared. It had never been anywhere but in the eye of the beholder to begin with.

So it is with political "market failure." How does one know that a political market, which appears to be democratic, is nevertheless "systematically malfunctioning"? I suspect one knows that because one dislikes the way the vote turned out. Ely assures us, however, that that is not what he means:

> Malfunction occurs when the *process* is undeserving of trust, when (1) the ins are choking off the channels of political change to ensure that they will stay in and the outs will stay out, or (2) though no one is actually denied a voice or a vote, representatives beholden to an effective majority are systematically disadvantaging some minority out of simple hostility or a prejudiced refusal to recognize commonalities of interest, and thereby denying that minority the protection afforded other groups by a representative system.[28]

The first of these forms of malfunction poses no special challenge to constitutional theory since it is the office of the first amendment's speech and press clauses to prevent anyone from closing the processes of politics and change. One may, of course, disagree with the particulars of Ely's version of the first amendment, as with some other matters in this connection, but that is another argument.

Ely's second form of malfunction—political market failure due to prejudice—is the concept that gets him into trouble. The concept is an elaboration of Justice Stone's suggestion that "discrete and insular minorities" may require special protection by the Court. The notion is an odd one, because certain minorities were intended to be protected from prejudiced legislation by those who ratified the Constitution and its various amendments. Ely and, one supposes, Stone suggest that still other minorities may be identified by the Court as not sufficiently protected by democratic processes. This is a function for judges that certainly does not come from the historic Constitution. It is an extrapolation of the various requirements of participation that Ely sees in the actual Constitution. It is, therefore, a line of reasoning remarkably similar to that by which Justice Douglas created the general "right of privacy" in *Griswold* v. *Connecticut:* There are a great many instances in the Constitution of what may be construed as protections for participation; these have emanations that form penumbras; the result is a general right of participation; people who keep losing in the legislative process because of "prejudice" that makes them "discrete and insular minorities" are subject to "systematic malfunctioning" and must be given special protection by the courts.

The *Griswold*-like nature of this creation of a new right is enough to show the argument's vulnerability. Once more, the ratifiers' creation of one set of rights is simultaneously a failure or refusal to create more. There is no basis for extrapolating from the rights they did create to produce rights they did not. One might as well say that the very large set of no-rights adds up to a general conclusion of no constitutional rights, thus erasing the Bill of Rights, as to do what Douglas and Ely have done.

But that is not the objection to Ely's theory I want to stress here. The minority he would have the courts protect is the one that "keeps finding itself on the wrong end of the legislature's classifications, for reasons that in some sense are discreditable."[29] To ask whether there exists unjustified hostility toward a group that has lost in the legislative process would be an invitation for courts to second-guess the legislature, so Ely asks simply whether there exists widespread hostility and then whether the group in question is likely to be perceived by legislators as different from themselves. This is what Ely calls the "we–they" contour. And it leads him to some extremely liberal versions of what the Constitution commands, striking down laws that disadvantage aliens,[30] homosexuals,[31] and all laws classifying by gender if the laws were enacted prior to 1920, when the nineteenth amendment provided female suffrage.[32] Affirmative action or reverse discrimination is constitutional because it involves a majority favoring people unlike themselves.[33] Capital punishment is a violation of the Constitution because people like "us" are not executed very often.[34] Many of Ely's prescriptions simply extend the Constitution in ways that were not intended by the ratifiers. Capital punishment, however, is recognized as an available penalty several times in the text of the Constitution. His "we–they" argument is thus capable of directly overriding the basic law—and why not? The ratifying conventions, to say nothing of the drafting convention at Philadelphia, were composed of men who were not of a class likely to be executed often.

The odd thing is this: Ely states that, of course, laws punishing burglars are constitutional, although, some opinion to the contrary notwithstanding, legislatures have few burglars in them. Ely's reason is that it is legitimate to discourage people from breaking into our homes. It certainly is, but that remark requires a theory of the legitimate ends of law that Ely does not supply. Why may a legislature not decide that aliens should not vote or be government employees on the ground that they are not part of the political community? Why may a legislature not decide that homosexuals should not teach primary school children or be allowed to adopt children on the ground that in some significant number of cases proselytizing may occur and the society wishes to discourage that out of moral disapproval? Ely's theory, which purports to take judges out of the business of making policy decisions, in fact plunges them into such decisions by requiring that they distinguish between cases in which groups lost in the legislative process for good reason (burglars) and those in which they lost for discreditable reasons (aliens, the poor, homosexuals, etc.). I fear that this is another point at which his system collapses. The results it produces turn out to be just another list of results on the liberal agenda which the Court must enact because legislatures won't.

In Ely's case, as in Bickel's, criticism confined to the structure of a theory necessarily overlooks many enlightening arguments and observations made in the course of the book.

Laurence Tribe

Laurence Tribe's constitutional theory is difficult to describe, for it is protean and takes whatever form is necessary at the moment to reach a desired result. This characteristic, noted by many other commentators, would ordinarily disqualify him for serious consideration as a constitutional theorist. But Tribe's extraordinarily prolific writings and the congeniality of his views to so many in the academic world and in the press have made him a force to be reckoned with in the world of constitutional adjudication. For that reason alone, he must be discussed.

Tribe's descriptions of his approach to the Constitution are quite misleading. In the preface to the second edition of his treatise *American Constitutional Law,* published in 1988, he states that his constitutional arguments are not a "cover for whatever liberal political views [he] might hold" but provide "ammunition to all combatants in the constitutional controversies of the day."[35] He writes that he has gained "a deeper appreciation of the very great difference between *reading* the Constitution we have and *writing* the Constitution some of us might wish to have."[36] Further, "My commitment to constitutional analysis is, in truth, neither particularly instrumental nor reflective of any specific philosophy."[37] These claims are shown by the rest of his book to be patently untrue. What makes Tribe interesting, as well as illustrative of the state of most constitutional scholarship today, is the fact that his writings are almost entirely an attempt to convert the Constitution to his political views. As Judge Richard Posner has said, Tribe's view is that "the Constitution is what we want it to be . . . and that what we should want it to be is the charter of a radically egalitarian society."[38]

Tribe states that he is not particularly concerned about questions of judicial capacity or the legitimacy of judicial rule.[39] These are the questions that lie at the center of all serious theories of the Constitution, and Tribe gives an odd reason for passing them by. He says that other actors in the governmental system must also employ their own understandings of the Constitution.[40] The answer is inadequate. Legislators and executives are not final; a court purporting to apply the Constitution is. The supremacy of unelected judges' decisions brings questions of judicial capacity and legitimacy to the center of constitutional law.

Tribe comes back to the subject somewhat later in his treatise, but only to treat it lightly again. He writes that his analysis will be "brief indeed; the subject is beyond the scope of an essentially doctrinal treatise."[41] That would be a sound response if the book were a doctrinal treatise, if Tribe had written merely a description of what courts have in fact decided. But that is not even remotely the purpose of his treatise. He had said, in the preface to the first edition of his treatise, reprinted in the second, that he is laying "a coherent foundation for an active, continuing, and openly avowed effort to construct a more just constitutional order."[42] No one can do that without saying what doctrine should be, and certainly no one can make the radical suggestions for vastly increased judicial power that Tribe does without addressing the capacity of judges and the limits to the legitimacy of judicial rule. His book is "doctrinal" only in the sense that he advocates doctrines, but those doctrines have no basis in the intentions of those who wrote and ratified the Constitution, no basis in the structure or history of the document, and, often enough, no basis in anything the Supreme Court has decided in the past. An effort that departs so drastically from all the usual criteria of constitutional adjudication requires, as its first and central element, a theory of what things judges may legitimately do.

Tribe tries to dispose of what he calls the "classical critics" by positing as the basis of their position a "dichotomy between a democratic political process and an antidemocratic adjudicatory process."[43] He then claims the dichotomy is not real because, over time, the adjudicatory process responds to the political climate and representative democracy diverges from the ideal. Indeed, he insists upon "the non-existence of *any* satisfactory form of representation,"[44] which "puts the burden of persuasion on those who assert that legislatures (or executives) deserve judicial deference as good aggregators of individual preference."[45] This certainly gets rid of the counter-majoritarian difficulty with judicial supremacy, but it does so only by denying that democracy has any claims that judges are bound to respect. If this nation were starting from scratch, we might argue about whether, as a general matter, judicial rule is to be preferred to democratic rule. I have no doubt that I would choose the latter. It appears from this passage that Professor Tribe would not. Much of the rest of his treatise confirms that hypothesis. In any event, we are not starting from scratch, and Tribe has told us that he has learned "the very great difference between *reading* the Constitution we have and *writing* the Constitution some of us might wish to have."[46] Well, the Constitution we have, on any coherent reading, leaves most areas of government to democracy and elected representatives, whether or not those representatives are "good aggregators of individual preference." If it matters, elected representatives are certainly better aggregators of individual preference than a majority of a committee of nine lawyers sitting in Washington.

The treatise is an enormously long book, running some 1,720 pages of text and footnotes, and there can be no attempt here to describe all of the approaches to judicial review that Tribe thinks the Court has tried in one era or another. Often he argues from the original understanding of the Constitution's provisions, but only when that does not hinder him from arriving at the result he thinks proper. When the original materials stand in the way, he generalizes the principle intended to such an extent that it loses all touch with the ratifiers' understanding of what they were doing. Since the equal protection clause of the fourteenth amendment was designed to prevent the legal subjugation of blacks, Tribe creates an "antisubjugation principle" that applies to people and situations the ratifiers of the amendment did not dream they were addressing.[47] This new principle (before his 1988 edition Tribe had not suspected its existence) is designed "to break down legally created or legally reenforced systems of subordination that treat some people as second-class citizens."[48] Not only does the antisubjugation principle make equal protection analysis unduly sweeping, but what Tribe means by "legally reenforced systems of subordination" makes the Constitution apply to much private action, although it explicitly applies only to action by government.[49]

The antisubjugation principle provides Tribe with his latest defense of *Roe* v. *Wade*, his three previous ones being now abandoned. He has had trouble finding a rationale for the decision but he is certain it is right. Abortion, he now writes, involves the "intensely public question of the subordination of women to men through the exploitation of pregnancy."[50] Making a woman carry her child to term is also like that "involuntary servitude" prohibited by the post–Civil War thirteenth amendment. The link to the thirteenth amendment, aimed primarily at protection of the newly freed slaves, "is underscored," according to Tribe, "by the historical parallel between the subjugation of women and the institution of slavery."[51]

> To give society—especially a male-dominated society—the power to sentence women to childbearing against their will is to delegate to some a sweeping and unaccountable authority over the lives of others. . . . Even a woman who is not pregnant is inevitably affected by her knowledge of the power relationships thereby created.[52]

The Justices who dissent from the abortion decisions are in "diametrical opposition to the central premises of reproductive autonomy."[53] The Constitution now seems to contain another unmentioned right, reproductive autonomy. No doubt there are many who wish it did, which seems to them reason enough to say that it does. I am told that Tribe's analysis here is entirely derivative from the work of feminist constitutional theorists. In fact, he claims much older roots than that. If *Roe* were overruled and the issue thus sent back for democratic resolution by the several states, he says, quoting a commentator, some states would trample the rights of women and others would sacrifice the rights of the unborn, which shows that allowing legislatures to resolve the issue is "the least legitimate alternative."[54]

If the fact that states may differ on moral issues makes their legislatures the least legitimate organs for decision, there is no excuse for having states. Everything should be decided at the national level and, presumably, by the Supreme Court rather than Congress. Tribe adds:

> It is worth recalling Abraham Lincoln's warning, voiced on a previous occasion when the nation was deeply divided over a different issue of fundamental liberty, that the Union could not long endure "half slave and half free."[55]

The preposterousness of citing Lincoln for the proposition that the Court should create a constitutional right of abortion apparently does not occur to Tribe. The abortion issue does not threaten the survival of the nation, and Lincoln certainly never suggested that the cure for a nation half slave and half free was for the Supreme Court to end slavery by inventing the thirteenth amendment. He knew that the solution had to be political, and ultimately it was. According to Tribe's formulation, whenever the various states disagree over a profound moral question, the Court should impose its resolution of the matter. That means the Court is to take all really important issues away from the people, whether or not it has in the Constitution any authority to do so. "Fundamental rights," Tribe says, cannot properly be reduced to political interests.[56] The entire question, of course, is whether abortion is a "fundamental right" under the Constitution or a moral issue to be decided democratically. Tribe makes it a fundamental right only by comparing the position of women to that of slaves.

Tribe is very upset by the decision in *Bowers* v. *Hardwick* that there is no constitutional right to homosexual conduct within the home. He thinks that such a right is part of a broader right to sexual intimacies between consenting adults. (Tribe argued the case for Hardwick in the Supreme Court.) "The Court's error in *Hardwick* was that it used the wrong level of generality to conceptualize the plaintiff's claim of liberty to test its pedigree."[57] How, one might ask, are we to know what level of generality is appropriate? "[I]n asking whether an alleged right forms part of a traditional liberty, it is crucial to define the liberty at a high enough level of generality to permit unconventional variants to claim protection along with mainstream versions of protected conduct."[58] This is entirely result-oriented. The Court must choose the level of generality at which it states "traditional liberty" at any level that results in a constitutional right for unconventional behavior. This bypasses the question of whether the Constitution contains protection for any sexual conduct or whether that is left to the moral sense of the people. It also fails to come to grips with the central question Bickel and Ely at least grappled with, albeit unsuccessfully: How can any individual, professor, judge, or moral philosopher tell us convincingly that, regardless of law or our own moral sense, certain forms of unconventional behavior must be allowed? There is no apparent reason why the Court should manipulate the level of generality to protect unconventional sexual behavior any more than liberty should be taken at a high enough level of abstraction to protect kleptomania. Tribe has more sympathy for one than for the other, but that hardly rises to the level of a constitutional principle.

Related to his discovery of a principle that makes "subjugation" unconstitutional is Tribe's discussion of rights of privacy and personhood.[59] These are rights of individual autonomy which inhere in the Constitution because that document is claimed to have an implicit idea of what it means to be fully human.[60] Quite aside from the dubious nature of that assertion, Tribe's version of what being human is turns out to be an extreme form of modern liberalism's moral relativism. Starting from the Court opinions saying that it is inconsistent with the first amendment for government to try to control men's minds, Tribe moves rapidly to the claim that the same sort of thing is involved when government attempts to regulate the way the mind processes the sensory data it receives from the world. He suggests that this is what happens when government is permitted to ban the use of "such psychoactive substances as marijuana."[61] He is not clear about the full range of "psychoactive substances" one might have a constitutional right to use, but he laments the fact that few courts have reached "the conclusion that the basic assertion of governmental power over the individual psyche in this area is illegitimate as a matter of due process. Typical was a North Carolina court's assertion that it is 'not a violation of [an individual's] constitutional rights to forbid him . . . to possess a drug which will produce hallucinatory symptoms similar to those produced in cases of schizophrenia, dementia praecox, or paranoia. . . .' "[62] Moving from a case in which the Court found a constitutional right to use pornography in the home, Tribe says that if it is offensive to have government rummage through a person's library to discover evidence of his mental and emotional tastes, it is not much less offensive for government to rummage through his medicine chest to discover his "chemical predilections."[63] "In either case, the offense is governmental invasion and usurpation of the choices that together constitute an individual's psyche."[64]

Although the Supreme Court protects pornography under the first amendment, it permits government to ban the most vile forms, termed "obscenity." Tribe disagrees and condemns even laws that suppress obscenity.

> [T]he attempt to single out some images or ideas for complete suppression . . . seems ultimately incompatible with the first amendment premise that awareness can never be deemed harmful in itself. . . . [S]uppression of the obscene persists because it tells us something about ourselves that some of us, at least, would prefer not to know. It threatens to explode our uneasy accommodation between sexual impulse and social custom—to destroy the carefully-spun social web holding sexuality in its place. . . . [T]he desire to preserve that web by shutting out the thoughts and impressions that challenge it cannot be squared with a constitutional commitment to openness of mind.[65]

The Constitution, according to Tribe, requires that the mind be open to both obscenity and narcotics. These conclusions follow from premises—awareness can never be deemed harmful, commitment to openness of mind, complete freedom of the psyche, etc.—that Tribe wants to be in the Constitution but that are not there.

But, fantastic though these conclusions will seem to most people familiar with the historic Constitution, it is on the subject of race that Tribe reveals the authoritarian side of his liberalism. Here the antisubjugation principle runs riot, flattening all the structures of our constitutional law. The Constitution's most fundamental distinction is that between what is public and what is private; it forbids government from doing certain things but lays almost no injunctions upon individuals. Thus, the equal protection clause of the fourteenth amendment forbids racial discrimination by any level or unit of government. It does not forbid private individuals from discriminating on any grounds they choose. That is why, when it was desired to end racial discrimination in privately owned restaurants, hotels, and the like, it was necessary to enact the 1964 Civil Rights Act. Tribe would obliterate this basic feature of the Constitution whenever "a situation of pervasive interdependence between a government actor and a private actor [makes] it appropriate to focus not on the substantively acceptable government decision to leave particular choices to the private actor, but on the substantively unacceptable way in which those choices are exercised in the specific case."[66] Thus, courts should order racial balance in institutions like schools, presumably busing children throughout a school system, even though the school system had never engaged in racial discrimination. If there is racial clustering, it cannot be a result of individual choice but must reflect a "system of subordination"[67] for which government must ultimately be held responsible. If people leave the area because of what the court is doing to their schools, the court should draw yet new boundaries to make possible the racial mix that Tribe thinks the Constitution always commands. Since Tribe analogizes the situation of women to that of blacks, and since the government is no less guilty of subjugation with respect to sex than it is with respect to race, one supposes courts could also impose sexual quotas throughout the society in the name of the Constitution.

There is much more of this sort of thing in Tribe's writings, but perhaps enough has been said to demonstrate that, while he professes to have no overarching theory of constitutional interpretation, Tribe is in fact a constitutional revolutionary who would overturn the Constitution we have. Judge Posner, reviewing another of Tribe's books, said: "As Tribe conceives constitutional 'interpretation,' the Constitution is flexible enough to embrace—to command—a partisan political position,"[68] and noted that his "method is to use the skills of a lawyer to make political choices for society in the name of a fictive constitution, as if the Supreme Court really were a superlegislature and government by lawyers had, at last, arrived."[69] Tribe's philosophy is that of a radical egalitarian, which is to say that he would require courts to impose moral relativism in such areas as pornography and drugs but would have courts also impose quotas in such areas as race and gender. As Professor Stanley Brubaker concluded, Tribe thinks the people should accord the Court authority to do whatever it thinks is right. "What he finds intolerable is a similar claim to authority by the people themselves. The 'mainstream' thinking preeminently articulated by Tribe is thus carrying us to a place in which there will be no room at all for self-government, and none for constitutional democracy."[70] It is a just comment.

More Liberal Revisionists of the Constitution

I have focused on Alexander Bickel, John Hart Ely, and Laurence Tribe because they are three quite different constitutional theorists.

They have different intellectual approaches and they vary enormously in the modesty or immodesty of the role they would assign to the Supreme Court. But they have in common the fact that they would depart, in varying degrees, from the actual Constitution of the United States. Their constitutions are more liberal, egalitarian, and socially permissive than either the actual Constitution or the legislative opinion of the American people. In that, they typify today's American professoriate, legal and nonlegal. What follows is a demonstration of that truth by sampling the views of other academic constitutional theorists.

Harvard is apparently a hotbed of revisionist law professors. In addition to Laurence Tribe, Professor Frank Michelman has long been working on a theory that would make welfare payments a constitutional right that would-be recipients could enforce in court.[71] Professor Richard Parker finds our present democracy in a state of "corruption," which asserted condition he regards as warrant enough for courts to use the Constitution to remake society. He promises a new constitutional theory that will "take seriously and work from (while, no doubt, revising) the classical conception of a republic, including its elements of relative equality, mobilization of the citizenry, and civic virtue."[72] This sounds a bit like a Court-managed version of the French Revolution.

Harvard law school is also a stronghold of Critical Legal Studies, a nihilistic neo-Marxist movement that views all law as oppressive and political. It is nihilistic because its members typically demand the destruction of current doctrine and hierarchies as illegitimate, but they acknowledge that they have no notion of what is to replace this society. To give the reader some flavor of the mood of these folk, I once attended a lecture by one of its leading Harvard proponents, which he concluded by saying: "The first year of law school is designed to destroy the minds of the students. It does that by asking them to reconcile the irreconcilable and to justify an obviously unjust society." He immediately left, saying he had a train to catch and could not stay for questions. Another leader of the movement at Harvard is Professor Duncan Kennedy. He states that he is against illegitimate hierarchy, domination, and oppression. What he is for is utopian speculation concerning an impossible Eden[73] which aspires to a "shared vision of a social harmony so complete as to obviate the need for any rules at all."[74] He has described his philosophy as a "utopian fragment" that is "very egalitarian" and "somewhat erotic and aesthetic."[75] That, presumably, is why he has suggested that

Harvard abolish all salary differences so that janitors and deans would be paid the same. Each member of the school should rotate through different jobs, janitors to teach sometimes and professors to mop floors.[76] Tenure should be abolished, admission to law school should be by lot, with quotas within the lottery for minority, female, and working-class students.[77] The purpose of the lottery device is to eliminate notions of merit and of better and poorer law schools.

Kennedy states his teaching goals as politicizing, in a leftward direction, as many students as possible. "[F]ind ways to use your . . . normal classroom interaction as a political tool, as a political weapon, as an aspect of political activist practice."[78] The Critical Legal Studies movement is, admittedly, an extreme case, but it is significant that it and its fellow travelers constitute about one-third of the Harvard faculty and that it is prominent at other law schools as well. Indeed, it is significant that it exists and survives at all. Prior to the 1960s generation in the universities, and many of the Crits are of that generation, the movement's mindless form of leftist politics, its crude anti-intellectualism, would not have been tolerated on any decent law school faculty. That it now thrives speaks volumes about the political and intellectual atmosphere in many of today's most prestigious law schools.

Dean Paul Brest of Stanford, where Ely also teaches, has written that "the controversy over the legitimacy of judicial review in a democratic polity . . . is essentially incoherent and unresolvable"[79] since "no defensible criteria exist" "to assess theories of judicial review."[80] Therefore, he concludes, "the Madisonian dilemma is in fact unresolvable."[81] One might suppose that a constitutional theorist who concludes that no defensible theory of judicial supremacy exists would at least entertain the idea that the institution is illegitimate and should be dropped. That is, there being no way to justify judicial power, courts should simply accept whatever legislatures produce. That is not Brest's conclusion, however. Instead, he lists a number of useful criteria the Court should employ in exercising the function of judicial review.

> Having abandoned both consent and fidelity to the text and original understanding as the touchstones of constitutional decision-making, let me propose a designedly vague criterion: How well, compared to possible alternatives, does the practice contribute to the well-being of our society—or, more narrowly, to the ends of constitutional government? Among other things, the practice

should (1) foster democratic government; (2) protect individuals against arbitrary, unfair, and intrusive official action; (3) conduce to a political order that is relatively stable but which also responds to changing conditions, values, and needs; (4) not readily lend itself to arbitrary decisions or abuses; and (5) be acceptable to the populace.[82]

Our actual constitutional order accomplishes these things, often by leaving such matters as responses to changing values and needs to the people and their elected officials. The difficulties with Brest's view are not only that, once the real Constitution is abandoned, the judge has no authority to impose any standards on legislators, but also that his set of criteria, agreeable though they may sound, are so vague, as he concedes, that judges are given virtually complete discretionary power to run the nation.

Another Stanford law professor, Thomas Grey, once urged courts to depart from the written Constitution on the theory that there is an unwritten law, a natural law, that judges should enforce. He sought to have it both ways, holding that judges can set aside democratic decisions because the Constitution is law and yet that judges are free to jettison that law by exceeding the Constitution's limits to enforce "deeply held but unwritten ideals."[83] Grey's arguments for a Court that departs from the historical meaning of the Constitution are essentially result-oriented: the results of departing from the Constitution are, as he sees it, politically good. Moreover, judges are best equipped to identify and enforce unwritten ideals, and the Founders intended judges to do just that. Those good results, one must suppose, if Grey thinks the historical record relevant, included not only *Roe* but such manifestations of the natural law as *Dred Scott* and *Lochner*. Moreover, if the Founders intended judges to apply natural law, they certainly kept quiet about it. Many historians are not even sure the Founders as a group contemplated any form of judicial review, even review confined to enforcement of the text, much less review according to an unmentioned natural law. No one at the time suggested any such power in the courts, and early courts made no claim that such a power had been delegated to them.

Grey gives us an idea of what his natural law, enforced through the Supreme Court—created right of privacy, can do for us. His own view appears to be that "one can discern the attitude most conducive to enshrinement of sexual freedom among our constitutional rights"[84] in "three disparate modern prophets":[85] Norman O. Brown, Michael Foucault, and Bertrand Russell. These gentlemen had not previously been regarded as constitutional theorists, but Grey's lengthy discussion of them strongly suggests that he thinks their call for celebration of Eros and the unlimited pleasure of the body should be elevated to constitutional principle. He forecasts, however, that the Supreme Court will reach the same results by responding to those conservative concerns for order and social stability that produced the contraception and abortion decisions! In any case, Grey agrees with such decisions and thinks it better to say that "their major premises come from such extra-textual sources as judicial precedent and the practices and ideals of social life."[86] Constitutional adjudication is viewed as guided, and correctly so, "in a relatively few cases, by the words of the Constitution."[87]

Grey leaves no doubt that the American people will not be consulted before their culture, morals, and ideas of the proper "practices and ideals of social life" are swept away by judges. One doubts somehow that this is what Madison and his colleagues had in mind.

Constitutional law becomes nothing other than moral philosophy, and that of a most peculiar kind, in the writings of David A. J. Richards of New York University law school.[88] Richards solves the Madisonian dilemma by contending that the central premise of our constitutional order is not democratic rule but moral principles of justice.

> [C]ontractarian theory explains why judicial review is not suspect, being, as it is, countermajoritarian. Majority rule is not the basic moral principle of the constitutional order. The basic moral principles are the principles of justice, including the principle of greatest equal liberty. Majority rule is justified only to the extent that it is compatible with this deeper moral principle. To the extent that judicial review enforces the requirements of a greatest equal liberty in a way that majority rule cannot, judicial review is morally justified.[89]

According to Richards, neither the text of the Constitution nor the history of its adoption can give real content to constitutional rights, so we must turn to a theory of human rights. This rests on two fundamental assumptions: "first, that persons have the capacity to be autonomous in living their life; second, that persons are entitled as persons, to equal concern and respect in exercising their capacities for living autonomously."[90] Richards gets further constitutional prin-

ciples from John Rawls's *A Theory of Justice*.[91] It might seem odd
that it is necessary to turn to a book published in 1971 to find the
meaning of a Bill of Rights ratified in 1791, but that may be done,
it seems, because Rawls is a contractarian and so were many of the
philosophers with whom the Framers were familiar. This takes account of neither the fact that the members of the ratifying conventions
may not have thought they were enacting any philosopher's views
nor the fact that contractarian philosophers can come to very different
conclusions. Robert Nozick, another modern contractarian, disagrees
basically with Rawls.

Rawls essentially asked what the social contract would look like
if framed by persons in the "original position" behind a "veil of
ignorance" as to their individual fates in the society they were planning. Assuming that all persons would be highly risk-averse, Rawls
concludes that the social contract drawn up would be very permissive
and egalitarian. There is no conceivable reason to think that judges
in our actual society are entitled to go about putting matters where
they would have been if a Rawlsian social contract had been entered
into. But Richards assumes just that and derives "the postulate of
constitutional morality that legally enforceable moral ideas [must]
be grounded on equal concern and respect for autonomy and demonstrated by facts capable of empirical validation."[92] He observes that
"humans use sexuality for diverse purposes" and concludes that:

> For the same reasons that notions of the unnatural are constitution-
> ally impermissible in decisions involving contraception, abortion,
> and the use of pornography in the home, these ideas are also
> impermissible in the constitutional assessment of laws prohibiting
> private forms of sexual deviance between consenting adults.[93]

Because sexual autonomy is profoundly related to basic self-respect,
Richards arrives at *"the principle of love as a civil liberty."*[94] In passing,
he finds a constitutional right to die,[95] a "good argument" that
dress and hair length are protected options as "basic life choices,"[96]
and that, perhaps, "soft drug use could be regarded as a form of
autonomous control of internal psychic space and attitudes, and thus
be fit within the rubric of [basic life choices]."[97] Since he thinks
there is a constitutional right to die, it is not apparent why hard
drug use should not also be permitted.

Richards thinks criminalization of homosexual conduct is like
punishing heresy:

Homosexuality is today essentially a form of political, social, and moral dissent on a par with the best American traditions of dissent and even subversive advocacy. For this reason, traditional liberal principles must protect this way of life from the worst American impulses of repressive nativism. Those that support criminalization find today in homosexuality what they found before in the family planning of Sanger, the atheism of Darwin, the socialism of Debs, or the Marxist advocacy of the American Communist Party.[98]

Not surprisingly, he finds that the suppression of hard-core pornography is "obnoxious in principle to the central moral purpose of the First Amendment."[99] Thus, "pornography can be seen as the unique medium of a vision of sexuality, a 'pornotopia'—a view of sensual delight in the erotic celebration of the body, a concept of easy freedom without consequences, a fantasy of timelessly repetitive indulgence. In opposition to the Victorian view that narrowly defines proper sexual function in a rigid way that is analogous to ideas of exremental [sic] regularity and moderation, pornography builds a model of plastic variety and joyful excess in sexuality. In opposition to the sorrowing Catholic dismissal of sexuality as an unfortunate and spiritually superficial concomitant of propagation, pornography affords the alternative idea of the independent status of sexuality as a profound and shattering ecstasy."[100]

Richards also writes, following to its logical conclusion the Warren Court's "fundamental interest" jurisprudence of the equal protection clause, that there is "no convincing moral justification for the refusal to constitutionalize the right to certain basic services."[101] He mentions school funding as a subject the courts should control, referring to the "rhetoric of local control" as a "moral harlequinade" and to "our moral immaturity as a people."[102]

The Constitution, as reconstructed by Richards's moral philosophy, requires that persons be judged in terms of their individual characteristics according to which moral discriminations can be made. "By contrast, viewing people in terms of morally irrelevant characteristics is to treat people as objects or tools having generalized characteristics that one may manipulate to advance one's purposes or ends."[103] Thus, race, sex, and homosexuality are not proper bases for legislative classification. But all of this gives way in the case of reverse discrimination (which he calls "preferential racial classifications"[104]). Evidently, only white males may be "treat[ed] . . . as objects or tools having generalized characteristics." It will hardly come as a surprise that the death penalty is unconstitutional since, despite popular support for a punishment that the Constitution clearly assumes to be available, "it fails to accord with the moral principles of punishment."[105]

So it is with others who purport to interpret the Constitution according to moral philosophy. Of these, one of the best known is Ronald Dworkin, who once taught at Yale law school and now teaches both at Oxford and the law school of New York University. Dworkin writes with great complexity but, in the end, always discovers that the moral philosophy appropriate to the Constitution produces the results that a liberal moral relativist prefers. One of his key distinctions, for example, is that between concepts and conceptions. He employs it to make the death penalty unconstitutional despite the fact that the Bill of Rights threw protections around the imposition of the punishment and thus clearly showed that the death penalty itself was constitutionally acceptable.[106] The eighth amendment, which is part of the Bill of Rights, states, "Excessive bail shall not be required, nor excessive fines imposed, nor cruel and unusual punishments inflicted."[107] But the fifth amendment, equally part of the Bill of Rights, three times assumes the availability of the death penalty: "No person shall be held to answer for a capital, or otherwise infamous crime, unless on a presentment or indictment of a Grand Jury . . . ; nor shall any person be subject for the same offence to be twice put in jeopardy of life or limb; . . . nor be deprived of life, liberty, or property, without due process of law. . . ."[108] When the fourteenth amendment was ratified in 1868, it contained the same requirement of due process for depriving a person of life. All of this, however, does not deter Dworkin:

> It would be a mistake for the Court to be much influenced by the fact that when the clause was adopted capital punishment was standard and unquestioned. That would be decisive if the framers of the clause had meant to lay down a particular conception of cruelty, because it would show that the conception did not extend so far. But it is not decisive of the different question the Court now faces, which is this: Can the Court, responding to the framers' appeal to the concept of cruelty, now defend a conception that does not make death cruel?[109]

The distinction between a concept and a conception is merely a way of changing the level of generality at which a constitutional provision may be restated so that it is taken to mean something it obviously did not mean. Why should we think that the ratifiers of 1791 legislated a concept whose content would so dramatically change over time that it would come to outlaw things that the ratifiers had no idea of outlawing? Even if we agree to call what they adopted a concept that might change in content, what is it that can legitimately work such a change? Can it be a change in the attitude of the American people? That will not do, because the American people, as shown by the laws they enact, generally favor capital punishment. And if they should come to feel it unacceptably cruel, they would have only to repeal the death penalty statutes. The Constitution does not require any state to have a death penalty. It does no good to dress the issue up as one in moral philosophy, because such philosophy gives no clear answer. Arguments have been made both ways and none is conclusive. Moreover, nothing in the Constitution empowers a judge to force a better moral philosophy upon a people that votes to the contrary. The only thing that has changed is that modern liberal elites dislike the punishment. That is no reason to declare that the Constitution bans it.

Dworkin's constitutional theory is perfectly congruent with the political positions of modern liberalism in its more extreme varieties. He thinks that reverse discrimination by government is constitutional, even that private reverse discrimination is lawful despite the 1964 Civil Rights Act, that there is a constitutional right to engage in homosexual conduct, and that laws limiting contraception are unconstitutional.[110]

Professor Mark Tushnet of Georgetown law school, after criticizing all theories of judicial review, added: "I am invariably asked, 'Well, yes, but how would *you* decide the X case?' . . . My answer, in brief, is to make an explicitly political judgment: which result is, in the circumstances now existing, likely to advance the cause of socialism? Having decided that, I would write an opinion in some currently favored version of Grand Theory."[111] Tushnet is at least candid about the fact that he would as a judge make a political decision and then deceive us. But also implicit in his statement is his confidence that Grand Theory can be made to reach any result. Indeed it can. The law school theorists we have examined prove that.

Bruce Ackerman of Yale law school says Bickel expresses "the central legal conclusion toward which the American academy had been struggling for generations: that, somehow or other, we must transcend the Framers' vision if we are to make our Constitution fit the needs of a modern democratic society."[112] Referring to the kind of theoretical efforts examined in this chapter, Ackerman states that "they all proceed from a common supposition—that classical conceptions of constitutional interpretation are so radically deficient as to be beyond hope of lawyerly reconstruction."[113] This apparently means that the Constitution's interpretation has undergone radical shifts in the past that cannot be accounted for by classical or lawyerly reasoning. That is certainly true, and to some of us it is a cause for regret. But Ackerman attempts to relieve our sorrow by assuring us that the Constitution may legitimately undergo "structural amendments" that bypass the amendment process specified in article V of the Constitution. Concentrating on the judicial activism of the 1930s Court, described in Chapter 2 of this book, Ackerman argues that the Court's retreat was caused by such a structural amendment. Such amendments need not be passed by the cumbersome procedures set in place by article V. Instead, in certain "constitutional moments," the American people "place a constitutional meaning upon a sustained series of electoral victories and legislative successes that is very different from the meaning ordinarily attached to any single episode."[114]

Thus Ackerman draws from the 1930s historical experience the lesson that when "a series of decisive victories at the polls permits the newly triumphant spokesmen of the People to proclaim their new higher law from *all three* of the branches" of government, there has been a legitimate ratification of a structural amendment to the Constitution.[115] He does not answer why, if the triumphant spokesmen of the People have enough power to influence all three branches of government, they do not have enough power to change the Constitution using the amendment process set forth in article V. Instead, Ackerman would have Supreme Court Justices watch the political scene closely, and if Congress and the President have, for some length of time, strongly agreed with an unconstitutional policy result, the Supreme Court may legitimately act as if a structural amendment has taken place. Although he accurately describes political and constitutional events in the 1930s, Ackerman's theory is, at bottom, an invitation for coup by judiciary. An eager Court may too easily decide that it stands at one of Ackerman's "constitutional moments" and proceed to amend the Constitution.

To recognize that the constitutional revolution worked by the New Deal Court was inevitable, moreover, is not quite the same thing as to concede its legitimacy. The combined forces of mortality and the power of appointment may enable a politically dominant movement to find Justices who will amend the Constitution from the bench. That is merely a description of power and the occasions when it can be exercised. The constitutional orthodoxy holds, however, that there is a Constitution with a historic meaning and that any individual is entitled to invoke that meaning to his aid no matter how many elections have gone against him. I wonder how many people would subscribe to the legitimacy of structural amendment if it were the first amendment's guarantees of religious freedom, free speech, and free press that were about to experience excision. The New Deal Court's refusal to set limits to national power is behind us, the consolidation of all power at the federal level is too firmly entrenched and woven into our governmental practices and private lives to be undone. That consolidation is, for that reason, now our effective constitutional law. There is nothing in that acceptance, however, that retroactively casts constitutional legitimacy about the way the change was accomplished.

Unlike most revisionists, Michael Perry of Northwestern University's law school believes that "[o]riginalism is fundamentally sound,"[116] and indeed he defends it admirably against some of the most common revisionist attacks.[117] The defects he sees in originalism "are not intrinsic, but comparative";[118] it is a fine theory, but his own is better.

Perry begins with the "axiomatic" premise "that the constitutional text is authoritative—indeed, supremely authoritative—in constitutional adjudication."[119] The problem, he thinks, is that one cannot axiomatically or unambiguously describe the meaning of "the constitutional text." One kind of meaning is of course the original meaning. However, some constitutional provisions—not all, but some—have an "aspirational" meaning in addition to their original meaning: that is, they "signify fundamental aspirations of the American political tradition."[120] If a judge believes that a particular provision signifies a fundamental aspiration and that the signified aspiration is worthwhile, the judge should bring that additional meaning to bear on the case before him.[121] If there is no aspirational meaning, or if the aspirational meaning does not prohibit the relevant legislative choice, the original meaning must govern. However, "the fundamental aspirations signified by the Constitution . . . are highly indeterminate,"[122] and in the end "the judge should rely on *her own beliefs* as to what the aspiration requires."[123]

Perry's book provides illuminating insights into many important questions of philosophy, politics, law, and religion, but it does not succeed as constitutional theory, because it fails clearly to identify the source of a judge's *authority* to invalidate legislative acts. If the authority stems from the moral worthiness of the particular "aspiration" brought to bear by the judge, then it would seem to be irrelevant whether the aspiration is or is not "signified" by the Constitution. If the authority instead stems from the Constitution's status as the supreme law of the land, deliberately adopted and maintained by the consent of the governed, then only the original meaning of the document can be legitimate material for the judge.[124] As Michael McConnell has summarized Perry's dilemma:

> The force of the originalist argument is that the people had a right to construct a Constitution, and that what they enacted should therefore be given effect, including the portions allocating powers to representative institutions. The force of the usual noninterpretivist argument is that judges should not be constrained in their quest to do good, either by the decisions of past generations . . . or the beliefs of the majority. . . . Professor Perry's intermediate position contradicts both these premises, but offers no persuasive normative argument of its own.[125]

Sanford Levinson, of the University of Texas law school, advances an extremely skeptical, indeed nihilistic, theory of "constitutional" interpretation. Levinson says that "The 'death of constitutionalism' may be the central event of our time, just as the 'death of God' was that of the past century."[126] In a major law review article, Levinson explains that "[f]or a Nietzschean reader of constitutions, there is no point in searching for a code that will produce 'truthful' or 'correct' interpretations; instead, the interpreter, in [philosopher Richard] Rorty's words, 'simply beats the text into a shape which will serve his own purpose.' " He admits that "[t]o put it mildly, there is something disconcerting about accepting the Nietzschean interpreter into the house of constitutional analysts, but I increasingly find it impossible to imagine any other way of making sense of our own constitutional universe."[127] Levinson goes on in the same article to argue that "[t]here are as many plausible readings of the United States Constitution as there are versions of *Hamlet,* even though each interpreter, like each director, might genuinely believe that he or she has stumbled onto the one best answer to the conundrums of the texts. That we cannot walk out of offending productions of our national epic poem, the Constitution, may often be anguishing, but that may be our true constitutional fate."[128] Thus, Levinson concludes in a later work that "[t]here is nothing that is unsayable in the language of the Constitution."[129]

Levinson does not explain why his view of the Constitution as non-law does not lead to the conclusion that judicial supremacy is without legitimacy. Nor does he explain why anyone, including legislators and lower court judges, should consider themselves bound by the decrees of a purely political Supreme Court. In reviewing Levinson's latest book, *Constitutional Faith,* political philosopher Thomas Pangle of the University of Toronto observed that:

> These are not the speculations of some distant or foreign observer; this is the strangely hopeful and exhilarated testimony of a pre-eminent (and by no means unrepresentative) teacher of the law. And, I submit, this book should be for all of us an alarm bell ringing in the night. Something ominous is afoot in the teaching of the law of this land.[130]

Unfortunately, although Levinson has some valuable insights to offer, Pangle's overall assessment seems correct.

Leonard Levy of Claremont Graduate School has recently published a book entitled *Original Intent and the Framers' Constitution,* which attacks a highly oversimplified version of the philosophy of original understanding that bears little resemblance to the theory set out in this book.[131] Thus, Levy goes to great pains to prove that: (1) the Framers did not mean for us to attach interpretive weight to their subjective intentions (hence Madison's secreting of his notes); (2) that the Framers did not mean to freeze the Constitution so that it would lose its character as a document intended to serve for ages to come; (3) that finding the original meaning of some constitutional provisions is quite difficult; and (4) that the Supreme Court has in fact ignored the constitutional text in many prior cases, behaving as if it were a sitting constitutional convention presiding over the writing of a judicial common law constitution.

No even moderately sophisticated originalist holds the view Levy refutes. Originalists, as explained in Chapter 7, do not seek the subjective intent of the Framers but rather the objective meaning that constitutional language had when it was adopted. This can be a difficult task, but permissible and impermissible ranges of meanings can be ascertained. Language is sometimes hard to interpret, but that does not suggest that it can be made to mean anything. Similarly, the fact that terms as originally understood must be applied to new circumstances and factual situations does not mean that we should conclude that those terms can be redefined to say absolutely anything we like. Levy demonstrates that the Court has in the past sometimes ignored the constitutional text, but does not, and I think could not, establish that the Court on such occasions behaved legitimately and should continue on that course.

Justice William J. Brennan, Jr.

In a 1985 speech at Georgetown University, Justice Brennan expounded his theory of constitutional interpretation and applied it specifically to his conclusion that the death penalty is unconstitutional.[132] As he noted, "Because judicial power resides in the authority to give meaning to the Constitution, the debate is really a debate about how to read the text, about constraints on what is legitimate interpretation."[133] He then illustrates how to read the text in a way that seems to contradict the text. He begins unexceptionably enough: "As augmented by the Bill of Rights and the Civil War Amendments, this text is a sparkling vision of the supremacy of the human dignity of every individual. . . . It is a vision that has guided us as a people throughout our history, although the precise rules by which we have protected fundamental human dignity have been transformed over time in response to both transformations of social condition and evolution of our concepts of human dignity."[134]

Justice Brennan traced the ways in which the various safeguards of the Constitution contribute to human dignity—the safeguards thrown around the criminal process; the principle of one person, one vote; rights of expression and conscience; and much more, including the decisions to apply the Bill of Rights to the states.

> I do not mean to suggest that we have in the last quarter century achieved a comprehensive definition of the constitutional ideal of human dignity. We are still striving toward that goal, and doubtless it will be an eternal quest. For if the interaction of this Justice and the constitutional text over the years confirms any single proposition, it is that the demands of human dignity will never cease to evolve.[135]

At this point, a vague unease begins to set in. The coupling in that paragraph of the constitutional text and the evolving demands of human dignity suggests that the meaning of the text must evolve, not by applying old principles to new circumstances but by changing the principles themselves. And that is precisely what Justice Brennan means, for he then identifies capital punishment as "one grave and crucial respect in which we continue, in my judgment, to fall short of the constitutional vision of human dignity. . . . As I interpret the Constitution, capital punishment is under all circumstances cruel and unusual punishment prohibited by the Eighth and Fourteenth Amendments."[136]

Human dignity thus becomes a clause of the Constitution that judges may apply in accordance with their own philosophies. That is clear because Justice Brennan concedes that his interpretation is not subscribed to by either a majority of his fellow Justices or a majority of his fellow Americans. In every capital punishment case, he votes that the death penalty is unconstitutional. "Because we are the last word on the meaning of the Constitution, our views must be subject to revision over time, or the Constitution falls captive, again, to the anachronistic views of long-gone generations."[137]

This thought is worth examination because of Justice Brennan's preeminence in forming our constitutional law for a third of a century. He would avoid, on the one hand, the mistake of adhering to the anachronistic views of past generations, the generations that gave us the Constitution, and also avoid, on the other hand, the majority vote of today's living generations. Having avoided both the original meaning of the Constitution and today's democratic choice, what is left? Only Justice Brennan's moral views on capital punishment. Those moral views are made relevant only by speaking as though the various manifestations of concern for aspects of human dignity in the provisions of the Constitution somehow added up to a human dignity clause that had no definition other than whatever definition a particular Justice chooses to give it. This, of course, is precisely the method by which Justice Douglas created a new right of privacy clause in *Griswold* v. *Connecticut*. The provisions of the Constitution may be said to exemplify concern for a great many general and admirable values. The technique used by Justices Brennan and Douglas is capable, therefore, of giving us a great many new clauses in the Constitution, clauses that bear little relationship either to the ratifiers' intentions or the desires of contemporary Americans.

If there were a human dignity clause in the Constitution of the sort Justice Brennan would import, it would not necessarily give the results he wants. A Justice of different temperament could as easily dwell upon the human dignity of the murderer's victim as upon the dignity of the murderer. The result of that exercise might be not merely to uphold the death penalty but to insist that states must use it. What concepts such as "dignity" and "privacy" mean in application depends entirely upon the sentiments of each judge.

10

The Theorists of Conservative Constitutional Revisionism

*T*hough the overwhelming preponderance of constitutional theorists are liberal to radical law school professors, there are a few who do not fit that category, and I have thought it well to discuss them separately.

The two most prominent theorists of what may be termed a conservative bent are Professor Bernard Siegan of the University of San Diego law school and Professor Richard Epstein of the University of Chicago law school. Siegan and Epstein, though they differ greatly from the liberal theorists just examined in the results their theories would produce, are, like them, revisionists. Though I am more in sympathy with their political ends than I am with the objectives of the ultraliberals, I do not think they establish satisfactorily that those ends may be reached through the Court.

Justice John Marshall Harlan, like Justice Brennan, also attempted a connected statement of theory that departs from the original understanding of the Constitution. Since Justice Harlan is generally regarded as moderately conservative, his theory is discussed in this chapter. The chapter concludes with the most recent debate among the Justices on the proper method of departing from the original understanding of the Constitution.

There are, of course, theorists who take the traditional position that the original understanding controls, scholars such as Raoul Berger, and Professors Michael McConnell, Lino Graglia, and Joseph Grano, of, respectively, the law schools of the University of Chicago, the University of Texas, and Wayne State University. There are other professors of constitutional law who work from originalist assumptions but have not argued the point. These persons are not discussed, since my object in this and the preceding chapter is simply to document the prevalence of revisionist theories, primarily in the law schools, and the flaws that inhere in them.

Bernard Siegan

A major difference between Professor Siegan, of the University of San Diego law school, and the liberal theorists is that he is not selective in the human freedoms he would have courts protect and does not display an egalitarian, redistributionist impulse. As the title of his book, *Economic Liberties and the Constitution,*[1] suggests, Siegan thinks economic liberties are undervalued in modern-day constitutional adjudication and he strives to make a case for increased protection. His strategy is to establish that economic liberties are no different, from a judicial point of view, from other freedoms not mentioned in the Constitution that the modern Court does see fit to protect. In this, he is surely correct. As Judge Learned Hand long ago pointed out,

> I cannot help thinking that it would have seemed a strange anomaly to those who penned the words in the Fifth [Amendment] to learn that they constituted severer restrictions as to Liberty than Property. . . . I can see no more persuasive reason for supposing that a legislature is *a priori* less qualified to choose between "personal" than between economic values; and there have been strong protests, to me unanswerable, that there is no constitutional basis for asserting a larger measure of judicial supervision over the first than over the second.[2]

Siegan would not necessarily decide for the claimed freedom in each case, but he does contend that one type of claim may not be preferred to the other merely because of the classification given it. In terms of judicial entertainment of claims to freedom, *Lochner* v. *New York*[3] and *Adkins* v. *Children's Hospital*[4] are as respectable as *Griswold* v. *Connecticut*[5] and *Roe* v. *Wade.*[6]

The logic is impeccable if one accepts *Griswold* and *Roe,* and much else in contemporary jurisprudence, as proper discharges of the judicial function. If not, then Siegan's case for unmentioned economic liberties is, by a parity of reasoning, defeated. Neither set of liberties being mentioned in constitutional materials, their claims for judicial consideration must stand or fall together. Of itself, the juridical equivalence of all extra-constitutional freedoms does not require Siegan's outcome. But it does require either his conclusion or mine—either substantive due process all the way or not at all. If we want *Griswold* and *Roe,* then *Lochner* and *Adkins* come with them. If we reject *Lochner* and *Adkins,* then we cannot have *Griswold* and *Roe.* My position is that the Court had no business undertaking to give a substantive answer to the claim of right in any of the four cases. There being nothing in the Constitution about maximum hours laws, minimum wage laws, contraception, or abortion, the Court should have said simply that and left the legislative decision where it was. Siegan chooses to accept, if not the results in all four cases, then the judicial approach in all four. The Court, he says, was right to decide each case on the merits and not merely say the subject matter was not covered by the Constitution.

The result is that Siegan places the Court in a stance of across-the-board libertarianism. Substantive due process becomes a policy of laissez faire, not just with respect to economics but with respect to all human activity. This by no means implies that Siegan would uphold the claimed freedom in each case, merely that he would have the Court examine the challenged legislation in a critical mood. He quotes approvingly Aaron Director's statement: "Laissez faire has never been more than a slogan in defense of the proposition that every extension of state activity should be examined under a presumption of error."[7] I, too, am an admirer of Director and accept the correctness of laissez faire, as so defined. The next question, however, is who is to apply the presumption of error, players in the political process or judges. My answer is the former; Siegan's is the latter.

Siegan lays out the model of judicial review he advocates. It is a comprehensive version of substantive due process and it is worth examining because Siegan, unlike most writers, makes clear what a rational version of substantive due process requires. What it requires is an impossible task. His model of review contains three steps:

In suits challenging the validity of restraints [upon human freedom], the government would have the burden of persuading a court . . . first, that the legislation serves important governmental objectives; second, that the restraint imposed by government is substantially related to achievement of these objectives, that is, . . . the fit between means and ends must be close; and third, that a similar result cannot be achieved by a less drastic means.[8]

The approach is libertarian because the burden is on the government to justify its law rather upon the claimant to show that the law is illegitimate. But no matter who must shoulder the burden, the task assigned is beyond the capacities of courts.

The first task requires the court to decide whether the "legislation serves important governmental objectives."[9] The idea of importance, in this context, necessarily connotes as well the idea of legitimacy. It is not to be supposed that a court would find the government's showing adequate if the objective was important but improper. It is necessary to be clear about the stupendous nature of the function thus assigned the judiciary. The court could not carry out the task assigned unless it had worked out a complete and coherent philosophy of the proper and improper ends of government with respect to all human activities and relationships. This philosophy must give answers to all questions social, economic, sexual, familial, political, moral, etc. It must be so detailed and well articulated, with all major and minor premises constructed and put in place, that it enables judges to decide infinite numbers of concrete disputes. It must also rest upon more than the individual preferences of judges. That is required both because a panel of nine judges, each voting his own preferences, would produce inconsistent results and because it is necessary to demonstrate the legitimacy of forcing a view of the ends of government chosen by judges upon elected representatives who have other ends of government in mind. No theory of the legitimate and important objectives of government that possesses all of these characteristics is even conceivable. No single philosopher has accomplished it, and nine Justices could not work it out and agree on it. Yet, upon the premise that a judge may not override democratic choice without an authority other than his own will, each of these qualities is essential.

Suppose that a challenge is made to a federal minimum wage law on the ground that though it advantages unions and workers whose productivity makes them worth the higher wage, it leads to unemployment for less productive workers. Let us suppose that the court is, as it should be, persuaded that the effects of the law are as described. But the government's counsel states that this does no more than show the statute was the result of interest group politics, which is inevitable in a large, pluralistic society. Or he states that Congress thought it best to moderate the speed of the migration of industry from the North to the South, since, in the legislators' estimation, it is more painful to lose a job you have held for twenty years than not to be offered a job you have never had and did not expect. Or that the minimum wage was part of a governmental policy to aid unionization and collective bargaining, employers being willing to bargain wages at higher levels when the alternative of nonunion labor is made economically less attractive, and unionization is considered desirable because of the social values unions have traditionally fostered. How is a court to demonstrate that none of these objectives is legitimate and important?

Suppose that the lawyer for Connecticut in *Griswold* argued that a majority, or even an intense and politically influential minority, regarded it as morally abhorrent that couples capable of procreation should copulate without the intention, or at least the possibility, of conception. Could the Court demonstrate that this moral view is wrong or that moral abhorrence is not an important and legitimate ground for legislation? The morality described is not one shared by most people, nor do I share it, but I would not know how to prove that a state that adopted such a moral stance had done something it must not be allowed to do. It seems to me a court would have no answer to the government lawyer in either the minimum wage or the contraception case. In the latter, it could say that most people do not feel that way, but that would not prove that people who do are wrong. I am quite clear that, as a legislator, I would vote against raising the minimum wage and against prohibiting the use of contraceptives, but that is because of my own moral views and not because of a principle that I think others with opposed views must accept even if they prove to be in the majority. Justice Holmes made a distinction like this one when he said that he had his "can't helps" but did not pretend they were universal laws. Thus, he said, he could not help preferring champagne to ditchwater but did not attribute that preference to the universe.[10]

Siegan's second stage of review is about ends and means. The court must be persuaded that the challenged law is "substantially related to achievement of [important] objectives."[11] In the case of most laws about which there is likely to be controversy, the social sciences are not up to the task assigned. Should the government insist that a minimum wage law is designed to improve the lot of workers generally, microeconomic theory and empirical investigation will demonstrate that the law does not achieve that objective. But if the government states that the law is designed to slow the transfer of industry from areas with experienced and highly paid workers to areas with inexperienced and less expensive workers because of an estimate about relative psychological hurts, or from unionized to nonunionized areas because of a belief about the social values that unions inculcate, the means will fit the ends.

Siegan has not directly addressed cost-benefit analysis, but it seems likely that a court employing his method of review would have to ask whether the benefits achieved were worth the costs incurred. Perhaps such an analysis is included in the requirement that there be a "substantial" relationship between the law and its objectives. If so, that introduces into the judicial calculus yet another judgment that can only be legislative and impressionistic in nature.

Siegan might contend that the superiority of microeconomics to other social sciences makes the case for substantive due process review of economic regulations stronger than the case for such review as it is now practiced with respect to noneconomic freedoms. In a sense, that is true. Assuming that judges acquire competence in microeconomics, they will be able to assess the asserted relationship between an economic regulation and its economic results better than they can the fit between other laws and objectives. But that leaves judicial review of laws with noneconomic objectives in an awkward position. In the case of laws about forms of sexuality, for instance, a claim that the law states a moral standard can never be rebutted and the government should always win. But if the objective is said to be something else, perhaps a decrease in violent acts attributed to the availability of pornography, the government may not be able to carry its burden of showing that the desired outcome is likely. Depending on which way the government states the objective, the law will be impossible to strike down or impossible to uphold.

The third step—that the government must show that a "similar result cannot be achieved by a less drastic means"[12]—is loaded with ambiguities and disguised tradeoff decisions. A "similar" result may be one whose tendency is the same but still not the full result desired by the legislature. Usually a lesser, though similar, result can be achieved by a lesser degree of coercion. Here cost-benefit analysis is in full blossom, and there is no way to quantify either the cost or the benefit when the law involves values that are not economic.

A court undertaking to judge such matters will have no guidance other than its own sense of legislative prudence about whether the greater result is worth the greater restriction.

The upshot is that any court undertaking the three-step analysis Siegan urges could not avoid exercising its powers in a purely legislative manner. For failures of the legislative process, which certainly occur, Siegan has devised a judicial process that must certainly fail. That the inevitable indeterminacy, and hence arbitrariness, of such judicial review is at least in the service of individual freedom is not a justification. Since it is not true, it is not even a plea in mitigation. In these matters, no matter whose theory of constitutionalism is under discussion, liberty is not exclusively on one side of the equation; it is on both. As well as the freedom of the individual challenging the law, there is also the freedom of the individuals who want the law upheld. We may not ignore the liberty of the individuals who make up a community to regulate their affairs as seems to them best, for objectives they regard as important, by means that seem to them effective, and for degrees of the objectives' attainment that seem to them to justify the degree of restriction.

It is only fair to say that Siegan's effort seems to me both valorous and superior to most constitutional theory. Unlike many writers, he lays out his assumptions candidly so that there is no difficulty, as there often is elsewhere, in discovering the structure of the argument beneath a flow of rhetoric. He refuses, moreover, to claim a difference between economic and other liberties. There is much to admire in Siegan, and I wish it were possible to agree that the virtue of intellectual integrity is sufficient to make a valid constitutional theory.

Richard A. Epstein

Professor Epstein, of the University of Chicago law school, has expounded a theory of the proper constitutional role of the federal courts which leads to libertarian results similar to those which Professor Siegan would reach under the due process clauses.[13] Epstein, however, advocates reliance on the takings clause of the fifth amendment[14] and the contract clause of article I, section 10.[15] In a sense, Epstein's approach is more satisfactory because he works with textually explicit constitutional provisions. He, like Siegan, performs the valuable function of directing attention to economic liberties, liberties that have been valued too lightly by our recent jurisprudence as well as in the theorizings of the professors. Epstein's statement of the theory as set out in Chapter 3 of his book *Takings* also presents a powerful defense of construing the clauses of the Constitution as they were originally understood.[16] He rejects the view that constitutional provisions are either too indeterminate to apply or that those provisions change in meaning with the passage of time.[17] Moreover, he finds no warrant for judges either to enforce any value that does not derive from the constitutional text or to refuse to enforce any value that does so derive.[18] With all of this I wholeheartedly agree. There appears, however, to be a rather severe disjunction between Epstein's description of the judge's task and his argument about the meaning of the clause of the fifth amendment providing that "private property [shall not] be taken for public use, without just compensation."[19] He concludes that a proper construction of the takings clause forbids all redistributionist legislation. Thus, he reads the clause to forbid progressive income taxation,[20] welfare,[21] and the National Labor Relations Act.[22] He concludes that compensation for unintentional torts by government officials is constitutionally mandated,[23] and that *Lochner* v. *New York*[24] and *Coppage* v. *Kansas*[25] were correctly decided.

My difficulty is not that Epstein's constitution would repeal much of the New Deal and the modern regulatory-welfare state but rather that these conclusions are not plausibly related to the original understanding of the takings clause. At first the reader thinks Epstein's argument will run essentially like this: the Founders greatly admired John Locke; it is plausible that the takings clause was intended to enact Locke's view of the proper relationship of governmental power to private property; we are, therefore, required to enforce that view as the meaning of the Constitution; and that meaning requires these results. But the argument then shifts to the nature of legislatures and to economic reasoning. As one sympathetic reviewer put it, "what starts out as a Lockean treatise ends up as an essay on public choice theory. . . . Epstein is not really a Lockean or a libertarian but a utilitarian with an especially grim view of majoritarian decisionmaking."[26] The upshot is that Epstein has written a powerful work of political theory, one eminently worth reading in those terms, but has not convincingly located that political theory in the Constitution.

Justice John Marshall Harlan

Justice Harlan offered a method of holding statutes unconstitutional, without recourse to any explicit provision, that many people find attractive. It seems to avoid, on the one hand, the obvious intellectual disingenuousness of some methods and, on the other, the necessity of allowing a bad law to stand. The occasion for Harlan's discourse was the case of *Poe* v. *Ullman*.[27] That was the previous challenge to Connecticut's anticontraception statute, and the Court, in an opinion by Justice Frankfurter, dismissed the appeal because, the statute almost never having been enforced, the case presented no live controversy.

Justice Harlan dissented, reached the merits of the claim, and concluded that the statute was unconstitutional.[28] He employed the due process clause of the fourteenth amendment since it was abundantly clear that nothing else in the Constitution could conceivably apply to the statute, and the due process clause has become the usual resort when no actual provision is available. He noted that the Court had rejected both the view that the clause guaranteed only procedural fairness in the application of law and the view that the clause's only substantive content came from incorporating part of the Bill of Rights.

Harlan, too, would accept neither version:

> Were due process merely a procedural safeguard it would fail to reach those situations where the deprivation of life, liberty or property was accomplished by legislation which by operating in the future could, given even the fairest possible procedure in application to individuals, nevertheless destroy the enjoyment of all three.[29]

That is a remarkable explanation of why due process is not a procedural guarantee alone: if it were, legislatures might enact laws that deprived people of life, liberty, or property. Of course, that is a major function of legislation, and Harlan was not objecting to such deprivations *per se*. He was objecting to those he disagreed with. He assumed that judges possess a legitimate method of deciding when the substance of a state law, even when applied fairly, *improperly* deprives people of life, liberty, and property. Such a method is also required to justify an undefined residue of judicial power outside the provisions of the Bill of Rights. For that reason, he turned next to the question of the proper method.

Conceding that the substantive content of due process "has not been reduced to any formula,"[30] Harlan went on: "The best that can be said is that through the course of this Court's decisions [substantive due process] has represented the balance which our Nation, built upon postulates of respect for the liberty of the individual, has struck between that liberty and the demands of organized society."[31] We have seen in the first four chapters of this book that *that* is exactly what cannot be said—unless, perhaps, the balance has swung wildly from one era to the next. Moreover, if it is "our Nation" that is striking the balance between liberty and order, it seems peculiar that the Court has to strike down the balance that the nation and various states have voted for. But Harlan referred to the traditions from which our country developed as well as those from which it broke, and said: "That tradition is a living thing. A decision of this Court which radically departs from it could not long survive, while a decision which builds on what has survived is likely to be sound. No formula could serve as a substitute, in this area, for judgment and restraint."[32] This is pure early Alexander Bickel. The primary safeguard against judicial willfulness seems to be a theory of the survival of the fittest decisions, a jurisprudential version of Darwinism. It is not explained what will kill off these constitutional mutations and how long that will take. By the same sort of reasoning, one might observe, there is no need for the judicial function described since it is even more plausible that, if a tradition is both real and valued, legislation that radically departs from it will not long survive the democratic process.

The "full scope of the liberty guaranteed by the Due Process Clause . . . is not a series of isolated points pricked out" by the Bill of Rights but is "a rational continuum which, broadly speaking, includes a freedom from all substantial arbitrary impositions and purposeless restraints and which also recognizes, what a reasonable and sensitive judgment must, that certain interests require particularly careful scrutiny of the state needs asserted to justify their abridgment." (He cited *Skinner* v. *Oklahoma* and *Bolling* v. *Sharpe*.)[33] The Justice must decide, that is, when the state has passed laws that are arbitrary and purposeless. It is rather odd to imagine a legislature enacting a statute that has no purpose.

The state of Connecticut offered a number of interests to support its anticontraception law, among them that the state considered the practice of contraception immoral in itself. That is a difficult state interest for the Court to overcome, for, as Justice Harlan said, much law is based on moral precepts.[34] But he adumbrated the Douglas of *Griswold,* arguing that enforcement of the law must mean arrests, searches and seizures, criminal charges, public trial, and testimony as to the marital relationship.[35] The privacy of the home is protected by the third amendment, relating to the quartering of soldiers, and by the fourth, prohibiting unreasonable searches and seizures. This was, he said, the "privacy" of the home.[36] It is, but that privacy which is constitutionally guaranteed is expressed in those amendments. That it is not general or absolute we know from the fact that many things done in the home are subject to both criminal and civil law. We had still to learn why, in constitutional terms, the Connecticut statute was different from physical abuse, conspiracy to commit a crime, or even marital incompatibility that would support a divorce action, all of which can occur in the home. Harlan, in fact, pointed out that the Connecticut statute would in all probability be "accomplished without any physical intrusion whatever into the home."[37] And he said that the right of privacy was not absolute. "Thus, I would not suggest that adultery, homosexuality, fornication and incest are immune from criminal inquiry, however privately practiced."[38]

The state, he said, could forbid these altogether, but marital intimacy was part of an institution which the state must allow and has always protected. Though the state had determined that the use of contraceptives is as evil as any extramarital sexual immorality, calling a husband and wife to account before a criminal tribunal is a very different thing from punishing those who practice intimacies the law has always forbidden and which have no claim to social protection. Harlan did not dispute the state's right to make its moral judgment, but it had not justified the "obnoxiously intrusive means it has chosen to effectuate that policy."[39] Indeed, the very fact that Connecticut had never enforced its law suggested it did not consider the policy very important or the means chosen to implement it appropriate or necessary. But what was conclusive was that no other state or nation, though many shared Connecticut's moral policy, had imposed a criminal prohibition on the use of contraceptives.

These are all very appealing sentiments, but as constitutional analysis the opinion will not wash. In a way, the case was too easy. Connecticut did not think its policy important and certainly did not think it appropriate to use criminal sanctions, or any sanctions, against married couples or anyone else. There was no serious moral policy whatever behind the law. And, admittedly, it was a lunatic law, which is precisely why nobody tried to enforce it. It was easy, therefore, to strike it down. The only things at stake were, on the one hand, the enlistment of the Court on one side of a cultural disagreement and, on the other, the maintenance of constitutional integrity.

Harlan's arguments were entirely legislative. The stark fact is that the Constitution has nothing whatever to do with issues of sexual morality. Those questions are left entirely to the morality of the people of the various states. Once, after I had given a talk on the Constitution at a law school, a student approached and asked whether I thought the Constitution prevented a state from abolishing marriage. I said no, the Constitution assumed that the American people were not about to engage in despotic insanities and did not bother to protect against every imaginable instance of them. He replied that he could not accept a constitutional theory that did not prevent the criminalization of marriage. It would have been proper to respond that in any society that had reached such a degenerate state of totalitarianism, one which the Cambodian Khmer Rouge would find admirable, it would hardly matter what constitutional theory one held; the Constitution would long since have been swept aside and the Justices consigned to reeducation camps, if not worse. The actual Constitution does not forbid every ghastly hypothetical law, and once you begin to invent doctrine that does, you will create an unconfinable judicial power.[40]

We are not framing a constitutional philosophy for a society imagined in a particularly horrible piece of science fiction. We are talking about our society, and in our society Harlan's vision of a due process clause guided by criteria such as the judge's view of the distinctions between contraceptive use and homosexuality means that there are effectively no limits to the judge's power to govern us. The Justice expressed sentiments about the uses of the criminal law that we all share, that, indeed, Connecticut shared, but the power to depart from the original understanding of the Constitution is not limited to the articulation and enforcement of views we all share. *Poe* v. *Ullman* led directly to the intellectual catastrophe of *Griswold* v. *Connecticut,* which led to the ukase of *Roe* v. *Wade,* which led to four Justices—and for a time they had the necessary fifth vote—finding a constitutional right to homosexual conduct. The Court or a substantial minority of it had come to do the very things that Justice Harlan had said of course it would not do. No matter what your moral views on any of these matters, nothing in the Constitution addresses them. Harlan's methodology, often admired by advocates of judicial restraint, turns out to offer no protection against judicial imperialism.

Some lawyers of a conservative disposition admire Harlan's *Poe* opinion for no better reason than that it invokes "tradition." But not all traditions are admirable, and none of them confines judges to any particular range of results. Former Stanford Dean John Ely begins his discussion of tradition as a source of constitutional doctrine with a quotation from Garry Wills: "Running men out of town on a rail is at least as much an American tradition as declaring unalienable rights."[41] Ely is excellent on the subject. "There is," he writes, "obvious room to maneuver, along continua of both space and time, on the subject of which tradition to invoke. Whose traditions count? America's only? Why not the entire world's? . . . And who is to say that the 'tradition' must have been one endorsed by a majority? Is Henry David Thoreau an invocable part of American tradition? John Brown? John Calhoun? Jesus Christ? It's hard to see why not."[42] The Constitution, he points out, is intended to check today's majorities, and it seems quite odd to check them with the views of yesterday's majorities.[43] I can think of no reason that rises to the level of constitutional argument why today's majority may not decide that it wants to depart from the tradition left by a majority now buried. Laws made by those people bind us, but it is preposterous to say that their unenacted opinions do.

A Judicial Philosophical Free-for-All

Matters have not improved since Justice Harlan wrote. In the spring of 1989 the Justices of the Supreme Court engaged in a debate about the meaning of the idea of substantive due process. The result was more confusion than ever about the sources and scope of a judicial power unrelated to the text of the Constitution.

The occasion for the debate was the case of *Michael H.* v. *Gerald D.*[44] The facts make clear why the full names of the parties were not given. Any of the more daring television soap operas would envy the plot. Gerald D., a top executive in a French oil company, married Carole D., an international model, in Las Vegas, appropriately enough. They settled in California. Two years later Carole entered an adulterous affair with Michael H., a neighbor. Two years after that, she conceived Victoria D. Gerald was shown as Victoria's father on the birth certificate and he always held himself out as that. But Carole told Michael he might be the father. Gerald moved to New York City for business reasons but Carole and Victoria remained in California. Blood tests then showed a 98.07 percent probability that Michael was Victoria's father. For three months, Carole visited Michael in St. Thomas, the site of his business, and there Michael held Victoria out as his child. Carole then returned to California with Victoria and took up residence with yet a third man, Scott K. Soon, she and Victoria spent time with Gerald in New York City and on vacation in Europe and then returned to Scott in California.

Michael filed an action in California to establish his paternity and right to visit Victoria. Carole was again living with Gerald in New York, but she soon returned to California and took up again with Michael. For eight months, when not in St. Thomas, Michael lived with Carole and Victoria and held the girl out as his daughter, but Carole then left Michael and rejoined Gerald in New York, where they lived with Victoria and had two other children.

The legal situation, unlike the human situation, was, initially at least, uncomplicated. A California statute provided that the child of a woman living with her husband is conclusively presumed, with some exceptions, to be her husband's child. The California court therefore gave judgment for Gerald, denying Michael's request to prove his paternity and for visitation. Michael challenged the constitutionality of the statute as a violation of his substantive due process rights and carried the case to the United States Supreme Court. There the constitutional situation proved as confused as everything else in the case. The only thing clear was that Gerald and Carole won and Michael lost.

The Court produced five opinions. No Justice took the position of Justice Hugo Black that, aside from incorporating the Bill of Rights, the due process clause of the fourteenth amendment was entirely a procedural guarantee and gave the Court no substantive powers. That, as pointed out in Chapter 1, is the only defensible view of the due process clause. Justice Scalia wrote an opinion which only Chief Justice Rehnquist joined in its entirety.[45] Justices O'Connor and Kennedy joined in all but a single footnote, but that footnote makes a great deal of difference.[46] Scalia began by saying "It is an established part of our constitutional jurisprudence that the term 'liberty' in the Due Process Clause extends beyond freedom from physical restraint." That, of course, means that the clause does not protect merely against being jailed without a fair trial but, to some unknown degree, gives freedom from other laws a legislature has enacted, that enabled Michael to challenge the California legislature's decision to presume that Victoria, having been born to Carole while the latter was married to Gerald, was Gerald's child. But Scalia worried that the assumption of such substantive power by judges might mean that the only limits were the predilections of those currently on the Court. He therefore turned to tradition and history and found that relationships such as that of Michael and Victoria had not been treated as a protected family unit while the marital family (Gerald, Carole, and Victoria) had.

In footnote 6, however, Scalia apparently attempted to provide a further safeguard against judicial constitution-making. Justice Brennan's dissent objected to using historical traditions specifically relating to the rights of an adulterous natural father rather than more general traditions relating to parenthood.[47] The dispute, as so often in constitutional law, was about the level of generality the Court should use in defining and applying a concept. Scalia and Rehnquist chose "the most specific level at which a relevant tradition protecting, or denying protection to, the asserted right can be identified." General traditions, he said, "provide such imprecise guidance [that] they permit judges to dictate rather than discern the society's views. . . . Although assuredly having the virtue (if it be that) of leaving judges free to decide as they think best when the unanticipated occurs, a rule of law that binds neither by text nor by any particular, identifiable tradition, is no rule of law at all."

Justice O'Connor, joined by Justice Kennedy, apparently wanted just such a free hand. Concurring in everything but Scalia's footnote 6, she wrote, "I would not foreclose the unanticipated by the prior imposition of a single mode of historical analysis."[48] Another name for the prior adoption of a single mode of analysis is, of course, "the rule of law."

It was left to Justice Brennan's dissent, joined by Justices Marshall and Blackmun, to claim unlimited judicial power to remake the substance of the Constitution in the name of a clause about fair procedures. He began his argument with Scalia's plurality by stating their position in order to give a very peculiar rebuttal: "Once we recognized that the 'liberty' protected by the Due Process Clause of the Fourteenth Amendment encompasses more than freedom from bodily restraint, today's plurality opinion emphasizes, the concept was cut loose from one natural limitation on its meaning."[49] Since that "recognition" involved transforming the clause from one about due process to one about due substance, without any guide in constitutional text, history, or structure as to what substance might be due, there was then no limitation on its meaning, natural or otherwise. The clause now "means" anything that can attract five votes on the Court.

Justice Brennan said, "This innovation paved the way, so the plurality hints, for judges to substitute their own preferences for those of elected officials."[50] Quite right, that is just what it does, and it is odd that, having stated the problem so succinctly, Brennan did not deny that it was true or offer a solution. Instead, he denied that the plurality's emphasis on "tradition" provided a limitation on judicial power: "this concept can be as malleable and as elusive as 'liberty' itself" and places no "discernible border around the Constitution. . . . [b]ecause reasonable people can disagree about the content of particular traditions, and because they can disagree even about which traditions are relevant to the definition of 'liberty.' "[51]

That is precisely what I said in criticizing Harlan's theory of substantive due process in *Poe* v. *Ullman*. I found that a conclusive reason to abandon the whole enterprise of substantive due process as an inherently lawless usurpation by judges of powers legitimately belonging to the people and their elected representatives. But Justice Brennan found it a conclusive reason to claim still more judicial power. Tradition was not irrelevant, he said, but

> [t]hroughout our decisionmaking in this important area runs the theme that certain interests and practices—freedom from physical restraint, marriage, childbearing, childrearing, and others— form the core of our definition of "liberty."[52]

Once more, we are tempted by good things, marriage and childbearing, to concede a power that is not legitimate. The "interests and practices" covered by the words "and others" included, of course, abortion and, in his view, homosexual sodomy. Had he cared to go back to prior Courts, the interests at the core of liberty would have included freedom from wages-and-hours legislation and freedom to own slaves. Even for the modern Court, his list is much too short.

Brennan gives a very odd reason for judicial protection of the freedoms the Court has chosen. "Our solicitude for these interests is partly the result of the fact that the Due Process Clause would seem an empty promise if it did not protect them, and partly the result of the historical and traditional importance of these interests in our society."[53] That sentence repays scrutiny. The due process clause would be an "empty promise" if it were limited to what it actually promised: due process. Not long afterward he rebuked the plurality for "mock[ing] those who, with care and purpose, wrote the Fourteenth Amendment."[54] Hugo Black would have replied that the mocking is done by those who take the clause as a grant of power that those who wrote it clearly did not intend. Nor is it clear why the historical and traditional importance of certain interests provides judges with power to set aside the assessment of their importance by elected representatives.

The dissent contains a paragraph that demonstrates the incoherence of substantive due process:

> In construing the Fourteenth Amendment to offer shelter only to those interests specifically protected by historical practice, moreover, the plurality ignores the kind of society in which our Constitution exists. We are not an assimilative, homogenous society, but a facilitative, pluralistic one, in which we must be willing to abide someone else's unfamiliar or even repellant practice because the same tolerant impulse protects our own idiosyncracies. Even if we can agree, therefore, that "family" and "parenthood" are part of the good life, it is absurd to assume that we can agree on the content of those terms and destructive to pretend that we do. In a community such as ours, "liberty" must include the freedom not to conform. The plurality today squashes this freedom by requiring specific approval from history before protecting anything in the name of liberty.[55]

A "freedom not to conform"? What can that possibly mean? Freedom from law? Law requires conformity within the subjects it covers. In this case, California's elected representatives had defined aspects of family and parenthood. Why is their agreement on those matters absurd and destructive? Why must Michael be free not to conform to the legislative and judicial determination that it was better for the family, including Victoria, not to give Michael the rights of a married father? Justice Brennan can say such things only by confusing the Court with the society so that what the actual society wants is of no importance compared with what the Court thinks it should want. And what the society should want is that the adulterous natural father be able to intrude upon the marital family. However one feels about that, the balance between the interests of the natural father and the marital family is surely a moral and prudential issue for the people and not for the unguided discretion of judges. But, having invented a Constitution that no one drafted or ratified, Justice Brennan topped matters off by accusing the Justices in the plurality of violating their sworn duty by not subscribing to his invented version: "I cannot accept an interpretive method that does such violence to the charter that I am bound by oath to uphold."[56] Brennan, it will be recalled from Chapter 9, created a "human dignity" clause, found nowhere in the Constitution, that makes unconstitutional the death penalty, which is found several times in the Constitution.

This is where matters now stand with respect to judicial revision of the Constitution. No Justice renounces the power to override democratic majorities when the Constitution is silent. It may be that Scalia and Rehnquist are trying to come as close as they can to that position by insisting on using the most specific tradition available. But even that assumes an illegitimate power, and the limitation will prove no restriction at all when there is only a general, unfocused tradition to be found. Seven Justices, in varying degrees, reject even that slight restriction on their powers. Nothing resembling an adequate justification has ever been, is now, or ever will be offered for this taking by judges of a power that is not theirs. The political seduction of the law continues apace.

11

Of Moralism, Moral Relativism, and the Constitution

*T*he theorists of left-liberal constitutional revisionism did not, of course, invent their ideas in a vacuum. They are best understood as the academic spokesmen for, and the rationalizers of, the dominant attitudes of what may be called the intellectual or knowledge class. They are, that is, rooted in a powerful American subculture whose opinions differ markedly from those of most Americans.

This disparity in attitudes and opinions is important because of the tendency of intellectual class attitudes to work their way into our constitutional law. Federal judges, who spend their lives working with ideas, are by definition members of the intellectual class. Perhaps because of their greater contact with the practical world, the world of business and commerce, the world of government and public affairs, judges usually do not share the values of the intellectual class to the same degree as their colleagues in the legal academic world. The judicial subculture, moreover, contains some ideas that tend to insulate the judge from the temptations of the intellectual class outlook, ideas such as adherence to the original understanding of the lawmakers, and the associated ideas of judicial restraint and the political and cultural neutrality of judges. But when the idea of the original understanding is consistently denigrated and its influence declines, the judge is left with the power of judicial review and little else. He is all too likely to begin to find "law" in the assumptions of the class and culture to which he is closest and with which he is most comfortable. Like most busy, practical people, judges often do not fully understand either the foundations or the ramifications of the assumptions of the culture in which they live.

The assumptions and ideas of the intellectual class regularly mutate, which means, to the extent that constitutional law incorporates those assumptions, our fundamental law will shift with intellectual fashion. As former Dean Ely said of suggestions that fundamental constitutional values be created by moral reasoning, "[e]xperience suggests that in fact there will be a systematic bias in judicial choice of fundamental values, unsurprisingly in favor of the values of the upper-middle, professional class from which most lawyers and judges, and for that matter most moral philosophers, are drawn."[1] The upper-middle, professional class is, of course, a major segment of the intellectual class and includes professors, journalists, and members of public interest organizations. As Ely said, "the values judges are likely to single out as fundamental . . . are likely to have the smell of the lamp about them."[2] I once referred to the tendency of such values to work their way into the law as the "gentrification of the Constitution."[3] The constitutional culture—those who are most intimately involved with constitutional adjudication and how it is perceived by the public at large: federal judges, law professors, members of the media, public interest groups—is not a cross-section of America politically, socially, or morally. The truth is that the judge who looks outside the historic Constitution always looks inside himself and nowhere else. And when he looks inside himself he sees an intellectual, with, as often as not, some measure of intellectual class attitudes.

The wide disparity between the left-liberal values of the intellectual class and the dominant values of bourgeois culture has existed and been widely recognized for a long time. For almost all of this century the "political weight of American intellectuals . . . has been disproportionately on the progressive, liberal, and leftist side."[4] The reasons for that disparity have been explored by a number of commentators, seem clear, and need not be rehearsed here.[5] One commentator has thus observed that American intellectuals display

> . . . almost in the manner of the livery of their vocational guild, an attitude of contempt and moral superiority toward the "business culture" of the United States, toward commerce, technology, and entrepreneurship. . . . They tend to regard themselves as being above the mundane practicalities of the worlds of trade, industry, and finance. In their teaching, and even more emphatically in their scholarship, there is a marked proclivity towards highly abstract theorizing and stridently censorious moralizing.[6]

Because of its stance in opposition to business-class or bourgeois values, indeed to the values of a majority of Americans, this class has been described as constituting an adversary culture.

There exists in this culture a significant disjunction in attitudes. The same people and organizations manage simultaneously to adopt positions of extreme moralism and extreme moral relativism. If one had to choose one organization to illustrate this feature of modern left-liberal culture, it would be the American Civil Liberties Union. Its positions resemble those of many other public interest groups, and it is the primary litigating arm of the adversary culture.* The ACLU's major asset with the general public is its claim that it is a nonpartisan civil liberties organization. That claim is demonstrably false.[7] The ACLU is in fact a highly political organization and is determined to advance an agenda through the courts that often has little or nothing to do with civil liberties found in the Constitution or our statutes.

As a list of its positions† demonstrates, the ACLU favors intrusive

---

* The ACLU is not unique among the activist public interest groups but it has the best-documented record of positions. It is one of the oldest of such organizations and its continuous involvement in litigation has created a much more complete public record of positions taken on a wider variety of issues than is the situation with respect to such organizations as People for the American Way, Planned Parenthood, or Common Cause.

† The most thorough documentation of the ACLU's positions is to be found in William Donohue's book, *The Politics of the American Civil Liberties Union*. The ACLU opposes laws outlawing gambling, the use of some narcotics (marijuana use is said to be constitutionally protected), homosexual conduct, pornography, abortion, and suicide. The ACLU thinks that in child custody proceedings, homosexuality may not even be considered by the court in determining the best interests of the child. The organization opposes state regulation of abortion. It thinks that while the production of child pornography may be prohibited, once it is produced, the first amendment requires its distribution free of state interference. The ACLU opposes laws that zone pornographic theaters away from churches and schools as well as laws that allow citizens to have the postmaster remove their names from mailing lists for pornographic material. It opposes metal detectors in airports. It does not favor mandatory incarceration, without the possibility of a sentence of probation, except perhaps for murder or treason and, of course, contends that the death penalty is unconstitutional. The ACLU has sued to have declared unconstitutional: the tax exempt status of churches and synagogues; the employment of chaplains by Congress, prisons, and the armed services; all displays of nativity scenes on public property; the singing of "Silent Night" in the classroom; and the words "under God" in the pledge of allegiance.

After the unfavorable references to it in the 1988 presidential campaign, the ACLU said it would reconsider some of its positions.

governmental action in the service of morality in some areas but insists that the Constitution mandates moral relativism in others. Reviewing *Our Endangered Rights: the ACLU Report on Civil Liberties Today,* Professor Jeremy Rabkin says, "Indeed, the most revealing thing in this book is the extraordinary scope the ACLU now gives to the term civil liberty."[8] It contains an essay on " 'Sexual Justice,' demanding special protection for homosexuals, legal recognition of homosexual marriages, and the rejection of any distinctions between men and women in the military. Then there is a neo-Marxist essay on 'Economic Justice,' demanding income redistribution and social control of corporate investment—in the name of enhancing liberty."[9] "[T]here are essays such as the one by Thomas Emerson on academic freedom, in which he endorses court challenges to the adoption of 'racist' school texts, while simultaneously endorsing court review of the 'censorship' involved in removing inflammatory books from school libraries."[10]

Another book describes such dogmatic "libertarians" as taking the most extreme positions in favor of free expression and freedom of life-style while also being strong advocates of equality, of business regulation, and of income redistribution, and tending to be indifferent to patriotism, personally uninterested in religion, and not very concerned about lawbreaking by citizens. Rabkin comments: "The ideological associations are so familiar, it is easy to forget how essentially incongruous they really are. Why do people who would trust government officials to control the allocation of vast resources with sensitivity and selflessness so often insist that government can never be trusted to distinguish unorthodox critics from inflammatory hate-mongers, or risqué entertainment from sadistic pornography? Why do people who insist that there can be no harm in a high-school teacher touting radical political causes, or flaunting a 'gay' lifestyle, object so strongly to any display of religious symbols in public schools? In general, why do those who boast of their determination to transform society through government action like to regard themselves as the greatest champions of liberty?"[11]

Attention must be paid to the apparent inconsistency of positions that seem to demand, simultaneously, governmental coercion in the service of certain moral values and individual freedom from law in the service of moral relativism.* Attention must be paid, because

---

* This ideological pattern is remarkably similar to the conclusions of the liberal academic constitutional theorists described in Chapter 9. They, too, combine a

that syndrome, advanced in litigation by the ACLU, other public interest organizations, and law professors, has entered into our constitutional jurisprudence.

Perhaps Professor Rabkin is correct, perhaps these positions are wildly inconsistent. Or perhaps their consistency is to be found only in that they are all hostile to the attitudes of middle-class, bourgeois culture. In that case, the consistency is hypocritical since these ideas would then have to be seen as held not for their own perceived merits but as weapons employed to damage the morale and erode the ascendancy of bourgeois culture in order to achieve the hegemony of the left-liberal culture.

There is, however, an alternative explanation, which I offer without entire confidence but for consideration. The groups under discussion hold strongly egalitarian social views. Whether that is a genuine commitment or simply a manifestation of hostility to bourgeois attitudes, the fact remains that this stance may at least suggest coherence in the ideas advanced.

An egalitarian morality naturally produces both extreme governmental restrictions of individual liberty and, simultaneously, the demand that government recognize the "right to be let alone." Egalitarian bureaucracies try to prohibit father–son banquets at high schools and insist that workers be denied promotion on merit in order to achieve proportional representation of the sexes and ethnic groups in the work force. As a friend of mine put it, "Whether the issue be racial balance in schools, seat belts on autos, or the rules for women's basketball in Iowa, the desires of the people to be affected are given little or no weight by the intellectual class." These are clearly coercions of individuals in order to implement a particular morality. Yet, this same segment of our culture emphatically denies the right of majorities to regulate abortion, homosexual conduct, pornography, or even the use of narcotics in the home. On the one hand, there appears to be a degree of morality so severe that it amounts to moralism, and, on the other, a hostility to morality so strong that it amounts to moral relativism. Each is the natural outcome of an egalitarian or redistributionist ethos.

Egalitarianism is hostile to hierarchies and distinctions. Hence law must be used to weaken or eliminate them, striking at private

---

taste for coercion in the service of moralism in some matters with an insistence upon moral relativism in others. That correspondence shows that we are indeed discussing a unified adversarial culture within our general culture.

morality and behavior that is not egalitarian. For entirely innocent reasons, the preferences and talents of people will not always produce equality of results. The egalitarian tendency is then to coerce equality of result by law. That tendency is, of course, frequently checked by public reaction, but it remains a tendency. Law may not be used, however, to enforce moral standards that are not egalitarian. This results in what may be seen as moral relativism or the privatization of morality. One person's morality being as good as another's, the community may not adopt moral standards in legislation. This viewpoint is often expressed by the common and wholly fallacious remark that "You can't legislate morality." Indeed, as discussed in Chapter 4, we legislate little else.

There is little doubt that this intellectual class bias has infiltrated our jurisprudence. The Court has, as we have seen, upheld government's use of gender preferences even though the applicable statute flatly prohibited that practice. In *Regents of the University of California* v. *Bakke,*[12] four members of the Court upheld the constitutionality of racial preferences in a state medical school's admission policies and the fifth Justice, whose position became the law, decided that race could not be an absolute criterion but that it could be a factor considered in giving preference to minority applicants.[13] There are a number of such holdings approving coercive governmental action in these areas.[14] This appears to be a moralism so strong that it overcomes positive law.

But the Court has also partially adopted the other prong of left-liberal ideology, moral relativism or the privatization of morality. This may be seen very dramatically in the Court's creation of the "right of privacy," which has little to do with privacy but a great deal to do with the freedom of the individual from moral regulation.[15] When privacy is not a plausible concept in the circumstance of a case, various Justices have, we have seen, invented other rights to free the individual from community standards: the right not to conform, the right to dignity, and the right to be left alone. All are expressions of rampant individualism and hence of moral relativism. The Constitution does protect defined aspects of an individual's privacy and it does privatize specified areas of moral behavior. The fourth amendment's protection of the privacy of the home from unreasonable searches is an illustration of the former, as is the first amendment's protection of the free exercise of religion of the latter. But the Court has erected individual autonomy into a constitutional principle that sweeps far beyond any constitutional provision, as it did in cases forbidding the regulation of the sale of contraceptives and drastically restricting the ability of state legislatures to regulate abortion. The relativity of morality was certainly expressed by the four Justices who voted that a community may not express its sexual morality in a law prohibiting homosexual conduct.[16] These examples do not depend upon one's view of the merits or morality of any of these pieces of legislation. The point is that nothing in the Constitution prevents such laws, and the Justices could vote against them only on the principle that sexual morality is a private matter with which the legislatures may not interfere.

As might be expected, intellectual class moral relativism is particularly evident in cases decided under the first amendment, which deals with religion and speech. These are subjects that lie at the center of our moral and political life as a nation. Due to decades of left-liberal dominance on the Supreme Court, moral relativism and untrammeled individualism are built into Court-created first amendment doctrine. That seems to me the only explanation possible for recent Court decisions, discussed in Chapter 4, holding that the speech clause protects the public burning of the American flag and the provision of pornographic telephone messages by the dial-a-porn industry. These are decisions in no way required by the historical guarantee of freedom of speech.

The same tendency may be seen in the Court's reading of the religion clauses of the first amendment. Under the clause prohibiting the passage of laws "respecting an establishment of religion," the Court has, quite unnecessarily, effectively banished religious symbolism from our public life. The severity of the Court's establishment of secularism as our official creed is illustrated by the case, also mentioned in Chapter 4, holding unconstitutional the display of a creche at Christmas time in a public building. The Court has, in fact, read the two religion clauses so expansively as to bring the prohibition of the establishment of religion into direct conflict with the guarantee of free exercise. The classic example is *Wisconsin* v. *Yoder*.[17] Amish parents objected to the state's school attendance laws, stating that their religion prohibited them from allowing their children to attend public school after the eighth grade. The Wisconsin statute required attendance to the age of sixteen and was in no way aimed at religion. The Supreme Court found the law a violation of religious freedom and held that the Amish children need not comply with it as other children must. Quite aside from the question of whether the decision was right or wrong, it makes plain that the religion clauses have been brought into conflict with each other. Had Wisconsin legislated an exception for the Amish, that favoritism clearly would have been held a forbidden establishment of religion. Thus, in the name of the free exercise of religion, the Supreme Court, according to its own criteria, itself established a religion.

This seems an example of the privatization of morality. Religion is regarded by most Americans as the sole or primary source of moral belief. The great expansion of the establishment clause serves to expunge official expressions of religious morality from our public life while the great expansion of the free exercise clause serves to reinforce individual autonomy even against laws that are in no way aimed at religion.

Moral relativism became explicit in the cases dealing with obscenity and pornography. *Cohen* v. *California*[18] threw first amendment protection around the behavior of a man who wore into a courthouse a jacket bearing words which suggested that the reader perform an act of extreme anatomical implausibility (copulation, to put it euphemistically) with the Selective Service System. Justice Harlan, writing for a majority of the Court, said the state could not ban such obscenity in public. "[T]he principle contended for by the State seems inherently boundless. How is one to distinguish this from any other offensive word?" From the perspective of moral relativism all words are the same. To take Harlan's line, one might as well say that the negligence standard of tort law is invalid because it is inherently boundless. How is one to distinguish the reckless driver from the safe one? The answer in both cases is by the standards of the community, applied through the common sense of the jury. Almost all judgments in law, as in life, are ones of degree. As Holmes said:

> [T]he law is full of instances where a man's fate depends on his estimating rightly, that is, as the jury subsequently estimates it, some matter of degree. If his judgment is wrong, not only may he incur a fine or short imprisonment, as here; he may incur the penalty of death. "An act causing death may be murder, manslaughter, or misadventure according to the degree of danger attending it" by common experience in the circumstances known to the actor.[19]

The law has never flinched from such judgments except when, as in the case of morals, judges seriously doubt the community's right to make moral judgments. But Harlan made it even clearer that moral relativism was the basis for the decision when he observed, and apparently thought the observation decisive: "[O]ne man's vulgarity is another's lyric."[20] If the statement that one man's moral judgment is as good as another's were taken seriously, it would be impossible to see how law on any subject could be permitted to exist. After all, one man's larceny is another's just distribution of goods.

Almost unlimited personal autonomy in these areas is defended with the shopworn slogan that the individual should be free to do as he sees fit so long as he does no harm to others. The formula is empty. The question is what the community is entitled to define as harm to others. It is difficult to know the origin of the peculiar notion that what the community thinks to be moral harm may not be legislated against. That notion has been given powerful impetus in our culture, as Gertrude Himmelfarb has shown, by John Stuart Mill's book, *On Liberty*.[21] As she demonstrates, Mill himself usually knew better than this. It is, in any event, an idea that tends to dissolve social bonds. As Lord Devlin said, "What makes a society is a community of ideas, not political ideas alone but also ideas about the way its members should behave and govern their lives."[22] A change in moral environment—in social attitudes toward sex, marriage, duties toward children, and the like—may surely be felt to be as harmful as the possibility of physical violence or the absence of proportional representation of ethnic groups in the work force. The Court has never explained, nor has anyone else, why what the community feels to be harm may not be counted as one.

These are not negligible matters. Any healthy society needs a view of itself as a political and moral community. The fact that laws about such matters are invalidated may be less important than the moral lesson taught. Traditional views of morality are under attack from many quarters. Attempts to change morality are constitutionally protected, but defiance of laws based upon morality should not be. In the arena of symbolism, which is how a culture defines itself, it hurts badly that the Justices, whom Eugene Rostow, former dean of the Yale law school, called "inevitably teachers in a vital national seminar,"[23] should teach the lesson that Americans' attempt to define their communities politically and morally through law is suspect, and probably pernicious.

It is unlikely, of course, that a general constitutional doctrine of the impermissibility of legislating moral standards will ever be framed. *Bowers* v. *Hardwick*,[24] which upheld the community's right to prohibit homosexual conduct, may be a sign that the Court is recovering its balance in these matters. I am dubious about making homosexual conduct criminal, but I favor even less imposing rules upon the American people that have no basis other than the judge's morality.

The worrisome aspect of the law just discussed, therefore, is less the particular decisions than it is the capacity of ideas, or even mere sentiments, that originate outside the Constitution to influence judges, often without their being aware of it, so that those attitudes are suddenly elevated to constitutional doctrine. Those ideas or sentiments seem to me to come from the intellectual culture associated with left-liberalism, but the phenomenon would be equally illegitimate whatever the origin or content of the ideas. Only the view that the judges are bound by the original understanding of the Constitution can prevent this osmosis of non-constitutional theories into the Constitution.

The intellectual class or, in Robert Nisbet's phrase, the clerisy of power is much more egalitarian than the American public and its elected representatives. In the past few decades, the Supreme Court has been located on this spectrum somewhere between the intellectual class and the general public. It has approved more coercion to achieve equality than the applicable law allows and has also created new rights, such as the "right of privacy," that demand moral relativism. But if the Court has done more of both than the public wants, or the law authorizes, it has not done as much of either as the intellectual class demands. It is to be hoped that the Court is on its way to neutrality in these political and cultural struggles. The philosophy of original understanding is the only approach that can produce that neutrality.

12

The Impossibility of All Theories that Depart from Original Understanding

*T*his chapter attempts to deal with revisionist constitutional theories on their own terms rather than in terms of prudence or the institutional incapacity of courts to develop and apply complex theories. The law school theorists seem to assume that the institutional incapacity of busy courts to develop complex theories is no problem since they, the professors, will work out the theories, and judges need only adopt the finished product. But the professors, too, will fail. No doubt some of what will be said here overlaps points already made, but most of it does not.

All theories of constitutional law not based on the original understanding contain inherent and fatal flaws. That is true whether the theories are liberal or conservative. All of the revisionist theories examined in the two preceding chapters must be judged to have failed, and it might be sufficient to extrapolate from a steady series of failures to a conclusion that all attempts will fail. But I mean something more than that. Just as it is possible to show that the invention of a perpetual motion machine will never occur, not because of the repeated failures to build one but because the laws of physics exclude any possibility of future success, so too can it be demonstrated that there is no possibility of a successful revisionist theory of constitutional adjudication in a constitutional republic.

Every one of the revisionist theories we have examined has involved major moral choices. At some point, every theory not based on the original understanding (and therefore involving the creation of new constitutional rights or the abandonment of specified rights), requires the judge to make a major moral decision. That is inherent in the nature of revisionism. The principles of the actual Constitution make the judge's major moral choices for him. When he goes beyond such principles, he is at once adrift on an uncertain sea of moral argument.

The revisionist theorist must demonstrate that judges have legitimate authority to impose their moral philosophy upon a citizenry that disagrees. If a warrant of that magnitude cannot be found, then, at a minimum, the judges must have a moral theory and persuade the public to accept it without simultaneously destroying the function of judicial supremacy. Moreover, the idea that the public, or even judges as a group, can be persuaded to agree on a moral philosophy necessarily rests upon a belief that not only is there a single correct moral theory but, in today's circumstances, all people of good will and moderate intelligence must accept that theory. None of these things is possible.

The first point we have already touched upon. There is no satisfactory explanation of why the judge has the authority to impose his morality upon us. Various authors have attempted to explain that but the explanations amount to little more than the assertion that judges have admirable capacities that we and our elected representatives lack. The utter dubiety of that assertion aside, the professors merely state a preference for rule by talented and benevolent autocrats over the self-government of ordinary folk. Whatever one thinks of that preference, and it seems to me morally repugnant, it is not our system of government, and those who advocate it propose a quiet revolution, made by judges.

Imagine how our polity could move from its present assumptions about democratic rule to the new form of government. The method apparently contemplated by the theorists is for judges slowly to increase the number of occasions on which they invalidate legislative decisions, always claiming that this is what the Constitution requires, until they effectively run the nation, or such aspects of policy as the professors care about. Not the least of the difficulties with that course is that it can succeed only by deception, which seems a dubious beginning for the reign of the higher morality. The other possibility, which does not require deception, is for judges to announce their decisions in opinions that state candidly: this decision bears no relation to the actual Constitution; we have invalidated your statute because of a moral choice we have made; and, for the following reasons, we are entitled to displace your moral choice with ours. The explanation of that last item is going to be a bit sticky. But that is what candor would require of a revisionist judge.

This brings us to the second difficulty with a constitutional jurisprudence based on judicial moral philosophizing. In order to gain the assent of the public, the judges' explanation of why they are entitled to displace our moral choices with theirs would require that the judges be able to articulate a system of morality upon which all persons of good will and adequate intelligence must agree. If the basic institution of our Republic, representative democracy, is to be replaced by the rule of a judicial oligarchy, then, at the very least, we must be persuaded that there is available to the oligarchy a systematic moral philosophy with which we cannot honestly disagree. But if the people can be educated to understand and accept a superior moral philosophy, there would be no need for constitutional judges since legislation would embody the principles of that morality. It may be thought that moral-constitutional judging would still be required because legislators might misunderstand the application of the philosophy to particular issues. In that case, however, there would be no reason for courts to invalidate the legislation; they need only issue an opinion explaining the matter, and the legislation will be amended to conform. The courts need use coercion only if their moral philosophy is not in fact demonstrably superior.

The supposition that we might all agree to a single moral system will at once be felt by the reader to be so unrealistic as not to be worth discussion. There is a reason for that feeling, and it brings us to the third objection to all theories that require judges to make major moral choices.

The impropriety is most apparent in those theories that simply assert what choices the judge should make, for this is obviously nothing more than a demand that the theorist's morality displace ours. But the same failure necessarily occurs in more elaborate theories that rest upon one or another of the various academic styles of moral philosophizing. (Though I think the argument that follows is correct, it is independent of the other reasons given for rejecting all nonoriginalist theories of judging.) The failure of the law school theories is, of course, merely a special instance of the general failure of moral philosophy to attain its largest objectives. I do not mean that moral philosophy is a failed or useless enterprise. I mean only that moral philosophy has never succeeded in providing an overarching system that commands general assent.

Nor do I mean that moral philosophy is alien to law and must be shunned in adjudication, but I do mean that it is valuable only at the retail level and disastrous at the wholesale. Moral reasoning can make judges aware of complexities and of the likenesses and dissimilarities of situations, all of which is essential in applying the ratifiers' principles to new situations. That is, in fact, the ordinary method of legal reasoning. Moral philosophy has a role to play in constitutional law, but the role it has to play is in assisting judges in the continuing task of deciding whether a new case is inside or outside an old principle. Thus, both moral philosophy and legal reasoning are useful only over limited ranges and must accept from outside their own disciplines the starting points for analysis. The function moral argument must not attempt is the creation of new constitutional principles.

The claim that moral philosophy cannot create primary rules, or major premises, that we will all come to accept may be supported in two ways. The first reason to doubt that moral philosophy can ever arrive at a universally accepted system is simply that it never has. Or, at least, philosophers have never agreed on one. The revisionist theorists of the law schools are merely semiskilled moral philosophers, and it seems all the more unlikely that they will succeed where for centuries philosophers of genius have failed. The state of affairs in moral theory is summed up, accurately so far as I can tell, by Alasdair MacIntyre. After canvassing the failure of a succession of thinkers to justify particular systems of morality, MacIntyre says that if all that were involved was the failure of a succession of particular arguments, "it might appear that the trouble was merely that Kierkegaard, Kant, Diderot, Hume, Smith and their other contemporaries were not adroit enough in constructing arguments, so that an appropriate strategy would be to wait until some more powerful mind applied itself to the problems. And just this has been the strategy of the academic philosophical world, even though many professional philosophers might be a little embarrassed to admit it."[1]

Though the names of the players in the legal academic world have rather less resonance than the names on McIntyre's list, the situation is the same in the world of law school moral philosophy. In fact, that is one of the most entertaining aspects of this doomed enterprise. Each of the moral-constitutional theorists finds the theories of all the others deficient—and each is correct, all the others, as well as his own, *are* deficient.

The incredible difficulty, amounting to an impossibility, of the task these theorists have set themselves seems not to occur to them. You might suppose that the mere recitation of the names of the people who have been at this work, not just for centuries but for millennia, would daunt the law professors. It does not appear to. The same bravado is observable in theorists of other branches of the law. Antitrust was for some time a body of incoherent doctrines. The situation was eventually retrieved in large measure through the application of decent economics to the rules governing competition and monopoly. But not everybody liked the new state of affairs. Articles written by lawyers claimed that microeconomic theory has little or no relation to the market reality it purports to describe and therefore should not be used in antitrust. I tried without success to persuade one or two such authors that if they were right, they had done a startling and wonderful thing. They had overthrown an intellectual discipline tracing back to Adam Smith and David Ricardo and forward to the likes of Milton Friedman and George Stigler. An intellectual upheaval of that magnitude ought not be hidden in some law review but should be published in a book directly attacking the entire body of price theory. If the attack is acknowledged a success, the author's name will live forever. We are still waiting.

So it is with the moral philosophers of constitutional law. None of them, so far as I know, proposes simply to apply Kant or Hume to create new constitutional rights. Instead, they begin again, albeit with the help of various moral philosophers, to construct the morality they would have judges use to devise new constitutional rights. It seems not to occur to most such academics that they are undertaking to succeed where the greatest minds of the centuries are commonly thought to have failed. It seems not to occur to them that they ought, if they are confident of success, to move from their law schools to the philosophy departments of their universities and work out the structure of a just society without the pretense, harmful on both sides, that what they are teaching their students is, in some real sense, law. But perhaps it would be best if they simply dropped this line of work altogether and took up one where the odds on success are better. If the greatest minds of our culture have not succeeded in devising a moral system to which all intellectually honest persons must subscribe, it seems doubtful, to say the least, that some law professor will make the breakthrough any time soon. It is my firm intention to give up reading this literature. There comes a time to stop visiting inventors' garages to see if someone really has created a perpetual motion machine.

The difficulty with the idea of perpetual motion, as I have said, is not the accumulation of disappointments in all those garages but that there was no point in going to look in the first place. There is never going to be such a machine. Similarly, the problem with overarching systems of morality is not simply that the law professors are not as bright as Kant, Hume, et al. The problem is that their enterprise is doomed to failure, no matter how intellectually adroit they are. Their quest is doomed for reasons given by MacIntyre:

> The most striking feature of contemporary moral utterance is that so much of it is used to express disagreements; and the most striking feature of the debates in which these disagreements are expressed is their interminable character. . . . [T]hey apparently can find no terminus. There seems to be no rational way of securing moral agreement in our culture.[2]

That is true, he says, because there is no longer a consensus about what man should become. Only a shared teleological view of the good for man can lead to common ground about which premises of morality are sound. Thus, MacIntyre is not claiming that moral knowledge is impossible or that there is not a correct moral view but only that, in our present circumstance, there is no possibility of agreement on the subject. In fact, our public moral debates over such matters as abortion and capital punishment have been interminable and inconclusive because we start from different premises and have no way of convincing each other as to which are the proper premises. In fact, the law professors themselves cannot agree on the premises from which they should begin to reason, and the surprising amount of agreement on outcomes is attributable to the shared liberal political culture of the universities today. They are as unlikely to convince me as I am to convince them. That is why, where the real Constitution is mute, we should vote about these matters rather than litigate them.

Without agreement on the moral final state we do not know where we should be going and hence cannot agree upon the starting place for reasoning. If we have no way of judging rival premises, we have no way of arguing to moral conclusions that should be accepted by all. "In a society where there is no longer a shared conception of the community's good as specified by the good for man, there can no longer either be any very substantial concept of what it is to contribute more or less to the achievement of that good."[3] The moral philosophers of constitutional revisionism will, for that reason, be unable to persuade all of us to accept either their premises or their conclusions. There is going to be no moral philosophy that can begin to justify courts in overriding democratic choices where the Constitution does not speak.

The judge who takes as his guide the original understanding of the principles stated in the Constitution faces none of these difficulties. His first principles are given to him by the document, and he need only reason from these to see that those principles are vindicated in the cases brought before him. Nor is it an objection that those who ratified the Constitution may have lacked a shared systematic moral philosophy. They were elected legislators and under no obligation to justify moral and political choices by a philosophy to which all must consent.

Some years ago I illustrated the difference between a judge and a legislator in a way that drew down a good deal of rhetorical abuse during the confirmation struggle. But being both stubborn and correct on this point, I shall employ the illustration once more and expand upon it. Given the fact that no provision of the Constitution spoke to the issue, my argument went, the Court could not reach its result in *Griswold*[4] in a principled fashion.* Given our lack of consensus on moral first principles, the reason is apparent. Every clash between a minority claiming freedom from regulation and a majority asserting its freedom to regulate requires a choice between the gratifications (or moral positions) of the two groups. When the Constitution has not spoken, the Court will be able to find no scale, other than its own value preferences, upon which to weigh the competing claims. Compare the facts in *Griswold* with a hypothetical suit by an electric utility company and two of its customers to void a smoke pollution ordinance as unconstitutional.

In *Griswold,* a husband and wife (it was actually a pair of doctors who gave birth control information) assert that they wish to have sexual relations without fear of unwanted children. The law prohibiting the use of contraceptives impairs their sexual gratifications. The state can assert, and at one stage in the litigation did assert, that the majority of Connecticut's citizens believes that the use of contra-

---

* The absence of any constitutional, as distinct from moral, footing for *Griswold*'s nullification of a statute prohibiting the use of contraceptives is discussed in Chapter 3.

ceptives is profoundly immoral. Knowledge that it is taking place
and that the state makes no attempt to inhibit it causes those in
the majority moral anguish and so impairs their gratifications.*

Let us turn to the challenge to the smoke pollution ordinance.
The electric utility asserts that it wishes to produce electricity at a
lower cost in order to reach a wider market and produce greater
income for its shareholders. The company is only the proxy for its
shareholders (as the doctors in *Griswold* were proxies for married
couples), who may be people in need of income for retirement, for
college tuition for their children, and for similar reasons. The two
utility customers who join in the challenge are a couple with very
little income who are having difficulty keeping their home warm
at high rates for electricity.

Neither the contraceptive nor the smoke pollution law is covered
specifically or by obvious implication by any provision of the Constitution. In *Griswold,* there is no way for a judge to say that the majority
is not entitled to its moral view; he can say only that he disagrees
with it, but his disagreement is not enough to make the law invalid.
This is Bickel's point about the man torturing puppies out of sight
of those who are morally offended by that practice.† Knowledge
that immorality is taking place can cause moral pain. The judge
has no way to choose between the married couple's gratifications
(or moral positions) and the majority's. He must, therefore, enforce
the law. Similarly, there is no principled way for a judge to prefer
the utility company's shareholders' or its two customers' gratifications
to those of the majority who prefer clean air. This law, too, must
be enforced.

We may put aside the objection, which seems to me itself dispositive, that the judge has no authority to impose upon society even a
correct moral hierarchy of gratifications. I wish to make the additional
point that, in today's situation, for the reasons given by MacIntyre,
there is no objectively "correct" hierarchy to which the judge can
appeal. But unless there is, unless we can rank forms of gratification,
the judge must let the majority have its way. There is, however,
no principled way to make the necessary distinctions. Why is sexual
gratification more worthy than moral gratification? Why is the gratifi-

---

* In order to make the point, I am overlooking the fact that the law in *Griswold*
was not enforced precisely because the majority in Connecticut did not hold the
view that contraception by married couples was immoral. If one assumes, for the
sake of the argument, that such a view was held, my conclusion follows.
† *See* p. 124, *supra.*

cation of low-cost electricity or higher income more worthy than the pleasure of clean air? Indeed, if the two somehow came into conflict, why is the sexual pleasure of a just-married couple nobler than a warm apartment to an indigent elderly couple? There is no way to decide these questions other than by reference to some system of moral or ethical principles about which people can and do disagree. Because we disagree, we put such issues to a vote and, where the Constitution does not speak, the majority morality prevails.

This line of argument, which I have made before, has led some commentators to label me a moral relativist or a radical moral skeptic. Nothing could be further from the truth. Like most people, I believe I have moral understanding and live and vote accordingly. I regard Connecticut's anticontraceptive law as wrong, would vote against it, and, when I lived in New Haven, had no idea the law even existed until it was challenged, for ideological and symbolic reasons, by professors I knew. I would probably also vote for the smoke control law, feel some sympathy for the shareholders, and vote for welfare payments to the indigent couple. Other people might make different choices, and the only way to settle the questions is by a vote, not a judge's vote but ours. This means that, where the Constitution does not apply, the judge, while in his robes, must adopt a posture of moral abstention (which is very different from personal moral relativism), but he and the rest of us need not and should not adopt such a posture when entering the voting booth. It is there that our differences about moral choices are to be decided, if not resolved, until the next election.

No matter how tirelessly and ingeniously the theorists of constitutional revisionism labor, they will never succeed in making the results of their endeavors legitimate as constitutional law.

13

In Defense of Legal Reasoning: "Good Results" vs. Legitimate Process

*T*he most common charge leveled against the idea of interpreting each provision of the Constitution according to the understanding of the generation of Americans who ratified and endorsed it is that better results can be, and have been, produced by ignoring what was intended. Often the accusation is stronger: The actual Constitution would allow *that* statute to stand, which would be intolerable.

This is the classic form of the eternal temptation: to trade the right of self-government for protection by benevolent judges. They are wiser and more humane than your fellow citizens, as shown by the fact that those citizens produced the statute which you and the judges abhor. What does legal reasoning matter if the judges know a good result when they see one?

This style of argumentation was used by almost every senator who opposed my confirmation. Senator Kennedy advanced it again and again in outraged tones. When I had criticized a judicial decision as unjustified by the Constitution he would listen to no constitutional argument but would express moral horror that anyone could say a particular law could stand. But this form of rhetoric was followed by almost all the opposition, albeit usually in less savage terms. That fact in itself is unremarkable. Many senators have no idea that constitutional law is about anything other than results they like.

What is more remarkable is that so much of the scholarly literature takes the same form. In article after article one reads arguments, offered as though they were devastating refutations, which consist of nothing more than a list of desirable decisions the principles of the historic Constitution could not have produced. The fact that this argument can be taken seriously indicates the decayed state of today's academy. It is a demonstration that law is being seduced by politics and is thereby losing its integrity as a discipline. If it continues on this course, law will cease to be what Holmes named it, the calling for thinkers, and become merely the province of emoters and sensitives.[1]

Consider the inversion of legal reasoning now in vogue. The orthodox style was to listen to a controversy between people, ascertain the facts, and then determine which side of the dispute was better supported by the relevant body of legal doctrine, whether that doctrine was expressed in judicial opinions, statutes, or the Constitution. The lawyer, judge, or professor asked what words were in the texts of these materials and what was the best interpretation of those words. The object was to frame a rule that was correct and that decided the case. A universal form of legal education and reasoning was to frame hypothetical situations to test the limits of the rule and to discover whether in such situations the rule embodied a sensible reading of the underlying text. This form of analysis makes sense only if the object is to carry the intended meaning of the legal text forward into the decision of real controversies. The rule comes out of the Constitution.

The person who judges constitutional law by results reverses this process. He asks what decision in each case is politically or morally attractive to him, devises a rule that achieves that result, and then works backward. The rule does not come out of, but is forced into, the Constitution. There is nothing that can be called legal reasoning in this. It is a process of personal choice followed by rationalization; the major and minor premises do not lead to a result, the result produces the major and minor premises. There is, furthermore, no point in testing those premises by hypotheticals to determine what results they might produce in the future, because the future results will be chosen by personal desire and the premises will be abandoned or reshaped to fit the new desired outcome.

We have seen precisely this process at work with the general right of privacy. In *Griswold*,[2] the Court wished to strike down a law forbidding the use of contraceptives and so fabricated a right of privacy whose rationale was the protection of the institution of marriage and "the sacred precincts of marital bedrooms."[3] A lawyer of the orthodox tradition, once he got past the impropriety of the creation of a new constitutional provision by judges, would begin to ask what other specific rights were necessary to protect the institution of marriage and the privacy of marital bedrooms. Did the inviolability of the marital bedroom protect the sexual abuse of women and children within its sacred precincts? Did these rationales protect all forms of sexuality within marriage, only those freely consented to, and so on? Did the protection of the institution of marriage require rights not directly related to sexuality, rights that would override laws about the rearing of children, about premarital agreements concerning property and other matters, about the custody of children and the division of property in the event of divorce, rights about the descent of property upon the death of a spouse?

The lawyer would be wasting his time. The reasoning of *Griswold* was not meant to be taken seriously by judges, only by the general public. *Eisenstadt* struck down a law regulating the retail distribution of contraceptives.[4] No invasion of the marital bedroom was even imaginable. And furthermore, the new right of privacy turned out to have nothing to do with protecting marriage, for the state was forbidden to place conditions on the sale of contraceptives to unmarried persons. The right of privacy now attached to the individual and enabled the individual to engage in a public transaction, a purchase. The result desired in *Eisenstadt* changed the rule that *Griswold* had placed in the Constitution. If the orthodox lawyer has not learned his lesson yet, he might start over to ask what was the scope of the amended right of privacy, "the right of the *individual,* married or single," to be free from a class of laws called "unwarranted governmental intrusion" and defined only by a single example, "intrusion into matters so fundamentally affecting a person as the decision whether to bear or beget a child." When *Roe*[5] was decided, we were not even told what was the rationale or the principle, simply that an operation by a physician to destroy a fetus was within the right of "privacy." *Eisenstadt* and *Roe* made it clear that the right of privacy had nothing to do with privacy. The dissent subscribed to by four Justices in *Bowers* v. *Hardwick* viewed the right as also not restricted to the decision to bear a child but, apparently, as broad enough to encompass sexual pleasure generally. *Griswold* turned out not to be about the police in the bedroom but the nose of the judicial camel in the people's tent. The premises for such decisions do not come out of the Constitution but are thrust into the Constitution and keep changing as the desired result changes.

The Court employs a sort of reverse syllogism: From the result we may infer the minor and major premises. It is hardly worth the bother of drawing the inference, however, because it is valid only for today's decision and will change with tomorrow's.

This results-first, premises-to-follow form of legal "reasoning" is to law what Robert Frost called free verse, "tennis with the net down."[6] There are no rules, only passions.

Well, why not? Aren't results more important to people than processes? Isn't the insistence upon reasoning from the actual principles of the Constitution an arid intellectualism that ignores human yearnings? An adherence to logical systems at the expense of social justice? One answer is that the result that is "good," though not justified by the Constitution, is not the result that the elected representatives of the people thought good. Thus, the ultimate answer is that legal reasoning is an intellectual enterprise essential to the preservation of freedom and democracy.

When a court strikes down a statute, it always denies the freedom of the people who voted for the representatives who enacted the law. We accept that more readily when the decision is based upon a fair reading of a constitutional provision. The Constitution, after all, was designed to remove a number of subjects from democratic control, subjects ranging from the composition of the Houses of Congress to the freedoms guaranteed by the Bill of Rights. But when the Court, without warrant in the Constitution, strikes down a democratically produced statute, that act substitutes the will of a majority of nine lawyers for the will of the people. That is what is always involved when constitutional adjudication proceeds by a concern for results rather than by concern for reasoning from original understanding. That is what is approved by law professors and politicians, two groups that are not as distinct as they once were, who assess decisions by sympathy or lack of sympathy with the results. For such people, a judicial nominee's character, professionalism, and intellectual capacity are far less important than that he follow the politically correct line.

Legal reasoning, which is rooted in a concern for legitimate process rather than preferred results, is an instrument designed to restrict judges to their proper role in a constitutional democracy. That style of analysis marks off the line between judicial power and legislative power, which is to say that it preserves the constitutional separation of powers, which is to say that it preserves both democratic freedom and individual freedom. Yet legal reasoning must begin with a body of rules or principles or major premises that are independent of the judge's preferences. That, as we have seen, is impossible under any philosophy of judging other than the view that the original understanding of the Constitution is the exclusive source for those exterior principles.

The person who understands these issues and nevertheless continues to judge constitutional philosophy by sympathy with its results must, if he is candid, also admit that he is prepared to sacrifice democracy in order that his moral views may prevail. He calls for civil disobedience by judges and claims for the Supreme Court an institutionalized role as a perpetrator of limited *coups d'état*. He believes in the triumph of the will. It is not clear why he does not advocate rioting or physical force, so long, of course, as the end is good as he sees the good. Such a man occupies an impossible philosophic position. What can he say of a Court that does not share his politics or his morality? What can an admirer of the Warren Court say if the Supreme Court should become dominated by conservative activists? What can he say of the Taney Court's *Dred Scott*[7] decision? He cannot say that the decision was the exercise of an illegitimate power because he has already conceded that power. There seems nothing he can say except that the Court is politically wrong and that he is morally justified in evading its rulings whenever he can and overthrowing it if possible in order to replace it with a body that will produce results he likes. In his view, the Court has no legitimacy as a legal institution. This being the case, the advocate of a political, value-choosing (rather than value-implementing) Court must answer another difficult question. Why should the Court, a committee of nine lawyers, be the sole agent for overriding democratic outcomes? The man who prefers results to processes has no reason to say that the Court is more legitimate than any other institution capable of wielding power. If the Court will not agree with him, why not argue his case to some other group, say the Joint Chiefs of Staff, a body with rather better means for enforcing its decisions? No answer exists.

III

THE BLOODY
CROSSROADS

On July 1, 1987, I stood beside President Ronald Reagan in the press room at the White House while he announced to the nation that he would place my name in nomination for the position of Associate Justice of the Supreme Court of the United States. The President's statement was brief:

> Well, it's with great pleasure and deep respect for his extraordinary abilities that I today announce my intention to nominate United States Court of Appeals Judge Robert H. Bork to be an Associate Justice of the Supreme Court.
>
> Judge Bork is recognized as a premier constitutional authority. His outstanding intellect and unrivaled scholarly credentials are reflected in his thoughtful examination of the broad, fundamental legal issues of our times. When confirmed by the Senate as an appellate judge in 1982, the American Bar Association gave him its highest rating: "exceptionally well qualified." On the bench, he has been well prepared, evenhanded, and openminded.
>
> In taking this action today, I'm mindful of the importance of this nomination. The Supreme Court of the United States is the custodian of our Constitution. Justices of the Supreme Court must not only be jurists of the highest competence; they must be attentive to the specific rights guaranteed in our Constitution and proper role of the courts in our democratic system.
>
> Judge Bork, widely regarded as the most prominent and

intellectually powerful advocate of judicial restraint, shares my view that judges' personal preferences and values should not be part of their constitutional interpretations. The guiding principle of judicial restraint recognizes that under the Constitution it is the exclusive province of the legislatures to enact laws and the role of the courts to interpret them.

We're fortunate to be able to draw upon such an impressive legal mind, an experienced judge and a man who already has devoted so much of his life to public service. He'll bring credit to the Court and his colleagues, as well as to his country and the Constitution.[1]

If the President overstated my judicial virtues, we did not have to wait long for an overstatement in the other direction. We left, and I went to Chief of Staff Howard Baker's office to make telephone calls to Senate leaders and to Justice Lewis Powell, who had just announced his departure from the Court and to whose seat I had been nominated. A television set was on in the office, and within forty-five minutes we watched Senator Edward Kennedy deliver a nationally televised speech from the floor of the Senate.

Robert Bork's America is a land in which women would be forced into back-alley abortions, blacks would sit at segregated lunch counters, rogue police could break down citizens' doors in midnight raids, schoolchildren could not be taught about evolution, writers and artists would be censored at the whim or [sic] government, and the doors of the Federal courts would be shut on the fingers of millions of citizens for whom the judiciary is often the only protector of the individual rights that are the heart of our democracy.[2]

We were incredulous. Not one line of that tirade was true. It had simply never occurred to me that anybody could misrepresent my career and views as Kennedy did. Nor did it occur to me that anybody would believe such charges. The conventional wisdom in Washington then and for some time afterward was that Kennedy had made a serious tactical blunder. His statement was so outrageous that everyone said it helped rather than hurt me. I should have known better. This was a calculated personal assault by a shrewd politician, an assault more violent than any against a judicial nominee in our country's history. As it turned out, Kennedy set the themes and the tone for the entire campaign.

Lionel Trilling once wrote of the bloody crossroads where politics and literature meet.[3] There is, as I was soon to learn, an even bloodier crossroads where politics and law meet. The next three chapters are about my experience there. It is important to describe the way the campaign against me was conducted and the seemingly ceaseless torrent of falsehoods about my views and record. It is important not for my own vindication (I have discovered that millions of Americans understand that they were lied to) but because of what the story tells about the people and groups who resorted to such tactics, of what it says about the desperation of the American left not only to continue to influence the direction of the courts but to prevent the articulation from our highest bench of the ideas I have articulated in the past and have explained once more in this book. The story, that is, illuminates not only the character of the left but the kind of constitutional rewriting they want judges to do. In that regard, the story lays bare the authoritarian character of that movement. There are few things more important for the American people to understand.

14

The Nomination and the Campaign

*M*y nomination was, as I have said, merely one battleground in a long-running war for control of our legal culture, which, in turn, was part of a larger war for control of our general culture. To describe the battle, however objectively, necessarily involves recounting personal experiences and reliving emotions. This is not an autobiography, but it may help to place the entire episode in at least the framework of a personal context.

Like many young people, I was drawn to the law because it seemed a calling in which one could remain intellectually active for a full lifetime. A professor of humanities who had studied law, Henry Rago, told me that law was philosophy carried into the market-place. Holmes and Brandeis offered models for what I and others thought a life in the law could be. The choice was between law and journalism, but, for reasons not relevant here, I chose to attend the law school of the University of Chicago. In June of 1952, upon returning from active duty in the Marine Corps and before the third year of law school, I married a college student, Claire Davidson. It was a very happy marriage, as I knew and as Claire told me when twenty-eight and one-half years later she knew that her death was imminent. A year working at the school on antitrust theory and then eight years in private practice, seven of them as associate and then partner with the Chicago firm of Kirkland & Ellis, followed graduation. During this time Claire and I had three children. Robert, Jr., was born on June 24, 1955; Charles on October 12, 1958; and Ellen on April 3, 1961. To practice with the Kirkland firm was to experience the practical aspect of the profession at its best. I made, and retain, some of my best friends in those years. After a time, however, the cases at the firm began to look alike, and I decided I wanted a rather broader intellectual life in the law. Yale law school offered me an associate professorship in 1962 and made me a professor in 1965. That was a period of great intellectual stimulation, and my time was divided between a full and happy family life and a busy schedule of teaching and writing, first in the field of antitrust and then in constitutional law. After his reelection in 1972, President Nixon offered me the post of Solicitor General of the United States, and the family moved to Washington in the spring of 1973. Most people are not very sure about what the Solicitor General does. Located in the Department of Justice, the Solicitor General is the chief legal officer of the United States. His duties include representing the United States before the Supreme Court.

My term in the office included some duties not listed in that job description, among them writing the briefs against Vice President Spiro Agnew, which Attorney General Elliot Richardson was kind enough to say may well have had the effect of persuading Agnew to plea bargain and leave the vice presidency rather than litigate further, and the firing of Special Prosecutor Archibald Cox in what was known as the Saturday Night Massacre. These are stories that may be left for another time. Because of what I regarded then and regard now as the peculiar taste in presidents the American people displayed in 1976, I left the job on January 20, 1977, and that summer the family moved back to New Haven. (The American people later came to agree about their choice and repaired matters in 1980). Claire had contracted cancer in 1971. By this time she was growing quite weak, and I spent all of my time, when not teaching, at home. After a struggle of nine and one-half years, she died in December 1980. The doctors were amazed that she had lived so long, and I am convinced that only her determination to see our children safely into adulthood kept her alive. Though I had known it was inevitable from the beginning, her death was devastating to me. I could not stay at Yale. The children were gone from home; my best friend, Alex Bickel, who made academic life a joy for me, had himself died of cancer in 1974. New Haven had too many shadows. I left and joined the Washington office of Kirkland & Ellis in the summer of 1981.

Very soon, however, the Administration approached me about accepting a judgeship on the United States Court of Appeals for the District of Columbia Circuit. The D.C. Circuit is not the local court of appeals for the District of Columbia. Most of the courts of appeals are numbered, the Second Circuit, for example, sits in New York City and hears appeals from the district courts, which are trial courts, located in the states of New York, Connecticut, and Vermont. The D.C. Circuit hears appeals from the district court located in the District of Columbia but also has a heavy workload reviewing the decisions of federal agencies, and the agency cases may arise from disputes anywhere in the United States. Since I had just rejoined Kirkland & Ellis after an interlude of nineteen years, I said no to the judgeship to the first two officials who approached me. But while I was back in New Haven to oversee the last of the moving, I received a lengthy telephone call from a very insistent Deputy Attorney General Edward Schmults and then a call from Attorney General William French Smith. My children finally decided the issue; they were unanimously in favor of my becoming a judge. I accepted and was sworn in on February 12, 1982. One of the judges asked why I had decided to leave practice for the bench. I told him that having just lost two cases, I decided I was losing my fastball and had better take up umpiring.

The years on the D.C. Circuit constitute a story worth telling, but not in this book. I was the first Reagan appointee on a very liberal court. There were then, I think, ten judges on the full court, and we sat in panels of three to hear appeals, except when a panel decision seemed both wrong enough and important enough to convene the entire court for an en banc rehearing. Relationships were quite cordial but gradually became less so as other Reagan appointees followed and achieved a majority on the full court. President Reagan has been accused of appointing judges with a political agenda, but that was most certainly not the case. He was committed to the idea that judges should not make up law but should interpret law. William French Smith barely knew me and had no idea of my personal views on most of the divisive issues of the time, but he knew that my idea of judging corresponded to his and Reagan's.

In June 1982 I had my great piece of good luck, the first, it seemed to me, in a long time. A Washington "think tank" called the Ethics and Public Policy Center had asked me to speak at one of its evening events twice before, and I had begged off. The third time I accepted. One member of the staff attended each event, and this time it was Mary Ellen Pohl's turn. She was working on Catholic studies at the Center and, until a year or so before, had been for fifteen years a nun in the Order of the Sacred Heart. We were married on October 30 in St. Matthew's Cathedral. Had I accepted either of the previous invitations to speak, we would never have met. This, too, has been an extremely happy marriage.

By the spring of 1987, I had developed serious doubts about remaining on the court of appeals for the remainder of my career. There were some very interesting cases with considerable legal significance, but a great part of our docket consisted of regulatory agency cases, many of which contained no significant legal issues to be explored and explicated. Though these cases were factually complex, in the end they often involved little more than examining the prudential judgment of one agency or another to make sure that it was not arbitrary. I liked judging very much—the oral arguments in the courtroom, particularly on days when both the lawyers and the judges were in good form, the discussions with my fellow judges, and working on opinions with my clerks. But I wanted engagement with larger ideas than the run of cases then brought before us. Mary Ellen and I discussed the matter with increasing frequency, and I finally chose a course that would leave my options open into 1988. Each judge has three clerks and usually hires them in the spring of the year, not for the coming fall term but for the one after that, about fifteen to eighteen months in advance. I decided not to hire clerks in the spring of 1987 since that would commit me to stay for the year they served, to the summer of 1990. I was confident that, if the decision was to continue as a judge, I could hire good clerks, perhaps from new recruits at law firms, in the spring of 1988. As it turned out, events made the decision for me.

At 10:00 A.M. on Friday, June 26, 1987, Associate Justice Lewis Powell held a press conference to announce his resignation as an Associate Justice of the Supreme Court of the United States. Powell, a courtly, soft-spoken man, had a distinguished career on the Court. As Solicitor General of the United States I had of course often argued before the Court. Powell's questions were invariably to the point, courteously put, but not so frequent as to prevent counsel from developing his argument in his own way.

The question I appreciated most came at the end of my argument for the constitutionality of the death penalty. A majority of the Court a few years back had held that capital punishment had become "cruel and unusual" and hence forbidden by the eighth amendment. When the issue came back in five challenges to new state death penalty statutes, I brought the federal government into the case as amicus curiae, or friend of the Court, to support the constitutionality of the laws. I asked for forty-five minutes, an unusually long period for one lawyer, particularly counsel for an amicus curiae, but the Court granted the time. Since the five state attorneys general stressed the horrors of the crimes involved, I argued the constitutional issues. No matter how much time he is given, counsel would always like more, but the Chief Justice will not grant an extra minute unless the lawyer is responding to a question from the bench. (There is a legend that Chief Justice Charles Evans Hughes once cut a lawyer off in the middle of the word "if.") My time expired and I was turning from the lectern when Justice Powell said he would like to ask me a question. Controlling his emotion over the incidence of murder with some difficulty, he recited the number of killings annually in America and then asked me to comment. It was a deliberately given license to make any additional points I wished in the form of a comment on his statement. I have never heard a question from the bench I liked better.

When Powell resigned in 1987, I had no particular expectation of being nominated. Not long after the resignation, four other judges met in my chambers to draft a joint dissent from our court's majority decision not to rehear four cases en banc. One of the judges asked if I thought I would be nominated, and I said there was now a well-entrenched tradition of passing me by and I thought not. When, at the time of my appointment as Solicitor General in 1973, I was first mentioned in the press, it seemed an unimaginably grand prospect. By the time I left that post almost four years later, familiarity with the Court's work had considerably reduced the glamour of the possibility. I had come to think of a seat on the Court as a position from which one could demonstrate the proper method of judging and articulate its principles in opinions that would have to be studied by the profession and, in particular, by law students. When Powell's announcement came, it seemed to me likely that the nomination would once more go elsewhere, but that thought did not disturb me.

I have since learned that the Department of Justice was actively working for my nomination, and, in the White House, Ken Cribb, the Assistant to the President for Domestic Affairs, was vigorous on my behalf. But at the time, I knew nothing of this.

The first inkling of any serious possibility came in a telephone call from the Counsel to the President, A. B. Culvahouse, on June 30, asking me to meet with him at 6:00 A.M. the next day. He wanted a place where we would not be observed by the press, and the "safe house" he chose was 716 Jackson Place, a row house facing Lafayette Square, which is across Pennsylvania Avenue from the White House. Former presidents often stay at 716 when visiting Washington. The next morning a young lawyer on Culvahouse's staff answered my knock, took me to a third-floor sitting room, and went into the kitchen to make coffee. Soon Culvahouse arrived, the aide left, and the two of us, now alone in the house, began an interview at the table in the third-floor dining room. Culvahouse, a capable and congenial young man, said that others were also being interviewed and that his purpose was to bring up to date the information developed by the Federal Bureau of Investigation when I had been nominated to the Court of Appeals. He had perhaps twenty questions that primarily concerned personal morality, questions about money, drugs, sex, wife or child abuse, and the like. It seemed somehow characteristic of Washington that many of these transgressions had gained proper names, as in, "Do you have the [name of a prominent person] problem?" After a number of questions, I said, "Look, I have led a very dull life." Culvahouse said, "Good. That's the way we like it." It must have been around 8:00 A.M. when I went to my chambers in the federal courthouse.

Sometime before noon, Howard Baker, Ronald Reagan's chief of staff, telephoned to say that the President would like to meet with me that afternoon to discuss nominating me to the Supreme Court. If he decided to go ahead, the announcement would be made right after the meeting. Once more, the object was to keep the press in the dark. The strategy chosen this time, however, left not only a good deal but almost everything to be desired. As arranged, about 1:30 P.M. my secretary, Mrs. Judy Carper, drove me to a street corner a few blocks from the courthouse in an area where nobody was likely to know me. I waited there for several minutes because John Tuck, an aide to Howard Baker, had gotten stuck in traffic. He finally picked me up in his own station wagon, which unfortunately, on that hot and humid Washington day, lacked any air conditioning. Tuck drove a roundabout route and came up Seventeenth Street to enter the gate to the Old Executive Office Building. He drove through the courtyard and into West Executive Avenue, a short street, guarded at both ends, that runs between the OEOB and the White House. Its disadvantage for security purposes is that reporters standing at the gates at both ends can easily see who gets in and out of cars. So, after our elaborate maneuvering, the press knew what was about to happen before we even got into the White House. Matters would have been no less secret, and I would have been a good deal more comfortable, if I had taken a taxi to the front door.

Upstairs, in Baker's office, I met him and several others of the White House staff. After a brief discussion we went to the Oval Office to meet the President. We had talked only once before, after his election in 1980 but before his inauguration, at a dinner party given by George and Madeleine Will. Now Reagan went to the point. He said he proposed to nominate me to fill Powell's seat and asked how I felt about that. I said I had been thinking about the idea for the past five or ten minutes and had decided I liked the idea. Reagan asked, "Does that mean 'yes'?" I said it did. There was much picture-taking by the official photographer as the President and I sat close together in wing chairs, trying, somewhat stiltedly, to make conversation. Then we and the others went to the press room, which was packed with reporters and television cameras. The President announced his intention to nominate me, and we left without taking questions.

Shortly afterward, I made telephone calls from Howard Baker's office to leading members of the Senate and others, including one to Lewis Powell. He said he was happy about the nomination and wished me well. I told him I would rather join him on the bench than replace him on it, to which he replied that he would be keeping chambers at the Court, as retired Justices do, and we would see a good deal of each other.

Next, there was a brief strategy session with members of the President's staff. It was stressed that my nomination was to be a White House rather than a Department of Justice operation. The Department of Justice had become quite unpopular with Democrats who controlled the Senate, a fact that was to prove a considerable handicap in the coming weeks. I returned to my chambers in the courthouse.

That evening, my children, Robert, Charles, and Ellen, were with Mary Ellen and me at home. Some neighbors and other friends dropped in to offer congratulations. I was pleased to have been nominated, of course, but also in a curiously subdued mood that I could not quite shake or explain, even to myself. The only explanation for this slightly somber mood I can think of was that the Court would be the last stage of my career. That may sound odd, even ungrateful, but I do not mean it that way. My professional life had involved just about every major facet of the law, from the intensely practical to the intensely intellectual, and I had enjoyed all of it, and not least the variety. An appointment to the Supreme Court would be a culmination, but it would also be an end, the beginning of the last stage. Perhaps it was the intimation of mortality implicit in that thought that subdued my spirits a bit.

It was also a night when we thought of Claire, who had been with us through so much and who was not here to share this. Mary Ellen, sensing what was on my daughter Ellen's mind, said to her, "Your mother knows about this," and Ellen replied, "Yes, I think she does, too." It was good to think that, and I was grateful to Mary Ellen for having said it.

Though we did not know it that night, we were two and one-half months from the hearing before the Senate Judiciary Committee. Since a delay of that length was virtually unprecedented, we had no reason to anticipate that the Democratic leaders in the Senate would insist upon it. The days that followed were enormously busy. The Department of Justice produced a series of huge briefing books so that I could review every aspect of my career: briefs filed in private practice, briefs filed and arguments made as Solicitor General, my role in the indictment of Vice President Agnew and then in the discharge of Archibald Cox as Special Prosecutor, my writings as a law professor, and my decisions and opinions as a judge. I had to arrange for witnesses to testify on my behalf. There was then, and may still be, a quaint White House institution with the reassuring name of "the murder board." The nominee sits at a table with perhaps a dozen or more members of the Administration and friendly lawyers from the outside and is subjected to savage questioning. The idea is to prepare him for the hearings to come, rather in the manner that a trainer repeatedly throws a medicine ball at a boxer's solar plexus. The questions are oversimplifications and put the nominee in the worst light, but, at that, "the murder board" fell well short of the distortions of the actual hearing. More of these sessions were planned, but I found the experience not terribly useful, since I was not concerned about withstanding brutality, and called the rest off. Instead, I had several sessions with lawyers from the White House and the Department of Justice, law school professors, and private practitioners, at which we discussed substantive legal issues.

It was important to discuss substantive issues, because I, unlike other nominees to the Court, would have to discuss them with senators during calls at their offices and with the Senate Judiciary Committee at the hearings. Most nominees are able to respond to substantive questions by saying something like "I cannot discuss legal issues because such matters might come before me as a judge." I could not take that line, because I had already discussed a great many such issues in print. Some people have said that I, too, should have declined to engage in discussion of legal issues, but that would have been disastrous or, perhaps I should say, even more disastrous than discussing them. It was apparent from Senator Kennedy's speech after the nomination, and from the public campaign that was already under way, that positions I had taken in the past would continue to be radically misrepresented. If I did not explain at the hearings, those misrepresentations would stand unanswered. A nominee who has not written on the relevant subjects can decline discussion. I could not.

During this period, as well as after the hearings, the public interest generated by the enormous campaign against me caused dozens of reporters to seek interviews, and television and radio talk programs repeatedly asked me to appear. Despite the unanswered hostile campaign, I decided that it was improper for a judicial nominee to wage a counter campaign by discussing his views on substantive issues anywhere but before the Senate, even if that meant letting slanders go unanswered. For that reason, I made it a rule of interviews by print reporters that I would not discuss issues, and I declined to appear at all on television or radio. Toward the end, when it was apparent that the nomination was in very serious trouble, a group of White House strategists proposed that Mary Ellen and I appear on Barbara Walters' television show. They were so insistent and unanimous in their opinion that we agreed to think about it overnight. But that night we decided we would rather go down than compromise ourselves with what would be, in effect, a personal media appeal. There were advisers who thought refusing to appear on various television shows was a serious mistake, including some who thought it cost me confirmation. However that may be, I continue to think that was the right decision. The entire process of a judicial confirmation was politicized more than ever before in America's history, but at least I did not contribute to that.

A great many people helped me during those months. Lloyd Cutler, a prominent liberal lawyer and President Carter's legal counsel, met with me shortly after the nomination and said, "You seem to frighten a lot of people, but I have read everything you've written and you don't frighten me." Cutler gave a great deal of wise counsel and supported my nomination in public on numerous occasions.

For that, he was widely criticized by his liberal allies, but he was unflinching and I admire his integrity.

A. Raymond Randolph, a younger lawyer and a top-flight advocate who had been one of my deputies in the Solicitor General's Office, gave advice, organized support, and spoke out. Leonard Garment, another prominent Washington attorney, tirelessly lobbied and organized the writing of position papers by lawyers in New York law firms. Carla Hills, now the Special Trade Representative in the Bush cabinet but then in private practice, organized prominent academics and others to write papers analyzing positions I had taken on a wide variety of topics to show that there was nothing extreme about them. Wm. Bradford Reynolds, the Assistant Attorney General for Civil Rights, and Mike Carvin, from the Office of Legal Counsel in the Department of Justice, not only advised me but worked day and night compiling information and responses to accusations made by various senators and liberal activists. My former clerks—Peter Keisler, who was then in the White House Counsel's Office; John Manning, Brad Clark, and Dan Troy of the Department of Justice; Steve Gilles, who came in from his Chicago law firm; Doug Mayer, who worked in the Washington office of the same firm; and Rebecca Swenson who was working in the Washington office of another firm—all labored mightily. My current clerks, Meg Tahyar, Clark Remington, and Andrew McBride, having no cases to work on since I gave up sitting during this period, also did enormous amounts of work. Dozens of other people were involved either full or part time, and I apologize to those I have not mentioned.

Tom Korologos, a well-known Washington lobbyist, was brought in by the White House to advise me and to supervise efforts to persuade individual senators. I had known Korologos when I was Solicitor General, and he was the Nixon White House's liaison to the Senate. He was a great support.

Those days of July, August, and the first two weeks of September proved enormously wearing. Not only was there the constant work of preparation and consultation but there were a great many courtesy calls on senators in their offices on Capitol Hill. One, which was obligatory on both sides, was a visit with Senator Kennedy. I went in with one or two persons from the White House assigned to accompany nominees. Kennedy had one or two aides with him in a small room. I was in a fairly cheerful mood but Kennedy seemed mildly depressed and was mostly silent. Others tried, without great success, to keep a conversation afloat. Every so often, Kennedy looked up at me—about three or four times, I suppose—and said, "Nothing personal."

Each courtesy call was different, and most were interesting. Senator Robert Packwood of Oregon told me he had no problems with any of the rest of my record but if there was the slightest chance I might vote to overturn *Roe* v. *Wade,* he would vote against my confirmation. He made it abundantly clear that that was the only issue. That seemed a trifle peculiar, because in his recent reelection campaign Packwood had been opposed by anti-abortion groups and he repeatedly said that a man should not be judged on a single issue but on his entire record. John Chafee of Rhode Island, like Packwood a Republican, also said that preserving *Roe* v. *Wade* was the overriding issue for him. Later, three Democratic senators, Bennett Johnston of Louisiana, Harry Reid of Nevada, and Dennis DeConcini of Arizona, in the course of explaining their intentions to vote against me, said I might *not* vote to overturn *Roe.*

Senator Jack Danforth of Missouri, who had been a student in the first class I taught at Yale, said he intended to support me and asked that at my hearing I make my position on the proper role of the judiciary entirely clear. He said he had seen too many nominees for various positions back away from their writings at hearings, and he thought it important that the American people understand that the issue was American self-government. I assured him that I would not begin endorsing the judicial creation of the Constitution.

During all of this time there was the incessant barrage of negative advertising, media coverage, a daily flood of mail, and constant telephone calls. The media varied, of course, but the reporting in the *New York Times,* the *Washington Post,* and the three network news programs was almost unrelievedly hostile, as, of course, were the advertisements. The campaign was having its effect. The Center for Media and Public Affairs coded 232 TV news and *Washington Post* stories and found that of 381 judgments by sources 63 percent were negative and 37 percent positive, and that proportion was almost identical at each of the networks and the *Post.* Sources discussing my ideas ran four to one negative at the *Post* and six to one at the networks, with CBS well out in front, at eight to one. Throughout July, August, and September, TV news carried eighty-six persons critical of my views and only sixteen who were favorable. After the hearings closed, TV carried twenty-nine critical statements and not one favorable statement.

It was not that so few defenders, or none, were available. Newspapers and television decide whom to ask and whose opinions to carry. According to a journalist, when a reporter wants to express his opinion in a news story, he goes to a source who agrees with him for a statement.[1] In that way, a pretense of objectivity is maintained. The Center also analyzed the tag lines of the television network news stories, because bias is usually manifested there. It reported that my nomination held the record for bias among all issues whose reporting the Center had monitored: 100 percent negative on all three networks. I later heard that polls were much more favorable to me among people who had watched the entire hearings than among those who saw only the nightly news.

We take three newspapers in the morning, and I became so sick of the coverage that I asked Mary Ellen not to hand me anything but the sports pages. Nor did I watch television news. The mail and the telephone callers, on the other hand, were almost unanimously friendly and supportive. There were so many letters that there was no possibility of answering the people who wrote, and we finally left the answering machine on day and night to avoid being on the telephone all of the time. We finally decided to go away for two weeks, but it was not much of a vacation since I spent the time with the briefing books and on the telephone. All in all, it was a relief when the date for the hearings drew close and the waiting was over.

What I did not know on July 1 was that activist groups of the left had begun preparing an all-out campaign against my confirmation well before President Reagan announced his nomination. Kennedy's speech that day was merely the opening salvo. Kennedy later told the *Boston Globe* that "The statement had to be stark and direct so as to sound the alarm and hold people in their places until we could get material together."[2] The people he wanted to hold in their places were senators who might commit themselves to vote for confirmation before the negative campaign could get rolling.

The campaign against the nomination was so enormous, varied, and widespread that this account can only provide an impression by discussing some of its main features. I shall not attempt to respond to the drumbeat of accusations here, because that went on through the hearings and after. The facts of the matters discussed are set out in Chapter 16. At this point, it is enough to say that every charge recounted was false.

Kennedy's first goal, according to his own account, was to gain time to organize. He met with three other extremely liberal Democratic senators: Joe Biden, the Chairman of the Judiciary Committee, Howard Metzenbaum, and Alan Cranston. They decided to postpone the committee's confirmation hearings until September 15, so that a total of seventy-seven days would pass between the President's announcement and the hearings, although the past average, I am told, had been fourteen days. Kennedy hired Anthony Podesta, the founding president of People for the American Way, whom the *Globe* identifies as a liberal lobbyist, to work on organizing opposition.

At this point Kennedy launched his Southern strategy to turn the votes of the crucial Southern Democratic senators. Since the Democrats had gained control of the Senate in 1986, the Republicans had to pick up some of these Democratic votes in order to win. Kennedy telephoned Democratic politicians around the South and concentrated on black ministers as well. According to the *Globe,* "Kennedy woke up Rev. Joseph Lowery at the Hyatt Hotel in New Orleans before the Southern Christian Leadership Conference's annual convention." As a result, "Lowery turned the entire day's meeting into an anti-Bork strategy session. From that meeting, the issue made its way into black churches throughout America."[3] One of Kennedy's aides is quoted as saying, "It has a special effect when Kennedy calls."[4]

He also called each of the thirty executive members of the AFL-CIO and held a conference call with forty state labor leaders to organize their opposition. He knew them well, because he is chairman of the Senate Labor Committee. Kennedy's other calls were to prominent liberal lawyers and law school professors. He created an enormous apparatus to fight the nomination.

But Kennedy was certainly not alone. A huge coalition of left activist groups, while of course cooperating with Kennedy and other ultraliberal senators, had been preparing and coordinating their efforts. The *New York Times* reported on July 9 that "civil rights activists had been keeping files on Judge Bork in anticipation of this moment."[5] The day before the nomination forty-five such organizations were represented at a strategy session held at the Washington office of the Leadership Conference on Civil Rights. The Conference's nomination statement referred to me as an "ultra conservative" whose confirmation would "jeopardize the civil rights achievements of the past three decades."[6]

The activist groups followed the same shock strategy that Kennedy did, and it was an unqualified success. The White House, unprepared for a campaign of this scope and ferocity, did little in the public arena, but the groups sent out wholly misleading information and lobbied the press as assiduously as they did undecided senators. The *New York Times* front page "news analysis" of July 2 sounded like the Leadership Conference's statement:

> Judge Bork's record suggests he would move the law of the land sharply to the right on issues like the death penalty, homosexual rights, government aid to religious schools, sexual harassment of women, access to the courts, Presidential power, the constitutionality of the special prosecutor law, antitrust and, perhaps, affirmative action.[7]

This was a peculiar analysis since the Court held positions very much like mine on most of those issues, and I could hardly change "the law of the land" on the others unless at least four Justices agreed with me.

The groups were also putting pressure on senators who might be undecided. Senator Biden told the *Philadelphia Inquirer* in November 1986, "Say the administration sends up Bork and after our investigation he looks a lot like another Scalia, I'd have to vote for him and if the groups tear me apart, that's the medicine I'll have to take, I'm not Teddy Kennedy."[8] My record was in fact almost identical to Scalia's. We voted the same way on the Court of Appeals 98 percent of the time, and on the one major case where we differed we did so because I favored a first amendment defense in a libel action. But seven days after my nomination, Biden was visited by representatives of the Leadership Conference on Civil Rights, the Alliance for Justice, the Women's Legal Defense Fund, and the National Association for the Advancement of Colored People Legal Defense and Education Fund, and he at once stated that he would oppose the nomination and would lead the fight in the Senate.[9]

At the NAACP convention in New York on July 6, opposition to the nomination became a litmus test for political support of candidates. Both former Governor Bruce Babbitt and Representative Richard Gephardt proclaimed their opposition. When Senator Daniel Moynihan told the convention he would reserve judgment until after the hearings, the reaction was swift. Hazel N. Dukes, an NAACP official, told the press, "I have the votes in New York to defeat him, when I get with his staff . . . I'll get what I want. It's strictly politics."[10]

The National Abortion Rights Action League held its annual convention in Washington on the weekend of July 11 and mapped a national campaign against confirmation.[11] Senator Howard Metzenbaum spoke as delegates wearing "Borkbusters" buttons chanted their opposition. The League's Washington lobbyist said it had drawn up a list of "target" senators, which included Howell Heflin, Dennis DeConcini, Robert Packwood, Daniel Evans, Lowell P. Weicker, Jr., and Arlen Specter. The League's executive director told the *New York Times* that the group planned "a series of demonstrations and letter-writing and telephone campaigns during the August congressional recess in the home states of senators seen as important to the effort."[12] The director of the New York affiliate said that the group had already begun a coordinated telephone and mailing campaign with a computerized system under which members had authorized the organization to send telegrams in their names without prior consultation.

People for the American Way mailed memoranda to editorial writers at nearly 1,700 newspapers.[13] PAW also began to run a series of radio ads in Washington and print ads in the major newspapers across the country. These struck the themes that were pounded into the hearings and beyond. "The Senate should learn why Mr. Bork criticized a congressional ban on literacy tests used to prevent minorities from voting."[14] The ad stated that I had "written in favor of a Virginia poll tax, against equal accommodations for black Americans, and against the principle of one man–one vote."[15] None of these charges was true (see pp. 324–326, *infra*). It then hit what was to become the centerpiece of the campaign: "The Senate must know whether Mr. Bork will try to roll back the clock on the civil rights gains of the last three decades."[16] The ad discussed "privacy" and stated that I said "the state could prevent married couples from using contraceptives at home."[17] My criticism of the *Griswold* case (see Chapter 3, where I have criticized it again) inspired that remark.

By the end of July, with more than six weeks to go to the first day of the delayed hearings, the group strategy could claim important successes. It had succeeded in creating the "sense of urgency" one spokesman said it needed, and it had spread the idea that the Senate should examine a nominee's positions on a wide range of constitutional issues. More importantly, it had repeatedly defined "judicial philosophy" not as the nominee's approach to constitutional interpretation and his conception of the role proper to judges but as simply a checklist of results that were to be assessed for political popularity. There was little or no response to this campaign. As the *Washington Post* reported later, "The hot, steamy days of July and August were filled with frantic activity—but only on the part of Bork's opponents."[18]

Kennedy's efforts with the AFL-CIO bore fruit in August when that organization put out a press release stating that I was:

> a man moved not by deference to the democratic process but by an overriding commitment to the interests of the wealthy and powerful in our society. He has never shown the least concern for working people, minorities, the poor or for individuals seeking the protection of the law to vindicate their political and civil rights.[19]

My public record (see Chapter 16) demonstrates that there was not a word of truth in this litany. The AFL-CIO pledged an undisclosed amount of money to oppose me. The week before, the American Federation of State, County and Municipal Employees (AFSCME) had contributed $40,000 to that effort, a contribution that was to be important.

The groups of the left waged a massive mail fundraising and "educational" drive. People for the American Way alone sent out 4.34 million anti-confirmation letters,[20] complete with opposition literature and preaddressed coupons to mail to senators. The letter stated that "the nomination of Judge Robert Bork . . . is one of the greatest threats to civil rights and civil liberties in three decades."[21] Of my philosophy of following the principles laid down by the ratifiers of the Constitution, readers were informed that " 'original intent' is the ideological code word . . . to justify *reversing* 30 years of Supreme Court law in the areas of search and seizure, civil rights and church and state."[22] PAW stated that it needed $1 million for its campaign. $450,000 was to go for newspaper and broadcast activities, $200,000 for legal costs and direct lobbying, and $350,000 for "the mail and telephone campaign that will mobilize America."[23]

In September the executive director of PAW said that it had wanted to raise $1 million but that it now looked more like $2 million. A direct mail consultant for five groups said that groups opposed to me had probably raised $6 million and might well collect $12 million before the fight was over.[24] It has been estimated that between $10 and $15 million was spent in the publicity campaigns against me. But perhaps the most shrewdly spent funds were the $40,000 donated by AFSCME. That contribution was used by others to finance a poll of 1,008 people, conducted from August

13 to August 17, to discover what issues troubled Americans most.[25] This was used to frame the issues to be used against me, and made particular reference to the South. The memo prepared argued that the public campaign and the hearings themselves should be built around three central themes:

> Bork poses the risk of reopening race relations battles which have been fought and put to rest. Bork flouts the southern tradition of populism. And (perhaps most surprising to some) Bork poses a challenge to a very strong pro-privacy sentiment among southern voters.[26]

These were indeed the themes stressed.

The first theme mentioned—that I would reopen all the old civil rights battles—was stressed again and again and yet again. The *Biden Report,* issued on September 2, stated that "Judge Bork's extensive record shows that he has opposed virtually every major civil rights advance on which he has taken a position. . . ."[27] The *Report* also converted my remarks some sixteen years earlier about advocacy of law violation into opposition to civil rights.

> The thrust of Judge Bork's theory is plainly directed at civil disobedience. Had his theory been the governing rule in the 1960s, the right of Martin Luther King, Jr. to advocate sit-ins at lunch counters segregated by law would have been left to the discretion of each legislature or town council. The same would have been true of advocacy of boycotts, marches, sermons and peaceful demonstrations—the tools that made possible the peaceful and lawful transformation in the South.[28]

Here, as elsewhere, the *Biden Report* so thoroughly misrepresented a plain record that it easily qualifies as world class in the category of scurrility.

The level of hysteria attained is shown by the Western Union priority letter sent on August 31 by the director of the American Civil Liberties Union. It contained statements in full capitals such as: "DETAILED RESEARCH REVEALS BORK FAR MORE DANGEROUS THAN PREVIOUSLY BELIEVED . . . WE RISK NOTHING SHORT OF WRECKING THE ENTIRE BILL OF RIGHTS . . . HIS CONFIRMATION WOULD THREATEN OUR SYSTEM OF GOVERNMENT. . . . TIME IS SHORT. . . . URGE YOU TO RUSH EMERGENCY CON-

TRIBUTION AT ONCE."[29] It is, in a perverse way, flattering to be regarded as so powerful as to be able to override eight other Justices and single-handedly wreck the entire Bill of Rights as well as the system of government. I assume the contributions were forthcoming.

People for the American Way, an organization founded and apparently guided by Norman Lear, was particularly energetic. To give merely one example of its work, for three weeks, prior to and during my testimony before the Senate Judiciary Committee, PAW ran sixty-second television spots featuring the easily recognizable voice of Gregory Peck.[30] Senator Biden later told the Senate that the ad ran eighty-six times and also received extensive media coverage of its own, coverage which, of course, repeated the charges made.[31] Peck, in a deep, sonorous voice, informed Americans that I "defended poll taxes and literacy tests, which kept many Americans from voting."[32] The implication was as clear as it was false: I favored keeping blacks away from the polls.

In any event, the effort to frighten black voters succeeded. They heard only one side of the story, and that from leaders they respected. As a leader in one of the groups told the *New York Times,* with some pride, "Black voters got the message quickly and acted on it."[33] As the same story in the *Times* put it, "a powerful lever was pulled when Judge Bork's opponents campaigned on the charge that he would 'turn back the clock' on civil rights."[34] No one wants to reopen old wounds, turn back the clock on civil rights, and so Southern whites as well as blacks were frightened of the prospect, which they were told was real, that I would do those things. People for the American Way ran an advertisement on radio and in newspapers that said: "The Senate should learn why Mr. Bork criticized a congressional ban on literacy tests used to prevent minorities from voting."[35] This was as false as the Gregory Peck ad.

The *Biden Report* also led the way with charges about my alleged hostility to women. "Judge Bork Has Indicated That The Constitution Does Not Protect Against Mandatory Sterilization"[36] and "Judge Bork Has Argued That Visitation Rights Of Non-Custodial Parents Are Not Constitutionally Protected."[37] Neither of those assertions was true. I have never said anything about mandatory sterilization or its constitutionality and, in a case involving visitation rights, had thought it unnecessary to reach the constitutional issue in order to uphold the rights.

The National Abortion Rights Action League ran an advertisement entitled "What women have to fear from Robert Bork." "Senate confirmation of Robert Bork to the Supreme Court might cost you the right to make your most personal and private decisions. His rulings might leave you no choice—in relationships, in childbearing, in your career. He must be stopped. Tell your Senators. Our lives depend on it."[38] The worst that could have happened to the women the League was trying to terrify was that abortion would once more have become a subject for state legislatures to govern. The rest is simply unintelligible. Planned Parenthood's ads accused me of "sterilizing workers." That, as shown by the discussion in Chapter 16 of the case referred to, was as flat a falsehood as could be imagined, except for the one next described.

My favorite accusation was contained in Planned Parenthood's full page advertisement that ran in newspapers across the country to inform the public that I was "an ultraconservative judicial extremist" who "uses obscure academic theory."[39] The theory is hardly obscure since Madison, Jefferson, and Story adhered to it, but it may certainly be obscure these days in the academy. The ad went on to misrepresent my academic writings and judicial decisions but reached a crescendo when it told Americans that I believed people could not choose their own relationships or living arrangements without fear of government intrusion. Planned Parenthood supported that remarkable assertion with the following: "Bork upheld a local zoning board's power to prevent a grandmother from living with her grandchildren because she didn't belong to the 'nuclear family.' Is this the sort of close-minded extremism we want on the Supreme Court?"[40]

I knew the case they were talking about. It was *Moore* v. *City of East Cleveland*,[41] and I was surprised to learn that I had ruled against the grandmother. The case was not heard by the court on which I sat but by a state appellate court for Cuyahoga County in Ohio. It was reviewed by the Supreme Court of the United States, and decided in favor of the grandmother, in 1977, five years before I even became a judge. Not only didn't I decide the case, I have never written about it or even discussed it. I can only suppose that Planned Parenthood was applying the familiar rule that equity regards as done that which ought to have been done. In their view, if I didn't make that ruling, I should have.

Several advertisements, and a report issued by the Feminist Men's Alliance, stated that I had testified before a Senate subcommittee in favor of the Human Life Bill.[42] The bill declared that human life began at conception and its object was to make it illegal for the states to tolerate abortions since such operations would be the deprivation of life without due process of law. Other publications expressed doubt about me on the opposite ground, that I had testified against the bill, which at least was true.

The record for deception, however, was probably established, one hopes for all time, by People for the American Way. Aside from its televised Gregory Peck spots, the organization ran a full-page ad on the day my hearings began. The ad, engagingly entitled "Robert Bork vs. The People," informed readers of my various depravities under boldface titles: "Sterilizing Workers"; "No Privacy"; "Big Business Is Always Right"; "Turn Back The Clock On Civil Rights?"[43] These were the themes stressed especially by Senators Kennedy and Metzenbaum. Metzenbaum pressed the subject of sterilization with such manic intensity that even viewers who knew the facts might almost have believed what he was saying. The ad's explanation was admirable for terse deceptiveness.

> A major chemical company was pumping so much lead into the workplace that female employees who became pregnant were risking having babies with birth defects. Instead of cleaning up the air, the company ordered all women workers to be sterilized or lose their jobs. When the union took the company to court, Judge Bork ruled in favor of the company. Five women underwent surgical sterilization. Within months, the company closed the dangerous part of the plant. And the sterilized women lost their jobs.[44]

Senator Metzenbaum at the hearings a few days later stated "I cannot understand how you as a jurist could put women to the choice of work or be sterilized."[45] What he would not understand, and would not have viewers understand, was, as shown in Chapter 16, that I had done nothing even resembling his accusations. Long after the vote, when he ran for reelection in Ohio, Metzenbaum continued saying that I favored forced sterilization of women workers.

Since I had criticized the general and undefined "right of privacy" invented in *Griswold* v. *Connecticut,*[46] opponents of my confirmation decided to charge that I did not think Americans should enjoy privacy. To make the charge effective, it was necessary to separate the right of privacy the Court invented from the purposes for which that right was actually used, creating a right to sell contraceptives, a right to abortion, and to urge a constitutional right to homosexual conduct. As Senator Biden told the *New York Times,* it was critical to the campaign against me that abortion not become a central issue in the debate.[47] Much of the campaign before and during the hearings was therefore devoted to asserting that I thought married couples had no right to privacy in their bedrooms. A full-page ad by Planned Parenthood informed the public that "Robert Bork is an extremist who believes you have no constitutional right to personal privacy."[48] From the charges made, a reader might reasonably have concluded that I wanted to sterilize the American people and then follow them into their bedrooms anyway to make sure they did not use contraceptives.

The *Biden Report* asserted that "Judge Bork's Opinions Show A Decidedly Pro-Business Pattern," and "Judge Bork's Opinions On Labor Issues Have Markedly Favored Employers."[49] In my book, *The Antitrust Paradox,*[50] I argued that the only proper purpose of the antitrust laws was to promote the welfare of consumers. Biden's group attempted to make that position seem actually hostile to consumers.

> It is important to recognize the special sense in which Bork uses the phrase "consumer welfare." It is a technical concept that relates to efficiency in an economy-wide sense. For example, if a practice resulted in efficiencies that led solely to greater profits for manufacturers, Judge Bork would call that "consumer welfare" even though consumers as a group paid higher prices.[51]

That, as will be seen in Chapter 16, was not merely false but an economic impossibility.

Ralph Nader's Public Citizen Group described as pro-business an opinion of mine that I had thought came out for the union. The union had refused to provide a lawyer for a nonunion employee when he was threatened with dismissal. A government agency tried to punish the union for a failure of representation. In a split decision, the panel held for the union, and my opinion held that the duty of representation was confined to matters covered by the collective bargaining contract, which this matter was not, and hence the union won. In order to give me a high pro-business batting average, Public Citizen classified the opinion as "pro-business" because, as they put it, unions are in the " 'business' of representing workers."[52] It also treated as "pro-business" a case in which I agreed that an individual ranch owner could collect damages for the government's intrusion on his land so as to make the land in large part unusable.[53]

So pervasive and intense was the politicization of the confirmation process that the American Bar Association, through its Committee on the Federal Judiciary, became a player in the game. The Department of Justice has for some years referred the names of judicial nominees to the committee for an assessment of each nominee's "competence, integrity, and judicial temperament."[54] It was understood that those terms did not authorize the committee to pass judgment on judicial philosophy or politics.[55] When President Reagan nominated me to the Court of Appeals for the District of Columbia Circuit, commonly said to be the second most important court in the nation, the ABA Committee unanimously gave me its highest rating. I expected no difficulty when nominated to the Supreme Court since I had not changed. But the committee had. To my surprise, I was told there would be several adverse votes. I asked why and was told that the committee now included members of groups vociferously opposed to me. They had been put on the committee, it was said, to ensure "political balance." But if the committee was to judge only professionalism and not philosophy, why was there a need for political balance? In the event, ten members of the committee again gave me the highest rating, one voted "not opposed," and four voted that I was unqualified on grounds of "judicial temperament." Persons casting negative votes were not identified but those familiar with the committee were pretty sure who they were. One committee member was also a member of the Democratic National Committee Finance Committee and a supporter of and contributor to Senator Joe Biden's campaign for the Democratic Party's presidential nomination. He remained on the committee and voted on my nomination after Biden had announced he would lead the fight against me. The split vote on the committee was extremely damaging to my nomination since the judgment was nominally about professionalism. In fact, according to the ABA's president, the dissenters disagreed with my "views respecting constitutional principles or their application, particularly within the ambit of the 14th Amendment."[56] Thus, my substantive views of the law were converted by a committee minority into a lack of "judicial temperament."

When Judge Douglas Ginsburg was nominated to the Court after my defeat, an anonymous leaker to the *Washington Post* said that a committee member referred to him as a "Borklet."[57] The leaker also said: "There are concerns that Ginsburg shares many of the conservative ideological beliefs that doomed the Bork nomination."[58] The ABA's committee became more deeply involved in controversy when it developed that it had leaked the names of Reagan nominees to liberal, but not to conservative, activist groups in advance of the public announcement of the nominations in order to get their views. That practice had, of course, the side effect, intended or not, of giving such groups additional time to prepare opposition.

This episode confirms, it must be feared, that none of the institutions of the law are free of the increasing politicization of our legal culture.

It has been possible to recount only a small fraction of the campaign that was waged. In addition to the advertisements in newspapers and on television and radio, the mass mailing and the telephone banks, the groups lobbied senators and their staffs and informed reporters and editorialists of their version of my career and views.

The campaign was summed up by Professor Robert W. Jenson, a Lutheran theologian whom, incidentally, I do not know, as "notable not only for its volume but for its scurrility and mendacity."[59] He wrote that much of the text of the newspaper and television ads had been "demonstrably false, misstating the matters at issue in cases decided by him and transforming statements that certain legal paths cannot lead to desired goals into statements that the goals are undesired. The misrepresentation has been so pervasive and its detection requires so little investigation, that either the sponsors and authors of these ads are astonishingly incompetent conceptually or they have simply lied."

Those who were helping me were concerned but kept saying that matters would be rectified when the hearings began and I had the chance to tell the facts as they were. We reckoned without the Democratic senators, the activist groups of the left, and the media.

15

The Hearings
and After

*I*t is called the Senate Caucus Room or, more prosaically, Room
SR-325 in the Russell Senate Office Building. A great deal of
history has been made there, and a good deal of blood shed. It
was the site of the Army–McCarthy hearings, at which Joseph Welch,
the Army's attorney, began the downfall of the senator from Wisconsin. It is also the room in which the Iran-Contra hearings had been
held, the room where Colonel Oliver North electrified a national
television audience with his testimony, although the congressmen
grilling him did not realize what was happening until too late.

That room held happy personal memories for me. I was sworn
in as Circuit Judge on February 12, 1982, in the ceremonial courtroom. A great many judges and friends were in attendance. The
oath was administered by Chief Justice Warren Burger, who had,
nine years previously, performed the same task when I became Solicitor General. It is customary on our court to have a speaker for the
occasion, and I had asked Edward Levi to do me the favor of making
the address. Edward had been my professor in law school and later
had been the Attorney General in Gerald Ford's administration, so
that he was my first professor and my last Attorney General. He
had also been Dean of the law school and President of the University
of Chicago. My entire family was present, including my mother.
My son Robert held the Bible as I took the oath. Mary Ellen was
not there. I have often reproached her for that, and she offers the
inadequate excuse that she did not know me then. Afterward we
went up the hill on Constitution Avenue to the Russell Building
and the Caucus Room, where friends from the Kirkland firm threw
a reception. A band played and the food, I am told, was magnificent.

But so many people stopped to congratulate me, each then going off to the buffet, that when I finally got there the food was gone. We rode home in a car filled with balloons that a friend had sent. All in all, a wonderful and happy occasion.

Now it was different. Green baize tables, cameras, hard lights, the room packed with people, the atmosphere of a Roman circus about to begin. The room had been rearranged since the Iran-Contra hearings so that there should be no danger that anything like the impact of Oliver North's testimony might happen again. The long table at which the Senate Judiciary Committee sat was lowered so that its members would not be seen looking down on the witness. The television cameras were moved off to the left and raised so that the angle would not be good for the witness, and the press photographers were forbidden to take frontal shots from below during the testimony, as they had when Colonel North was the witness. The Judiciary Committee Democrats need not have worried. I did not have the histrionic talents of North and, if I had, would not have employed them. The emotional and rhetorical style that is entirely appropriate to a man in his position is not, in my view, appropriate to a federal judge or to any judicial nominee. I had prepared myself to answer questions matter-of-factly and to explain my view of judging fully.

That day, Tuesday, September 15, 1987, Room SR-325 in the Russell Senate Office Building was jammed. Sitting at the committee table was the Chairman, Senator Joe Biden (Delaware), in the center and, as I faced them, to my right, the Democratic members, Senators Edward Kennedy (Massachusetts), Robert C. Byrd (the Senate majority leader, West Virginia), Howard Metzenbaum (Ohio), Dennis DeConcini (Arizona), Patrick J. Leahy (Vermont), Howell Heflin (Alabama), and Paul Simon (Illinois). To my left sat the Republican members, next to Biden the senior and Ranking Member, Senator Strom Thurmond (South Carolina), and then Senators Orrin G. Hatch (Utah), Alan K. Simpson (Wyoming), Charles E. Grassley (Iowa), Arlen Specter (Pennsylvania), and Gordon J. Humphrey (New Hampshire). I had talked to all of the senators in their offices before the hearing, as is customary, and had formed very different impressions of them as individuals. I was to come to know them much better over the five long days of my testimony. Ranged against the wall behind the committee were various staffers who aided the senators with their questioning during the testimony.

I sat alone at a small table facing the committee. Behind me sat my wife, Mary Ellen, and my children, Robert, Charles, and Ellen. Sitting with them was Mrs. Potter Stewart, known as Andy, the widow of the late Justice Potter Stewart. Andy Stewart had asked if she could sit with the family as a way of showing her support. We were, of course, delighted with her gesture. Tom Korologos sat with the family as well. In the remainder of the seats were various clerks of mine, people from the Department of Justice, and people from the White House staff.

Behind them, separated by a rail, at tables perpendicular to the committee table, were perhaps a hundred reporters from the print and electronic media. Still farther back was a small section for members of the public. There were far fewer seats than there were interested people, so those in part of this section were rotated in and out during the entire process.

One had only to look at the committee to see the nature of the problem. Three of the Democrats had already announced vehement opposition to me before the hearings began: Biden, Kennedy, and Metzenbaum. Two of them, Biden and Simon, had announced their candidacies for the Democratic presidential nomination. That necessarily meant that Simon, as well as Biden, would vote against me. The voters in the Democratic primaries are far more liberal than the main part of the Democratic Party, and that is particularly true of those who participate in the Iowa caucuses, the first primary test, which was still ahead. No Democrat who voted for me would stand a chance in the party's primaries. We were not sure about the other Democrats, but, as the campaign against my nomination by groups important to the Democratic Party intensified, some Democrats who had appeared favorable prior to the Senate's recess were displaying signs of coolness. We also had to worry about Kennedy's tactic of frightening black voters, because the black vote is essential to Democratic senators from the South.

Joining me before the committee on that first day to introduce me and recommend my confirmation were former President Gerald R. Ford, Senator Robert Dole (Minority Leader, Kansas), Senator John C. Danforth (Missouri), and Representative Hamilton Fish, Jr. (New York). President Ford knew me from the days when I was Solicitor General in his Administration. Jack Danforth was in the first class I ever taught at Yale. I remember him well, not only because he was a fine student, but because my terror at facing a class for the first time was so great that I can still see all of their faces looking at me.

The introductions need not be repeated here, but I found them thoroughly enjoyable, as would anyone upon whom praise is heaped. The senators made their opening statements, some lavish in their praise, some lavish in their denunciations, some lavish in their equivocations. It was apparent that not one person but several were being described by the senators. Kennedy stated that my public record showed that I was "hostile to the rule of law"[1] and that I had "harshly opposed"[2] and was now "publicly itching to overrule"[3] Supreme Court decisions that seek to fulfill the promise of justice for all Americans. If that were not enough, I was "instinctively biased against the claims of the average citizen and in favor of concentrations of power, whether that is governmental or private."[4] Kennedy struck all the themes he had sounded in his initial denunciation of me and all those the groups had used in the public campaign. President Reagan had not chosen "a real judicial conservative"[5] but "an activist of the right whose agenda would turn us back to the battles of a bitterly divided America."[6] He charged racism and sexism.[7] It was an ugly performance, and he repeated it again and again as the hearings progressed.

Senator Hatch said that, given my career and the witnesses who were to testify for me, "it is hard to understand why your nomination would generate controversy. The answer is found in one word, which is tragic in this judicial context, and that word is 'politics.' "[8] He said the great danger "in the impending ideological inquisition is injury to the independence and integrity of the Supreme Court and the whole federal judiciary."[9] If judges began to decide according to political criteria, "we will have lost the reasoning processes of the law which have served us so well to check political excesses and fervor over the past 200 years."[10] Hatch quoted Hodding Carter, who had been high in President Carter's administration: "The nomination of Judge Bork forces liberals like me to confront a reality we don't want to confront, which is that we are depending in large part on the least democratic institution, with a small 'd,' in government to defend what it is we no longer are able to win out there in the electorate."[11]

Senator Simpson began, "Here we go again," and referred to the process as "the 4-H Club of hype, hoorah, hysteria and hubris."[12] "Since this man's name was proposed by the President, the various interest groups have been salivating at the chops. . . . I referred to them once as 'bug-eyed zealots.' I have no reason to change that opinion at all."[13] Since a great deal of the campaign against me insisted that I would disturb the balance of the Court in replacing Lewis Powell, Simpson noted that in cases where Powell voted on my decisions, he agreed with me in nine out of ten. "Let's not miss that. Do not let that go off the wall or skip off the puddle."[14] He reminded his colleagues that the Senate Judiciary Committee had unanimously recommended my confirmation and the full Senate had unanimously voted confirmation twice, once when I was nominated for Solicitor General in 1973 and again when I was nominated for a seat on the court of appeals in 1982.[15] The academic writings which now formed the basis for accusations all predated those confirmations.

Senator Grassley said, "Make no mistake about it, the critics of this; [sic] nominee know the law they prefer is judge-made, and therefore susceptible to change by other judges. Their loud protests underscore that the law they prefer is not found in the Constitution or the statutes."[16] If it were, "they would have no fear of any new judge pledged to live by the credo of judicial restraint. Instead, these critics prefer judges who will act as some kind of 'super legislature' who will give them victories in the courts when they lose in the legislature."[17]

Senator Humphrey stated, "I have been around this city for 9 years, and the charges against Judge Bork are the worst infestation of politics this Senator has ever seen."[18] He reviewed my record and quoted former Chief Justice Warren Burger: "I do not think in more than 50 years since I was in law school there has ever been a nomination of a man or woman any better qualified than Judge Bork."[19] Humphrey went on to point out that the year before the Senate had confirmed Antonin Scalia to the Supreme Court by a unanimous vote, though Scalia and I had served on the same court for four years and had voted the same way 98 percent of the time. "Does that make Scalia an extremist, too? Of course not. It means instead that these charges against Bork are political poppycock, pure political poppycock, 99.9 percent pure, so pure it floats."[20]

The reader may have gathered by now that I enjoy quoting the senators who supported me, but I think my enjoyment is understandable. Up until now I have been quoting denunciations of me in the public campaign against my confirmation. Everyone is entitled to some relief from quoting his enemies against himself. And it is surely a mitigating factor that I have not quoted the more extravagant praises.

Finally, it was my turn. I introduced my family and Andy Stewart,

mentioned that my mother, Elizabeth Bork, was watching on television, thanked the President for nominating me and those who had
introduced me for their warm remarks.[21] I then turned to what I
took to be the central point of the hearings, the question of judicial
philosophy, and made remarks about "the role of a judge in a constitutional democracy"[22] that seemed to me correct then and seems so
now:

> The judge's authority derives entirely from the fact that he is
> applying the law and not his personal values. That is why the
> American public accepts the decisions of its courts, accepts even
> decisions that nullify the laws a majority of the electorate or
> their representatives voted for. The judge, to deserve that trust
> and that authority, must be every bit as governed by law as is
> the Congress, the President, the state Governors and legislatures,
> and the American people. No one, including a judge, can be
> above the law. Only in that way will justice be done and the
> freedom of Americans assured.
>
> How should a judge go about finding the law? The only
> legitimate way, in my opinion, is by attempting to discern what
> those who made the law intended. . . .
>
> If a judge abandons intention as his guide, there is no law
> available to him and he begins to legislate a social agenda for
> the American people. That goes well beyond his legitimate power.
>
> He or she then diminishes liberty instead of enhancing it.
> . . . [W]hen a judge goes beyond [his proper function] and
> reads entirely new values into the Constitution, values the framers
> and the ratifiers did not put there, he deprives the people of
> their liberty. That liberty, which the Constitution clearly envi-
> sions, is the liberty of the people to set their own social agenda
> through the processes of democracy. . . .
>
> My philosophy of judging, Mr. Chairman, as you pointed
> out, is neither liberal nor conservative. It is simply a philosophy
> of judging which gives the Constitution a full and fair interpreta-
> tion but, where the Constitution is silent, leaves the policy strug-
> gles to the Congress, the President, the legislatures and executives
> of the 50 states, and to the American people.[23]

I have set out my statement with some fullness because this was
the central controversy in the hearings. I stressed the necessity that

the judge adhere to a process that did not involve him in making unguided policy. My opponents stressed the necessity that the judge make good policy, that the results he reaches be politically correct.

The hearings take up five thick printed volumes, and there can be no possibility of recapturing their mood or restating all of even the main features. In their opening statements various senators had said that the main issue was judicial philosophy, and I had agreed. I was now to learn that there is no possibility of an adequate judgment of judicial philosophy by a group of senators, nor is that fact surprising. Aside from my years as a judge, I had spent decades analyzing and assessing courts and their performance in a wide variety of contexts. Senators, even the best of them, and the best are very good, simply do not have much experience with constitutional law, either as practitioners or as professors. The worst of them know only what they like and suppose that is the Constitution. Here, I shall illustrate the point with a few exchanges with senators who chose to engage in constitutional dialogue.

The Democrats and one Republican, Arlen Specter, professed horror at the thought that a judge must limit his rulings to the principles of the actual Constitution. Joe Biden, the Chairman, would throw his arms up in the air and announce, "I have [rights] because I exist."[24] It did no good to tell him that might be true, but a judge was not empowered to enforce rights not to be found in law. Senator Simon, in a particularly nasty piece of innuendo, mentioned that he had recently read Taney's *Dred Scott* opinion and said, "It sounded an awful lot like Robert Bork."[25] Since Taney employed, and probably invented, substantive due process, my views and his could not be further apart (see Chapter 1).

The hearings also illustrated the point that most senators would do well not to attempt to judge a nominee by engaging in a detailed discussion of legal doctrine. Whatever the "advice and consent" function of the Senate may legitimately encompass, prudence suggests that it not consist of an attempt to argue the outcome of specific issues. The only senator who engaged in that enterprise at the hearings was Senator Arlen Specter, who questioned me on the subject of the first amendment's guarantee of freedom of speech. It is worth examination because Specter and others have said that this kind of examination should set a pattern for future confirmation hearings. We must hope that it does not, for our exchange produced a striking instance of a dialogue run amok. If the passage you are about to read seems not to make sense, that is probably because it doesn't.

Since I had written that I did not think the first amendment,

properly interpreted, protected pornography, Specter wanted to
know if I disagreed with then Justice Rehnquist's opinion in *Jenkins*
v. *Georgia*,[26] holding that the state could not convict a person for
showing the movie *Carnal Knowledge*. I said I did not know the
movie, but perhaps the Court had looked at it and decided it was
not pornographic.[27] In the discussion, each of us sometimes used
the words "pornography" and "obscenity" interchangeably, as I explained at another point in the hearings. I had written that I thought
pornography as well as its more extreme form, obscenity, did not
deserve constitutional protection, that its availability should be left
to the political community. But that was not what Specter was
driving at. He had somehow gotten into his head the erroneous
notion that something I had written meant that the Court could
not decide for itself whether books or films are obscene or pornographic in the process of deciding whether they are to receive first
amendment protection.

SENATOR SPECTER. The question, Judge Bork, is, you have a
Georgia statute on obscenity, you have a jury verdict, you have
a conviction, you have it upheld by the State Supreme Court,
and then you have the U.S. Supreme Court, Justice Rehnquist
saying first amendment protection stops that prosecution.

All of your writings say—and you affirm it here this afternoon—that the first amendment does not reach pornography or
obscenity to stop majority rule in a State court determination.
And I am saying to you that that pretty clearly places you at
variance, at least on that issue, with Justice Rehnquist, or, I
am asking you if it does.

JUDGE BORK. With respect, Senator, I think it does not at
all, because merely because a particular State defines something
as pornographic does not mean that the Supreme Court has to
accept that definition.

In order to protect the first amendment, the Supreme Court
has to apply a definition of pornography of its own. Otherwise,
the States could define literary works, or even political speech
as pornographic.

SENATOR SPECTER. Well, but you are then saying that it is
appropriate for the Supreme Court to strike down a conviction
on First Amendment grounds where it is pornographic.

JUDGE BORK. No, no, Senator. I am not making myself clear. I will try to be clearer in what I say. The determination of what is pornographic for first amendment purposes has to be made by the Supreme Court, or by the lower Federal courts.

Otherwise, if you let a State's definition of what is pornographic govern, things that are not pornographic, in a constitutional sense, might be banned.

. . .

SENATOR SPECTER. Judge Bork, if you are saying that, then you are saying that the majority, Madisonian majoritarianism which you write about so extensively, does not apply in that situation. That we are not allowing the legislature to make a definition, a definition which a conviction is entered on, but that the Supreme Court has the authority, legitimacy—your term—to come in and upset that conviction.

JUDGE BORK. Senator, with respect, that is entirely consistent with my position on what I have called the Madisonian dilemma, and that is that the Supreme Court must, by applying the Constitution, define what things the majority may rule, and what things the majority may not rule, where the individual, or the minority, must be left freedom.

Now free speech is perhaps the most central freedom in the Constitution. That means that the Supreme Court, ultimately the Supreme Court, the Federal Judiciary, when it says pornography is not protected, it must make sure that what the State calls pornography is pornography, and that is why they are entitled to examine a State determination that "Carnal Knowledge" is pornography and to reverse it.

. . .

SENATOR SPECTER. But your writings are exactly to the contrary, as recently as 1985.

JUDGE BORK. Senator, I do not understand. I am missing some aspect of this, because in 1985, I said the first amendment protection did not extend to pornography. All I am saying now is, that the Supreme Court must decide what is pornography, and what is not, in order to apply the first amendment protection.

. . .

SENATOR SPECTER. But you have written that the Court does not have legitimacy in using the first amendment to interfere with what a State has done.

JUDGE BORK. Senator, I never said that the first amendment—the Court did not have a legitimate role, under the first amendment, to interfere with what the State has done. Now, the State may say we are regulating pornography, but it may be regulating things that the Supreme Court does not think are pornography. Therefore, the Supreme Court must make sure that it is pornography, before it allows the State to ban it.

SENATOR SPECTER. Judge Bork, with all due respect, I think you are putting the rabbit in the hat. The Supreme Court has to take the issue to decide what is involved. Now you have written, going back to the Indiana Law Review article, "There is no basis for judicial intervention to protect that variety of expression we call obscene or pornographic."

Now you cannot have a determination as to whether it is obscenity or pornographic until the Court takes it up, but you say, flatly here, that there is no basis for judicial intervention.

Here Specter confused the idea that the Supreme Court should let the community decide whether it wanted to ban pornography, which I had expressed, with the notion that the Supreme Court could not even look at a case to determine whether what the community had banned actually should be classified as pornography, a position neither I nor anyone else had ever taken. The latter position would destroy the possibility of judicial review.

· · ·

JUDGE BORK. All right. The Court must protect speech that the first amendment covers. It must not protect speech that the first amendment does not cover and which a community wishes to outlaw. A community's definition, or characterization of a particular magazine, or book, or movie as "pornographic" cannot be taken as final.

The Supreme Court must have its own definition of what is pornographic, and, indeed, it does, and then look at the book, or the speech, to see whether it is pornographic, and hence, subject to State regulation.

. . .

SENATOR SPECTER. And the thrust of your writings have been that the Court may not make those interpretations, absent some specific constitutional right. That it is really the same area of judicial action, and Supreme Court determination, Supreme Court legitimacy.

JUDGE BORK. Senator, in the pornography case we are talking about, there is absolutely no problem, because the Supreme Court has the first amendment and its guarantee of free speech and free press to apply, and it must apply it.

So that there is no question of judicial legitimacy in the first amendment area. There is a constitutional provision which must be applied.

SENATOR SPECTER. But it all depends on whether the Court, legitimately, may apply the first amendment to pornography cases, and you have said that they should not.[28]

. . .

This exchange was longer than the portion reproduced here but the rest merely repeated and repeated the central confusion. When I said the Supreme Court should allow local communities to control pornography, Specter could not grasp my further statement that the Court would have to define what is pornography for first amendment purposes and take cases to make sure that the community was not banning non-pornographic works. He seemed to think my position was that once a state legislature called something pornography the Court was bound by that.

Senator Specter spent hours attempting to demonstrate that he was engaged in a weighty discussion of constitutional theory, but episodes like this made it apparent that he had at best quite erroneous notions of my views on the Constitution and the relationship of judicial supremacy to democracy. Shortly after that, we got into a discussion of *Bolling* v. *Sharpe*,[29] the companion case to *Brown*[30] that outlawed segregated schools in the District of Columbia. I explained, as I have explained in Chapter 3, that the segregation laws of the District had been written by Congress, which governed the District; and that the equal protection clause, under which *Brown* had been decided, was not applicable.[31] The Court, however, invented a new part of the fifth amendment's due process clause, importing into that clause an equal protection component. *Bolling* has been cited ever since for having accomplished that.[32] Specter denied it.[33] He was simply wrong on a point that is clear to every constitutional lawyer. But the point of his insistence turned out to be a desire to establish that it was common, and thus in his view proper, for courts to decide cases without reference to the Constitution. He picked up my prior remark that sooner or later the appointment power would mean that the commerce clause would be interpreted in accordance with "the needs of the nation."[34] But instead of drawing from that the conclusion I had, which is that the Court cannot stand forever against what a strong political movement perceives as the nation's needs, Specter was prepared to make that a constitutional principle, saying that was "a very broad articulation of what the Supreme Court does, meeting the needs of the nation. That certainly is not concrete and that certainly is not specified in the Constitution."[35] He then somehow got the idea that I had approved of *Bolling* v. *Sharpe* and the expansion of the commerce clause by the New Deal Court. I had to explain once more that I accepted the expansion of the commerce clause "because what has happened is irreversible."[36] It did no good, however; he continued to come back to "the needs of the nation" as though that phrase provided some kind of warrant for judges to act without constitutional authority and as though I had accepted the idea.[37]

I spent almost seven hours all told with Senator Specter, at the hearings and in his offices, discussing constitutional law, all of it at his request. To the end, he could not comprehend what I was saying about the first amendment, the equal protection clause, the need to construe the Constitution in the light of the original understanding, or the dangers of letting judges decide cases with no more authority or guidance than a phrase not in the Constitution, such as "fairness" or "the needs of the nation." Because I was, out of necessity, patient with him, a lot of people not versed in constitutional law got the impression that this was a serious constitutional discussion.

Nor was there any serious discusson of law with the Democratic senators. Kennedy simply kept insisting that I was against everybody's rights. He and Metzenbaum tried to establish, but could not, that my discharge of Archibald Cox was illegal.[38] They dropped that subject when it became apparent that the work of the Office of the Special Prosecutor had not been hindered in any way and continued as planned after Cox left. It was left to Metzenbaum, however, to make some of the most egregious accusations about my attitudes toward women.[39] He insisted that in one of my decisions I had put women employees to the choice of losing their jobs or being sterilized in order to allow the company to achieve a safer workplace.[40] The accusation was so outrageously at odds with the facts of record that I could hardly believe it was being made, but Metzenbaum made it over and over again long after it had been conclusively answered. It is answered once more in the next chapter.

And so on it went, through five long days, Democratic senators making accusations over and over again, not deterred in the least by testimony or facts, and Republican senators, with the exception of Specter, bringing out my record as a judge and as Solicitor General to show that the charges were false. Strom Thurmond, Orrin Hatch, Al Simpson, Charles Grassley, and Gordon Humphrey labored at length to expose the misrepresentations, and I remain grateful to each of them. But it became clearer and clearer that the hearings were changing no one's mind on the committee. The same questions, the same charges were answered and rebutted over and over again. The process resembled more a war of attrition than an exploration of views.

During the hearings, Senator Biden's presidential aspirations came to a sudden end, probably for all time. The campaign staff of Governor Michael Dukakis gave the press videotapes demonstrating that Biden had plagiarized speeches by other politicians such as Britain's Neal Kinnock.[41] In addition, the press learned that Biden had misrepresented his law school record.[42] As the damaging facts began to pile up, Biden at first tried to explain and finally had to hold a press conference at which he withdrew as a candidate for his party's nomination.[43] Shortly after that, during a break in the hearings, Biden came over to my table and said, with every appearance of sympathy, "You know, your situation and mine are a lot alike." I didn't think there was any comparison but managed not to tell him so.

At last, on a Saturday, my testimony came to an end. Biden asked me if it had been fair.[44] I said it had, meaning that he had let me answer every accusation, but it had not been a "hearing" at all, since nobody heard.

The hearings were undoubtedly harder on my family than on me. I at least had the opportunity to speak in response to what was being said, while they had to sit for hours on end and listen to the calumnies. Every evening, at home, we discussed that day's developments. My family was a great source of strength during the entire proceeding. After my part was over, Mary Ellen and I were offered the use of a country place in Middleburg, Virginia, by Dr. and Mrs. Walter Abendschein. We went down for two or three days of utter inactivity. The hearings continued with witnesses for and against me, but we were so repelled and wearied by the entire experience that we could not watch even the friendly witnesses on television.

As a matter of fact, a lot of the friendly witnesses were not much on television or reported in the papers either.[45] Joe Biden and the Democrats structured the proceedings to keep them off. For example, the opposition had two former Attorneys General of the United States testify against my confirmation. Seven former Attorneys General were to testify in favor of confirmation. The nine were taken early in the morning to the office of the Vice President in the Capitol to await their turn. They were given breakfast there, then lunch, and the day dragged on toward dinner. Biden had the two opposed AG's testify during the day and kept the seven favorable ones waiting until the deadline for the evening TV news programs and the morning newspapers had passed. One of them, William Saxbe, with whom I had served in the Department of Justice, was a former senator and became so incensed at this treatment that in late afternoon he walked out. Edward H. Levi, William French Smith, William P. Rogers, Herbert Brownell, Griffin B. Bell, and Elliot Richardson testified but were not, of course, seen on the evening news or reported in the next day's papers. These reported only the two AGs in opposition. Nor did the media go back the next day to report what they had missed. Tactics like this were intended to, and did, give the public a greatly distorted view of the opposition and the support.*

Throughout the hearings the negative advertisements kept up, with almost no answering ads. By and large, the major media outlets were very hostile. They did not trouble to analyze the assertions made in the advertisements on television, radio, and in print, though the falsity of the charges could easily be shown. In fact, the steady

---

* A future Attorney General and former Governor of Pennsylvania, Dick Thornburgh, also testified for me. Justice John Paul Stevens publicly endorsed my nomination at least twice and Justice Byron White allowed a news commentator to state that White favored my confirmation. The names of these and other persons who supported the nomination demonstrate the emptiness of the claim that my views were "outside the mainstream"; these were people whose careers have defined the American legal mainstream.

barrage of lies would have been a major story, but it went largely (on the networks and in the two major East Coast papers, entirely) unreported and unanalyzed. Nor was the major media's own reporting unbiased.[46] Instead, most of the major media institutions simply reported the accusations and made no attempt to report the facts that were misrepresented. There were some exceptions. The *Wall Street Journal* editorial page answered the smears in detail, though its news pages were unfriendly. The *Chicago Tribune* and other papers also were fair. So enormous were the negative advertising and the bias in the major media organs that to this day I am astounded that so many Americans saw through them and understood that I was not the ogre painted.

In any event, the nomination began to unravel. Senator after senator announced against me long before the Senate debate was scheduled to begin. A number of them made statements that came right out of the advertising campaign and had nothing to do with either the hearings or my record. Senators said that I favored school prayer (a subject I have never addressed), that I believed individuals had no right of privacy in their own homes (I had testified that the fourth amendment guaranteed that privacy), that I rejected legal rights for noncustodial parents and grandparents to visit their children and grandchildren (a confusion of a case I had decided and Planned Parenthood's false assertion that I had ruled in *Moore* v. *East Cleveland*). Senator Lloyd Bentsen, who was shortly to run for vice president, said he could not vote for a man who believed there was no constitutional right to privacy, especially in the home. He had evidently not read anything I had written or my testimony, where I repeatedly said that the Constitution protected many aspects of privacy of the home. Senator Conrad produced an outrageous parody of the philosophy of original understanding, saying that I would "confine the constitutional search for justice to an 18th century world where women could not vote and slaves were property."[47] He thus purported to believe that I would somehow overrule the thirteenth, fourteenth, fifteenth, and nineteenth amendments to the Constitution. On and on the misrepresentations rolled. The repetition of the ad campaign's charges as though they represented my views became so ridiculous that even some Democrats who voted against me complained that the Senate process of debate was being subverted and positions taken from thirty-second television spots.

A majority of senators announced that they would vote against me before the debate even began. This can only have reflected the heavy political pressure they were under from the activist groups and from constituencies that had been misled as to my views. Otherwise, even if a senator were determined to vote against confirmation, it would have been politically wiser to appear to listen and deliberate. But the left wanted its victory nailed down immediately, and it became politically expedient to announce against at once. Senator Exon, who voted against me, said "The rush to judgment day accelerated as pressures and demands from special interest groups mounted to record proportions."[48]

The crucial bloc were the Southern Democrats. Kennedy's strategy of arousing blacks with lies about my positions had put these senators in an awkward position. Southern Democrats do not win elections without an almost unanimous black vote in their favor. Southern blacks had been told that I wanted to "reopen the wounds" of the civil rights struggles. That falsehood also worried Southern whites as well, since nobody in his right mind would want to refight those issues. The columnists Evans and Novak reported that both Dennis DeConcini of Arizona and John Shelby of Alabama had left Washington in August expecting to vote for confirmation. "[DeConcini] returned a different man, as was shown in hostile questioning of Bork. The explanation is massive pressure against Bork by . . . [l]abor, feminists and particularly blacks."[49]

The Southern senators held a caucus and decided to vote against me as a bloc. Senator J. Bennett Johnston was apparently the main figure in this decision. According to the *Washington Post,* Johnston said to Shelby:

> This nomination is going to go down because people like you are going to vote against it. You're going to vote against it because you're not going to turn your back on 91 percent of black voters in Alabama who got you here.[50]

The same story stated that many Southern senators cited Johnston as important to their final decision to oppose the nomination. Kennedy's racial politics had succeeded.

From the day I was nominated, the press had set up a watch at our home in Washington, print reporters and television crews camping in the street from very early in the morning until I returned home at night. Now that defeat was assured they set up a "death watch," apparently convinced that I would announce my withdrawal. They shouted questions at me whenever I appeared. Two motorcyclists and a man in an automobile were stationed on the street and followed our car wherever we went, from home to the office and back. They worked for the three networks. My son Robert usually drove us in the family car. The route between office and home runs behind the White House and past the gate that most people use. Toward the end, we drove that way with the whole family in the car, the motorcyclists and the car driver right behind us. They must have radioed ahead that we were headed for the White House, and as we got there a great rush of reporters and cameramen sprinted toward the gate, but we drove on past and Robert signaled happily to the followers that they had been fooled.

The question of withdrawing now became a very real one. Defeat was certain. We received advice from a great many people, and almost all of it was to withdraw rather than take a bad Senate vote. President Reagan said he would prefer that I stay in but clearly left the decision up to me. Vice President Bush issued a statement expressing the hope that I would stay, and the Republicans in the Senate urged the same course. At one point, Mary Ellen and I attended a meeting with Republican senators in the offices of the Minority Leader, Robert Dole. The senators were enthusiastic about fighting it out. Only Allan Simpson said that he was not sure I should stay in because I would have to live with a fairly decisive defeat. One of the other senators said that if they had known Simpson was going to talk that way, they wouldn't have invited him to the meeting. At the conclusion, someone said, "Let's all accompany Judge Bork to his car." They formed a group around us and we went together out to the front of the Senate, where a great many reporters and people were waiting. The senators applauded as we got in the car and were driven away. Later they sent me a pair of signed photographs of the occasion.

It was fairly clear that most of the White House staff wanted me to pull out and end the episode so they could get on to a new nominee. But the people I listened to most were personal friends who obviously had no political calculations in mind but were concerned only for my well-being. They were virtually unanimous in urging withdrawal before the vote. One couple of whom we are especially fond cited Theodore Sorenson's withdrawal of his nomination to head the CIA under President Carter. Largely because of the advice of personal friends, Mary Ellen and I were leaning toward withdrawal. We were both very weary from more than three months of struggle and unremitting attack. It is hard to think clearly under such conditions, but we carefully weighed the pros and cons. Finally, getting out seemed probably the best course.

On Thursday, October 8, I sat at my desk in my chambers

and began tentatively preparing a withdrawal statement. Mary Ellen and my sons, Robert and Charles, were having coffee in a room across the hall. I had trouble composing the statement. It did not feel right. At that moment Al Simpson called from his hotel room in Denver. Simpson said he had been rethinking his suggestion that it might be better to withdraw. If I did, the matter would be closed, but if I stayed in, he and the other Republicans could make a permanent record in the debates that would tell the facts for history. Shortly before Simpson hung up, Mary Ellen, Robert, and Charles walked into my chambers, looking like a delegation come to make a statement. When I had hung up, and before I could tell them what Al Simpson had said, Mary Ellen said, "We got to talking and we barged in to tell you what we think." She gestured toward Charles, who said he had always been against withdrawing. Robert then said he thought I should not quit. Mary Ellen then said, "I don't think you should withdraw. Why should you?" I told them what Simpson had said, which seemed to me to make a good deal of sense. But what made the difference, I think, was a simple emotional reaction that we shared, that it was better to fight than to run, even though defeat was certain. I had been subjected to unbelievable amounts of abuse and lies, and I was not going to reward the people who had done it. As soon as the decision was made, we all felt much better and more cheerful.

I telephoned Ray Randolph, told him the decision, and asked him to stop by my house on his way home. At the house we worked on a statement to be made the next day since a public decision could be postponed no longer. The next morning we met again in my chambers, and as we bent over the draft, Ray lifted his head and asked, "Do you have any doubts about this?" I said, "No." Ray said, "Neither do I," and we bent over the draft again. Robert and Charles came in and began working with us. Both of them made good suggestions. Later my daughter, Ellen, came in. She agreed but had not wanted to say anything while we were in the process of deciding. We had notified the White House that we were coming over, though they did not know what I had decided. We finished the draft just as the cars arrived, and the family plus Ray Randolph got into the cars and went.

The press, of course, saw us arrive and immediately assumed that I had come to announce my withdrawal. That impression was supported by the fact that my family was with me. It is common, I am told, for a nominee to have his family with him when he surrenders. I wanted mine with me because we—I do not say I but we—were not going to surrender. By this time the whole business had become very much a family enterprise. The President was upstairs at a farewell luncheon for a cabinet member, so we were put in the downstairs Map Room, just inside the back door. Soon George Bush joined us, as did Edwin Meese, the Attorney General. Conversation was rather desultory, we drank coffee, and I did a moderate amount of pacing about the room. Finally, word came that I was to join the President and staff members upstairs in the family quarters. The Vice President and the Attorney General, of course, also came. Mary Ellen, Robert, Charles, Ellen, and Ray remained in the Map Room.

The President sat in an armchair and I on a sofa perpendicular to his chair. Bush and Meese knew my decision, but the others did not. I said that we had considered the matter very carefully and had decided that I should not withdraw. Reagan said that was the way he wanted it, but I thought some of the staff looked unhappy. In any event, I said I had a statement I wanted to make in the White House press room. One of the staff took it and went off to have copies made for distribution to the press. Soon my family was brought up to meet Reagan, and he chatted pleasantly with them until the copies were ready. Then we went down and I walked alone into a packed press room. Once more still cameras were flashing and television cameras rolling. The reporters were leaning forward; they thought it was the end. I then read the following statement:

> More than three months ago, I was deeply honored to be nominated by the President for the position of Associate Justice of the Supreme Court of the United States.
>
> In the 100 days since then, the country has witnessed an unprecedented event. The process of confirming Justices for our nation's highest Court has been transformed in a way that should not, indeed must not, be permitted to occur ever again.
>
> The tactics and techniques of national political campaigns have been unleashed on the process of confirming judges. That is not simply disturbing. It is dangerous.
>
> Federal judges are not appointed to decide cases according to the latest opinion polls. They are appointed to decide cases impartially according to law. But when judicial nominees are assessed and treated like political candidates the effect will be

to chill the climate in which judicial deliberations take place, to erode public confidence in the impartiality of our judges, and to endanger the independence of the judiciary.

In politics the opposing candidates exchange contentions in their efforts to sway the voters. In the give and take of political debate, the choice will, in the end, become clear. A judge, however, cannot engage. Political campaigning and the judge's function are flatly incompatible. In two hundred years, no nominee for Justice has ever campaigned for that high office. None ever should. And I will not.

This is not to say that my public life—the decisions I have rendered, the articles I have written—should be immune from consideration. They should not. Honorable persons can disagree about these matters. But the manner in which the debate is conducted makes all the difference. Far too often the ethics that should prevail have been violated and the facts of my professional life have been misrepresented.

It is, to say no more, unsatisfying to be the target of a campaign that by necessity must be one-sided, a campaign in which the "candidate," a sitting federal judge, is prevented by plain standards of his profession, from becoming an energetic participant. Were the fate of Robert Bork the only matter at stake, I would ask the President to withdraw my nomination.

The most serious and lasting injury in all of this, however, is not to me. Nor is it to all of those who have steadfastly supported my nomination and to whom I am deeply grateful. Rather, it is to the dignity and integrity of law and of public service in this country.

I therefore wish to end the speculation. There should be a full debate and final Senate decision. In deciding on this course, I harbor no illusions. But a crucial principle is at stake. That principle is the way in which we select the men and women who guard the liberties of all the American people. That should not be done through public campaigns of distortion. If I withdraw now, that campaign would be seen as a success and it would be mounted against future nominees.

For the sake of the federal judiciary and the American people that must not happen. The deliberative process must be restored.

In the days remaining I ask only that voices be lowered, the facts respected, and the deliberations conducted in a manner that will be fair to me and to the infinitely larger and more important cause of justice in America.[51]

I walked out without taking questions. Afterward a White House car took us back to the courthouse, still followed by the press automobile and the two motorcyclists. In a moment, I was handed the car telephone. It was Senator Dole and two other Republican senators calling to congratulate me on the decision to stay in the fight. Still later, the car took us home, and now an oddly cheering minor event occurred. The people following us, particularly the goggled motorcyclists, had always seemed ominous and hostile, but, as I looked back, one of the press motorcycle riders lifted his gloved right hand and gave me a thumbs-up salute.

Not long afterward, the President made two speeches on the subject. In one he quoted the columnist David Broder: "To subject judges and judicial appointees to propaganda torture tests does terrible damage to the underlying values of this democracy and the safeguards of our freedoms."[52] In the other, he said, "The principal errors in recent years have nothing to do with the intent of the framers who finished their work 200 years ago last month. They've had to do with those who have looked upon the courts as their own special province to impose by judicial fiat what they could not accomplish at the polls."[53]

Within a few days the Senate began its non-debate. There was hardly a vote on either side that had not already been announced, and once senators announce, they do not change. That was why the activist groups applied so much pressure to get announcements of opposition before the debate began.

A number of senators made strong speeches on my behalf. All of them cannot be mentioned but Jack Danforth of Missouri obtained a full hour and made a magnificent speech, expressing, among other things, his anger at the travesty of a process the Senate had produced.[54] Mary Ellen and my sons sat in the gallery to watch the debate. Mary Ellen was so moved by Danforth's speech that she could watch no more. A great many senators on both sides spoke, and the question arose when to cut off the debate. Al Simpson telephoned at night to say that there were more Republicans who would speak but he thought the points had all been made and there was danger of having the whole thing sag into anticlimax. There was also the possibility that Senator Byrd would postpone the remaining speeches for a week or two to take up other matters. He asked what I wanted them to do. The prospect of leaving the Court without a new nominee was worrisome. The Court can get along with eight members for a time by scheduling argument only in cases that promise not to divide the Justices evenly, but that tactic can be used only so long. I told Simpson that I had no objection to closing down the debate and would accept his and the others' judgment about the best time to do that.

October 23 was chosen as the day for the vote, very nearly four months after the nomination. Mary Ellen and I had no desire to watch. We invited Walter Berns, a friend and prominent political scientist, to have lunch with us at the Madison Hotel. We knew the vote was over when a reporter from the *Washington Post* interrupted our lunch by standing at the table and asking how I felt about being rejected. I told her I would like to have lunch in peace.

We did not actually have any particular reaction to the Senate vote, because we had known the certain outcome for quite some time. Later, when I had time to reflect, I felt regret that I was now effectively barred from public life, a life which I enjoy and for which, I confess, I feel suited. But there was no sadness at not being on the Supreme Court. There is the opportunity now to study and to write and to speak. When Alex Bickel was in the last stages of his illness he told me that on a house visit his doctor had expressed some sharp opinions about the slowness of the procedures by which Richard Nixon was being impeached but that he had persuaded the doctor to think otherwise, to recognize the immense importance of process. I expressed surprise that Alex, who was then half-blind and paralyzed on his right side, should have made such an effort. He drew himself up as well as he could in the chair he now never left and said, "I'm a teacher." The happiness and pride with which he said it were both entirely justified. It is a great calling to be a teacher—of true things.

Only once since the day of the vote did I feel a pang of sadness. Mary Ellen and I were getting ready to go out for the evening and she came to show me a new dress. I liked it very much and told her so. She said, "This is the dress I bought for your swearing in. I hadn't the slightest doubt it would happen." The poignancy of that moment had nothing to do with my career but with her, and since I could not explain it, I said nothing and the moment passed.

In the months that followed the vote I resumed sitting as a court of appeals judge and discussed with my family the course we should take in the future. It seemed clearer now than ever that I should leave the court for reasons that I expressed in my January letter of resignation to President Reagan.

January 7, 1988

Dear Mr. President:

Six years ago you appointed me to the United States Court of Appeals for the District of Columbia Circuit. That was a great honor and I continue to be grateful to you for it. The task of serving the law and the ends of justice has made the last six years absorbing and fulfilling.

It is, therefore, with great reluctance, and only after much thought and discussion with my family, that I have now decided to step down from the bench. This decision is the more difficult because of what I owe to you, to the many Americans who have written to me in the last six months to express their support, and, indeed, to all Americans our system of justice serves. Because I recognize these debts and obligations, I want to explain the course I have chosen.

The crux of the matter is that I wish to speak, write, and teach about law and other issues of public policy more extensively and more freely than is possible in my present position. As a sitting judge on a very busy court, I cannot devote the time and energy I wish to public discourse. Moreover, constraints of propriety and seemliness limit the topics a federal judge may address and the public positions he may advocate. My experience as your nominee for Associate Justice of the Supreme Court of the United States made me acutely aware of the restrictions on my ability to address issues. For several months various highly vocal groups and individuals systematically misrepresented not only my record and philosophy of judging but, more importantly, the proper function of judges in our constitutional democracy. This was a public campaign of miseducation to which, as a sitting federal judge, I felt I could not publicly respond. What should have been a reasoned national debate about the role of the courts under the Constitution became an essentially unanswered campaign of misinformation and political slogans. If, as a judge, I cannot speak out against this attempt to alter the traditional nature of our courts, I think it important to place myself where I can.

You nominated me to my present court and to the Supreme Court precisely because I do speak for the traditional view of the judge's role under the Constitution. It is a view that goes back to the founding of our nation and was ably articulated by, among others, James Madison, Thomas Jefferson, Alexander Hamilton, and Joseph Story. It has been espoused by the greatest judges in our history. That view, simply put, is that a judge must apply to modern circumstances the principles laid down by those who adopted our Constitution but must not invent new principles of his own.

A few years ago I said:

> In a constitutional democracy the moral content of law must be given by the morality of the framer or the legislator, never by the morality of the judge. The sole task of the latter—and it is a task quite large enough for anyone's wisdom, skill, and virtue—is to translate the framer's or the legislator's morality into a rule to govern unforeseen circumstances. That abstinence from giving his own desires free play, that continuing and self-conscious renunciation of power, that is the morality of the jurist.

That was my view then. It is my view now. Though there are many who vehemently oppose it, that philosophy is essential if courts are to govern according to the rule of law rather than whims of politics and personal preference. That view is essential if courts are not to set the social agenda for the nation, and if representative democracy is to maintain its legitimate sphere of authority. Those who want political judges should reflect that the political and social preferences of judges have changed greatly over our history and will no doubt do so again. We have known judicial activism of the right and of the left; neither is legitimate.

My desire to participate in the public debate on these matters is what prompts my decision to leave the bench at this time. I had considered this course in the past but had not decided until the recent confirmation experience brought home to me just how misfocused the public discourse has become. A great many supporters have written to urge that I continue in public service. The decision I have made will, I believe, allow me to do just that. My views on these matters are of long standing. Because of my experience as your nominee, I am now in a better position to address the issues than ever before.

Though I am sure this decision is the correct one, I find, as the time of my departure draws near, that the prospect of leaving the federal judiciary fills me not merely with reluctance but with sadness. Any lawyer should be deeply honored to be a federal judge and to serve with a nationwide corps of the most dedicated men and women one is likely ever to meet. The work of an appellate judge may be the aspect of the legal profession for which I am best suited. I have actively enjoyed the day-to-day work of judging—the exchanges with lawyers at oral argument, the discussions with colleagues and clerks in arriving at a correct decision, and the effort to craft the best opinion one can. Trying with all one's capacities to do justice according to law is a deeply satisfying experience, both intellectually and emotionally. I will miss it more than I can say. I find some consolation in leaving behind a record of which I believe I may be proud, and one by which I am content to be judged.

In choosing a date for my departure, I have considered, among other factors, the desirability of leaving time for the nomination and confirmation of my successor as well as the importance of beginning my new work without undue delay. It will, however, take a few weeks to complete work on hand. I ask, therefore, that you accept my resignation as Circuit Judge, United States Court of Appeals for the District of Columbia Circuit, effective at the close of business, Friday, February 5, 1988.

With deep gratitude for your confidence in me, for appointing me to this court and nominating me to the Supreme Court, I will always remain

> Yours truly,
> Robert H. Bork

The President responded with a very warm letter accepting my resignation.

> January 14, 1988

Dear Bob:

It is with deep sadness that I accept your decision to resign as United States Circuit Judge for the District of Columbia Circuit, effective February 5, 1988. In my many appointments to the Federal bench, I have attempted to select men and women of uncommon intellect, unimpeachable integrity, and a strong, steady temperament—men and women with special gifts for communication and reasoning and with an abiding courage of conviction. You, Bob, epitomize these virtues at their very finest—which is why I turned to you to fill Justice Lewis Powell's seat on the Supreme Court.

The unprecedented political attack upon you which resulted in the regrettable Senate action was a tragedy for our country. All Americans are the poorer today for not having your extraordinary talents and legal skills on the High Court.

And yet, as I read your letter of resignation, I cannot help but feel a warm admiration for the difficult decision you have made. There is, as you state, a lively public debate brewing in this country, fueled in no small part by your confirmation hearings—a debate over the proper role of the judiciary in our system of representative self-government. That debate has advocates who view the courts and the Constitution as mere instruments for political advantage. Effective advocacy of a more traditional approach to the judicial function occurs too infrequently. Your recent experience, against a background of unswerving commitment to the doctrine of judicial restraint, makes you uniquely well suited to carry that debate forward.

For your many years of dedicated public service, especially the last six on the Court of Appeals, your country and I thank you. For your courageous adherence to conviction and refusal to forsake your ideals, your country and I salute you. For daring to embark on this new course in selfless service of the cause of truth and justice in the public arena, your country and I remain in your debt.

While your public service on the Court of Appeals will be sorely missed, I am confident that your writings and other contributions as a private citizen are destined to have a most profound and lasting impact on the Nation.

Best wishes for success in your future endeavors.

Sincerely,
/s/ Ronald Reagan

I left my chambers for the last time on a Friday. Just as I was preparing to go, a number of my former clerks surprised me by coming in to throw a small departure party. That was a joy because my relationships with my clerks were one of the happiest aspects of judging. On Monday, I assumed my new position as the John M. Olin Scholar in Legal Studies at the American Enterprise Institute, a scholarly Washington think tank. AEI's scholars include (to mention only those I know at least moderately well) Walter Berns, Christopher DeMuth (the president), Suzanne Garment, Robert Goldwin, Jeane Kirkpatrick, Irving Kristol, Michael Novak, Herbert Stein, and Ben Wattenberg. There are others, equally prominent, whom I intend to get to know when this book is done. Being at AEI is like being on a first-rate university faculty, in the days before politicization of the campuses, but without the necessity of grading examinations.

In the time since I left the court, I have spoken to audiences all around the country. Mary Ellen and I have enormously enjoyed the people we have met and the warmth with which they have greeted us. People come up to me everywhere, in airports, hotel lobbies, on the street, to express sympathy or outrage at the process I have been through. Fortunately, only the friendly ones come up. I cherish those encounters, but there is one I cherish above all others. I was standing in a bookstore in Chicago when a woman came up behind me and tapped me on the shoulder. I turned, and she said very earnestly, "Sir, we are heeding your warnings." Puzzled, I thought for a moment, and asked, "What warnings?" She said, "You're the Surgeon General." Such is the capacity for even quite dissimilar beards to confuse identification. Dr. Koop, I am told, is frequently stopped by strangers who tell him they are sorry he didn't make it.

16

The Charges and the Record: A Study in Contrasts

*I*t is important to understand the degree to which the charges leveled against me during the confirmation battle were false and known to be so by those who made them. That is so because, in the struggle for dominance in the legal culture and in the general culture, this episode is a revealing case study. The flat impossibility of reconciling the accusations hurled with the actual record demonstrates the nature of the forces ranged on the other side of those struggles. They are relentlessly disingenuous in advancing their agenda. In the guise of "protecting our civil rights," an idea that most Americans approve, they urge the courts to adopt as "civil rights" positions on a host of controversial issues that in fact divide public opinion and are nowhere to be found in the Constitution or the statutes of the United States—and which in fact, the American people will not allow their legislators to enact.

The charges reviewed here were made variously by Senators Biden, Kennedy, and Metzenbaum, the consultants who helped Biden put out his *Report,* the American Civil Liberties Union, People for the American Way, Planned Parenthood, the National Women's Law Center, the National Organization of Women, the Feminist Men's Alliance, Ralph Nader's Public Citizen Litigation Group, the AFL-CIO, and many others.[1]

Just as the left early on identified themes it would stress in the campaign against me, I shall organize this discussion around those same themes.

The Civil Rights of Racial Minorities

As we have seen, following my nomination the nation was treated to a host of charges that I was hostile to the civil rights of racial minorities, wanted to roll back the clock, and would reopen old wounds. How one Justice out of nine could wreak so much havoc was not explained. It was said that I had opposed every major civil rights decision on which I had taken a position and that I had always opposed civil rights "when it counted."[2]

The facts are otherwise. They are, in fact, so otherwise that it is hard to know where to begin. Perhaps as good a place as any is with *Brown* v. *Board of Education*.[3] I have always supported the proposition that racial segregation by government is unconstitutional, and in the 1971 article of which so much was made[4] I attempted to construct a rationale for *Brown,* one that the Court neglected, to show its legitimacy. It is true that I had criticized *Shelley* v. *Kraemer,*[5] which invalidated private racially restrictive covenants (and I have done so again in this book, in Chapter 7), but then so have most legal scholars who have discussed the case.[6] Most of the evidence for the assertion that I had opposed virtually all decisions advancing the rights of blacks came from criticisms after the fact in one sixteen-year-old article that was devoted to analyzing decisions that I thought had no constitutional rationale, only some of them involving minority civil rights. I continue to consider those cases examples of political impulse rather than legal reasoning. In fact, there are many cases favoring the rights of blacks that I have taught as correct in my constitutional law course, cases such as *South Carolina* v. *Katzenbach,*[7] which upheld key provisions of the Voting Rights Act of 1965.

Gregory Peck's commercial, on behalf of People for the American Way, stating that I favored poll taxes and literacy tests, which had been used to keep black Americans from voting, was a particularly egregious falsehood. I have never said a word in favor of poll taxes. I did object to the ruling in *Harper* v. *Virginia State Board of Elections,*[8] which struck down a small poll tax in a case where racial discrimination was not even alleged, thus rewriting the Constitution and overturning years of consistent precedent. Three Justices of the Supreme Court agreed that the majority decision was wrong— Hugo Black, John Marshall Harlan, and Potter Stewart.[9] Fifteen years earlier, eight Justices took the position I did: Hugo Black, Felix Frankfurter, Robert Jackson, Stanley Reed, Harold Burton,

Tom Clark, Sherman Minton, and Chief Justice Fred Vinson.[10] I also objected to *Katzenbach* v. *Morgan,*[11] not because it eliminated a literacy test, again in a case where racial discrimination was not charged, but because it allowed Congress to change the interpretation the Court had given to a constitutional provision by statute. Justices Harlan and Stewart took the same position I did.[12] Dissenting in another case, so did Justice Powell.[13] Indeed, for that same reason I testified against the Human Life Bill in 1981, because it attempted to overturn *Roe* v. *Wade,*[14] a decision for which I feel no sympathy whatsoever, by statute. (A number of conservatives were angered by that. The Feminist Men's Alliance, on the other hand, issued a report stating, falsely, that I had testified in favor of the bill.) Similarly, in 1972, in a monograph supporting President Nixon's bill to set some limits on busing, I noted that it could be supported by *Morgan* but refused to rely upon that rationale.[15]

The statement that I favored poll taxes and literacy tests, with the strong implication that I did so because they had been used to keep blacks from voting, was, in all respects, a flat falsehood.[16] People for the American Way has a good many lawyers; it is inconceivable this charge could have been made, and endlessly repeated, by mistake. I have no idea whether Mr. Peck knew then, or knows to this day, that the lines he read were false and can only have been deliberately so. At a guess, he probably trusted the people who handed him the script and believed what he intoned. Norman Lear, the founder of PAW, however, when questioned about that ad, said that he had reviewed it and was satisfied with it. He may well be satisfied with it; he can hardly believe that it was true.

Aside from my earlier theoretical writings as a professor, there was the fact that I had an extensive public record on matters of racial equality both as Solicitor General of the United States and as a United States Circuit Judge. I will not repeat that record in detail since it may be found in published works by others, but it is worth noting that as Solicitor General I filed briefs in or argued a number of cases in favor of minority civil rights and never took a position less favorable to the minority than the position the Supreme Court adopted. The Court rejected some of my positions as too favorable to minorities. The National Association for the Advancement of Colored People filed briefs in ten cases in which I participated and agreed with my position in nine.[17] As an appellate judge, I often voted for minority claims.[18]

Many opponents of my confirmation argued that my public record meant nothing because as Solicitor General I upheld the position of the Administration and as a judge I was bound by Supreme Court precedent.[19] No person of any legal sophistication could believe that. The Solicitor General has a great deal of discretion about the positions he takes, and I did not have to enter many of the cases I did. Moreover, in those cases where I felt bound to take a position I did not agree with, I sent a deputy to make the oral argument. In those years, I did that in almost all antitrust cases. But in the minority rights cases, when the United States was not an amicus curiae but a party, I did make the oral argument.[20] The freedom of a judge is even greater. If the meaning of Supreme Court precedent was always clear, there would be no need for lower court judges; everybody would know the law. I sometimes voted for racial minorities and sometimes did not, because I thought the law sometimes supported the minority and sometimes did not.

Enough has been said to show that the allegations of opposition to black and other minority civil rights were wholly false. If there was one thing that angered me about the campaign against me more than all others, it is that millions of black Americans were lied to and made to believe that I was their enemy in the courts. That charge, if one knew the record, could be made only by someone who believes that the minority claimant should always win regardless of the law, not by anyone who believes in law rather than political result so that the minority claimant wins when the law supports him and does not win when the law does not.

The Civil Rights of Women

The assertion that I am opposed to the rights of women was made again and again, and summarized by Senator Metzenbaum's refrain that "the women of America" were afraid of me.[21]

This part of the campaign was based upon my criticism of *Roe* v. *Wade,* my opinion in *American Cyanamid,*[22] and my statements that the ratifiers of the fourteenth amendment did not intend to treat women as a special class deserving protection as they did intend with respect to blacks. In Chapter 4, I have shown once more why *Roe* is not supported by the Constitution. That conclusion has nothing to do with an attitude toward women, only with an attitude toward law. If it matters, many women are intensely opposed to *Roe,* so that it is impossible to say that any position with respect to that case is pro- or anti-women.

The *American Cyanamid* decision was grossly distorted during the campaign and the hearings. The facts were quite otherwise than People for the American Way and Metzenbaum indicated.[23] The charge was that the company was pumping lead into the air of the workplace so that the fetuses of pregnant female employees were endangered and that I had permitted the company to achieve a safe workplace by telling the women they must be sterilized or fired. The charge was false in every particular. The statement that I had put women to this unhappy choice was wrong. The women who underwent voluntary sterilization did so four years before I became a judge. The only issue before me and the other two judges on the panel was whether a relatively small fine should be assessed against the company long after the fact. The company was not pumping lead into the workplace, a statement by PAW that implies willfulness on the part of the employer. The unavoidable consequence of one stage of the manufacturing process was to produce lead in the air. Nor, as PAW asserted, did the company have the alternative of "cleaning up the air." The factual finding of the administrative law judge, which we were bound to accept because it was not challenged on appeal, was that no technology existed which would allow the company to remove enough lead from the air to make that department safe for pregnant women.

The company was therefore faced with an unsafe condition of the workplace, as that is defined by the Occupational Safety and Health Act. Not being able to remove the lead, it had to remove women of childbearing age. There being only a few other openings in the plant, some of the women would have been transferred to lower-paying jobs and some would have been discharged. If the company had simply transferred or discharged the women, there would have been no violation of law. Indeed, there would have been full compliance with the law. But some of the women apparently wanted to keep these jobs, and the company informed them that sterilization was an option. Five of them chose that option.

There is, I am sure, a moral question whether the company should have made that choice known to the women. Perhaps it should have said that some were transferred, some were fired, and that it would not retain a woman even if she were sterilized. How far, as a matter of morality, the company was obliged to make the moral decision for the women, a decision that would have run against the wishes of some of them, or how far the company was obliged to treat the women as free adults capable of making their own choices is one of those questions about which people may differ.

Fortunately, no such knotty question of morality was put before the appeals panel. The only question before us was a legal one: whether offering the women the information to enable them to make a choice constituted an "unsafe condition of the workplace" as defined by the Occupational Safety and Health Act. Unanimously, we thought it absolutely clear that the offer of a choice was not an unsafe working condition. Given the statutory language and the legislative history, there could be no doubt on that score. The administrative law judge who first heard the case stated, "There's a law that covers this, and it's not the Occupational Safety and Health Act."* He found it "clear that Congress conceived of occupational hazards in terms of processes and materials which cause injury or disease by operating directly upon employees as they engage in work or work-related activities." He was affirmed by the Occupational Safety and Health Review Commission, whose decision we reviewed and affirmed. The Secretary of Labor had the right to appeal from the Commission and chose not to do so. The union did appeal but after our decision did not seek en banc review by the full Court of Appeals and did not petition the Supreme Court for review. It was a perfectly cut-and-dried case and no one who troubled to learn the facts and the law could have thought otherwise. Under the statute, a policy of offering women a choice was not a "hazardous condition of the workplace." The judges who joined me in that decision were Justice, then Judge, Scalia and Senior District Judge Williams. When Judge Scalia was up for confirmation to the Supreme Court, no member of the Senate Judiciary Committee asked him even one question about his vote in *American Cyanamid.* Howard Metzenbaum's moral outrage was nowhere in evidence.†

The accusation that I thought the Constitution does not protect women is, of course, wrong. The Constitution protects people, women equally with men. The real question is whether the Constitution singles out women for special protection in the way that it does racial minorities. The relevant constitutional text is the equal protection clause of the fourteenth amendment. The proponents of

---

* My opinion noted that the company's action might constitute an unfair labor practice or a form of employment discrimination under other statutes. Indeed, the women and the union had sued American Cyanamid under the law prohibiting employment discrimination and the company had settled the case.

† The case was *Oil, Chemical & Atomic Workers Int'l Union* v. *American Cyanamid, Co.,* reported at 741 F.2d 444 (D.C. Cir. 1984), and anyone who wishes to learn the truth of the matter may read it.

the Equal Rights Amendment assume that the equal protection clause has no special application to women or, if it does, the clause does not provide adequate protection.

It is clear that the ratifiers of the fourteenth amendment did not think they were treating women as an oppressed class similar in legal disadvantages to the newly freed slaves. That is an entirely modern notion and written into our jurisprudence only recently by the Supreme Court.[24] That innovation has raised a number of difficulties since courts cannot treat women in the same way that they do racial minorities. As explained in Chapter 3, the application of the equal protection clause to racial minorities very properly led eventually to a rule that government may not provide different treatment or facilities to the races (leaving aside the unsettled question of discrimination against white males). No such rule can be framed with respect to men and women, because our society feels very strongly that relevant differences exist and should be respected by government. To take the most obvious examples, no city could constitutionally provide separate toilet facilities for whites and blacks but certainly may do so for men and women. Similarly, the armed forces could not exempt one racial group from combat duty but surely may keep women from combat.[25] This means that a court that applies the fourteenth amendment to women as a special group, rather than as part of the human race, must make cultural and political choices that it need not make when applying the amendment to racial groups. That fact argues in favor of leaving such choices to the body politic. As attitudes about the respective roles of men and women change, those changes will be reflected in legislation. Women are certainly not a "discrete and insular minority" but are, in fact, a slight majority of the population.[26]

To say that women (and men) are not protected as such by the fourteenth amendment raises its own difficulties. Though the intentions of the ratifiers of the fourteenth amendment may have been narrow, the language they used is broad: "No State shall . . . deny to *any person* within its jurisdiction the equal protection of the laws."[27] Very early on, the Supreme Court expanded the protection of the clause beyond the class of newly freed slaves. *Yick Wo* v. *Hopkins,*[28] decided in 1886, held unconstitutional discrimination by the city of San Francisco against a native and subject of China. The discrimination was racial, but the central purpose of the amendment had been to protect a different race. Still, the decision seems within the general intention of the clause, and it raises no question about courts making political and cultural choices since the rule can be applied to all areas of life.

The question becomes how far the protection of the clause may be extended beyond race and ethnicity. The clause has, in one sense, been extended to every subject that law covers since the Supreme Court has long required that any challenged legislative distinction have a rational basis. For the most part, that has been a requirement easily met but it does provide some foundation for scrutinizing legislative distinctions between the sexes. I had taken the position that, except for this rational basis test, the equal protection clause should be restricted to race and ethnicity because to go further would plunge the courts into making law without guidance from anything the ratifiers understood themselves to be doing.[29] The Court's present law of equal protection is unsatisfactory because there is no adequate explanation for its choice of groups entitled to equal protection or for the differing degrees of protection it affords to the various groups. Thus, the Court has stated that some legislative distinctions, such as that between races, require strict scrutiny while others, such as distinctions between economic interests, deserve only minimal scrutiny. But the Court's various members have gone on to articulate various and varying intermediate levels of scrutiny for distinctions made as to other groups, such as the sexes. The result has been an incoherent body of case law, as anyone who has tried to teach it knows. It seemed to me that the best way of clarifying what can only be described as a mess was to adopt Justice John Paul Stevens' suggestion that all legislative distinctions between persons be reasonable.[30] That comports with the language of the equal protection clause and would produce doctrine relating to distinctions between the sexes quite similar to current doctrine. There is unlikely to be much work for the equal protection clause to do with respect to governmental distinctions between the sexes because legislators are hardly likely to impose invidious discriminations upon a group that comprises a slight majority of the electorate. Justice Stevens' formulation might not in fact cause any major changes in the application of the equal protection clause but it would focus judges' attention on the reasonableness of distinctions rather than on a process of simply including or excluding groups on criteria that can only be subjective and arbitrary.

In this area as well, I had a public record both as Solicitor General and as a Circuit Judge, and that record displays not the least hostility to the rights of women.[31] I have argued in the Supreme

Court for women's rights and, as in the case of race, never advanced a position less favorable to those rights than the position the Court adopted. Similarly, as a judge, I have often ruled in favor of women's claims.[32] One of the more ironic aspects of the charges made was that Senator Metzenbaum kept saying that when he flew he learned that airline stewardesses were afraid of me. That seemed ironic. The fact is that I participated in a decision and wrote part of the opinion holding that Northwest Airlines had discriminated against stewardesses and must pay damages as well as give them equal pay in the future.[33] Nobody could look at that record objectively and see anything but an attempt to apply the law as it is written. The groups and many of the senators in opposition nonetheless purported to see something else, and they broadcast it far and wide. When Senator Metzenbaum asked former Attorney General William French Smith to account for the fact that millions of Americans, including women, feared me, Smith replied that "to the extent that fear exists, I think a large part of it is due to the misrepresentations and the distortions and the propaganda that has been put out about this man."[34] Pressed, he said "that is false, and it borders on dishonesty, and it borders on lying to the American public."[35]

Big Business, Government, and Labor

The charge was repeatedly made that in my judicial decisions I always favored government, except when it opposed big business, always favored big business over small business, and usually ruled against labor. None of this bore any relation to the truth.

We may begin with antitrust law. The *Biden Report* attempted to convert my view that the antitrust laws should be interpreted to promote consumer welfare into a pro-business, anti-consumer philosophy.[36] The *Report* said consumer welfare was a technical concept that allowed business to attain greater efficiency even if that means higher prices for consumers.[37] Not only is that not my view, it is an impossibility. Consumer welfare refers to the most efficient distribution and employment of society's resources so that total output, as consumers value it, is maximized. It is a standard concept in economics and is not pro-business. As a matter of fact, Biden's example is economic nonsense. If manufacturers achieve greater efficiencies, they maximize their own returns by increasing output, which necessarily lowers prices, and that is true under monopolistic as well as competitive conditions. Prices can rise only if the new efficiency takes the form of an addition to the product being sold, but that means consumers are pleased to get more for the additional price. If consumers are not pleased, there is no increase in efficiency but a decline. The Supreme Court now takes the position that consumer welfare is the goal of antitrust and has cited my book *The Antitrust Paradox*[38] in support of that conclusion.[39]

My decisions in administrative law and regulatory matters have been analyzed by others. Professor Richard B. Stewart of Harvard stated that while he disagreed with a number of my opinions, they "are well within the mainstream of current judicial thinking and practice in the federal appeals courts and, especially, the Supreme Court. . . . If we are to judge by his decisions in regulatory and administrative law, claims that Judge Bork is a radical revolutionary of the right are simply ludicrous."[40] Professor Robert A. Anthony of George Mason, a former Chairman of the Administrative Conference of the United States, analyzed my decisions (in cases where another judge wrote the opinion) in forty-eight cases involving regulatory issues and eight cases involving claims for benefits from government.[41] Of twelve cases in which business opposed a regulatory agency, Anthony found that I decided seven for the agencies, four for the business interests, and one had mixed results.[42] Often in an appeal from an agency action, business interests are on both sides of the dispute. Of twelve cases in this category, Anthony found that I reversed the agency in only four.[43] In twenty-four cases in which nonbusiness interests challenged agency action, nine favored the citizen or public organization, fifteen favored the agency. The parties in whose favor I ruled "included a public housing tenants' group, environmental action organizations, a labor union, Navajo Indian groups, a radio listeners' group, consumer organizations, and a state asserting its right to regulate beyond the federal minimum."[44]

Though the *Biden Report* charged that I favored government against the individual, Professor Anthony noted that not a single case was cited in support of the charge.[45] Anthony thought any such bias should show up in cases involving administration of federal benefits entitlement programs. There were eight decisions in this category. In the three cases where an agency had denied the claims of individuals, I ruled for the individuals and against the agency in all three.[46] In three others where organizations representing individuals challenged the agency action, I held for the recipients' group once, for the agency in a second, and dismissed the third because

Congress had precluded court review by statute.[47] In two cases of hospital claims for increased reimbursement under Medicare, I voted once for the hospital and once for the agency.[48] Anthony concluded the "cases were decided on the merits, not on politics or ideology."[49]

In my tenure on the Court of Appeals, I participated in forty-six labor cases and dissented from majority opinions only twice. In those forty-six decisions, I voted nineteen times in favor of the union or the employee and nineteen times for the employer; eight cases are difficult to classify because the results were ambiguous or mixed in terms of a "pro-business"–"pro-labor" dichotomy.[50]

Freedom of Speech Under the First Amendment

The charges that I was opposed to freedom of speech were entirely based on an article I had written some sixteen years previously. The article opened and closed with admonitions that it was theoretical, tentative, and speculative.[51] In the intervening years, I had created a public record in this field, too, but that was ignored by the opposition as if it did not exist.

In the course of that wide-ranging article, I had argued two points that infuriated the opposition. The first was that of all the functions speech served, only one was different from the functions of other, unprotected, human activities, and that was the discovery and spread of political truth. There was, therefore, I argued, no reason to throw constitutional protection around speech that was not political. I later abandoned that position, not because the observation about the functions of speech was not true, but because it results in an unworkable rule.[52] Almost any speech could be made protected by simply adding a policy proposal at the end. Moreover, the discovery and spread of what we regard as political truth is assisted by many forms of speech and writing that are not explicitly political.

My second contention was that there is no constitutional reason to protect speech advocating forcible overthrow of the government or speech advocating the violation of law. The reason for that conclusion is plain. The Constitution creates a republican form of government in which political speech is essential to arrive at consensus on various issues. Majorities make up their minds and either do or do not enact laws. In such a government, speech advocating the forcible overthrow of the government and the seizure of power by a minority has no value because it contradicts the premises of constitutional democracy. If the speech succeeds, democracy and individual freedom are at an end. For the same reason, speech that advocates violation of the law or civil disobedience is an attempt to defeat by lawlessness what the majority has decided. In our form of government, everyone is always free to advocate changing the law by the regular legislative processes. Because we are a constitutional democracy, there is one exception to the idea that speech advocating violation of the law is illegal. If the object of the disobedience advocated is to frame a challenge in the courts to the constitutionality of the law, and if the law proves to be unconstitutional, then the speaker may not be punished.

We may have done at once with the charge that my position would have made illegal the advocacy of boycotts, marches, sermons, and peaceful demonstrations during the civil rights struggle in the South. Customer boycotts are not usually illegal and advocating them would not be. Marches, sermons, and peaceful demonstrations do not involve incitement to break the law and are themselves expressive conduct protected by the first amendment. The suggestion that I thought any of these things illegal was flatly false.[53] That leaves the case of Martin Luther King, Jr. Dr. King, so far as I am aware, rarely advocated lawbreaking except in an effort to challenge the constitutionality of the law. When he himself violated a law, he accepted the punishment that ensued, as his *Letter from the Birmingham Jail* attests.[54] There is surely no reason to think it is proper to punish those who violate the law but improper to punish the person who persuades them to do so.

Indeed, bringing Dr. King's name into the question of the legality of advocating lawbreaking was merely part of the tactic of claiming that I was opposed to civil rights. If the advocacy of civil disobedience is to receive first amendment protection, that protection cannot be confined to Dr. King. The courts cannot apply the first amendment selectively, deciding which advocate of law violation is a good man and which a bad man, extending the protection of the Constitution to the former but not the latter. That is not law but politics, and not of a very respectable type at that. Nor does it seem satisfactory to frame a rule that all advocacy of lawbreaking is protected by the first amendment. There may well come times when society cannot tolerate such a rule. Inciting a mob to lynch a prisoner would be protected speech under such a rule. The Supreme Court has never enunciated such a standard or even flirted with it. After trying various formulas, the Supreme Court in *Brandenburg* v. *Ohio* (1969) adopted the principle that "the constitutional guarantees of free speech and free press do not permit a State to forbid or proscribe advocacy of the use of force or of law violation except where such advocacy is directed to inciting or producing imminent lawless action and is likely to incite or produce such action."[55] That rule, which the preparers of the *Biden Report* would presumably endorse, and which was adopted by a liberal Supreme Court, would not protect one who advocated a sit-in at a segregated lunch counter if the segregation was lawful and the advocacy produced a sit-in.

The claim that I had suggested a legal formulation that would have punished advocacy of illegal conduct that the Supreme Court would protect was, as the example given shows, false. But, in the academic writings referred to, I did suggest that there was no reason for courts to protect any advocacy of law violation since that is merely advocacy of a piecemeal overthrow of the democratic system. Such speech, in a republican form of government, has little, if any, value. Whether it should be tolerated as a matter of prudence seems to me essentially a political rather than a judicial choice. The law was once very close to that position, and there was no occasion to make it appear that what I had written some time ago was outside the realm of respectable discussion. And that is what the old article relentlessly cited was, a theoretical discussion by a law professor. When I told the Judiciary Committee that as a judge I would abide by the current state of the law, that was treated as a conversion made in an effort to be confirmed.

But there was a public record on freedom of speech and the press under the first amendment that came after my one theoretical writing on the subject. I extended the press's protection from libel actions in cases such as *Ollman* v. *Evans*[56] and *McBride* v. *Merrell Dow & Pharmaceuticals Inc.*[57] In *Telecommunications Research & Action Center* v. *FCC*,[58] I not only held that the fairness doctrine, generally disliked by broadcasters and approved by many conservatives, was not statutorily required, but called on the Supreme Court to reexamine its position that the electronic media may be constitutionally subjected to restrictions that cannot be applied to the print media because of the first amendment. In *Quincy Cable TV* v. *FCC*,[59] I joined a decision that the restrictions, in my view wrongly, applied to the electronic media did not apply to cable television. In *FTC* v. *Brown & Williamson Tobacco Corp.*,[60] I wrote an opinion protecting commercial advertising. These and other decisions and opinions were said to show nothing about my first amendment views because the protection was given to business interests, which libel defendants, being media corporations, usually are, or to conservatives. That dismissal of my work as a judge rings hollow since in *Lebron* v. *Washington Metropolitan Area Transit Authority*[61] I found that an artist who wanted to put up in the subways stations a poster harshly critical of Ronald Reagan had a first amendment right to do so. And in *Finzer* v. *Barry,*[62] I found against the free speech claim of a conservative Episcopalian priest who wanted to demonstrate against the Soviets immediately outside their embassy. Those decisions cannot possibly be explained by my personal views. The poster denouncing Reagan, the man who had appointed me to the Court of Appeals, seemed to me harsh and untrue, and I have never been particularly known for sympathy to the Soviet government. People may legitimately disagree with any or all of those decisions, but one thing they cannot truthfully say is that the pattern shows a hostility to freedom of speech or is explained by a preference for conservatives.

*   *   *

This analysis of the charges made could be extended indefinitely, for the number of charges made sometimes seemed to approach the infinite, and a great many of them were more vicious than those recounted here. To recount and rebut all of them would fill an entire book, but that is not my object. The purpose of this chapter is to demonstrate that key charges were not only false but should have been, must have been, known to be false by the individuals and groups that made them and repeated them even after they were answered with facts. That, as I said at the outset of this book, is the way the war for control of our legal culture is being fought.

17

Why the Campaign Was Mounted

We have seen how the opposition behaved and the tactics it saw fit to use. The question that must be answered is why. Why was there an explosion of fury at my nomination? Why did the public interest organizations, so many academics, and most of the major media display blatant hostility and misrepresent facts?

Most immediately, of course, many of these groups were energized by issues such as abortion and sexual permissiveness. *Roe* v. *Wade*[1] imposed on the United States rules permitting more widespread abortion than is allowed by the laws of any other Western democracy.[2] The possibility that the case would be overturned meant that greater regulation might occur here. On this and related social issues the Court was perceived to be at a tipping point, and Justice Powell, whom I would have replaced, had one year before my nomination provided a crucial fifth vote to retain *Roe*.[3] The real fear that I would vote the other way may also have brought into play accusations about hostility to civil rights as a means of adding other groups to the opposition coalition.

But the fear of the opposition was more general than that. *Roe* is a symbol for a constellation of attitudes about social issues that are typical of the groups that came together in a great coalition to organize the opposition. The battle was ultimately about whether intellectual class values,[4] which are far more egalitarian and socially permissive, which is to say left-liberal, than those of the public at large and so cannot carry elections, were to continue to be enacted into law by the Supreme Court. That was why this nomination became the focal point of the war within our culture. The behavior of the people involved reflects a left-liberal culture in near despair.

The members of that culture know they are a minority, and they were desperate not to lose a battle in which symbolism as much as substance was at stake. The left-liberal culture commands much of the institutional high ground in our society. Until recently, one of its major strongholds was the Supreme Court of the United States. Being a minority, that culture must control such institutions, including counter-majoritarian institutions such as the federal courts, to have any hope of winning its cultural battles. As Lloyd Cutler, a prominent liberal lawyer and Counsel to President Carter, and a man who publicly supported me, said afterward, "Your enemies did not really think you would overturn all the decisions they like. But they have an entitlements agenda for the future—things like constitutional rights to welfare and to education—and they knew you wouldn't give it to them."[5] If so, they were right. I would not have enacted that agenda for them, not because I disagree with those positions politically or morally but because they are not to be found in the actual Constitution. If the groups' programs are to become law, they must be enacted by legislatures.

We have discussed the sharp, long-standing difference between intellectual class attitudes and the values of most Americans in Chapter 11. Only recently, however, have intellectual class policies been advanced with the ferocity and, it must be said, the intellectual dishonesty that was manifested in the nomination campaign. What is new is the addition to the intellectual class of a group associated with, indeed responsible for, the rebelliousness and turmoil in the universities in the late 1960s. The members of "the 60s generation," as this small group of the total population of the same age is known, are now in mid-career but, in large measure, retain the attitudes they formed in youth. One member of the Columbia College class of 1968 observed at the class's twentieth reunion:

> "I'm amazed at how many people *haven't* been depoliticized. . . . Against the odds of a decade of greed and cynicism, an unbelievable number are still involved in socially committed work."[6]

As would be expected, they have avoided careers in business and professions not directly concerned with policymaking. Instead, today they are tenured in the universities, strongly represented in the media, far more active than other Americans in politics, where they have found their home in the Democratic Party, and, as I shall discuss below, man an enormous range of activist public interest groups. Another member of the Columbia class of 1968, now teaching Shakespeare at the university, made this point in telling fashion:

"What has changed most since 1968 has been the faculty, especially the junior faculty. They are the children of the 60's. They were marching then, but now the political action takes place in the classroom, and in scholarly books dedicated to social change."[7]

Others as well have made this same observation. Thus Harold Taylor has commented:

"Many of the students involved in the reform movements in the early and middle 1960s have gone on to the graduate schools with no slackening in their enthusiasm for the causes with which they were identified as undergraduates. . . . [T]heir social views, especially on questions of race and poverty, are radical, and at the same time are becoming politically respectable."[8]

Balch and London observe that today the radical left is "comfortably ensconced within a network of journals and professional organizations, university departments and academic programs"[9] where they may be distinguished from their colleagues by their view that "scholarship and teaching are preeminently, and unavoidably, extensions of politics."[10] This general academic phenomenon is observable in the law faculties as well. Thus one law professor writes:

In the late 1960s and early 1970s, many of us entered law teaching with liberal or even radical views and the faith that legal scholarship and law teaching would enable us to translate our values into social reform.[11]

Indeed, the adherents of the radical Critical Legal Studies movement, mentioned in Chapter 9, themselves agree that the typical CLS professor was a college and law student in the late 1960s and early 1970s whose political attitudes were shaped by the antiwar and other radical activities of that period.[12]

The 60s generation originated as an adversary culture—indeed, many of them then described themselves as the "counterculture"— and they remain cultural revolutionaries, but now they occupy positions from which they can heavily influence and alter the general culture, and they have. The New Left, a congeries of radicals so named to distinguish them from the historic American left, collapsed as a political movement, but its adherents are still with us and arguably have more effect on our politics and policies than ever.

The defining experience of this group was, of course, opposition to the war in Vietnam. George Bush, in his inaugural address, pointed to that experience as still dividing the parties in Congress. "There has grown a certain divisiveness. We have seen the hard looks and heard the statements in which not each other's ideas are challenged but each other's motives. And our great parties have too often been far apart and untrusting of each other. It's been this way since Vietnam. That war cleaves us still."[13] If the President sees that effect in our politics, it is not implausible—indeed it is obvious—that a similar effect, of the war and of the radicalism that surrounded that issue, is present elsewhere in our culture.

The influence of this new left (I have dropped the capitals to indicate that it is no longer a political movement) is greatly increased by the fact that many such persons claim to be merely liberals of the old-fashioned variety. The claim is false, but it increases the credibility of this group with traditional liberals. The most important aspects of the new left are that it is unprogrammatic and that it is alienated.

Because it has no cohesive program, this form of radicalism finds outlets in a variety of single-issue organizations. As Arch Puddington said:

> The [contemporary left's] job has been simplified by the absence of serious left-wing parties whose ideologies, programs, or foreign links might elicit public scrutiny—and hostility. Instead of working through organized parties, the Left presses its agenda through single-issue projects—on the misconduct of the CIA, the menace of nuclear power, Central American "war crimes," multinational corporate greed, U.S.–Soviet relations. At any given time, it has going literally hundreds of projects, coalitions, committees, task forces, and commissions of inquiry. Many achieve little beyond a few newspaper clippings; a few, however, have changed the very complexion of American politics.[14]

The single-issue groups also include those who attack American business through extreme forms of environmentalism, feminism, product safety, health concerns, and the like. Each of these is recognized by Americans of all persuasions as a meritorious cause, but each can be pushed to extremes so great that it is difficult not to conclude that more than concern for the stated cause is at work. That "more" often seems to be an antibusiness or antibourgeois mind set.

The new left is probably unprogrammatic because it is frustrated by its inability to articulate its natural policy preferences. The new left adopts Marxist critiques of American society because Marxism offers the most fully developed and prestigious adversarial system ready to hand. Yet the new left cannot afford to put forward a Marxist program. There is really no alternative to a capitalistic, bourgeois society other than some form of socialism. But socialism is widely, almost universally, recognized to be a practical and intellectual failure, a set of policies now so thoroughly discredited that in America no movement with any ambition to achieve power or even influence can afford to embrace it. There are of course repackaged varieties of socialism, such as industrial planning, but they quickly lose appeal when seen for what they are. The result is that those who dislike this society have only a policy of severe criticism without an alternative program they can articulate.

The other fact to be noted about the new left and some other segments of the intellectual class is that it is enormously mistrustful of this society and its institutions, a mistrust so deep that some commentators have characterized it as a state of alienation.

Every study of the new left and sympathetic members of the intellectual class shows their attitudes to be as I have described. S. Robert Lichter and Stanley Rothman studied the attitudes of leaders or top staffers in 74 public interest organizations, including the American Civil Liberties Union, Center for Law and Social Policy, Common Cause, Consumers Union, Environmental Defense Fund, Public Citizen, and major public interest law firms. Lichter and Rothman found:

> The liberalism of public interest leaders shades into profound dissatisfaction with the American social and economic order. . . . In fact their alienation was one of our most striking findings. . . . Three out of four believe the very structure of our society causes alienation, and over 90% say our legal system favors the wealthy. . . . Only about half the public interest leaders believe the system can be salvaged.[15]

Ninety-six percent of the public interest elite sampled voted for George McGovern.[16] That last statistic is staggering. Richard Nixon in 1972 won an enormous landslide in the nation as a whole, but at the same time the public interest elite gave his leftist opponent a landslide of the proportions usually seen only in Communist bloc nations. Figures of the same general magnitude are displayed by media and academic elites. The general class of intellectuals who display views of this sort numbers in the millions.

A culture that is at once moralistic, self-righteous, alienated, and in a minority will constantly be tempted to break the rules of political discourse—indeed to conduct its struggles in ways that preclude the use of the word "discourse"—and to gain its ends by deception or outright falsehoods. Policy disputes are disguised and take the form of moral assault. As President Bush said, the disputants challenge not each other's ideas but each other's motives. Max Lerner observed that our politics today are more Jacobin than at any time since the 1960s.[17] Saul Bellow noted that the "heat of the dispute between Left and Right has grown so fierce in the last decade that the habits of civilized discourse have suffered a scorching."[18] This form of behavior was certainly a prominent feature of the 60s generation's tactics as students. Alexander Bickel, in describing those tactics, complained of

> . . . the abandonment of reason, of standards, of measure, the loss of balance and judgment. Among its symptoms were the incivility and even violence of rhetoric and action that academics and other intellectuals domesticated into their universe of discourse. . . . Our recent revolutionists have offered us hatred. They despise and dehumanize the persons, and they condemn the concerns and the aspirations, of the vast majority of their countrymen. They have offered for the future, so far as their spokesmen have been able to make clear, the Maypole dance and, in considerable tension if not contradiction, a vision of "liberated" masses adjuring profit, competition, personal achievement, and any form of gratification not instantly and equally available to all.[19]

It is a sign that an important part of this society has accepted, or become resigned to, both the values and tactics of the new left that assaultive rhetoric of the kind Bickel describes is now allowed to pass with little resistance or comment from the media and other institutions of the intellectual class.

People who are alienated obviously will not respect the basic institutions of a society they regard as illegitimate. Lectures about the right of self-government, judicial restraint, and the separation of powers will seem irrelevant if not reactionary. Thus Bickel also noted that such people prefer an activist, imperialistic Supreme Court as a means of displacing democratic choice by moral principle.[20]

This explains why it is that the intellectual left reacts with fury when its influence with the courts is threatened. The rise or, more accurately, the resurrection of a jurisprudence of original understanding threatens this "natural order," hence it is illegitimate and may be assailed.

As our cultural war intensifies, it is necessarily reflected in our politics. It is obvious that our parties are becoming increasingly polarized on social issues, especially at the level of presidential elections, which means that the two parties are coming to represent opposite sides of our cultural class warfare in their political struggles. That is why George Bush attacked Michael Dukakis on the symbolic cultural and class issues of the pledge of allegiance and the Governor's pride in being a "card-carrying member of the ACLU."

That, I think, was why the groups of left-liberalism came together in an enormous coalition to oppose me. I had been, of course, an academic and a professor of constitutional law for a number of years and a dissident to the left orthodoxy that prevails in the academy. Perhaps the fury is explained partly by the feeling that I was a traitor. If the philosophy of political judging is a heresy in the American system of government, it is the orthodoxy of the law schools and of the left-liberal culture. I would have done well to remember that in the old days nobody burned infidels, but they did burn heretics.

Yet in the final analysis, the furor and the venom were less about me than about the issue of whether the Court would become dominated by the neutral philosophy of original understanding and thus decisively end its long enlistment on one side of the war in our culture. As *Time* said, "All at once the political passions of three decades seemed to converge on a single empty chair."[21] That battle is over but the war in both our legal and general culture goes on. There will be more blood at the crossroads where law and politics meet.

18

Effects for the Future

What does the political campaign against my confirmation promise for the future of the nomination process? What does the possible permanent deterioration of that process mean for the future of the Court and the Constitution? It is too soon to be certain, but some important tendencies are apparent.

Some of what happened is specific to my situation and not necessarily instructive. I was nominated by a President who had lost much of his political power on Capitol Hill both because of the approaching end of his term and because he had been badly damaged in the Iran-Contra affair. This was an opportune time for the Democrats to administer a defeat to Ronald Reagan. (The President himself generously took that view in my conversations with him, but I prefer to take some of the credit and to think that I qualified as a target in my own right.) The Republicans, moreover, had lost control of the Senate in the 1986 elections. Finally, the liberals, who have always regarded the federal judiciary as their particular ally in government, needed to stop my confirmation in particular. Because of my writings I had become perhaps the most visible proponent of adhering to what the Constitution actually says and of pointing out that where the Constitution is silent, the people must decide through legislation. That view is anathema to liberals who have come to view the courts as the branch that will enact their policies when legislatures won't. Quite aside from the effect of my vote on the Court, I was a symbol that they needed to destroy. They needed to prove that a liberal imperialistic Court is legitimate and that any other view is outside what they insist is "the mainstream."

A political attack of similar dimensions may or may not happen to future nominees, but even so it seems likely that the way the campaign and the hearings were conducted will have long-term effects—effects on the judicial nomination process of the future, effects upon the substance of our law, particularly our constitutional law, and effects upon the intellectual life of the law.

Because I had written on relevant subjects, I was subjected to intensive questioning about what I had said years before. Some of the senators regard this as a precedent for inquiring into the nominees' views even if he has not written or otherwise created a track record. The confirmation hearings to which Justice Kennedy was subjected are hardly conclusive on the question of how the Senate and the Judiciary Committee will approach these matters in the future. Kennedy was questioned about his views and felt obliged to give answers. The fact that he was permitted to give quite general answers does not mean that others will be. The Senate cannot stage too many of these circuses consecutively. Some senators, particularly the Southern Democrats, knew they eventually had to confirm a nominee perceived as being conservative. Moreover, the activist groups that had spent millions and months in a hysterical campaign against me could not reach that peak of frenzy twice in a row. When some of the groups wanted to mount such a campaign against Justice Kennedy, one senator said, "Nobody wants to go through that again. There's just too much blood on the floor."[1] But, after some time has passed, they may well be able to mount such a campaign against a future nominee.

The greatest impact of what occurred, however, may not be simply the precedent set but what the knowledge that such a campaign is always possible will do to the calculations of other actors in the process.

The senators are now accustomed to insisting upon answers to doctrinal questions. If they continue that practice, they will effectively compel nominees to make campaign promises or face the possibility of rejection. It is amusing that some senators claimed that the White House imposed a litmus test for the President's nominees. No one in the Administration asked me a single question about my views on any topic of law. They were satisfied that they knew my approach to judging. By contrast, various senators not only asked my views but insisted that I adopt what they thought the correct position. At one point we counted about seventeen propositions that senators wanted me to agree to, some of them highly controversial. I did not agree to them and lost votes as a result. If senators are able to get future nominees to agree, the Senate and not the Supreme Court will come to control the substance of our constitutional law. Perhaps "control" is too strong a word, but the Senate will certainly influence Supreme Court decisions in a variety of areas. That is not our constitutional form of government. If the Court has often erred by encroaching upon the legislative domain, it is equally inconsistent with the American constitutional design when the Senate encroaches upon areas left to the legitimate authority of the Court.

But there is another way in which this episode may affect both the course of the law and the intellectual life of the law. It is impossible to know how many opinions, articles, and books will be written differently because of this episode. That some will seems certain. My 1971 article in the *Indiana Law Journal*[2] was, even before the hearings, one of the most discussed and cited law review articles in our history. It accomplished what I, as a professor, had hoped: It generated debate and fresh theoretical inquiry. But despite its explicitly tentative and speculative nature, and despite years of a subsequent record in public service, that article, in badly misrepresented form, became the single most effective weapon used against me. I remain glad that I wrote it. Most of it still seems to me entirely correct. But it is possible to wonder what the effect will be on men and women who observed the political use made of an academic writing.

In the short run, the pool of potential nominees is likely to shrink and change in composition. A president who wants to avoid a battle like mine, and most presidents would prefer to, is likely to nominate men and women who have not written much, and certainly nothing that could be regarded as controversial by left-leaning senators and groups. People who have thought much about the role proper to judges are likely, however, to have written or spoken on the subject. The tendency, therefore, will be to nominate and confirm persons whose performance once on the bench cannot be accurately, or perhaps even roughly, predicted either by the President or by the Senate.

In the longer run, the anticipation that campaigns such as this may be waged is likely to affect both the course of the law and the intellectual life of the law. There are in this country a great many men and women who are potential Supreme Court nominees; there are a great many more who imagine that they are potential nominees; and many more than that who may be unwilling early in their careers permanently to rule out the possibility of a federal judgeship. It is quite conceivable that some lower court judges may be affected in the decisions they make and in the opinions they write. The panel's decision and my opinion in *American Cyanamid,*[3] the case of the women given the option of sterilization, was, for example, ruthlessly misrepresented. Perhaps a judge faced with a similarly exploitable issue will decide the case the other way and write an opinion filled with popular sentiments. I am sure most judges will not consciously yield to that temptation, but the career hazards involved in deciding a case according to the law ought not even be in the back of any judge's mind. Now, I fear, that is inevitable.

Lawyers and professors have been encouraged to think twice or three times about what they write. Criticizing the reasoning of a politically popular decision, particularly one popular with the senators and activist groups of the left, may be a significant hindrance to attaining a career on the bench. I have already learned of instances of lawyers withdrawing articles from magazines for this very reason. One magazine had two such episodes. One lawyer withdrew an article he had submitted altogether, explicitly on the grounds of my experience, and the other, at last report, was resisting editorial changes that would make his points clearer.

My nomination did not, of course, create these trends. It merely brought them into the open in a way that had never previously occurred but was bound to happen sooner or later as conservative presidents, armed with the nomination power, begin to threaten the liberal hegemony over the courts. This book has traced the increasingly political nature of the Supreme Court, which reached its zenith with the Warren Court, and the increasing, by now almost overwhelming, politicization of the law schools, where much constitutional scholarship is now only politics. When the Court is perceived as a political rather than a legal institution, nominees will be treated like political candidates, campaigns will be waged in public, lobbying of senators and the media will be intense, the nominee will be questioned about how he will vote, and he will be pressed to make campaign promises about adhering to or rejecting particular doctrines.

This is a logical development as law becomes politicized. Why, then, since the Warren Court began over thirty years ago, did the development not occur sooner? One answer is that it did, but some earlier battles, while essentially political, were not overtly so. Judge Clement Haynesworth's defeat in the Senate was very largely political but was presented as concern about a quite trivial ethical matter. The old forms and procedures had considerable staying power because to engage in ideological battle is to admit publicly that the Court is at least partially politicized and that you accept that condition. In my case, after the most minute scrutiny of my personal life and professional record, all that was available to the opposition was ideological attack, and so politics came fully into the open. I had criticized the Warren Court, and this was the revenge of the Warren Court.

Though I hope it is not true, the forms and restraints of the Senate confirmation process in which the nominee was judged on professional ability and integrity alone have probably been weakened. It will be easier in the future to be explicitly ideological in support of or opposition to a nominee. But whether that ideological testing is overt or covert, it will continue so long as courts are seen as political. And they will be seen that way so long as their behavior invites such a perception.

There seems to be no immediate prospect that the steady politicization of the law and its institutions will slow, much less be reversed. Too many people have come to see as crucial the capture of the law and its deployment as a political weapon. This explains the recent battles over lower court appointments and even over appointments to the Department of Justice. One effect of the political struggle over my nomination was to heighten awareness of what is at stake, and the effects may be seen everywhere. When the Supreme Court recently handed down rather moderate civil rights and abortion decisions, we witnessed an explosion of inflammatory rhetoric from activist groups surpassing in violence anything witnessed for over thirty years. Insults to particular Justices and threats of civil disobedience were bandied freely.

Nor should this be surprising. We have been moving in this direction for a long time. No legal system can produce increasingly political results without at some point ceasing to be, or earning the respect due, a legal system. Groups that have been taught to see the courts as their reliable political ally, as their branch of government, react in fury when courts begin to apply law instead. The Supreme Court is our preeminent symbol of the rule of law. If the Court comes to seem illegitimate, the legitimacy of law itself declines and the moral obligation to obey it is cast into doubt. What the future holds in this respect is unclear. What is clear is that we have come close to a tipping point and we must draw back.

Conclusion

*T*he Constitution has been many things to Americans. It has been and remains an object of veneration, a sacred text, the symbol of our nationhood, the foundation of our government's structure and practice, a guarantor of our liberties, and a moral teacher.

But the Constitution is also power. That is why we see political struggle over the selection of the judges who will wield that power. In our domestic affairs and even to some degree in our foreign dealings, the Constitution provides judges with the ultimate coercive power known to our political arrangements. In the hands of judges, words become action: commands are issued by courts, obeyed by legislatures, and enforced by executives. The reading of the words becomes freedoms and restrictions for us; the course of the nation is confirmed or altered; the way we live and the ways we think and feel are affected.

It will not do to overstate the matter. We are an incredibly complex and intricate society and no power is without checks, some obvious and direct in operation, some subtle and intangible. But a major check on judicial power, perhaps the major check, is the judges' and our understanding of the proper limits to that power. Those limits may be pressed back incrementally, case by case, until judges rule areas of life not confided to their authority by any provision of the Constitution or other law. We have, in fact, witnessed just that process. The progression of political judging, judging unrelated to law, has been recounted in this book. This progression has greatly accelerated in the past few decades and now we see the theorists of constitutional law urging judges on to still greater incursions into Americans' right of self-government.

This is an anxious problem and one that can be met only by understanding that judges must always be guided by the original understanding of the Constitution's provisions. Once adherence to the original understanding is weakened or abandoned, a judge, perhaps instructed by a revisionist theorist, can reach any result, because the human mind and will, freed of the constraints of history and "the sediment of history which is law," can reach any result. As we have seen, no set of propositions is too preposterous to be espoused by a judge or a law professor who has cast loose from the historical Constitution.

The judge's proper task is not mechanical. "History," Cardinal Newman reminded us, "is not a creed or a catechism, it gives lessons rather than rules."[1] No body of doctrine is born fully developed. That is as true of constitutional law as it is of theology. The provisions of the Constitution state profound but simple and general ideas. The law laid down in those provisions gradually gains body, substance, doctrines, and distinctions as judges, equipped at first with only those ideas, are forced to confront new situations and changing circumstances. It is essential, however, that the new developments always be weighed in the light of the lessons history provides about the principles meant to be enforced. Doctrine must be shaped and reshaped to conform to the original ideas of the Constitution, to ensure that the principles intended are those which guide and limit power, and that no principles not originally meant are invented to deprive us of the right to govern ourselves. The concept of original understanding itself gains in solidity, in articulation and sophistication, as we investigate its meanings, implications, and requirements, and as we are forced to defend its truths from the constitutional heresies with which we are continually tempted.

Among the stakes is the full right of self-government that the Founders bequeathed us and which they limited only as to specified topics. In the long run, however, there may be higher stakes than that. As we move away from the historically rooted Constitution to one created by abstract, universalistic styles of constitutional reasoning, we invite a number of dangers. One is that such styles teach disrespect for the actual institutions of the American nation. A great many academic theorists state explicitly, and some judges seem easily persuaded, that elected legislators and executives are not adequate to decide the moral issues that divide us, and that judges should therefore take their place. But, when Americans are morally divided, it is appropriate that our laws reflect that fact. The often untidy responses of the elected branches possess virtues and benefits that the "principled" reactions of courts do not. Our popular institutions, the legislative and executive branches, were structured to provide safety, to achieve compromise when we are divided, to slow change, to dilute absolutisms. They both embody and produce wholesome inconsistencies. They are designed, in short, to do the very things that abstract generalizations about moral principle and the just society tend to bring into contempt. That is a dangerous civics lesson to teach the citizens of a republic. As Edmund Burke put it:

> All government, indeed every human benefit and enjoyment, every virtue, and every prudent act, is founded on compromise and barter. We balance inconveniences; we give and take; we remit some rights, that we may enjoy others; and, we choose rather to be happy citizens, than subtle disputants.[2]

It may be significant that this passage is from Burke's speech on *Moving His Resolutions for Conciliation With the Colonies,* delivered to Parliament in 1775. The English government elected to stand on abstract principles of sovereignty and lost the American colonies.

The attempt to define individual liberties by abstract moral philosophy, though it is said to broaden our liberties, is actually likely to make them more vulnerable. I am not referring here to the freedom to govern ourselves but to the freedoms from government guaranteed by the Bill of Rights and the post–Civil War amendments. Those constitutional liberties were not produced by abstract reasoning. They arose out of historical experience with unaccountable power and out of political thought grounded in the study of history as well as in moral and religious sentiment. Attempts to frame theories that remove from democratic control areas of life our nation's Founders intended to place there can achieve power only if abstractions are regarded as legitimately able to displace the Constitution's text and structure and the history that gives our legal rights life, rootedness, and meaning. It is no small matter to discredit the foundations upon which our constitutional freedoms have always been sustained and substitute as a bulwark only the abstract propositions of moral philosophy. To do that is, in fact, to display a lightmindedness terrifying in its frivolity. Our freedoms do not ultimately depend upon the pronouncements of judges sitting in a row. They depend upon their acceptance by the American people, and a major factor in that acceptance is the belief that these liberties are inseparable from the founding of the nation. The moral systems urged as constitutional law by the theorists are not compatible with the moral beliefs of most Americans. Richard John Neuhaus wrote that law is "a human enterprise in response to human behavior, and human behavior is stubbornly entangled with beliefs about right and wrong."[3] Law will not be recognized as legitimate if it is not organically related to "the larger universe of moral discourse that helps shape human behavior." Constitutional doctrine that rests upon a parochial and class-bound version of morality, one not shared by the general American public, is certain to be resented and is unlikely to prove much of a safeguard when crisis comes.

Robert Bolt's play about Thomas More, *A Man For All Seasons,* makes the point. When More was Lord Chancellor, his daughter, Margaret, and his son-in-law, Roper, urged him to arrest a man they regarded as evil. Margaret said, "Father, that man's bad." More replied, "There is no law against that." And Roper said, "There is! God's law!" More then gave excellent advice to judges: "Then God can arrest him. . . . The law, Roper, the law. I know what's legal not what's right. And I'll stick to what's legal. . . . I'm *not* God. The currents and eddies of right and wrong, which you find such plain sailing, I can't navigate. I'm no voyager. But in the thickets of the law, oh, there I'm a forester."[4]

Roper would not be appeased and he leveled the charge that More would give the Devil the benefit of law.

> MORE. Yes. What would you do? Cut a great road through the law to get after the Devil?
>
> ROPER. I'd cut down every law in England to do that!
>
> MORE. . . . Oh? . . . And when the last law was down, and the Devil turned round on you—where would you hide, Roper, the laws all being flat? . . . This country's planted thick with laws from coast to coast—man's laws, not God's—and if you cut them down— . . . d'you really think you could stand upright in the winds that would blow then? . . . Yes, I'd give the Devil benefit of law, for my own safety's sake.[5]

This is not a romanticized version of the man, for the historic More is reported to have said of his duty as a judge: "[I]f the parties will at my hands call for justice, then, all were it my father stood on the one side, and the Devil on the other, his cause being good, the Devil should have right."[6] It is a hard saying and a hard duty, but it is the duty we must demand of judges.

Judges will always be tempted to apply what they imagine to

be "God's law," cutting a great road through man's law. When they have done, when man's law has been thoroughly weakened and discredited, and when powerful forces have a different version of God's law or the higher morality, we may find that the actual rights of the Constitution and the democratic institutions that protect us may have all been flattened.

The difference between our historically grounded constitutional freedoms and those the theorists, whether of the academy or of the bench, would replace them with is akin to the difference between the American and the French revolutions. The outcome for liberty was much less happy under the regime of the abstract "rights of man" than it has been under the American Constitution. What Burke said of the abstract theorists who produced the calamities of the French Revolution might equally be said of those, judges and professors alike, who would remake our constitution out of moral philosophy: "This sort of people are so taken up with their theories about the rights of man that they have totally forgotten his nature."[7] Those who made and endorsed our Constitution knew man's nature, and it is to their ideas, rather than to the temptations of utopia, that we must ask that our judges adhere.

APPENDIX

The Constitution of the United States of America

We the People of the United States, in Order to form a more perfect Union, establish Justice, insure domestic Tranquility, provide for the common defence, promote the general Welfare, and secure the Blessings of Liberty to ourselves and our Posterity, do ordain and establish this Constitution for the United States of America.

ARTICLE I.

SECTION 1. All legislative Powers herein granted shall be vested in a Congress of the United States, which shall consist of a Senate and House of Representatives.

SECTION 2. The House of Representatives shall be composed of Members chosen every second Year by the People of the several States, and the Electors in each State shall have the Qualifications requisite for Electors of the most numerous Branch of the State Legislature.

No Person shall be a Representative who shall not have attained to the Age of twenty five Years, and been seven Years a Citizen of the United States, and who shall not, when elected, be an Inhabitant of that State in which he shall be chosen.

Representatives and direct Taxes shall be apportioned among the several States which may be included within this Union, according to their respective Numbers, which shall be determined by adding to the whole Number of free Persons, including those bound to Service for a Term of Years, and excluding Indians not taxed, three fifths of all other Persons. The actual Enumeration shall be made within three Years after the first Meeting of the Congress of the United States, and within every subsequent Term of ten Years, in such Manner as they shall by Law direct. The Number of Representatives shall not exceed one for every thirty Thousand, but each State shall have at Least one Representative; and until such enumeration shall be made, the State of New Hampshire shall be entitled to chuse three, Massachusetts eight, Rhode Island and Providence Plantations one, Connecticut five, New-York six, New Jersey four, Pennsylvania eight, Delaware one, Maryland six, Virginia ten, North Carolina five, South Carolina five, and Georgia three.

When vacancies happen in the Representation from any State, the Executive Authority thereof shall issue Writs of Election to fill such Vacancies.

The House of Representatives shall chuse their Speaker and other Officers; and shall have the sole Power of Impeachment.

SECTION 3.   The Senate of the United States shall be composed of two Senators from each State, chosen by the Legislature thereof, for six Years; and each Senator shall have one Vote.

Immediately after they shall be assembled in Consequence of the first Election, they shall be divided as equally as may be into three Classes. The Seats of the Senators of the first Class shall be vacated at the Expiration of the second Year, of the second Class at the Expiration of the fourth Year, and of the third Class at the Expiration of the sixth Year, so that one third may be chosen every second Year; and if Vacancies happen by Resignation, or otherwise, during the Recess of the Legislature of any State, the Executive thereof may make temporary Appointments until the next Meeting of the Legislature, which shall then fill such Vacancies.

No Person shall be a Senator who shall not have attained to the Age of thirty Years, and been nine Years a Citizen of the United States, and who shall not, when elected, be an Inhabitant of that State for which he shall be chosen.

The Vice President of the United States shall be President of the Senate, but shall have no Vote, unless they be equally divided.

The Senate shall chuse their other Officers, and also a President pro tempore, in the Absence of the Vice President, or when he shall exercise the Office of President of the United States.

The Senate shall have the sole Power to try all Impeachments. When sitting for that Purpose, they shall be on Oath or Affirmation. When the President of the United States is tried the Chief Justice shall preside: And no Person shall be convicted without the Concurrence of two thirds of the Members present.

Judgment in Cases of Impeachment shall not extend further than to removal from Office, and disqualification to hold and enjoy any Office of honor, Trust or Profit under the United States: but the Party convicted shall nevertheless be liable and subject to Indictment, Trial, Judgment and Punishment, according to Law.

Section 4.   The Times, Places and Manner of holding Elections for Senators and Representatives, shall be prescribed in each State by the Legislature thereof; but the Congress may at any time by Law make or alter such Regulations, except as to the Places of chusing Senators.

The Congress shall assemble at least once in every Year, and such Meeting shall be on the first Monday in December, unless they shall by Law appoint a different Day.

Section 5.   Each House shall be the Judge of the Elections, Returns and Qualifications of its own Members, and a Majority of each shall constitute a Quorum to do Business; but a smaller Number may adjourn from day to day, and may be authorized to compel the Attendance of absent Members, in such Manner, and under such Penalties as each House may provide.

Each House may determine the Rules of its Proceedings, punish its Members for disorderly Behaviour, and, with the Concurrence of two thirds, expel a Member.

Each House shall keep a Journal of its Proceedings, and from time to time publish the same, excepting such Parts as may in their Judgment require Secrecy; and the Yeas and Nays of the Members of either House on any question shall, at the Desire of one fifth of those Present, be entered on the Journal.

Neither House, during the Session of Congress, shall, without the Consent of the other, adjourn for more than three days, nor to any other Place than that in which the two Houses shall be sitting.

Section 6. The Senators and Representatives shall receive a Compensation for their Services, to be ascertained by Law, and paid out of the Treasury of the United States. They shall in all Cases, except Treason, Felony and Breach of the Peace, be privileged from Arrest during their Attendance at the Session of their respective Houses, and in going to and returning from the same; and for any Speech or Debate in either House, they shall not be questioned in any other Place.

No Senator or Representative shall, during the Time for which he was elected, be appointed to any civil Office under the Authority of the United States, which shall have been created, or the Emoluments whereof shall have been encreased during such time; and no Person holding any Office under the United States, shall be a Member of either House during his Continuance in Office.

Section 7. All Bills for raising Revenue shall originate in the House of Representatives; but the Senate may propose or concur with amendments as on other Bills.

Every Bill which shall have passed the House of Representatives and the Senate, shall, before it become a Law, be presented to the President of the United States; If he approve he shall sign it, but if not he shall return it, with his Objections to that House in which it shall have originated, who shall enter the Objections at large on their Journal, and proceed to reconsider it. If after such Reconsideration two thirds of that House shall agree to pass the Bill, it shall be sent, together with the Objections, to the other House, by which it shall likewise be reconsidered, and if approved by two thirds of that House, it shall become a Law. But in all such Cases the Votes of both Houses shall be determined by yeas and Nays, and the Names of the Persons voting for and against the Bill shall be entered on the Journal of each House respectively. If any Bill shall not be returned by the President within ten Days (Sundays excepted) after it shall have been presented to him, the Same shall be a Law, in like Manner as if he had signed it, unless the Congress by their Adjournment prevent its Return, in which Case it shall not be a Law.

Every Order, Resolution, or Vote to which the Concurrence of the Senate and House of Representatives may be necessary (except on a question of Adjournment) shall be presented to the President of the United States; and before the Same shall take Effect, shall be approved by him, or being disapproved by him, shall be repassed by two thirds of the Senate and House of Representatives, according to the Rules and Limitations prescribed in the Case of a Bill.

SECTION 8.   The Congress shall have Power To lay and collect Taxes, Duties, Imposts and Excises, to pay the Debts and provide for the common Defence and general Welfare of the United States; but all Duties, Imposts and Excises shall be uniform throughout the United States;

To borrow Money on the credit of the United States;

To regulate Commerce with foreign Nations, and among the several States, and with the Indian Tribes;

To establish an uniform Rule of Naturalization, and uniform Laws on the subject of Bankruptcies throughout the United States;

To coin Money, regulate the Value thereof, and of foreign Coin, and fix the Standard of Weights and Measures;

To provide for the Punishment of counterfeiting the Securities and current Coin of the United States;

To establish Post Offices and post Roads;

To promote the Progress of Science and useful Arts, by securing for limited Times to Authors and Inventors the exclusive Right to their respective Writings and Discoveries;

To constitute Tribunals inferior to the supreme Court;

To define and punish Piracies and Felonies committed on the high Seas, and Offenses against the Law of Nations;

To declare War, grant Letters of Marque and Reprisal, and make Rules concerning Captures on Land and Water;

To raise and support Armies, but no Appropriation of Money to that Use shall be for a longer Term than two Years;

To provide and maintain a Navy;

To make Rules for the Government and Regulation of the land and naval Forces;

To provide for calling forth the Militia to execute the Laws of the Union, suppress Insurrections and repel Invasions;

To provide for organizing, arming, and disciplining, the Militia, and for governing such Part of them as may be employed in the Service of the United States, reserving to the States respectively, the Appointment of the Officers, and the Authority of training the Militia according to the discipline prescribed by Congress;

To exercise exclusive Legislation in all Cases whatsoever, over such District (not exceeding ten Miles square) as may, by Cession of particular States, and the Acceptance of Congress, become the Seat of the Government of the United States, and to exercise like Authority over all Places purchased by the Consent of the Legislature of the State in which the Same shall be, for the Erection of Forts, Magazines, Arsenals, dock-Yards, and other needful Buildings;— And

To make all Laws which shall be necessary and proper for carrying into Execution the foregoing Powers, and all other Powers vested by this Constitution in the Government of the United States, or in any Department or Officer thereof.

Section 9.   The Migration or Importation of such Persons as any of the States now existing shall think proper to admit, shall not be prohibited by the Congress prior to the Year one thousand eight hundred and eight, but a Tax or duty may be imposed on such Importation, not exceeding ten dollars for each Person.

The Privilege of the Writ of Habeas Corpus shall not be suspended, unless when in Cases of Rebellion or Invasion the public Safety may require it.

No Bill of Attainder or ex post facto Law shall be passed.

No Capitation, or other direct, Tax shall be laid, unless in Proportion to the Census or Enumeration herein before directed to be taken.

No Tax or Duty shall be laid on Articles exported from any State.

No Preference shall be given by any Regulation of Commerce or Revenue to the Ports of one State over those of another: nor shall Vessels bound to, or from, one State, be obliged to enter, clear, or pay Duties in another.

No Money shall be drawn from the Treasury, but in Consequence of Appropriations made by Law; and a regular Statement and Account of the Receipts and Expenditures of all public Money shall be published from time to time.

No Title of Nobility shall be granted by the United States: And no Person holding any Office of Profit or Trust under them, shall, without the Consent of the Congress, accept of any present, Emolument, Office, or Title, of any kind whatever, from any King, Prince or foreign State.

Section 10.   No State shall enter into any Treaty, Alliance, or Confederation; grant Letters of Marque and Reprisal; coin Money; emit Bills of Credit; make any Thing but gold and silver Coin a Tender in Payment of Debts; pass any Bill of Attainder, ex post facto Law, or Law impairing the Obligation of Contracts, or grant any Title of Nobility.

No State shall, without the Consent of the Congress, lay any Imposts or Duties on Imports or Exports, except what may be absolutely necessary for executing its inspection Laws: and the net Produce of all Duties and Imposts, laid by any State on Imports or Exports, shall be for the Use of the Treasury of the United States; and all such Laws shall be subject to the Revision and Controul of the Congress.

No State shall, without the Consent of Congress, lay any Duty of Tonnage, keep Troops, or Ships of War in time of Peace, enter into any Agreement or Compact with another State, or with a foreign Power, or engage in War, unless actually invaded, or in such imminent Danger as will not admit of delay.

ARTICLE II.

SECTION 1. The executive Power shall be vested in a President of the United States of America. He shall hold his Office during the Term of four Years, and, together with the Vice President, chosen for the same Term, be elected, as follows

Each State shall appoint, in such Manner as the Legislature thereof may direct, a Number of Electors, equal to the whole Number of Senators and Representatives to which the State may be entitled in the Congress: but no Senator or Representative, or Person holding an Office of Trust or Profit under the United States, shall be appointed an Elector.

The Electors shall meet in their respective States, and vote by Ballot for two Persons, of whom one at least shall not be an Inhabitant of the same State with themselves. And they shall make a List of all the Persons voted for, and of the Number of Votes for each; which List they shall sign and certify, and transmit sealed to the Seat of the Government of the United States, directed to the President of the Senate. The President of the Senate shall, in the Presence of the Senate and House of Representatives, open all the Certificates, and the Votes shall then be counted. The Person having the greatest Number of Votes shall be the President, if such Number be a Majority of the whole Number of Electors appointed; and if there be more than one who have such Majority, and have an equal Number of Votes, then the House of Representatives shall immediately chuse by Ballot one of them for President; and if no Person have a Majority, then from the five highest on the List the said House shall in like Manner chuse the President. But in chusing the President, the Votes shall be taken by States, the Representation from each State having one Vote; a quorum for this Purpose shall consist of a Member or Members from two thirds of the States, and a Majority of all the States shall be necessary to a Choice. In every Case, after the Choice of the President, the Person having the greatest Number of Votes of the Electors shall be the Vice President. But if there should remain two or more who have equal Votes, the Senate shall chuse from them by Ballot the Vice President.

The Congress may determine the Time of chusing the Electors, and the Day on which they shall give their Votes; which Day shall be the same throughout the United States.

No Person except a natural born Citizen, or a Citizen of the United States, at the time of the Adoption of this Constitution, shall be eligible to the Office of President; neither shall any Person be eligible to that Office who shall not have attained to the Age of thirty five Years, and been fourteen Years a Resident within the United States.

In Case of the Removal of the President from Office, or of his Death, Resignation, or Inability to discharge the Powers and Duties of the said Office, the Same shall devolve on the Vice President, and the Congress may by Law provide for the Case of Removal, Death, Resignation or Inability, both of the President and Vice President, declaring what Officer shall then act as President, and such Officer shall act accordingly, until the Disability be removed, or a President shall be elected.

The President shall, at stated Times, receive for his Services, a Compensation, which shall neither be increased nor diminished during the Period for which he shall have been elected, and he shall not receive within that Period any other Emolument from the United States, or any of them.

Before he enter on the Execution of his Office, he shall take the following Oath or Affirmation:—"I do solemnly swear (or affirm) that I will faithfully execute the Office of President of the United States, and will to the best of my Ability, preserve, protect and defend the Constitution of the United States."

SECTION 2. The President shall be Commander in Chief of the Army and Navy of the United States, and of the Militia of the several States, when called into the actual Service of the United States; he may require the Opinion, in writing, of the principal Officer in each of the executive Departments, upon any Subject relating to the Duties of their respective Offices, and he shall have Power to grant Reprieves and Pardons for Offenses against the United States, except in Cases of Impeachment.

He shall have Power, by and with the Advice and Consent of the Senate, to make Treaties, provided two thirds of the Senators present concur; and he shall nominate, and by and with the Advice and Consent of the Senate, shall appoint Ambassadors, other public Ministers and Consuls, Judges of the supreme Court, and all other Officers of the United States, whose Appointments are not herein otherwise provided for, and which shall be established by Law: but the Congress may by Law vest the Appointment of such inferior Officers, as they think proper, in the President alone, in the Courts of Law, or in the Heads of Departments.

The President shall have Power to fill up all Vacancies that may happen during the Recess of the Senate, by granting Commissions which shall expire at the End of their next Session.

SECTION 3. He shall from time to time give to the Congress Information of the State of the Union, and recommend to their Consideration such Measures as he shall judge necessary and expedient; he may, on extraordinary Occasions, convene both Houses, or either of them, and in Case of Disagreement between them, with Respect to the Time of Adjournment, he may adjourn them to such Time as he shall think proper; he shall receive Ambassadors and other public Ministers; he shall take Care that the Laws be faithfully executed, and shall Commission all the Officers of the United States.

SECTION 4. The President, Vice President and all Civil Officers of the United States, shall be removed from Office on Impeachment for, and Conviction of, Treason, Bribery, or other high Crimes and Misdemeanors.

ARTICLE III.

SECTION 1. The judicial Power of the United States, shall be vested in one supreme Court, and in such inferior Courts as the Congress may from time to time ordain and establish. The Judges, both of the supreme and inferior Courts, shall hold their Offices during good Behaviour, and shall, at stated Times, receive for their Services, a Compensation, which shall not be diminished during their Continuance in Office.

SECTION 2. The judicial Power shall extend to all Cases, in Law and Equity, arising under this Constitution, the Laws of the United States, and Treaties made, or which shall be made, under their Authority;—to all Cases affecting Ambassadors, other public Ministers and Consuls;—to all Cases of admiralty and maritime Jurisdiction;—to Controversies to which the United States shall be a Party;—to Controversies between two or more States;—between a State and Citizens of another State;—between Citizens of different States;—between Citizens of the same State claiming Lands under Grants of different States, and between a State, or the Citizens thereof, and foreign States, Citizens or Subjects.

In all Cases affecting Ambassadors, other public Ministers and Consuls, and those in which a State shall be Party, the Supreme Court shall have original Jurisdiction. In all the other Cases before mentioned, the supreme Court shall have appellate Jurisdiction, both as to Law and Fact, with such Exceptions, and under such Regulations as the Congress shall make.

The Trial of all Crimes, except in Cases of Impeachment; shall be by Jury; and such Trial shall be held in the State where the said Crimes shall have been committed; but when not committed within any State, the Trial shall be at such Place or Places as the Congress may by Law have directed.

SECTION 3. Treason against the United States, shall consist only in levying War against them, or in adhering to their Enemies, giving them Aid and Comfort. No Person shall be convicted of Treason unless on the Testimony of two Witnesses to the same overt Act, or on Confession in open Court.

The Congress shall have Power to declare the Punishment of Treason, but no Attainder of Treason shall work Corruption of Blood, or Forfeiture except during the Life of the Person attainted.

ARTICLE IV.

SECTION 1. Full Faith and Credit shall be given in each State to the public Acts, Records, and judicial Proceedings of every other State; And the Congress may by general Laws prescribe the Manner in which such Acts, Records and Proceedings shall be proved, and the Effect thereof.

SECTION 2.   The Citizens of each State shall be entitled to all Privileges and Immunities of Citizens in the several States.

A Person charged in any State with Treason, Felony, or other Crime, who shall flee from Justice, and be found in another State, shall on Demand of the executive Authority of the State from which he fled, be delivered up, to be removed to the State having Jurisdiction of the Crime.

No Person held to Service or Labour in one State, under the Laws thereof, escaping into another, shall, in Consequence of any Law or Regulation therein, be discharged from such Service or Labour, but shall be delivered up on Claim of the Party to whom such Service or Labour may be due.

SECTION 3.   New States may be admitted by the Congress into this Union; but no new State shall be formed or erected within the Jurisdiction of any other State; nor any State be formed by the Junction of two or more States, or Parts of States, without the Consent of the Legislatures of the States concerned as well as of the Congress.

The Congress shall have Power to dispose of and make all needful Rules and Regulations respecting the Territory or other Property belonging to the United States; and nothing in this Constitution shall be so construed as to Prejudice any Claims of the United States, or of any particular State.

SECTION 4.   The United States shall guarantee to every State in this Union a Republican Form of Government, and shall protect each of them against Invasion; and on Application of the Legislature, or of the Executive (when the Legislature cannot be convened) against domestic Violence.

ARTICLE V.

The Congress, whenever two thirds of both Houses shall deem it necessary, shall propose Amendments to this Constitution, or, on the Application of the Legislatures of two thirds of the several States, shall call a Convention for proposing Amendments, which, in either Case, shall be valid to all Intents and Purposes, as Part of this Constitution, when ratified by the Legislatures of three fourths of the several States, or by Conventions in three fourths thereof, as the one or the other Mode of Ratification may be proposed by the Congress; Provided that no Amendment which may be made prior to the Year One thousand eight hundred and eight shall in any Manner affect the first and fourth Clauses in the Ninth Section of the first Article; and that no State, without its Consent, shall be deprived of its equal Suffrage in the Senate.

ARTICLE VI.

All Debts contracted and Engagements entered into, before the Adoption of this Constitution, shall be as valid against the United States under this Constitution, as under the Confederation.

This Constitution, and the Laws of the United States which shall be made in Pursuance thereof; and all Treaties made, or which shall be made, under the Authority of the United States, shall be the supreme Law of the Land; and the Judges in every State shall be bound thereby, any Thing in the Constitution or Laws of any State to the Contrary notwithstanding.

The Senators and Representatives before mentioned, and the Members of the several State Legislatures, and all executive and judicial Officers, both of the United States and of the several States, shall be bound by Oath or Affirmation, to support this Constitution; but no religious Test shall ever be required as a Qualification to any Office or public Trust under the United States.

ARTICLE VII.

The Ratification of the Conventions of nine States, shall be sufficient for the Establishment of this Constitution between the States so ratifying the Same.

*　　　　　*　　　　　*

ARTICLES IN ADDITION TO, AND AMENDMENT OF, THE CONSTITUTION OF THE UNITED STATES OF AMERICA, PROPOSED BY CONGRESS, AND RATIFIED BY THE SEVERAL STATES, PURSUANT TO THE FIFTH ARTICLE OF THE ORIGINAL CONSTITUTION.

AMENDMENT I [1791].

Congress shall make no law respecting an establishment of religion, or prohibiting the free exercise thereof; or abridging the freedom of speech, or of the press, or the right of the people peaceably to assemble, and to petition the Government for a redress of grievances.

AMENDMENT II [1791].

A well regulated Militia, being necessary to the security of a free State, the right of the people to keep and bear Arms, shall not be infringed.

AMENDMENT III [1791].

No Soldier shall, in time of peace be quartered in any house, without the consent of the Owner, nor in time of war, but in a manner to be prescribed by law.

AMENDMENT IV [1791].

The right of the people to be secure in their persons, houses, papers, and effects, against unreasonable searches and seizures, shall not be violated, and no Warrants shall issue, but upon probable cause, supported by Oath or affirmation, and particularly describing the place to be searched, and the persons or things to be seized.

AMENDMENT V [1791].

No person shall be held to answer for a capital, or otherwise infamous crime, unless on a presentment or indictment of a Grand Jury, except in cases arising in the land or naval forces, or in the Militia, when in actual service in time of War or public danger; nor shall any person be subject for the same offence to be twice put in jeopardy of life or limb, nor shall be compelled in any criminal case to be a witness against himself, nor be deprived of life, liberty, or property, without due process of law; nor shall private property be taken for public use without just compensation.

AMENDMENT VI [1791].

In all criminal prosecutions, the accused shall enjoy the right to a speedy and public trial, by an impartial jury of the State and district wherein the crime shall have been committed; which district shall have been previously ascertained by law, and to be informed of the nature and cause of the accusation; to be confronted with the witnesses against him; to have compulsory process for obtaining witnesses in his favor, and to have the assistance of counsel for his defence.

Amendment VII [1791].

In Suits at common law, where the value in controversy shall exceed twenty dollars, the right of trial by jury shall be preserved, and no fact tried by a jury shall be otherwise re-examined in any Court of the United States, than according to the rules of the common law.

Amendment VIII [1791].

Excessive bail shall not be required, nor excessive fines imposed, nor cruel and unusual punishments inflicted.

Amendment IX [1791].

The enumeration in the Constitution of certain rights shall not be construed to deny or disparage others retained by the people.

Amendment X [1791].

The powers not delegated to the United States by the Constitution, nor prohibited by it to the States, are reserved to the States respectively, or to the people.

Amendment XI [1795].

The Judicial power of the United States shall not be construed to extend to any suit in law or equity, commenced or prosecuted against one of the United States by Citizens of another State, or by Citizens or Subjects of any Foreign State.

Amendment XII [1804].

The Electors shall meet in their respective states and vote by ballot for President and Vice President, one of whom, at least, shall not be an inhabitant of the same state with themselves; they shall name in their ballots the person voted for as President, and in distinct ballots the person voted for as Vice-President, and they shall make distinct lists of all persons voted for as President, and of all persons voted for as Vice-President, and of the number of votes for each, which lists they shall sign and certify, and transmit sealed to the seat of the government of the United States, directed to the President of the Senate;—The President of the Senate shall, in the presence of the Senate and House of Representatives, open all the certificates and the votes shall then be counted;—The person having the greatest number of votes for President, shall be the President, if such number be a majority of the whole number of Electors appointed; and if no person have such majority, then from the persons having the highest numbers not exceeding three on the list of those voted for as President, the House of Representatives shall choose immediately, by ballot, the President. But in choosing the President, the votes shall be taken by states, the representation from each state having one vote; a quorum for this purpose shall consist of a member or members from two-thirds of the states, and a majority of all the states shall be necessary to a choice. And if the House of Representatives shall not choose a President whenever the right of choice shall devolve upon them, before the fourth day of March next following, then the Vice-President shall act as President, as in the case of the death or other constitutional disability of the President—The person having the greatest number of votes as Vice-President, shall be the Vice-President, if such number be a majority of the whole number of Electors appointed, and if no person have a majority, then from the two highest numbers on the list, the Senate shall choose the Vice-President; a quorum for the purpose shall consist of two-thirds of the whole number of Senators, and a majority of the whole number shall be necessary to a choice. But no person constitutionally ineligible to the office of President shall be eligible to that of Vice-President of the United States.

AMENDMENT XIII [1865].

SECTION 1.   Neither slavery nor involuntary servitude, except as a punishment for crime whereof the party shall have been duly convicted, shall exist within the United States, or any place subject to their jurisdiction.

SECTION 2.   Congress shall have power to enforce this article by appropriate legislation.

Amendment XIV [1868].

Section 1.   All persons born or naturalized in the United States and subject to the jurisdiction thereof, are citizens of the United States and of the State wherein they reside. No State shall make or enforce any law which shall abridge the privileges or immunities of citizens of the United States; nor shall any State deprive any person of life, liberty, or property, without due process of law; nor deny to any person within its jurisdiction the equal protection of the laws.

Section 2.   Representatives shall be apportioned among the several States according to their respective numbers, counting the whole number of persons in each State, excluding Indians not taxed. But when the right to vote at any election for the choice of electors for President and Vice President of the United States, Representatives in Congress, the Executive and Judicial officers of a State, or the members of the Legislature thereof, is denied to any of the male inhabitants of such State, being twenty-one years of age, and citizens of the United States, or in any way abridged, except for participation in rebellion, or other crime, the basis of representation therein shall be reduced in the proportion which the number of such male citizens shall bear to the whole number of male citizens twenty-one years of age in such State.

Section 3.   No person shall be a Senator or Representative in Congress, or elector of President and Vice President, or hold any office, civil or military, under the United States, or under any State, who, having previously taken an oath, as a member of Congress, or as an officer of the United States, or as a member of any State legislature, or as an executive or judicial officer of any State, to support the Constitution of the United States, shall have engaged in insurrection or rebellion against the same, or given aid or comfort to the enemies thereof. But Congress may by a vote of two-thirds of each House, remove such disability.

Section 4.   The validity of the public debt of the United States, authorized by law, including debts incurred for payment of pensions and bounties for services in suppressing insurrection or rebellion, shall not be questioned. But neither the United States nor any State shall assume or pay any debt or obligation incurred in aid of insurrection or rebellion against the United States, or any claim for the loss or emancipation of any slave; but all such debts, obligations and claims shall be held illegal and void.

SECTION 5. The Congress shall have power to enforce, by appropriate legislation, the provisions of this article.

AMENDMENT XV [1870].

SECTION 1. The right of citizens of the United States to vote shall not be denied or abridged by the United States or by any State on account of race, color, or previous condition of servitude.

SECTION 2. The Congress shall have power to enforce this article by appropriate legislation.

AMENDMENT XVI [1913].

The Congress shall have power to lay and collect taxes on incomes, from whatever source derived, without apportionment among the several States, and without regard to any census or enumeration.

AMENDMENT XVII [1913].

The Senate of the United States shall be composed of two Senators from each State, elected by the people thereof, for six years; and each Senator shall have one vote. The electors in each State shall have the qualifications requisite for electors of the most numerous branch of the State legislatures.

When vacancies happen in the representation of any State in the Senate, the executive authority of such State shall issue writs of election to fill such vacancies: *Provided,* That the legislature of any State may empower the executive thereof to make temporary appointments until the people fill the vacancies by election as the legislature may direct.

This amendment shall not be so construed as to affect the election or term of any Senator chosen before it becomes valid as part of the Constitution.

AMENDMENT XVIII [1919].

SECTION 1. After one year from the ratification of this article the manufacture, sale, or transportation of intoxicating liquors within, the importation thereof into, or the exportation thereof from the United States and all territory subject to the jurisdiction thereof for beverage purposes is hereby prohibited.

SECTION 2. The Congress and the several States shall have concurrent power to enforce this article by appropriate legislation.

SECTION 3. This article shall be inoperative unless it shall have been ratified as an amendment to the Constitution by the legislatures of the several States, as provided in the Constitution, within seven years from the date of the submission hereof to the States by the Congress.

AMENDMENT XIX [1920].

The right of citizens of the United States to vote shall not be denied or abridged by the United States or by any State on account of sex.

Congress shall have power to enforce this article by appropriate legislation.

AMENDMENT XX [1933].

SECTION 1. The terms of the President and Vice President shall end at noon on the 20th day of January, and the terms of Senators and Representatives at noon on the 3d day of January, of the years in which such terms would have ended if this article had not been ratified; and the terms of their successors shall then begin.

SECTION 2. The Congress shall assemble at least once in every year, and such meeting shall begin at noon on the 3d day of January, unless they shall by law appoint a different day.

SECTION 3. If, at the time fixed for the beginning of the term of the President, the President elect shall have died, the Vice President elect shall become President. If a President shall not have been chosen before the time fixed for the beginning of his term, or if the President elect shall have failed to qualify, then the Vice President elect shall act as President until a President shall have qualified; and the Congress may by law provide for the case wherein neither a President elect nor a Vice President elect shall have qualified, declaring who shall then act as President, or the manner in which one who is to act shall be selected, and such person shall act accordingly until a President or Vice President shall have qualified.

SECTION 4.   The Congress may by law provide for the case of the death of any of the persons from whom the House of Representatives may choose a President whenever the right of choice shall have devolved upon them, and for the case of the death of any of the persons from whom the Senate may choose a Vice President whenever the right of choice shall have devolved upon them.

SECTION 5.   Sections 1 and 2 shall take effect on the 15th day of October following the ratification of this article.

SECTION 6.   This article shall be inoperative unless it shall have been ratified as an amendment to the Constitution by the legislatures of three-fourths of the several States within seven years from the date of its submission.

AMENDMENT XXI [1933].

SECTION 1.   The eighteenth article of amendment to the Constitution of the United States is hereby repealed.

SECTION 2.   The transportation or importation into any State, Territory, or possession of the United States for delivery or use therein of intoxicating liquors, in violation of the laws thereof, is hereby prohibited.

SECTION 3.   This article shall be inoperative unless it shall have been ratified as an amendment to the Constitution by conventions in the several States, as provided in the Constitution, within seven years from the date of the submission hereof to the States by the Congress.

AMENDMENT XXII [1951].

SECTION 1.   No person shall be elected to the office of the President more than twice, and no person who has held the office of President, or acted as President, for more than two years of a term to which some other person was elected President shall be elected to the office of the President more than once. But this Article shall not apply to any person holding the office of President when this Article was proposed by the Congress, and shall not prevent any person who may be holding the office of President, or acting as President, during the term within which this Article becomes operative from holding the office of President or acting as President during the remainder of such term.

SECTION 2. This article shall be inoperative unless it shall have been ratified as an amendment to the Constitution by the legislatures of three-fourths of the several States within seven years from the date of its submission to the States by the Congress.

AMENDMENT XXIII [1961].

SECTION 1. The District constituting the seat of Government of the United States shall appoint in such manner as the Congress may direct:

A number of electors of President and Vice President equal to the whole number of Senators and Representatives in Congress to which the District would be entitled if it were a State, but in no event more than the least populous State; they shall be in addition to those appointed by the States, but they shall be considered, for the purposes of the election of President and Vice President, to be electors appointed by a State; and they shall meet in the District and perform such duties as provided by the twelfth article of amendment.

SECTION 2. The Congress shall have power to enforce this article by appropriate legislation.

AMENDMENT XXIV [1964].

SECTION 1. The right of citizens of the United States to vote in any primary or other election for President or Vice President, for electors for President or Vice President, or for Senator or Representative in Congress, shall not be denied or abridged by the United States or any State by reason of failure to pay any poll tax or other tax.

SECTION 2. The Congress shall have power to enforce this article by appropriate legislation.

AMENDMENT XXV [1967].

SECTION 1. In case of the removal of the President from office or of his death or resignation, the Vice President shall become President.

SECTION 2. Whenever there is a vacancy in the office of the Vice President, the President shall nominate a Vice President who shall take office upon confirmation by a majority vote of both Houses of Congress.

Section 3. Whenever the President transmits to the President pro tempore of the Senate and the Speaker of the House of Representatives his written declaration that he is unable to discharge the powers and duties of his office, and until he transmits to them a written declaration to the contrary, such powers and duties shall be discharged by the Vice President as Acting President.

Section 4. Whenever the Vice President and a majority of either the principal officers of the executive departments or of such other body as Congress may by law provide, transmit to the President pro tempore of the Senate and the Speaker of the House of Representatives their written declaration that the President is unable to discharge the powers and duties of his office, the Vice President shall immediately assume the powers and duties of the office as Acting President.

Thereafter, when the President transmits to the President pro tempore of the Senate and the Speaker of the House of Representatives his written declaration that no inability exists, he shall resume the powers and duties of his office unless the Vice President and a majority of either the principal officers of the executive department or of such other body as Congress may by law provide, transmit within four days to the President pro tempore of the Senate and the Speaker of the House of Representatives their written declaration that the President is unable to discharge the powers and duties of his office. Thereupon Congress shall decide the issue, assembling within forty-eight hours for that purpose if not in session. If the Congress, within twenty-one days after receipt of the latter written declaration, or, if Congress is not in session, within twenty-one days after Congress is required to assemble, determines by two-thirds vote of both Houses that the President is unable to discharge the powers and duties of his office, the Vice President shall continue to discharge the same as Acting President; otherwise, the President shall resume the powers and duties of his office.

Amendment XXVI [1971].

Section 1. The right of citizens of the United States, who are eighteen years of age or older, to vote shall not be denied or abridged by the United States or by any State on account of age.

Section 2. The Congress shall have power to enforce this article by appropriate legislation.

Notes

WHERE there is reference to only a few passages in a case or other writing, all the pages referred to are placed in a single note. Where there are too many references to make that convenient, each passage has its own note.

INTRODUCTION

1. 410 U.S. 113 (1973).
2. H. Belloc, *The Great Heresies* 10 (Trinity Communic. ed. 1987) (1938).
3. J. Story, *Commentaries on the Constitution of the United States* vi (Carolina Academic Press 1987) (1833).
4. *Id.* at 135.
5. *See* E. Sergeant, "Justice Touched With Fire," in *Mr. Justice Holmes* 206–07 (F. Frankfurter ed. 1931); H. Shriver, *What Gusto: Stories and Anecdotes About Justice Oliver Wendell Holmes* 10 (privately printed 1970).
6. *Hohri* v. *United States,* 793 F.2d 304, 313 (D.C. Cir. 1986) (Bork, J., dissenting from denial of reh. en banc), *rev'd,* 482 U.S. 64 (1987).
7. G. McDowell, "The Politics of Original Intention," in *The Constitution, the Courts, and the Quest for Justice* 2 (R. Goldwin & W. Schambra eds. 1989).
8. A. MacIntyre, *After Virtue* 253 (2d ed. 1984).
9. M. Lerner, "Cleaning Up the Mess," *The Washington Times,* June 27, 1988, at D1.
10. H. Belloc, *supra* note 2, at 12.

1. THE SUPREME COURT AND THE TEMPTATIONS OF POLITICS

1. *See, e.g.,* I. Kristol, *Two Cheers for Capitalism* 25–31 (1978).

1. CREATION AND FALL

1. 3 U.S. (3 Dall.) 386, 387–89 (1798).

2. 3 U.S. (3 Dall.) at 398–99 (Iredell, J., concurring).

3. U.S. CONST. art. II, § 4.

4. U.S. CONST. art. III, § 1.

5. *See* L. Tribe, *American Constitutional Law* 64 n.7 (2d ed. 1988).

6. Letter from Thomas Jefferson to Judge Spencer Roane (Sept. 6, 1819), *reprinted in* 15 *The Writings of Thomas Jefferson* 212–16 (A. Lipscomb ed. 1903).

7. 5 U.S. (1 Cranch) 137, 148 (1803) (emphasis omitted).

8. 2 U.S. (2 Dall.) 409 (1792).

9. 5 U.S. (1 Cranch) at 176, 177, 179–80 (emphasis in original).

10. 10 U.S. (6 Cranch) 87, 134 (1810).

11. U.S. CONST. art. I, § 10.

12. 10 U.S. (6 Cranch) at 135, 136.

13. *Fletcher* v. *Peck,* 10 U.S. (6 Cranch) at 143, 144 (Johnson, J., concurring).

14. 22 U.S. (9 Wheat.) 1 (1824).

15. 27 U.S. (2 Pet.) 245 (1829).

16. 17 U.S. (4 Wheat.) 316 (1819).

17. 32 U.S. (7 Pet.) 243 (1833).

18. D. Currie, *The Constitution in the Supreme Court: The First Hundred Years 1789–1888,* at 197 (1985).

19. P. Boller, *Presidential Anecdotes* 69 (1981), *citing* W. Sumner, *Andrew Jackson* 227 n. (1882).

20. 60 U.S. (19 How.) 393 (1857).

21. *See, e.g.,* U. Phillips, *American Negro Slavery: A Survey of the Supply, Employment and Control of Negro Labor as Determined by the Plantation Regime* 359–401 (1918); E. Genovese, *The Political Economy of Slavery: Studies in the Economy and Society of the Slave South* (1965). This view was also espoused by Charles William Ramsdell. The brilliant and controversial study by Robert William Fogel and Stanley L. Engerman, *Time on the Cross: The Economics of American Negro Slavery* 89–94 (1974), however, has argued that slavery was economically viable and would have survived.

22. Speech, Springfield, Illinois, July 17, 1858 *reprinted in* 2 *The Collected Works of Abraham Lincoln, 1848–1858* 504, 514 (R. Basler ed. 1953).

23. 60 U.S. (19 How.) at 449, 450.

24. J. Ely, *Democracy and Distrust* 18 (1980) (footnote omitted).

25. *In re Winship,* 397 U.S. 358, 377, 378–80, 382, 384, 378 (1970) (Black, J., dissenting).

26. D. Currie, *supra* note 18, at 271 (footnotes omitted).

27. 198 U.S. 45 (1905).

28. 410 U.S. 113 (1973).

29. The saying is apparently a standard German expression which Lenin might have picked up during his time in Munich or Zurich. *See Langenscheidt's Encyclopaedic Dictionary of the English and German Languages, Based on the Original Work by Prof. Dr. E. Muret and Prof. D. Sanders, Part II: German-English, First Volume A-K* 1 (1974).

30. 60 U.S. (19 How.) at 564, 620–21 (1856) (Curtis, J., dissenting).

31. Fehrenbacher, "Dred Scott v. Sandford," in 2 *Encyclopedia of the American Constitution* 584, 586 (1986).

32. 75 U.S. (8 Wall.) 603, 604, 614, 622, 623 (1870) (quoting *McCulloch* v. *Maryland*).

33. U.S. CONST. preamble.

34. U.S. CONST. amend. XIV, § 1.

35. 83 U.S. (16 Wall.) 36, 71, 78, 80–81 (1872).

36. 83 U.S. (16 Wall.) 83, 96, 97, 110 (1872) (Field, J., dissenting) (emphasis in original).

37. 83 U.S. (16 Wall.) 111, 119, 122 (1872) (Bradley, J., dissenting).

38. D. Currie, *supra* note 18, at 346–47 (footnote omitted).

39. 83 U.S. (16 Wall.) at 123.

40. C. Fairman, "Reconstruction and Reunion: 1864–88," *History of the Supreme Court of the United States* 1270 (1971).

41. 25 Wis. 167, 194 (1870).

42. 20 Mich. 452, 470, 473, 487, 494 (1870).

43. 87 U.S. (20 Wall.) 655, 662, 663, 666 (1874).

44. 87 U.S. (20 Wall.) 667, 668–69 (1874) (Clifford, J., dissenting) (footnotes omitted).

45. 96 U.S. 97, 105, 102, 104 (1877).

46. 165 U.S. 578, 591, 589, 590 (1897).

47. 198 U.S. 45, 61, 53, 58 (1905) (citation omitted).

48. 3 U.S. (3 Dall.) 398–401 (1798).

49. 198 U.S. 74, 75, 76 (1905) (Holmes, J., dissenting) (emphasis added).

50. 208 U.S. 161 (1908).

51. 236 U.S. 1 (1915).

52. 261 U.S. 525, 553 (1923).

53. 261 U.S. at 567, 569–70 (Holmes, J., dissenting).

54. 262 U.S. 390, 399, 400 (1923) (citations omitted).

55. 262 U.S. at 412 (Holmes, J., dissenting).

56. 268 U.S. 510, 535 (1925).

57. 198 U.S. at 59.

2. THE NEW DEAL COURT
AND THE CONSTITUTIONAL REVOLUTION

1. 295 U.S. 495 (1935).

2. U.S. CONST. amend. X.

3. *Railroad Retirement Board* v. *Alton Railroad Co.,* 295 U.S. 330 (1935).

4. *Carter* v. *Carter Coal Co.,* 298 U.S. 238 (1936).

5. *United States* v. *Butler,* 297 U.S. 1 (1936).

6. Radio address by President Roosevelt, Mar. 9, 1937, *reprinted in* G. Gunther, *Cases and Materials on Constitutional Law* 151 (10th ed. 1980).

7. Attributed. Lincoln explained and defended his policy of occasionally suspending the right to habeas corpus in his July 4, 1861 message to Congress. *See* 4 *The Collected Works of Abraham Lincoln* 429–31 (R. Basler ed. 1953) (reprinting Lincoln's Message to Congress in Special Session, July 4, 1861) ("are all the laws, *but one,* to go unexecuted, and the government itself go to pieces, lest that one be violated? Even in such a case, would not the official oath be broken, if the government should be overthrown, when it was believed that disregarding the single law, would tend to preserve it?").

8. 347 U.S. 483 (1954).

9. Report of the Senate Judiciary Committee, June 14, 1937, *reprinted in* G. Gunther, *supra* note 6, at 152.

10. This quote was apparently derived from a similar statement attributed to the young New Dealer Abe Fortas, "a switch in time serves nine." *See The New York Times,* June 15, 1937, at A19.

11. 317 U.S. 111, 128 (1942).

12. U.S. CONST. art. I, § 8.

13. U.S. CONST. amend. X.

14. 291 U.S. 502, 537 (1934).

15. *Id.* at 539, 554, 556 (1934) (McReynolds, J., dissenting).

16. 300 U.S. 379 (1937).

17. *Adkins* v. *Children's Hospital,* 261 U.S. 525 (1923).

18. 304 U.S. 144 (1938).

19. *Id.* at 152–53 n.4 (citations omitted).

20. 313 U.S. 236, 247 (1941).

21. Okla. Stat. Ann. tit. 57, §§ 171, *et seq.;* L. 1935, pp. 94 *et seq., quoted in Skinner* v. *Oklahoma* 316 U.S. 535, 536–37 (1942).

22. 316 U.S. 535 (1942).

23. 83 U.S. (16 Wall.) 36 (1872).

24. 274 U.S. 200, 208 (1927).

25. *Id.* at 207. *But see* Lombardo, *Three Generations, No Imbeciles: New Light on Buck v. Bell,* 60 N.Y.U.L. Rev. 30 (1985) (arguing that the factual assertions the Supreme Court relied on were false. Carrie Buck, her mother, and daughter were not in fact mentally retarded.).

26. 316 U.S. at 540, 541, 543.

27. 83 U.S. (16 Wall.) at 123 (Bradley, J., dissenting).

28. 316 U.S. at 541.

3. The Warren Court: The Political Role Embraced

1. Schlesinger, *The Supreme Court: 1947,* Fortune, vol. 35, Jan. 1947, at 73, 201–02.

2. A. Bickel, *The Least Dangerous Branch* 80 (1962).

3. *Ibid.*

4. *Id.* at 84.

5. *Levy* v. *Louisiana,* 391 U.S. 68 (1968).

6. *Griffin* v. *Illinois,* 351 U.S. 12 (1956).

7. *Shapiro* v. *Thompson,* 394 U.S. 618 (1969).

8. *Miranda* v. *Arizona,* 384 U.S. 436, 479 (1966).

9. *Mapp* v. *Ohio,* 367 U.S. 643 (1961).

10. *See generally* R. Bork, *The Antitrust Paradox: A Policy at War with Itself* (1978).

11. Handler, *The Supreme Court and the Antitrust Laws: A Critic's Viewpoint,* 1 Ga. L. Rev. 339, 350 (Spring 1967).

12. 347 U.S. 483 (1954).

13. 163 U.S. 537, 551 (1896).

14. 163 U.S. 552, 557, 559 (1896) (Harlan, J., dissenting).

15. 347 U.S. at 494.

16. *Mayor of Baltimore* v. *Dawson,* 350 U.S. 877 (1955).

17. *Holmes* v. *Atlanta,* 350 U.S. 879 (1955).

18. *New Orleans City Park Imp. Ass'n* v. *Detiege,* 358 U.S. 54 (1958).

19. *Johnson* v. *Virginia,* 373 U.S. 61 (1963).

20. *See, e.g.,* Pollak, *Racial Discrimination and Judicial Integrity: A Reply to Professor Wechsler,* 108 U. Pa. L. Rev. 1 (1959). *See also* Deutsch, *Neutrality, Legitimacy, and the Supreme Court: Some Intersections Between Law and Political Science,* 20 Stan. L. Rev. 169 (1968).

21. Wechsler, *Toward Neutral Principles of Constitutional Law,* 73 Harv. L. Rev. 1 (1959).

22. *Id.* at 19.

23. L. Jaffe, *English and American Judges As Lawmakers* 38 (1969).

24. Wechsler, *supra* note 21, at 31–32, 34 (footnote omitted).

25. Bork, *The Supreme Court Needs a New Philosophy,* FORTUNE, vol. 78, Dec. 1968, at 138.

26. Bork, *Civil Rights—A Challenge,* THE NEW REPUBLIC, vol. 149, Aug. 31, 1963, at 21.

27. 347 U.S. 497 (1954).

28. J. Ely, *Democracy and Distrust* 32 (1980) (The notion "that the Due Process Clause of the Fifth Amendment incorporates the Equal Protection Clause of the Fourteenth . . . is gibberish both syntactically and historically.").

29. *See, e.g., Buckley* v. *Valeo,* 424 U.S. 1, 93 (1976); *Weinberger* v. *Wiesenfeld,* 420 U.S. 636, 638 n.2 (1975). *See also* Note, *A Madisonian Interpretation of the Equal Protection Doctrine,* 91 Yale L.J. 1403 (1982).

30. 369 U.S. 186 (1962).

31. U.S. CONST. art. IV, § 4.

32. 377 U.S. 533, 573, 574, 580 (1964).

33. 377 U.S. 713 (1964).

34. 377 U.S. 744, 745, 746, 750,753, 754 (1964) (Stewart, J., dissenting).

35. *Gaffney* v. *Cummings,* 412 U.S. 735 (1973).

36. A. Cox, *The Court and the Constitution* 290 (1987).

37. 302 U.S. 277 (1937).

38. 383 U.S. 663 (1966).

39. *Id.* at 669–70 (emphasis in original).

40. 383 U.S. at 670, 676–77 (Black, J., dissenting).

41. 383 U.S. 663, 680, 686 (Harlan, J., dissenting).

42. 384 U.S. 641 (1966).

43. *Id.* at 651 n.10.

44. *Adamson* v. *California,* 332 U.S. 46, 68, 71–72, 90–92 (1947) (Black, J., dissenting) ("one of the chief objects that the provisions of the [Fourteenth] Amendment's first section, separately, and as a whole, were intended to accomplish was to make the Bill of Rights applicable to the states.").

45. 338 U.S. 25 (1949).

46. 367 U.S. 643 (1961).

47. 384 U.S. 436 (1966).

48. 384 U.S. at 499, 504, 526 (Clark, Harlan, Stewart, and White, JJ., dissenting).

49. *Engel* v. *Vitale,* 370 U.S. 421 (1962); *Abington School District* v. *Schempp,* 374 U.S. 203 (1963).

50. *See Wallace* v. *Jaffree,* 472 U.S. 38 (1985).

51. 381 U.S. 479 (1965).

52. *Id.* at 485–86.

53. 357 U.S. 449 (1958).

54. 381 U.S. at 486.

55. *Id.* at 481–482.

56. 381 U.S. at 507, 508, 510 (Black, J., dissenting).

57. 381 U.S. at 527, 530 n.7 (Stewart, J., dissenting).

4. AFTER WARREN: THE BURGER AND REHNQUIST COURTS

1. 401 U.S. 424, 431 (1971).

2. *See, e.g., United Steelworkers of America* v. *Weber,* 443 U.S. 193, 209–16 (1979) (Blackmun, J., concurring).

3. 401 U.S. at 431, 436.

4. 443 U.S. 193 (1979).

5. 443 U.S. at 216 (Burger, C.J., dissenting).

6. 443 U.S. at 219 (Rehnquist, J., dissenting).

7. 480 U.S. 616, 620, 641–42 (1987).

8. 42 U.S.C. § 2000e-2(a).

9. 480 U.S. at 660 (1987) (Scalia, J., dissenting).

10. M. Mayer, *Today and Tomorrow in America* 3–4 (1975).

11. T. Sowell, *"Weber* and *Bakke,* and the Presuppositions of 'Affirmative Action,' " *Discrimination, Affirmative Action, and Equal Opportunity* 35, 44–50 (W. Block & M. Walker eds. 1981); T. Sowell, *Civil Rights: Rhetoric or Reality?* 77–79 (1984).

12. 57 U.S.L.W. 4132 (U.S. Jan. 23, 1989).

13. 57 U.S.L.W. at 4145 (Kennedy, J., concurring).

14. 57 U.S.L.W. at 4148, 4157 (Marshall, J. and Blackmun, J., dissenting).

15. Will, "Backing Out of a Swamp," *The Washington Post,* Jan. 29, 1989, at D7.

16. 57 U.S.L.W. 4583, 4586 (U.S. June 5, 1989).

17. 381 U.S. 479 (1965).

18. 405 U.S. 438, 453 (1972).

19. 410 U.S. 113 (1973).

20. *Id.* at 130.

21. *Id.* at 148.

22. *Id.* at 152–53.

23. 316 U.S. 535 (1942).

24. 405 U.S. 438 (1972).

25. 268 U.S. 510 (1925).

26. 262 U.S. 390 (1923).

27. 321 U.S. 158 (1944).

28. 388 U.S. 1 (1967).

29. 410 U.S. at 153, 164–65.

30. 410 U.S. at 171, 172 (Rehnquist, J., dissenting).

31. 410 U.S. at 221–22 (White, J., dissenting).

32. 57 U.S.L.W. 5023 (U.S. July 3, 1989).

33. *Id.* at 5025 (plurality op. of Rehnquist, C.J.).

34. *Id.* at 5034 (Scalia, J., concurring).

35. *Id.* at 5031 (O'Connor, J., concurring).

36. 478 U.S. 186 (1986).

37. *Id.* at 190.

38. *Id.* at 191.

39. 302 U.S. 319, 325, 326 (1937).

40. 431 U.S. 494, 503 (1977).

41. 478 U.S. at 194.

42. 478 U.S. at 199 (Blackmun, J., dissenting).

43. *Id.* at 204.

44. 478 U.S. at 196.

45. 478 U.S. at 206 (Blackmun, J., dissenting); 195–96 (opinion of the Court).

46. 478 U.S. at 206, 208 (Blackmun, J., dissenting).

47. *Id.* at 211–12 (emphasis added).

48. 57 U.S.L.W. 4770, 4774 (U.S. June 21, 1989).

49. *Id.* at 4775.

50. 57 U.S.L.W. at 4776, 4779 (Rehnquist, C.J., dissenting).

51. *Sable Communications of California, Inc.* v. *FCC,* 57 U.S.L.W. 4920 (U.S. June 23, 1989).

52. *County of Allegheny* v. *ACLU,* 57 U.S.L.W. 5045 (U.S. July 3, 1989).

53. *Texas Monthly, Inc.* v. *Bullock,* 57 U.S.L.W. 4168 (U.S. Feb. 21, 1989).

5. THE SUPREME COURT'S TRAJECTORY

1. A. Bickel, *The Morality of Consent* (1975).
2. *Id.* at 120–21 (emphasis in original).
3. *Ibid.*
4. *Id.* at 121.

II. THE THEORISTS

1. *See, e.g.,* J. Story, *Commentaries on the Constitution of the United States* (Carolina Academic Press 1987) (1833); T. Cooley, *Constitutional Limitations* (2d ed. 1871).
2. *See, e.g.,* Chapter 9, *infra.*
3. J. Story, *supra* note 1, at vi.
4. A. Bloom, *The Closing of the American Mind* (1987).
5. Kramer, *Studying the Arts and the Humanities: What Can Be Done,* THE NEW CRITERION, vol. 7, Feb. 1989, at 1, 3.
6. Letter from Gertrude Himmelfarb to Robert H. Bork (May 4, 1989).
7. H. Schlossberg, *Idols for Destruction* 204 (1983).

6. THE MADISONIAN DILEMMA
AND THE NEED FOR CONSTITUTIONAL THEORY

1. Letter from Lord Acton to Bishop Mandell Creighton (Apr. 5, 1887), *quoted in* G. Himmelfarb, *Lord Acton: A Study in Conscience and Politics* 160–161 (1952).

7. THE ORIGINAL UNDERSTANDING

1. Monaghan, *Stare Decisis and Constitutional Adjudication,* 88 Colum. L. Rev. 723, 725–27 (1988) ("The relevant inquiry must focus on the *public* understanding of the language when the Constitution was developed. Hamilton put it well: 'whatever may have been the intention of the framers of a constitution, or of a law, that intention is to be sought for in the instrument itself, according to the usual & established rules of construction.' " [emphasis in original; footnotes omitted]).
2. 17 U.S. (4 Wheat.) 316, 407 (1819).
3. 5 U.S. (1 Cranch) 137, 177–79 (1803).
4. *See also* Scalia, *Originalism: The Lesser Evil,* 57 U. Cin. L. Rev. 849, 853 (1989) (It is a canard to interpret Marshall's observation in *McCulloch* as implying that our interpretation of the Constitution must change from age to age. "The real implication was quite the opposite: Marshall

was saying that the Constitution had to be interpreted generously because the powers conferred upon Congress under it had to be broad enough to serve not only the needs of the federal government originally discerned but also the needs that might arise in the future. If constitutional interpretation could be adjusted as changing circumstances required, a broad initial interpretation would have been unnecessary.").

5. U.S. CONST. art. VI.

6. 347 U.S. 483 (1954).

7. *See* Chapter 3, *supra,* at 78–84.

8. Schlesinger, *The Supreme Court: 1947,* FORTUNE, vol. 35, Jan. 1947, at 73, 201–02.

9. U.S. CONST. amend. I.

10. *Griswold* v. *Connecticut,* 381 U.S. 479 (1965).

11. Brest, *The Fundamental Rights Controversy: The Essential Contradictions of Normative Constitutional Scholarship,* 90 Yale L.J. 1063, 1091–92 (1981) (footnotes omitted).

12. *Slaughter-House Cases,* 83 U.S. (16 Wall.) 36 (1873).

13. *See* Chapter 3, *supra,* at 78–84.

14. 334 U.S. 1 (1948).

15. *Id.* at 19.

16. Bork, *Neutral Principles and Some First Amendment Problems,* 47 Ind. L.J. 1 (1971).

17. *Runyon* v. *McCrary,* 427 U.S. 160 (1976).

18. P. Bator, P. Mishkin, D. Meltzer & D. Shapiro, *Hart and Wechsler's The Federal Courts and the Federal System* 7 (3d ed. 1988) quoting 1 Farrand, *The Records of the Federal Convention* 21 (May 29) (1911).

19. *Ibid., quoting* 1 Farrand, *The Records of the Federal Convention* 97–98, 109 (June 4) (1911).

20. *Ibid.*

21. *The Federalist* No. 78, at 465–66 (A. Hamilton) (C. Rossiter ed. 1961).

22. Monaghan, *supra* note 1, at 727.

23. *Id.; see also* Bittker, *The Bicentennial of the Jurisprudence of Original Intent: The Recent Past,* 77 Calif. L. Rev. 235 (1989).

24. *See* Scalia, *supra* note 4, at 861–65.

25. Monaghan, *supra* note 1, at 741–43; Maltz, *Some Thoughts on the Death of Stare Decisis in Constitutional Law,* 1980 Wis. L. Rev. 467, 494–96 ("It seems fair to say that if a majority of the Warren or Burger Court has considered a case wrongly decided, no constitutional precedent—new or old—has been safe.").

26. *Helvering* v. *Hallock,* 309 U.S. 106, 119 (1940).

27. *Mitchell* v. *W. T. Grant Co.*, 416 U.S. 600, 627–28 (1974) (Powell, J., concurring).

28. 75 U.S. (8 Wall.) 603 (1870).

29. 79 U.S. (12 Wall.) 457 (1871).

30. 41 U.S. (16 Pet.) 1 (1842).

31. 304 U.S. 64 (1938).

32. 163 U.S. 537 (1896).

33. 347 U.S. 483 (1954).

34. *Compare Maryland* v. *Wirtz,* 392 U.S. 183 (1968); *National League of Cities* v. *Usery,* 426 U.S. 833 (1976); *Garcia* v. *San Antonio Metropolitan Transit Authority,* 469 U.S. 528 (1985).

35. 469 U.S. 528, 547 (1985).

36. *Graves* v. *New York,* 306 U.S. 466, 491–92 (1939) (Frankfurter, J., concurring).

37. U.S. CONST. art. VI, cl. 2.

38. U.S. CONST. art. III, § 1.

39. *See* R. Berger, *Death Penalties* 82–83 n. 29 (1982) (Berger makes this statement while referring to a Supreme Court decision that in my judgment is unquestionably correct. His misapplication of the biblical command in this context, however, does not detract from his general point about *stare decisis*—that past errors in particular cases should not be expanded and elaborated simply because they cannot be undone).

40. Scalia, *supra* note 4, at 861.

41. F. Frankfurter, *The Commerce Clause* 80–81 (1937).

8.   OBJECTIONS TO ORIGINAL UNDERSTANDING

1. J. Ely, *Democracy and Distrust* 12 (1980).

2. Speech by Justice William J. Brennan, Jr. to the Text and Teaching Symposium, Georgetown University, Washington, D.C. (Oct. 12, 1985), *reprinted in The Great Debate: Interpreting Our Written Constitution* 11 (The Federalist Society 1986).

3. *Id.* at 14.

4. J. Ely, *supra* note 1, at 1–2 (footnote omitted).

5. Ted Koppel, Commencement Address at Duke University, Durham, North Carolina (May 10, 1987) (emphasis added).

6. 5 U.S. (1 Cranch) 137 (1803).

7. *IIT* v. *Vencap, Ltd.*, 519 F.2d 1001, 1015 (2d Cir. 1975).

8. *Hanoch Tel-Oren* v. *Libyan Arab Republic,* 726 F.2d 774 (D.C. Cir. 1984) (per curiam) (concurring ops. filed by Edwards, Bork, and Robb, JJ.).

9. 726 F.2d at 775–98 (Edwards, J., concurring).

10. 726 F.2d at 815 (Bork, J., concurring).

11. *Ollman* v. *Evans,* 750 F.2d 970, 993 (D.C. Cir. 1984) (en banc) (Bork, J., concurring).

12. *Id.* at 995–96 (with slight adaptations).

13. U.S. CONST. amend. IV.

14. Sandalow, *Judicial Protection of Minorities,* 75 Mich. L. Rev. 1162, 1183 (1977).

15. Brest, *The Misconceived Quest for the Original Understanding,* 60 B.U.L. Rev. 204, 234 (1980).

16. *Id.* at 225 (footnotes omitted).

17. *Ibid.* (footnotes omitted).

18. U.S. CONST. art. VI, cl. 2.

19. U.S. CONST. art. VI, cl. 3.

20. Speech at Elmira, New York (May 3, 1907).

21. *Quoted in* Thayer, *The Origin and Scope of the American Doctrine of Constitutional Law,* 7 Harv. L. Rev. 129, 152 (1893), and *in* L. Levy, *Original Intent and the Framers' Constitution* 56 (1988).

22. Dworkin, *The Forum of Principle,* 56 N.Y.U.L. Rev. 469, 470 (1981).

23. R. Bork, *Tradition and Morality in Constitutional Law,* The Francis Boyer Lectures on Public Policy 11 (American Enterprise Institute, Dec. 1984).

24. J. Ely, *supra* note 1, at 11.

25. *Id.* at 12.

26. *Id.* at 12–13.

27. *Id.* at 15 (emphasis in original; footnotes omitted).

28. *Id.* at 22.

29. *Id.* at 28.

30. 4 Wash. C.C. 371, 6 F.Cas. 546 (C.C.E.D. Pa. 1823).

31. 60 U.S. (19 How.) 393 (1856).

32. J. Ely, *supra* note 1, at 32.

33. *See, e.g., Sugarman* v. *Dougall,* 413 U.S. 634, 642–43 (1973) (alienage); *Graham* v. *Richardson,* 403 U.S. 365, 376 (1971) (same); *Trimble* v. *Gordon,* 430 U.S. 762, 773 (1977) (illegitimacy); *Levy* v. *Louisiana,* 391 U.S. 68 (1968) (same); *Craig* v. *Boren,* 429 U.S. 190, 202 (1976) (gender); *Reed* v. *Reed,* 404 U.S. 71 (1971) (same).

34. 347 U.S. 497 (1954).

35. U.S. CONST. amend. IX.

36. U.S. CONST. amend. X.

37. J. Ely, *supra* note 1, at 45.

38. Caplan, *The History and Meaning of the Ninth Amendment,* 69 Va. L. Rev. 223 (1983).

39. J. Ely, *supra* note 1, at 35–36 (emphasis added), *quoting* 1 Annals of Cong. 439 (1789).

9. THE THEORISTS OF LIBERAL CONSTITUTIONAL REVISIONISM

1. A. Bickel, *The Least Dangerous Branch* (1962).

2. G. McDowell, *Curbing the Courts: The Constitution and the Limits of Judicial Power* 15 (1988).

3. A. Bickel, *supra* note 1, at 16.

4. *Id.* at 18.

5. *Id.* at 27.

6. *Id.* at 24.

7. *Id.* at 64.

8. *Id.* at 25–26.

9. *Id.* at 236.

10. *Id.* at 236–37.

11. *Id.* at 239.

12. *Id.* at 258.

13. *Id.* at 236.

14. *Id.* at 237.

15. D. MacDonald, "The Triumph of the Fact: An American Tragedy," *The Anchor Review,* vol. 2, at 113, 124 (New York: Doubleday, 1957), *quoted in* A. Bickel, *supra* note 1, at 237.

16. J. Ely, *Democracy and Distrust* (1980).

17. *Id.* at 73.

18. *Id.* at 43–72.

19. *Id.* at 75.

20. 304 U.S. 144, 152–53 n.4 (1938).

21. *Ibid.*

22. J. Ely, *supra* note 16, at 87.

23. *Id.* at 88–101.

24. *Id.* at 98–99.

25. *Id.* at 99.

26. *Id.* at 102–03.

27. *Id.* at 105–16.

28. *Id.* at 103.

29. *Id.* at 152.

30. *Id.* at 161–62.

31. *Id.* at 162–64.

32. *Id.* at 167.

33. *Id.* at 170–72.

34. *Id.* at 176.

35. L. Tribe, *American Constitutional Law* iii (2d ed. 1988).

36. *Ibid.* (emphasis in original).

37. *Ibid.*

38. Posner, *The Constitution as Mirror: Tribe's Constitutional Choices,* 84 Mich. L. Rev. 551 (1986).

39. L. Tribe, *supra* note 35, at 15–16.

40. *Id.* at 16.

41. *Id.* at 62.

42. *Id.* at vii.

43. *Id.* at 63.

44. *Id.* at 65 n.11 (emphasis in original).

45. *Id.* at 12 n.6.

46. *Id.* at iii (emphasis in original).

47. *Id.* at 1514–21.

48. *Id.* at 1515.

49. *Id.* at 1518–20.

50. *Id.* at 1353.

51. *Id.* at 1354 n.13.

52. *Id.* at 1354.

53. *Id.* at 1347.

54. *Id.* at 1351.

55. *Ibid.*

56. *Ibid.*

57. *Id.* at 1427.

58. *Id.* at 1428.

59. *Id.* at 1302–08.

60. *Id.* at 1308.

61. *Id.* at 1324.

62. *Id.* at 1324–25 (footnote omitted).

63. *Id.* at 1326.

64. *Ibid.*

65. *Id.* at 919 (footnotes omitted).

66. *Id.* at 1715.

67. *Id.* at 1488–1502; 1515.

68. Posner, *supra* note 38, at 559.

69. *Id.* at 567.

70. Brubaker, *Rewriting the Constitution,* COMMENTARY, vol. 86, Dec. 1988, at 36, 42.

71. Michelman, *Welfare Rights in a Constitutional Democracy,* 1979 Wash. U.L.Q. 659; Michelman, *In Pursuit of Constitutional Welfare Rights: One View of Rawls' Theory of Justice,* 121 U. Pa. L. Rev. 962 (1973).

72. Parker, *The Past of Constitution Theory—And Its Future,* 42 Ohio St. L.J. 223, 259 and 258 n.146 (1981).

73. Schwartz, *With Gun and Camera,* 36 Stan. L. Rev. 413, 426 (1984).

74. Kennedy, *Form and Substance in Private Law Adjudication,* 95 Harv. L. Rev. 1685, 1746 (1976).

75. Kennedy, *First Year Teaching as Political Action,* 1 J.L. & Soc. Prob. 47, 49, 52 (1980), *quoted in* Schwartz, *supra* note 73, at 419.

76. Schwartz, *supra* note 73, at 413.

77. *Ibid.*

78. Kennedy, SALT Conference on Goals in Law Teaching (Dec. 16, 1979) 8, *quoted in* Schwartz, *supra* note 73, at 434 n.88.

79. Brest, *The Fundamental Rights Controversy: The Essential Contradictions of Normative Scholarship,* 90 Yale L.J. 1063 (1981).

80. *Id.* at 1065.

81. *Id.* at 1097.

82. Brest, *The Misconceived Quest for the Original Understanding,* 60 B.U.L. Rev. 204, 226 (1980).

83. Grey, *Do We Have an Unwritten Constitution?,* 27 Stan. L. Rev. 703, 706 (1975); *see generally,* Grey, *Origins of the Unwritten Constitution: Fundamental Law in American Revolutionary Thought,* 30 Stan. L. Rev. 843 (1978); Grey, *The Constitution as Scripture,* 37 Stan. L. Rev. 1 (1984).

84. Grey, *Eros, Civilization and the Burger Court,* 43 Law & Contemp. Probs. 83, 97 (1980).

85. *Ibid.*

86. Grey, *The Constitution as Scripture,* 37 Stan. L. Rev. 1, 5 (1984).

87. *Id.* at 25.

88. Richards, *Sexual Autonomy and the Constitutional Right to Privacy: A Case Study in Human Rights and the Unwritten Constitution,* 30 Hastings L.J. 957 (1979) [hereinafter *Sexual Autonomy*]; Richards, *Constitutional Privacy and Homosexual Love,* 14 N.Y.U. Rev. L. & Soc. Change 895 (1986); Richards, *Constitutional Privacy, the Right to Die and the Meaning of Life: A Moral Analysis,* 22 Wm. & Mary L. Rev. 327 (1981). D. Richards, *The Moral Criticism of Law* (1977).

89. D. Richards, *The Moral Criticism of Law* 50–51 (1977).

90. Richards, *Sexual Autonomy, supra* note 88, at 964 (emphasis omitted).

91. *Id.* at 970. *See* J. Rawls, *A Theory of Justice* (1971).

92. Richards, *Sexual Autonomy, supra* note 88, at 981.

93. *Id.* at 980, 982.

94. *Id.* at 1005 (emphasis in original).

95. Richards, *Sexual Autonomy, supra* note 88, at 1015 n.245; Richards, *Constitutional Privacy, the Right to Die and the Meaning of Life: A Moral Analysis, supra* note 88, at 408 (1981).

96. Richards, *Sexual Autonomy, supra* note 88, at 1015 n.245.

97. *Ibid.*

98. Richards, *Constitutional Privacy and Homosexual Love, supra* note 88, at 905 (1986).

99. D. Richards, *supra* note 89, at 67.

100. *Id.* at 71 (footnotes omitted).

101. *Id.* at 143.

102. *Id.* at 159.

103. *Id.* at 168.

104. *Id.* at 172.

105. *Id.* at 256.

106. R. Dworkin, *Taking Rights Seriously* 135–36 (1978).

107. U.S. CONST. amend. VIII.

108. U.S. CONST. amend. V.

109. R. Dworkin, *supra* note 106, at 135–36.

110. *Id.* at 223–239; R. Dworkin, *A Matter of Principle* 291–331 (1985) (discussing reverse discrimination. *See* R. Dworkin, *A Matter of Principle* at 67–68 (discussing laws based on "popular convictions about private sexual morality").

111. Tushnet, *The Dilemmas of Liberal Constitutionalism,* 42 Ohio St. L.J. 411, 424 (1981).

112. Ackerman, *The Storrs Lectures: Discovering the Constitution,* 93 Yale L.J. 1013, 1015 (1984).

113. *Id.* at 1045.

114. *Id.* at 1055–56.

115. *Id.* at 1056 (emphasis in original).

116. M. Perry, *Morality, Politics, and Law* 130 (1988).

117. *See id.* at 123–28.

118. *Id.* at 131.

119. *Ibid.* (footnote omitted).

120. *Id.* at 133 (footnote omitted).

121. *See id.* at 134–35.

122. *Id.* at 149.

123. *Ibid.* (emphasis in original).

124. *See* McConnell, *Book Review,* 98 Yale L.J. 1501, 1528 (1989):

> If one necessary (even if not sufficient) condition for the Constitution to be authoritative is that it was adopted by the people, then it follows that principles never adopted by the people cannot be authoritative, even if they have some linguistic plausibility. Functionally, to apply an unintended meaning is no different from introducing a principle that has no textual basis whatsoever. The only difference between the unintended meaning and the extratextual principle is verbal happenstance. Perhaps an unintended—an accidental—meaning can be said to be "better," or will seem so to the judge. Precisely the same can be said of other "worthwhile aspirations" that are "not signified by" the text. None of these principles were the product of the people's "reflection and choice." None of these principles properly can be said to be law.

125. *Id.* at 1529.

126. S. Levinson, *Constitutional Faith* 52 (1988).

127. Levinson, *Law as Literature,* 60 Tex. L. Rev. 373, 385 (1982).

128. *Id.* at 391–92 (footnote omitted).

129. S. Levinson, *supra* note 126, at 191.

130. Pangle, Book Review, " 'Post Modernist' Thought," *The Wall Street Journal,* Jan. 5, 1989, at A8. *See also* Amar, *Civil Religion and Its Discontents,* 67 Tex. L. Rev. 1153 (1989).

131. L. Levy, *Original Intent and the Framers' Constitution* (1988).

132. Speech by Justice William J. Brennan, Jr. to the Text and Teaching Symposium, Georgetown University, Washington, D.C. (Oct. 12, 1985), *reprinted in The Great Debate: Interpreting Our Written Constitution* 11 (The Federalist Society 1986).

133. *Id.* at 14.

134. *Id.* at 18–19.

135. *Id.* at 23.

136. *Ibid.*

137. *Id.* at 24.

10. THE THEORISTS OF CONSERVATIVE CONSTITUTIONAL REVISIONISM

1. B. Siegan, *Economic Liberties and the Constitution* (1980).

2. L. Hand, *The Bill of Rights* 50–51 (1958).

3. 198 U.S. 45 (1905).

4. 261 U.S. 525 (1923).

5. 381 U.S. 479 (1965).

6. 410 U.S. 113 (1973).

7. B. Siegan, *supra* note 1, at 154, *quoting* Director, *The Parity of the Economic Market Place,* 7 J.L. & Econ. 1, 2 (1964).

8. *Id.* at 324.

9. *Ibid.*

10. Letter from Oliver Wendell Holmes, Jr. to William James (Mar. 24, 1907), *reprinted in* R. Perry, *The Thought and Character of William James: As Revealed in His Unpublished Correspondence and Notes Together With His Other Writings,* 2 *Philosophy and Psychology* 459 (1935). Also *reprinted in* E. Sergeant, "Oliver Wendell Holmes: Justice Touched with Fire," in *Fire Under the Andes: A Group of Literary Portraits* 318–19 (1927).

11. B. Siegan, *supra* note 1, at 324.

12. *Ibid.*

13. R. Epstein, *Takings: Private Property and the Power of Eminent Domain* (1985); Epstein, *Toward a Revitalization of the Contract Clause,* 51 U. Chi. L. Rev. 703 (1984).

14. U.S. CONST. amend. V.

15. U.S. CONST. art. I, § 10, cl.1.

16. R. Epstein, *Takings, supra* note 13, at 19–31.

17. *Id.* at 20–25.

18. *Id.* at 19–20, 29–31.

19. U.S. CONST. amend. V.

20. R. Epstein, *Takings, supra* note 13, at 99–100, 295–303.

21. *Id.* at 314–24.

22. *Id.* at 328.

23. *Id.* at 41–46.

24. 198 U.S. 45 (1905).

25. 236 U.S. 1 (1915).

26. Merrill, *Review Essay on Takings: Private Property and the Power of Eminent Domain, by Richard A. Epstein,* 80 NW. U.L. Rev. 1561, 1578 (1986).

27. 367 U.S. 497 (1961).

28. 367 U.S. at 522 (Harlan, J., dissenting).

29. *Id.* at 541.

30. *Id.* at 542.

31. *Ibid.*

32. *Ibid.*

33. *Id.* at 543 (citations omitted).

34. *Id.* at 545–47.

35. *Id.* at 548.

36. *Id.* at 549.

37. *Ibid.*

38. *Id.* at 552.

39. *Id.* at 554.

40. J. Ely, *Democracy and Distrust* 181–83 (1980).

41. *Id.* at 60, *quoting* G. Wills, *Inventing America* xiii (1978) (paraphrasing Willmoore Kendall).

42. *Id.* at 60.

43. *Id.* at 62.

44. 57 U.S.L.W. 4691 (U.S. June 15, 1989).

45. *Id.* at 4691–96.

46. *Compare* plurality op. at 4695–96 n.6 *with* concurring op. at 4696–97.

47. *Id.* at 4698.

48. *Id.* at 4697.

49. *Id.* at 4698.

50. *Ibid.*

51. *Ibid.*

52. *Ibid.*

53. *Ibid.*

54. *Id.* at 4699.

55. *Ibid.*

56. *Ibid.*

11. OF MORALISM, MORAL RELATIVISM, AND THE CONSTITUTION

1. J. Ely, *Democracy and Distrust* 58–59 (1980). *See also* R. Dahl, *Democracy in the United States* 24 (3d ed. 1976) ("After nearly twenty-five centuries, almost the only people who seem to be convinced of the advantages of being ruled by philosopher-kings are . . . a few philosophers.").

2. J. Ely, *supra* note 1, at 59.

3. "Federalism and Gentrification," Speech before The Federalist Society at Yale University, Apr. 24, 1982.

4. E. Ladd, Jr. & S. Lipset, *The Divided Academy: Professors and Politics* 14 (1975) *citing* R. Hofstadter, *Anti-intellectualism in American Life* 39 (1963).

5. J. Schumpeter, *Capitalism, Socialism and Democracy* (1942); Holland, *A Hurried Perspective on the Critical Legal Studies Movement: The Marx Brothers Assault the Citadel,* 8 Harv. J.L. Pub. Pol'y 239, 245 (1985) *citing* L. Trilling, *Beyond Culture: Essays on Literature and Learning* (1965).

6. Holland, *supra* note 5, at 245.

7. W. Donohue, *The Politics of the American Civil Liberties Union* (1985). *See also* Vigilante & Vigilante, *Taking Liberties: The ACLU Strays from its Mission,* POLICY REVIEW, Fall 1984, at 28.

8. Rabkin, *Class Conflict Over Civil Liberties,* THE PUBLIC INTEREST, no. 77 Fall Books Supp., Fall 1984, at 119.

9. *Id.* at 120.

10. *Ibid.*

11. *Id.* at 121.

12. 438 U.S. 265 (1978).

13. *Id.* at 319–20 (opinion of Powell, J.).

14. *Johnson* v. *Transportation Agency, Santa Clara County,* 480 U.S. 616 (1987); *United Steelworkers of America* v. *Weber,* 443 U.S. 193 (1979).

15. *Roe* v. *Wade,* 410 U.S. 113 (1973); *Griswold* v. *Connecticut,* 381 U.S. 479 (1965).

16. *Bowers* v. *Hardwick,* 478 U.S. 186, 199 (1986) (Blackmun, J., joined by Brennan, Marshall, and Stevens, JJ., dissenting).

17. 406 U.S. 205 (1972).

18. 403 U.S. 15, 25 (1971).

19. *Nash* v. *United States,* 229 U.S. 373, 377 (1913).

20. 403 U.S. at 25.

21. *See* G. Himmelfarb, *On Liberty and Liberalism: The Case of John Stuart Mill* (1974).

22. P. Devlin, *The Enforcement of Morals* 89 (1965).

23. Rostow, *The Democratic Character of Judicial Review,* 66 Harv. L. Rev. 193, 208 (1952).

24. *Bowers* v. *Hardwick,* 478 U.S. 186 (1986).

12. THE IMPOSSIBILITY OF ALL THEORIES THAT DEPART FROM ORIGINAL UNDERSTANDING

1. A. MacIntyre, *After Virtue* 51 (2d ed. 1984).

2. *Id.* at 6.

3. *Id.* at 232.

4. *Griswold* v. *Connecticut,* 381 U.S. 479 (1965).

13. In Defense of Legal Reasoning: "Good Results" vs. Legitimate Process

1. Speech, "The Profession of the Law," *reprinted in Speeches by Oliver Wendell Holmes* 22 (1st ed. 1913).

2. *Griswold v. Connecticut,* 381 U.S. 479 (1965).

3. *Id.* at 485.

4. *Eisenstadt v. Baird,* 405 U.S. 438 (1972).

5. *Roe v. Wade,* 410 U.S. 113 (1973).

6. R. Frost, Address at Milton Academy, Milton, Massachusetts (May 17, 1935).

7. *Dred Scott v. Sandford,* 60 U.S. (19 How.) 393 (1856).

III. The Bloody Crossroads

1. President's Remarks Announcing the Nomination of Robert H. Bork to be an Associate Justice, 23 Weekly Comp. Pres. Doc. 761 (July 1, 1987).

2. 133 Cong. Rec. S9188-S9189 (daily ed. July 1, 1987) (statement of Sen. Kennedy).

3. L. Trilling, *The Liberal Imagination* 10 (1979).

14. The Nomination and the Campaign

1. *The New York Times,* May 12, 1989, at B8.

2. *Boston Globe,* Oct. 11, 1987, at 22.

3. *Ibid.*

4. *Ibid.*

5. *The New York Times,* July 9, 1987, at A24.

6. *The New York Times,* July 2, 1987, at A22.

7. Taylor, "Robert Heron Bork: A Committed Conservative with a Rare Opportunity," *The New York Times,* July 2, 1987, at A22.

8. *Philadelphia Inquirer,* Nov. 16, 1986, at A13.

9. *The New York Times,* July 9, 1987, at A1.

10. *The Washington Post,* July 9, 1987, at A1; *The New York Times,* July 9, 1987, at A1.

11. *The New York Times,* July 13, 1987, at A12.

12. *Ibid.*

13. *The New York Times,* July 9, 1987, at A24.

14. *The Washington Post,* Aug. 5, 1987, at A20.

15. *Ibid.*

16. *Ibid.*

17. *Ibid.*

18. *The Washington Post,* Oct. 24, 1987, at A16.

19. *The New York Times,* Aug. 18, 1987, at A16.

20. *The New York Times,* Sept. 11, 1987, at A20.

21. Letter from Arthur J. Kropp, on behalf of People for the American Way Action Fund, at 3.

22. *Id.* at 4.

23. *Id.* at 45.

24. *The New York Times,* Sept. 11, 1987, at A20.

25. *The Washington Post,* Oct. 24, 1987, at A16.

26. *The Washington Post,* Oct. 4, 1987, at A1.

27. *Biden Report,* 9 Cardozo L. Rev. 219, 231 (1987).

28. *Id.* at 253.

29. Business reply letter from ACLU Foundation (Aug. 31, 1987), *reprinted in* Myers, *Advice and Consent on Trial: The Case of Robert H. Bork,* 66 Den. U.L. Rev. 201, 215 n.68 (1989).

30. *The Washington Post,* Sept. 26, 1987, at A6.

31. 133 Cong. Rec. S14721 (daily ed. Oct. 21, 1987).

32. The text of this commercial is reprinted in Dowd, *Winning One from the Gipper,* FORTUNE, vol. 116, Nov. 1987, at 125, 128.

33. *The New York Times,* Oct. 8, 1987, at A1.

34. *Ibid.*

35. *The Washington Post,* Aug. 5, 1987, at A20.

36. *Biden Report,* 9 Cardozo L. Rev. at 246.

37. *Id.* at 247.

38. *The New York Times,* Sept. 13, 1987, at 7.

39. *The Washington Post,* Sept. 14, 1987, at A9.

40. *Ibid.*

41. 431 U.S. 494 (1977).

42. See Rotunda, *The Confirmation Process for Supreme Court Justices in the Modern Era,* 37 Emory L.J. 559, 581 (1988) *citing* Sullivan, "The Bork Screw," THE NEW REPUBLIC, vol. 197, Oct. 1987, at 16.

43. *The New York Times,* Sept. 15, 1987, at A21.

44. *Ibid.*

45. *Nomination of Robert H. Bork to be Associate Justice of the Supreme Court of the United States: Hearings Before the Senate Comm. on the Judiciary,* 100th Cong., 1st Sess. 467 (1987).

46. 381 U.S. 479 (1965).

47. *The New York Times,* July 23, 1987, at A21.

48. *The Washington Post,* Sept. 14, 1987, at A9.

49. *Biden Report,* 9 Cardozo L. Rev. at 264–66.

50. R. Bork, *The Antitrust Paradox: A Policy At War With Itself* (1978).

51. *Biden Report,* 9 Cardozo L. Rev. at 259.

52. *Public Citizen Report,* 9 Cardozo L. Rev. 297, 310 (1987).

53. *Id.* at 338.

54. Allen, *Judgment Day for a Judging Panel,* INSIGHT, Mar. 20, 1989, at 46.

55. "Screen Test for Judges," *The Detroit News,* Apr. 2, 1989.

56. "Screening New Judges," *The Washington Post,* Apr. 17, 1989, at A18.

57. "Lest Ye Be Judged," *The Wall Street Journal,* Jan. 28, 1988 at 22.

58. *Ibid.*

59. Jenson, "Churchly Honor and Judge Bork," DIALOG, vol. 27, Winter 1988, at 3.

15. THE HEARINGS AND AFTER

1. *Nomination of Robert H. Bork to be Associate Justice of the Supreme Court of the United States: Hearings Before the Senate Comm. on the Judiciary,* 100th Cong., 1st Sess. 33 (1987) [hereinafter *Hearings*] (opening statement of Senator Edward M. Kennedy).

2. *Ibid.*

3. *Ibid.*

4. *Ibid.*

5. *Id.* at 34.

6. *Ibid.*

7. *Ibid.*

8. *Hearings* at 36 (opening statement of Senator Orrin G. Hatch).

9. *Ibid.*

10. *Ibid.*

11. *Id.* at 37.

12. *Hearings* at 47 (opening statement of Senator Alan K. Simpson).

13. *Id.* at 48–49.

14. *Id.* at 49.

15. *Id.* at 48.

16. *Hearings* at 59, 61 (opening statement of Senator Charles E. Grassley).

17. *Ibid.*

18. *Hearings* at 85 (opening statement of Senator Gordon J. Humphrey).

19. *Id.* at 86.

20. *Id.* at 88.

21. *Hearings* at 103 (opening statement of Robert H. Bork to be Associate Justice of the U.S. Supreme Court).

22. *Ibid.*

23. *Id.* at 103–05.

24. *Hearings* at 320.

25. *Hearings* at 314.

26. 418 U.S. 153 (1974).

27. *Hearings* at 280.

28. *Hearings* at 280–83.

29. 347 U.S. 497 (1954).

30. 347 U.S. 483 (1954).

31. *Hearings* at 284.

32. J. Ely, *Democracy and Distrust* 32 (1980) ("[T]he Court held, in essence, that the Due Process Clause of the Fifth Amendment incorporates the Equal Protection Clause of the Fourteenth Amendment."). *See, e.g., Buckley* v. *Valeo,* 424 U.S. 1, 93 (1976); *Weinberger* v. *Wiesenfeld,* 420 U.S. 636, 638 n.2 (1975).

33. *Hearings* at 284–85.

34. *Id.* at 285.

35. *Ibid.*

36. *Id.* at 287.

37. *Id.* at 287–88.

38. *Id.* at 194–236.

39. *Id.* at 467–69.

40. *See, e.g., Oil, Chemical & Atomic Workers Int'l Union* v. *American Cyanamid Co.,* 741 F.2d 444 (D.C. Cir. 1984).

41. Kaus, *Biden's Belly Flop,* NEWSWEEK, Sept. 28, 1987, at 23.

42. *Ibid.*

43. Alter & Fineman, *The Fall of Joe Biden,* NEWSWEEK, Oct. 5, 1987, at 28.

44. *Hearings* at 860.

45. *The New York Times,* Sept. 28, 1987, at B7 ("The Committee Democrats . . . kept anti-Bork witnesses with impeccable credentials in the spotlight, pushing many of the best pro-Bork witnesses into the evening hours.").

46. 1 *Media Monitor* No. 7, at 1, 5–6 (Center for Media and Public Affairs, Oct. 1987).

47. 133 Cong. Rec. S13743 (daily ed. Oct. 7, 1987) (Sen. Conrad).

48. 133 Cong. Rec. S13708 (daily ed. Oct. 7, 1987) (Sen. Exon).

49. *The Washington Post,* Sept. 21, 1987, at A15.

50. *The Washington Post,* Oct. 8, 1987, at A1.

51. Statement of Robert H. Bork, White House Press Room, Washington, D.C., Oct. 9, 1987.

52. Radio Address to the Nation on the Nomination of Robert H. Bork to be an Associate Justice, Oct. 10, 1987, 23 Weekly Comp. Pres. Doc. 1158 (Oct. 19, 1987).

53. Address to the Nation on the Nomination of Robert H. Bork to be an Associate Justice, Oct. 14, 1987, 23 Weekly Comp. Pres. Doc. 1171, 1172 (Oct. 19, 1987).

54. 133 Cong. Rec. S14941 (daily ed. Oct. 23, 1987) (Sen. Danforth).

16. THE CHARGES AND THE RECORD: A STUDY IN CONTRASTS

1. The *Biden Report* and the *Report of the Public Citizen Litigation Group* are reprinted in 9 Cardozo L. Rev. 219, 297 (1987). Statements by the other groups listed may be found in *Nomination of Robert H. Bork to be Associate Justice of the Supreme Court of the United States: Hearings before the Senate Comm. on the Judiciary,* 100th Cong., 1st Sess. [hereinafter *Hearings*], 370, 1335, 1630, 1725, 1880, 1936, 3978, 3995, 4003, 4053, 4531, 4739, 4908, 5266, 5307, 5588, 5701, 5913 (1987).

2. *Hearings* at 157.

3. 347 U.S. 483 (1954).

4. Bork, *Neutral Principles and Some First Amendment Problems,* 47 Ind. L.J. 1 (1971).

5. 334 U.S. 1 (1948).

6. Professors Wechsler and Henkin, both of Columbia, have noted the lack of a neutral principle behind *Shelley. See* Wechsler, *Toward Neutral Principles of Constitutional Law,* 73 Harv. L. Rev. 1, 29 (1959); Henkin, *Shelley v. Kraemer, Notes for a Revised Opinion,* 110 U. Pa. L. Rev. 473, 474 (1962). In addition, the Supreme Court has repeatedly refused to extend *Shelley. See, e.g., Evans* v. *Abney,* 396 U.S. 435 (1970); *Moose Lodge No. 107* v. *Irvis,* 407 U.S. 163 (1972); *San Francisco Arts & Athletics, Inc.* v. *United States Olympic Comm.,* 483 U.S. 522 (1987).

7. 383 U.S. 301 (1966).

8. 383 U.S. 663 (1966).

9. 383 U.S. at 670 (Black, J., dissenting); 383 U.S. at 680 (Harlan, Stewart, JJ., dissenting).

10. *Butler* v. *Thompson,* 341 U.S. 937 (1951).

11. 384 U.S. 641 (1966).

12. 384 U.S. at 659 (Harlan, Stewart, JJ., dissenting).

13. *City of Rome* v. *United States,* 446 U.S. 156, 200 (1980).

14. 410 U.S. 113 (1973).

15. R. Bork, *Constitutionality of the President's Busing Proposals* 8–13 (1972).

16. *See, e.g., Hearings* at 3135–45.

17. *See A Response to the Critics of Judge Robert H. Bork,* 9 Cardozo L. Rev. 373, 438 (1987).

18. *See The White House Report: Information on Judge Bork's Qualification, Judicial Record & Related Subjects,* 9 Cardozo L. Rev. 187.

19. *Hearings* at 469.

20. *United Jewish Organizations* v. *Carey,* 430 U.S. 144 (1977).

21. *Hearings* at 469.

22. *Oil, Chemical & Atomic Workers Int'l Union* v. *American Cyanamid Co.,* 741 F.2d 444 (D.C. Cir. 1984).

23. *See, e.g., Hearings* at 3135–45.

24. *Reed* v. *Reed,* 404 U.S. 71 (1971) (first Supreme Court decision analyzing gender classification under emerging intermediate standard of review).

25. *Rostker* v. *Goldberg,* 453 U.S. 57 (1981).

26. J. Ely, *Democracy and Distrust* 164 (1980).

27. U.S. CONST. amend. XIV, § 1.

28. 118 U.S. 356 (1886).

29. *See also Craig* v. *Boren,* 429 U.S. 190, 217 (1976) (Rehnquist, J., dissenting); *Trimble* v. *Gordon,* 430 U.S. 762, 777 (1977) (Rehnquist, J., dissenting).

30. *City of Cleburne, Texas* v. *Cleburne Living Center,* 473 U.S. 432, 451 (1985) (Stevens, J., concurring).

31. *Justice Department Report,* 9 Cardozo L. Rev. 373, 454–68 (1987).

32. *Id.* at 454 n.105.

33. *Laffey* v. *Northwest Airlines,* 740 F.2d 1071 (D.C. Cir. 1984) (per curiam).

34. *Hearings* at 1135.

35. *Id.* at 1136.

36. *Biden Report,* 9 Cardozo L. Rev. 219, 258–64 (1987).

37. *Id.* at 259.

38. R. Bork, *The Antitrust Paradox: A Policy at War With Itself* (1978).

39. *See Justice Department Report,* 9 Cardozo L. Rev. 373, 486 (1987), observing that *The Antitrust Paradox* has been cited approvingly in: *Cargill, Inc.* v. *Monfort of Colorado, Inc.,* 479 U.S. 104, 121 n.17 (1986) (Brennan, J.); *Matsushita Elec. Indus.* v. *Zenith Radio Co.,* 475 U.S. 574 (1986) (Powell, J.); *Aspen Skiing Co.* v. *Aspen Highlands Skiing Corp.,* 472 U.S. 585 (1985) (Stevens, J.); *NCAA* v. *Board of Regents,* 468 U.S. 85, 101 (1984) (same); *Reiter* v. *Sonotone Corp.,* 442 U.S. 330, 343 (1979) (Burger, C.J.); *United States* v. *United States Gypsum Co.,* 438 U.S. 422, 442 (1978) (same).

40. Stewart, *The Judicial Performance of Robert H. Bork in Administrative and Regulatory Law,* 9 Cardozo L. Rev. 135, 138 (1987).

41. Anthony, *Judge Robert H. Bork's Decisions in Which he Wrote No Opinion: An Analysis of the Regulatory and Benefit Cases,* 9 Cardozo L. Rev. 159 (1987).

42. *Id.* at 161.

43. *Id.* at 164.

44. *Id.* at 165.

45. *Id.* at 171.

46. *Ibid.*

47. *Id.* at 172.

48. *Ibid.*

49. *Id.* at 174.

50. *Justice Department Report,* 9 Cardozo L. Rev. 373, 476–77 (1987).

51. Bork, *Neutral Principles and Some First Amendment Problems,* 47 Ind. L.J. 1 (1971).

52. *See, e.g.,* Letter, "Judge Bork Replies," ABA JOURNAL, Feb. 1984, at 132.

53. *See Hearings* at 271–77.

54. King, *Letter from the Birmingham Jail,* ATLANTIC MONTHLY, Aug. 1963, at 78–88.

55. 395 U.S. 444, 447 (1969).

56. *Ollman* v. *Evans,* 750 F.2d 970, 973 (D.C. Cir. 1984) (en banc) (Bork, J., concurring).

57. *McBride* v. *Merrell Dow & Pharmaceuticals, Inc.,* 717 F.2d 1460 (D.C. Cir. 1983).

58. *Telecommunications Research & Action Center* v. *FCC,* 801 F.2d 501 (D.C. Cir. 1986).

59. *Quincy Cable TV* v. *FCC,* 768 F.2d 1434 (D.C. Cir. 1985).

60. *FTC* v. *Brown & Williamson Tobacco Corp.,* 778 F.2d 35 (D.C. Cir. 1985).

61. *Lebron* v. *Washington Metropolitan Area Transit Authority,* 749 F.2d 893 (D.C. Cir. 1984).

62. *Finzer* v. *Barry,* 798 F.2d 1450 (D.C. Cir. 1986).

17. WHY THE CAMPAIGN WAS MOUNTED

1. 410 U.S. 113 (1973).

2. M. A. Glendon, *Abortion and Divorce in Western Law: American Failures, European Challenges* 2 (1987).

3. *Thornburgh* v. *American College of Obstetricians & Gynecologists,* 476 U.S. 747 (1986); *Biden Report,* 9 Cardozo L. Rev. 219, 234 (1987) ("this particular vacancy—occurring at this particular time—carries historical weight").

4. For a description and definition of the intellectual or "new class," *see* I. Kristol, *Two Cheers for Capitalism* 25–31 (1978).

5. Conversation with Lloyd Cutler, May 20, 1989, New York, New York.

6. Tom Hurwitz *quoted in* Dickstein, "Columbia Recovered," *New York Times Sunday Magazine,* May 15, 1988, at 32.

7. *Id.,* quoting James Shapiro, at 68.

8. D. Bok, *Beyond the Ivory Tower: Social Responsibilities of the Modern University* 83 (1982), *quoting* H. Taylor, *Students Without Teachers: The Crisis in the University* 128 (1969).

9. Balch & London, *The Tenured Left,* COMMENTARY, vol. 82, Oct. 1986, at 41, 43.

10. *Id.* at 45.

11. Kissam, *The Decline of Law School Professionalism,* 134 U. Pa. L. Rev. 251, 271 (1986).

12. Parker, *The Past of Constitutional Theory—And Its Future,* 42 Ohio St. L.J. 223, 257 (1981); Schlegel, *Notes Toward an Intimate, Opinionated, and Affectionate History of the Conference on Critical Legal Studies,* 36 Stan. L. Rev. 391, 406 (1984).

13. Inaugural Address, Jan. 20, 1989, 25 Weekly Comp. Pres. Doc. 99, 100 (Jan. 27, 1989).

14. Puddington, *The Soul of the Left's Machine,* THE NATIONAL INTEREST, no. 13, Fall 1988, at 111.

15. As *quoted in* P. Hollander, *The Survival of the Adversary Culture* 151–52 (1988).

16. *Id.* at 152.

17. Lerner, "Cleaning Up the Mess," *The Washington Times,* June 27, 1988, at D1.

18. Introduction to A. Bloom, *The Closing of the American Mind* 18 (1987).
19. A. Bickel, *The Morality of Consent* 137, 140 (1975).
20. *Id.*
21. Lacayo, *The Battle Begins,* TIME, July 13, 1987, at 10.

18. EFFECTS FOR THE FUTURE

1. *The Washington Post,* Nov. 13, 1987, at A11.
2. Bork, *Neutral Principles and Some First Amendment Problems,* 47 Ind. L.J. 1 (1971).
3. *Oil, Chemical & Atomic Workers Int'l Union* v. *American Cyanamid Co.,* 741 F.2d 444 (D.C. Cir. 1984).

CONCLUSION

1. J. H. (Cardinal) Newman, *The Development of Christian Doctrine* 7 (1968).
2. E. Burke, Speech on Moving His Resolutions for Conciliation With the Colonies (Mar. 22, 1775), *reprinted in* 1 *The Works of the Right Hon. Edmund Burke* 181, 200 (H. G. Bohn ed. 1841).
3. R. Neuhaus, *The Naked Public Square: Religion and Democracy in America* 255 (1984).
4. R. Bolt, *A Man For All Seasons* 65–66 (1962).
5. *Id.* at 66.
6. R. W. Chambers, *Thomas More* 268 (1962).
7. E. Burke, *Reflections on the Revolution in France* 74 (T. Mahoney ed. 1955).

Table of Works Cited

References are to text pages where note is cited.

Ackerman, *The Storrs Lectures: Discovering the Constitution,* 93 Yale L. J. 1013 (1984), 214, 215

ACLU Foundation, business reply letter (Aug. 31, 1987) in Myers, *Advice and Consent on Trial: The Case of Robert H. Bork,* 66 Den. U. L. Rev. 201 (1989), 287–88

Acton, Lord. Letter to Bishop Mandell Creighton (Apr. 5, 1887) in G. Himmelfarb, *Lord Acton: A Study in Conscience and Politics* (1952), 141

Allen, *Judgment Day for a Judging Panel,* INSIGHT, Mar. 20, 1989, at A18, 292

Alter & Fineman, *The Fall of Joe Biden,* NEWSWEEK, Oct. 5, 1987, 307

Amar, *Civil Religion and Its Discontents,* 67 Tex. L. Rev. 1153 (1989), 218

Anthony, *Judge Robert H. Bork's Decisions in Which He Wrote No Opinion: An Analysis of the Regulatory and Benefit Cases,* 9 Cardozo L. Rev. 159 (1987), 332–33

Balch & London, *The Tenured Left,* COMMENTARY, vol. 82, Oct. 1986, 339

Bator, P., P. Mishkin, D. Meltzer & D. Shapiro, *Hart and Wechsler's The Federal Courts and the Federal System* (3d ed. 1988) *quoting* 1 Farrand, *The Records of the Federal Convention* (1911), 154

Belloc, H., *The Great Heresies* (1987), 4, 11

Berger, R., *Death Penalties* (1982), 159

Bickel, A., *The Least Dangerous Branch* (1962), 71, 72, 188, 189, 190, 191, 192

―――― *The Morality of Consent* (1975), 131–32, 342

Biden Report, 9 Cardozo L. Rev. 219 (1987), 287, 288, 291, 331, 337

Bittker, *The Bicentennial of the Jurisprudence of Original Intent: The Recent Past,* 77 Calif. L. Rev. 235 (1989), 154

Bloom, A., *The Closing of the American Mind* (1987), 137, 342

Bolt, R., *A Man For All Seasons* (1962), 354

Bork, R. Letter. *Judge Bork Replies,* ABA JOURNAL, (Feb. 1984) at 132, 333

―――― *Neutral Principles and Some First Amendment Problems,* 47 Ind. L. J. 1 (1971), 152, 324, 333, 347

―――― *The Antitrust Paradox: A Policy at War With Itself* (1978), 73, 291, 332

―――― *Civil Rights—A Challenge,* THE NEW REPUBLIC, vol. 149 (1963), 80

―――― *Constitutionality of the President's Busing Proposals* (1972), 325

―――― Conversation with Lloyd Cutler,

May 20, 1989, New York, New York, 338

———— Speech. "Federalism and Gentrification," before The Federalist Society, Yale University, Apr. 24, 1982, 242

———— Statement. White House Press Room, Washington, D. C., Oct. 9, 1987, 314–15

———— *Tradition and Morality in Constitutional Law,* Francis Boyer Lectures on Public Policy 11 (American Enterprise Institute, Dec. 1984), 178

———— *The Supreme Court Needs a New Philosophy,* FORTUNE, vol. 78 (Dec. 1968), 80

Boston Globe, Oct. 11, 1987, 282, 283

Brennan, William J., Jr. Speech to the Text and Teaching Symposium, Georgetown University, Washington, D.C. (Oct. 12, 1985) reprinted in *The Great Debate: Interpreting Our Written Constitution* (Federalist Society, 1986), 162, 219, 220

Brest, *The Fundamental Rights Controversy: The Essential Contradictions of Normative Constitutional Scholarship,* 90 Yale L. J. 1063 (1981), 148–49, 208

———— *The Misconceived Quest for the Original Understanding,* 60 B. U. L. Rev. 204 (1980), 171–72, 208–9

Brubaker, *Rewriting the Constitution,* COMMENTARY, vol. 86 (Dec. 1988), 206

Burke, E., *Reflections on the Revolution in France* (T. Mahoney, ed., 1955), 354

———— Speech on Moving His Resolutions for Conciliation with the Colonies (Mar. 22, 1775) in *The Works of the Right Hon. Edmund Burke* (H.G. Bohn ed. 1841), 353

Bush, Inaugural Address, Jan. 20, 1989, 25 Weekly Comp. Pres. Doc. 99 (Jan. 27, 1989), 340

Caplan, *The History and Meaning of the Ninth Amendment,* 69 Va. L. Rev. 223 (1985), 184

Chambers, R.W., *Thomas More* (1962), 354

133 Cong. Rec. S13708, S13743 (daily ed. Oct. 7, 1987), 309–310

133 Cong. Rec. S14721 (daily ed. Oct. 21, 1987), 288

133 Cong. Rec. S14941 (daily ed. Oct. 23, 1987), 315

Cooley, T., *Constitutional Limitations* (2d ed. 1871), 134

Cox, A., *The Court and the Constitution* (1987), 89

Currie, D., *The Constitution in the Supreme Court: The First Hundred Years, 1979–1888* (1985), 27, 32, 39

Dahl, R., *Democracy in the United States* (3d ed. 1976), 242

The Detroit News, "Screen Test for Judges," April 2, 1989, 292

Deutsch, *Neutrality, Legitimacy and the Supreme Court: Some Intersections Between Law and Political Science,* 20 Stan. L. Rev. 169 (1968), 78

Devlin, P., *The Enforcement of Morals* (1965), 249

Director, *The Parity of the Marketplace,* 7 J. L. & Econ. 1 (1964), in Siegan, B., *Economic Liberties and the Constitution* (1988), 225–26

Donohue, W., *The Politics of the American Civil Liberties Union* (1985), 243

Dowd, *Winning One From the Gipper,* FORTUNE, vol. 116, Nov. 1987, 288

Dworkin, R., *A Matter of Principle* (1985), 214

———— *Taking Rights Seriously* (1978), 213, 214

———— *The Forum of Principle,* 56 N. Y. U. L. Rev. 469 (1981), 176–77

Ely, J., *Democracy and Distrust* (1980), 32, 83, 161, 162, 178, 179, 180, 182, 184, 185, 194, 195, 196, 197, 198, 234, 242, 306, 329

Epstein, R., *Takings: Private Property*

and the Power of Eminent Domain (1985), 230

_____ *Toward a Revitalization of the Contract Clause,* 51 U. Chi. L. Rev. 703 (1984), 229

Fairman, C., "Reconstruction and Reunion: 1864–88," *History of the Supreme Court of the United States* (1971), 39

Fehrenbacher, D., "Dred Scott v. Sandford" in 2 *Encyclopedia of the American Constitution* (1986), 34

Fogel, R. & S. Engerman, *Time on the Cross: The Economics of American Negro Slavery* (1974), 29

Fortas, A., *The New York Times,* June 15, 1937, 55

Frankfurter, F., *The Commerce Clause* (1937), 160

Frost, R., Address, Milton Academy, Milton, Massachusetts, May 17, 1935, 264

Genovese, E., *The Political Economy of Slavery: Studies in the Economy and Society of the Slave South* (1965), 29

Glendon, M.A., *Abortion and Divorce in Western Law: American Failures, European Challenges* (1987), 337

Grey, *Do We Have an Unwritten Constitution?* 27 Stan. L. Rev. 703 (1975), 209

_____ *Eros, Civilization and the Burger Court,"* 43 Law & Contemp. Probs. 83 (1980), 209–10

_____ *Origins of the Unwritten Constitution: Fundamental Law in American Revolutionary Thought,* 30 Stan. L. Rev. 843 (1978), 209

_____ *The Constitution as Scripture,* 37 Stan. L. Rev. 1 (1984), 209, 210

Hamilton, A., *The Federalist,* No. 78 (C. Rossiter ed. 1961), 154

_____ Quoted in L. Levy, *Original Intent and the Framers' Constitution* (1988), 176

_____ Quoted in Thayer, *The Origin*

and Scope of the American Doctrine of Constitutional Law,* 7 Harv. L. Rev. 129 (1893), 176

Hand, L., *The Bill of Rights* (1958), 224

Handler, *The Supreme Court and the Antitrust Laws; A Critic's Viewpoint,* 1 Ga. L. Rev. (1967), 73

Henkin, *Shelley v. Kraemer, Notes for a Revised Opinion,* 110 U. Pa. L. Rev. 473 (1962), 324

Himmelfarb, G., Letter to R. Bork (May 4, 1989), 137

_____ *On Liberty and Liberalism: The Case of John Stuart Mill* (1974), 249

Hofstadter, R., *Anti-intellectualism in American Life* (1963) *quoted in* Ladd, E. Jr., and S. Lipset, *The Divided Academy: Professors and Politics* (1975), 242

Holmes, O. Letter to William James (Mar. 24, 1907) in Perry, R., *The Thought and Character of William James: As Revealed in His Unpublished Correspondence . . .* 2 Philosophy and Psychology 459 (1935), 227

_____ Letter to William James (Mar. 24, 1907) in Sergeant, E., *Fires Under the Andes: A Group of Literary Portraits* (1927), 227

_____ Speech. "The Profession of the Law," in Speeches by Oliver Wendell Holmes, 1st ed. (1913), 262

Hughes, Speech, Elmira, New York (May 3, 1907), 175

Hurwitz, T. *quoted in* Dickstein, "Columbia Recovered," *The New York Times Magazine,* May 15, 1988, at 32, 338

Jaffe, L., *English and American Judges As Lawmakers* (1969), 78

Jefferson, Thomas. Letter to Judge Spencer Roane (Sept. 6, 1819) in 15 *The Writings of Thomas Jefferson,* A. Lipscomb, ed. (1903), 22

Jenson, *Churchly Honor and Judge Bork,* DIALOG, vol. 27 (Winter 1988), 293

Justice Department Report, 9 Cardozo L. Rev. 373 (1987), 330–31, 333

Kaus, *Biden's Belly Flop,* Newsweek, Oct. 5, 1987, at 28, 307

Kennedy, E., Statement, 133 Cong. Rec. S9188 (daily ed. July 1, 1987), 268

⸺ *First Year Teaching as Political Action,* 1 J. L. & Soc. Prob. 47 (1980), in Schwartz, *With Gun and Camera,* 36 Stan. L. Rev. 413 (1984), 207

⸺ *Form and Substance in Private Law Adjudication,* 95 Harv. L. Rev. 1685 (1976), 207

⸺ SALT Conference on Goals in Law Teaching (Dec. 16, 1979) in Schwartz, *With Guns and Camera,* 36 Stan. L. Rev. 413 (1984), 208

King, *Letter from the Birmingham Jail,* Atlantic Monthly, (Aug. 1963), 334

Kissam, *The Decline of Law School Professionalism,* 134 U. Pa. L. Rev. 251 (1984), 339

Koppel, T. Commencement address at Duke University, Durham, North Carolina (May 10, 1987), 164

Kramer, *Studying the Arts and the Humanities: What Can Be Done,* The New Criterion, vol. 7 (Feb. 1989), 137

Kristol, I., *Two Cheers for Capitalism* (1978), 18, 337

Kropp, A. Letter on behalf of People for the American Way Action Fund, 286

Lacayo, *The Battle Begins,* Time, July 13, 1987, 343

Langenscheidt's Encyclopedic Dictionary of the English and German Languages, Part II: German-English, Vol. I (1974), 32

Lerner, "Cleaning Up the Mess," *The Washington Times,* June 27, 1988, 9, 342

Levinson, S., *Law as Literature,* 60 Tex. L. Rev. 373 (1982), 217

⸺ *Constitutional Faith* (1988), 217, 218

Levy, L., *Original Intent and the Framers' Constitution* (1988), 218

Lichter and Rothman, quoted in P. Hollander, *The Survival of the Adversary Culture* (1988), 341

Lincoln, A. Message to Congress, July 4, 1861 in R. Basler, 4 *The Collected Works of Abraham Lincoln* (1953), 54

⸺ Speech, Springfield, Illinois, July 17, 1858 in R. Basler, ed., 2 *The Collected Works of Abraham Lincoln,* (1953), 29

Lombardo, *Three Generations, No Imbeciles: New Light on Buck v. Bell,* 60 N. Y. U. L. Rev. (1985), 63

McConnell, M., Book review, 98 Yale L. J. 1528 (1989), 217

MacDonald, *The Triumph of the Fact: An American Tragedy,* The Anchor Review, vol. 2, 113 (1957) in A. Bickel, *The Least Dangerous Branch* (1962), 192

McDowell, G., *Curbing the Courts: The Constitution and the Limits of Judicial Power* (1988), 188

⸺ "The Politics of Original Intention" in *The Constitution, the Courts, and the Quest for Justice,* R. Goldwin and W. Schambra, eds. (1989), 8

MacIntyre, A., *After Virtue* (2d ed. 1984), 8, 10, 254, 256–57

Maltz, *Some Thoughts on the Death of Stare Decisis in Constitutional Law,* Wis. L. Rev. 467 (1980), 155–56

Mayer, M., *Today and Tomorrow in America* (1975), 106

1 Media Monitor, No. 7, Oct. 1987, 309

Merrill, Review essay on *Takings: Private Property and the Power of Eminent Domain* by R. Epstein, 80 Nw. U. L. Rev. 1561 (1986), 230

Michelman, *In Pursuit of Constitutional Welfare Rights: One View of Rawls' Theory of Justice,* 121 U. Pa. L. Rev. 962 (1973), 207

⸺ *Welfare Rights in a Constitutional Democracy,* Wash. U. L. Q. 659 (1979), 207

Monaghan, *Stare Decisis and Constitutional Adjudication,* 88 Colum. L. Rev. (1988), 144, 153, 155–56

Neuhaus, R., *The Naked Public Square: Religion and Democracy in America* (1984), 354

Newman, J. H. (Cardinal), *The Development of Christian Doctrine* (1968), 352

The New York Times, July 2, 1987, 283
_____ July 9, 1987 at A1, 283, 284, 285
_____ July 13, 1987, 284–85
_____ July 23, 1987, 291
_____ August 18, 1987, 286
_____ Sept. 11, 1987, 286
_____ Sept. 13, 1987, 289
_____ Sept. 15, 1987, 290
_____ Sept. 28, 1987, 308
_____ Oct. 8, 1987, 288
_____ May 12, 1989, 282

Nomination of Robert H. Bork to be Associate Justice of the Supreme Court of the United States: Hearings Before the Senate Comm. on the Judiciary, 100th Cong., Ist sess. 467 (1987), 290, 298–307, 324, 325, 326, 327, 331, 334

Note, *A Madisonian Interpretation of the Equal Protection Doctrine,* 91 Yale L. J. (1982), 84

Pangle, Book review. " 'Post Modernist' Thought," *The Wall Street Journal,* Jan. 5, 1989, 218

Parker, *The Past of Constitutional Theory—and Its Future,* 42 Ohio St. L.J. 223 (1981), 207, 339

Perry, M., *Morality, Politics and Law* (1988), 216

Philadelphia Inquirer, Nov. 16, 1986, 284

Phillips, A., *American Negro Slavery: A Survey of the Supply, Employment and Control of Negro Labor as Determined by the Plantation Regime* (1918), 29

Pollak, *Racial Discrimination and Judicial Integrity; A Reply to Professor*

Wechsler, 108 U. Pa. L. Rev. 1 (1959), 78

Posner, *The Constitution as Mirror: Tribe's Constitutional Choices,* 84 Mich. L. Rev. 551 (1986), 200, 206

Public Citizen Report, 9 Cardozo L. Rev. 297 (1987), 291–92

Puddington, *The Soul of the Left's Machine,* THE NATIONAL INTEREST, No. 13, Fall 1988, at 111, 340

Rabkin, *Class Conflict Over Civil Liberties,* THE PUBLIC INTEREST, No. 77, Fall Book Supp. (1984), 244

Rawls, J., *A Theory of Justice* (1971), 210–11

Reagan, R., Radio address to the Nation. Nomination of Robert H. Bork to be an Associate Justice, Oct. 14, 1987, 23 Weekly Comp. Pres. Doc. 1158, 1171 (Oct. 19, 1987), 315
_____ Remarks announcing the nomination of Robert H. Bork to be an Associate Justice, 23 Weekly Comp. Pres. Doc. 761 (July 1, 1987), 267–68

Report of the Senate Judiciary Committee, June 14, 1937 in G. Gunther, *Cases and Materials on Constitutional Law,* 55

A Response to the Critics of Judge Robert H. Bork, 9 Cardozo L. Rev. 373 (1987), 325

Richards, D., *Constitutional Privacy, the Right to Die and the Meaning of Life: A Moral Analysis,* 22 Wm. & Mary L. Rev. 327 (1981), 210, 211
_____ *Constitutional Privacy and Homosexual Love,* 14 N.Y.U. Rev. L. & Soc. Change 895 (1986), 210, 211, 212, 213
_____ *The Moral Criticism of Law* (1977), 210
_____ *Sexual Autonomy and the Constitutional Right to Privacy: A Case Study in Human Rights and the Unwritten Constitution,* 30 Hastings L. J. 957 (1979), 210, 211

Roosevelt, Franklin D., Radio address, Mar. 9, 1937, in G. Gunther, *Cases and Materials on Constitutional Law,* 10th ed. (1980), 54

Rostow, *The Democratic Character of Judicial Review,* 66 Harv. L. Rev. 193 (1952), 249

Sandalow, *Judicial Protection of Minorities,* 75 Mich L. Rev. 1162 (1977), 171

Scalia, *Originalism: The Lesser Evil,* 57 U. Cin. L. Rev. 849 (1989), 145, 155, 159

Schlegel, *Notes Toward an Intimate, Opinionated and Affectionate History of the Conference on Critical Legal Studies,* 36 Stan. L. Rev. 391 (1984), 339

Schlesinger, *The Supreme Court: 1947,* Fortune, vol. 35, Jan. 1947, 69, 146

Schlossberg, H., *Idols for Destruction* (1983), 138

Schumpeter, J., *Capitalism, Socialism and Democracy* (1942), 242

Schwartz, *With Gun and Camera,* 36 Stan. L. Rev. 413 (1984), 207, 208

Sergeant, F., "Justice Touched With Fire" in *Mr. Justice Holmes,* F. Frankfurter, ed. (1931), 6

Shriver, H., *What Gusto: Stories and Anecdotes About Justice Oliver Wendell Holmes* (1970), 6

Siegan, B., *Economic Liberties and the Constitution* (1980), 224, 227–28

Sowell, T., *Civil Rights: Rhetoric or Reality?* (1984), 107

―――― "*Weber* and *Bakke,* and the Presuppositions of 'Affirmative Action,'" in W. Block and M. Walker, eds., *Discrimination, Affirmative Action, and Equal Opportunity* (1981), 107

Stewart, *The Judicial Performance of Robert H. Bork in Administrative and Regulatory Law,* 9 Cardozo L. Rev. 135 (1987), 332

Story, J., *Commentaries on the Constitution of the United States,* 1833 (1987), 5, 6, 134

Sullivan, *The Bork Screw,* The New Republic, vol. 197, 16 (Oct. 1987) in Rotunda, *The Confirmation Process for Supreme Court Justices in the Modern Era,* 37 Emory L. J. 559 (1988), 289

Sumner, W., *Andrew Jackson* (1882) in Boller, P., *Presidential Anecdotes* (1981), 28

Taylor, H., *Students Without Teachers: The Crisis in the University* (1969) quoted in D. Bok, *Beyond the Ivory Tower: Social Responsibilities of the Modern University* (1982), 339

―――― "Robert Heron Bork: A Committed Conservative with a Rare Opportunity," *The New York Times,* July 2, 1987, 284

Tribe, L., *American Constitutional Law,* 2d ed. (1988), 22, 199–200, 201, 202, 203, 204, 205, 206

Trilling, L., *Beyond Culture: Essays on Literature and Learning* (1965) in Holland, *A Hurried Perspective on the Critical Legal Studies Movement: The Marx Brothers Assault the Citadel,* 8 Harv. J. L. Pub. Pol'y 239 (1985), 242

―――― *The Liberal Imagination* (1979), 269

Tushnet, *The Dilemmas of Liberal Constitutionalism,* 42 Ohio St. L. J. 411 (1981), 214

Vigilante and Vigilante, *Taking Liberties: The ACLU Strays From Its Mission,* Policy Review, vol. 28 (Fall 1984), 243

The Wall Street Journal, "Lest Ye Be Judged," Jan. 28, 1988, at 22, 292–93

The Washington Post, July 9, 1987, 284

―――― August 5, 1987, 285, 288

―――― Sept. 14, 1987, 289, 291

―――― Sept. 21, 1987, 310

―――― Sept. 26, 1987, 288

―――― Oct. 4, 1987, 287

_____ Oct. 8, 1987, 310

_____ Oct. 24, 1987, 285–86, 287

_____ Nov. 13, 1987, 346

_____ "Screening New Judges," April 17, 1989, 292

Wechsler, *Toward Neutral Principles of Constitutional Law,* 73 Harv. L. Rev. 1 (1959), 78, 79, 324

The White House Report: Information on Judge Bork's Qualifications, Judicial Record & Related Subjects, 9 Cardozo L. Rev. 187 (1987), 325

Will, "Backing Out of a Swamp," *The Washington Post,* Jan. 29, 1989, 108

Wills, G., "Inventing America," in J. Ely, *Democracy and Distrust* (1980), 235

Table of Cases

Index